WITHDRAWN

Organization

WILFRED BROWN

Organization

HEINEMANN · LONDON

Heinemann Educational Books Ltd

LONDON EDINBURGH MELBOURNE
TORONTO AUCKLAND JOHANNESBURG HONG KONG
SINGAPORE IBADAN NAIROBI NEW DELHI

ISBN 0 435 85103 9

Published by Heinemann Educational Books Ltd
48 Charles Street, London WIX 8AH

Printed in Great Britain by
Fletcher & Son Ltd, Norwich

Preface

TEN YEARS AGO I tried to set down in writing all that I had learnt from being chief executive of an engineering company and from collaborating with my colleagues and with Elliott Jaques in a study of organization in the Glacier Metal Company. The result was published in *Exploration in Management* in 1960.

Opportunity for learning more has occurred since then. I left Glacier in 1965, after thirty-four years' service, to become a Minister of State in the Board of Trade, with special responsibility for exports and overseas trade relations. Professor Jaques has continued his association with Glacier and, as Head of the School of Social Sciences at Brunel University, has carried out analyses of organization both in Government departments and elsewhere.

So, again, I attempt to pull together in one volume as much as possible of all that has been learnt. With Jaques's agreement I have made constant use of material from his work without specific acknowledgement on each occasion. Had I made such acknowledgement the book would have been cluttered with references.

When I left industry I was entirely convinced that clearer understanding and consistent use of the role-relationships and institutions that the Glacier Project had described and defined had proved of major help to the progress of the Company and to the satisfaction of its employees. The most striking aspect of the situation was the co-existence of full participation by representatives of all employees in policy-making and the full authority of managers to manage. Contrary to much conventional thinking, it had become clear that these two situations were complementary, not mutually exclusive.

I wondered, when I joined the Government, whether working with the Civil Service and with a much broader spectrum of industry would modify my convictions. For five years my thoughts have never left the subject of organization as I observed the Civil Service and many hundreds of industrial companies at work. I was usually impressed with the personal calibre of the people I met, but dismayed

by the extent to which lack of organizational clarity seemed to undermine their efforts and waste their time. My convictions about the
importance of describing and defining organization were thus
strengthened rather than weakened. I therefore resolved to write this
book as soon as opportunity occurred—as it did when the Labour
Government lost the 1970 election.

Exploration in Management was subjected to two major criticisms by
academics. I must attempt to answer them, for this book may well be
similarly criticized.

The first was that I took too little account of psychological factors in
considering organization. Personal motivation, personal relationships,
behaviour, the culture of groups and other psychological factors have
direct relevance to organization problems. But much research has been
done in this area and hundreds of excellent books are available record-
ing the results. I have nothing unique to contribute on the subject, but
I do want to try and contribute in the far less well-tilled field of roles,
role-relationships, organization and social institutions. My selection of
one of these fields of study is no indication that I under-value the other.

The second criticism was lack of reference in my writing to the
works of others. This I accept, though I am unable to make amends.
I have been fully extended as a chief executive and as a Minister
since 1939. I have read widely but not sufficiently. I make my apology
now to those whose works I should have but have not quoted.

I have some defence however, for I have found great difficulty in
discovering reports of work done on organization. There is some
degree of confusion in the use of terms. Too many of the books I have
read are not so much about organization as I understand the term,
as about psychological factors within organizations. Many new works
appear each year about 'organization', but the subjects they deal
with are not those I expect.

I can find very few writers interested in definition of roles, role-
relationships and role systems, and who build models of the social
mechanisms and institutions whose study I, as a manager, have
found very rewarding because they are among the most important
factors affecting the behaviour of people at work.

I close this Preface by expressing my gratitude to Mark Arnold-
Foster for doing so much detailed work to improve the literary style
of this book, to Marjorie Davis who has spent much of her leisure
time typing, correcting and from her long experience, commenting
on content, and last but not least to my wife. I could not write any
book without the happy environment which she creates in our home.

1971   W.B.

Contents

PART TWO   POWER GROUPS, PARTICIPATION
AND WAGE DIFFERENTIALS

against giving foremen managerial authority: examples, piecework, clocking in, absence of appeals systems and absence of written policies. Supervisors are half-rank managers. Their role needs clarifying. The proliferation of charge-hands, leading hands, supervisors and assistant foremen. Supervisor role defined. Every employee must have access to a manager who knows him.

levels is demoralizing. Titling of roles in industry quite inconsistent with level of work and between companies. Clarification of ranking notions and measurement of level of work could lead to reduction of number of management levels in many companies.

Part One

The Anatomy of Employment Systems

CHAPTER ONE

Introduction

'*For there is no creature whose inward being is so strong that it is not greatly determined by what lies outside it.*'—GEORGE ELIOT, *Middlemarch*

STARTING BOOKS IS very difficult both for the reader and the writer. It is difficult for me to dive straight into my subject without some rather broad preliminary observations, setting out the underlying themes that motivate me. But some readers want to get at the meat quickly to discover whether the book is worth reading at all. So, if you are one of these, my advice is to skip this chapter and go straight to chapter two. If you finish the book you may then think it worth while to come back and read this chapter.[1]

I am completely convinced of the validity of two important ideas. (I will deal with the first at length before stating the second.)

(1) *Specific individual behaviour at work is as likely to arise from the nature of the role which the individual occupies, its relation with other roles, and with the entire structure of the social system within which that role is positioned, as from the personality of the individual.* There are many variables which affect human behaviour. Society used to regard inherited characteristics as predominant, but today it is recognized that early family environment plays a very important part in the formation of character and behaviour. A hundred years ago this was not recognized, and it must

---

[1] The book is in four parts:

    (1) The Anatomy of Employment Systems
    (2) Power-groups, Participation and Wage Differentials
    (3) Operational Work and Techniques
    (4) Personnel Work and Techniques

If you are as anxious about industrial justice, industrial strikes, participation in policy-making, wages problems and the decline of managerial authority as I am, you may wish to read part two first and then come back to part one.

often have caused despair. For example, mental illness was called insanity, and the cause was consistently attributed to inherited characteristics. Environment was seldom regarded as a contributory factor.

When people assume that human behaviour is an heredity-based fixed quantity then they are stuck with it, until the individual dies. Once, however, it came to be recognized that the variable of early family environment was affecting individual behaviour later in life, then particular types of undesirable behaviour were no longer inevitable. The spread of this realization, and of knowledge of what forms of early environment make people behave anti-socially, changed the whole mode of upbringing of children by parents. This appreciation of the effects of early environment changed society. That, I think, is a dramatic example of how a gain in psychological insight can lead to very widespread changes in human behaviour and in society itself.

I am not suggesting that organizational environment has nearly as important an effect on individual behaviour as early family environment. Family environment during childhood produces virtually permanent effects on the character of the person, and I do not suggest that organizational environment at work changes personality. On the other hand, I do contend that work environment does affect day-to-day behaviour profoundly. I can no more 'prove' this than Freud was able to prove that early environment affected subsequent individual character. I can only ask people to consult their own experience. Is it not observable that when a man changes from one role to another, or from one employment hierarchy to another, his behaviour often seems to change quite dramatically? Of course, the change may be due to the fact that his behaviour in his first situation was the result of a personal relationship with his manager or his colleagues. This is a very important factor governing behaviour. But do we not too readily attribute all behaviour to inbuilt character and to *personal* relationship? Why should we so often tend to exclude organizational environment as an important factor? My own experience is that clearly structured role-relationships, explicitly clear allocation of authority and accountability, clear-cut institutions for the investigation of feelings of injustice and for giving explicit opportunities of helping to form the rules and regulations governing working life, result in much less anxiety, frustration and hostility than an ill-defined environment. That the behaviour of large numbers of people is seriously affected by their organizational environment is, to me, beyond doubt.

Kurt Lewin, the famous German-American psychologist, in his book *A Dynamic Theory of Personality*,[1] describes the continuing tendency, even for psychologists, to ascribe all behaviour to the nature of the individual rather than to the individual plus his environment. Lewin asserts that Aristotelian thinking is still largely the current mode and describes this thinking like this: 'The vectors which determine an object's movements are completely determined by the object. That is, they do not depend upon the relation of the object to the environment, and they belong to that object once and for all, irrespective of its surroundings at any given time.'

Lewin then contrasts this Aristotelian attitude with that of modern *physical* scientists who are always concerned to explain phenomena in terms of the object *and* its relationship to its environment. He (Lewin) then gives many examples of continued failure to study human phenomena in this context and says: 'The dynamic of the processes is always to be derived from *the relation of the concrete individual to the concrete situation* [my italics] and, so far as internal forces are concerned, from the mutual relations of the various functional systems that make up the individual.'

Here is a variable—organizational environment—which is under our control; that means that we can affect our daily behaviour by the way we design employment hierarchies and the manner in which we set up all the sub-institutions within them. This is exciting because it opens up a field where progress can be made in helping millions to lead happier lives, to carry out work more efficiently and thus to increase their standard of living.

Contrast this prospect with the despair of those who believe that the country is going to the dogs, that human nature is not what it was, that we will not improve until human nature changes, that we live in a materialistic society (as though we have not always done so) and that as long as this is so, human behaviour will continue to grow less and less acceptable as one year follows another.

Over the last century there has been a massive movement of population into employment. Up to the nineteenth century most people worked, if they were employed at all, in one-family agricultural holdings, in small family businesses, on itinerant or seasonal jobs, on genuine piecework, or in that special category called 'being in service'.

---

[1] McGraw-Hill, 1935. The quotations come from one essay in his book entitled 'The Conflict between Aristotelian and Galileian Modes of Thought in Contemporary Psychology'.

With industrialization there has been wholesale moves into ever larger employment hierarchies. In 1970 the *Reader's Digest* conducted an analysis of economic conditions in the UK and the member countries of the European Economic Community. Less than 5 per cent of the working population of the UK were either self-employed or employers, the analysis said. If these figures are correct it means that over 90 per cent of our population are now employed in employment hierarchies. These hierarchies are continually growing in size, and the larger they become the greater the need for understanding.

In small employment hierarchies—in the garage, the farm, the local shop or the professional firm—tension and hostility seem to occur much less often than in those employing larger numbers. But hierarchies are growing in size very rapidly as a response to economic and technological pressures, and tension grows with size. Everyone worries today about the increase of anti-social conduct in society generally. But what we may be observing is an overspill of feeling caused by unsatisfactory relations at work, an overspill that affects society itself.

(2) My second conviction follows on from my first. This is it: *that in order to create an environment at work that will stimulate social as opposed to anti-social behaviour, we must be able to describe that environment in objective terms, and we must establish a clear language in which all of us can communicate with each other, so that we share the same mental models of the many social institutions within which we take up different roles.* It is not possible to gain control of our working environment if we lack concepts and defined language. It was lack of these which for so long held back the description of our physical environment. It was the emergence of shared and defined concepts such as mass, velocity, density, atom, volt, force and energy which laid the basis of the international language of science. Using these means of communication scientists built up a shared picture of our universe and began to control it. This led to the harnessing of material resources and to a great surge forward in material standards of living.

An analogous effort to establish a common and defined language about our social environment could lead to a surge forward in our psychological standards of living. There is today too much tension, greed, readiness to resort to force and hate in employment. These tendencies seem to grow rather than diminish. If that is due to the innate character of all the individuals concerned, then we are stuck with it during our lifetime, for character-change in a population takes generations. But I do not believe that. I think that the average individual is generous and reasonable. He wants to contribute to society by working creatively and efficiently, but is held back by the environment at work.

So I am optimistic—because I believe that we can change that work environment. That is what this book is about.

CHAPTER TWO

Discipline in Thinking and Language

'It is certainly a reasonable hypothesis that one of the principal causes of confusion, misery and fear is blind adherence to outworn notions, pathological suspicion of any form of critical self-examination, frantic efforts to prevent any degree of rational analysis of what we live by and for.'—SIR ISAIAH BERLIN

WALTER BAGEHOT PUBLISHED *The English Constitution* in 1867. Its importance to me lies in the fact that Bagehot was one of the first to adopt a detailed and objective scientific attitude towards specific social institutions. Instead of accepting the conventional wisdom of his time he began to look at the English Constitution and compare what he saw with the assumptions that people had made about it. Here are his words:

> The literature which has accumulated upon it [the English Constitution] is huge. But an observer who looks at the living reality will wonder at the contrast to the paper description. He will see in the life much which is not in the books: and he will not find in the rough practice many refinements of the literary theory.

He goes on to discuss the constitution, and comes to this conclusion:

> In such constitutions there are two parts (not indeed separable with microscopic accuracy for the genius of great affairs abhors nicety of division): first, those which excite and preserve the reverence of the population—*the dignified parts*, if I may call them so: and next, *the efficient parts*—those by which it, in fact, works and rules.

Later Bagehot draws attention to the fact that 'it is laid down as a principle of the English polity that in it the legislative, the executive and the judicial powers are quite divided . . . that no one of these can at all interfere with the work of the other'. After discussing the situation he points out that in fact 'the efficient secret of the English Constitution may be described as the close union, the nearly complete fusion of the executive and legislative powers'.

This may sound a strange introduction to a work on organization, but I claim that what is needed today is a Bagehot-like analysis of all our institutions. I use the term 'institution' in a broad sense to refer to a single role like that of a manager or a shop-steward, to a network of roles like that of an employment hierarchy or a trade union, to an institution which allows of an interaction of two systems of roles, such as a joint negotiating body between management and representatives, and to a vast complex like, say, the National Health Service, the railways, or a large industrial group.

It is the way these institutions are set up that largely constitutes our environment at work. The clarity or lack of clarity with which accountability and authority are allocated to individual roles, the relationship between roles, the authority of one system of roles as opposed to the power emanating from another system, determine our conditions of work, our pay, our authority, our accountability, our freedom to get on with the job or our lack of it, our relations with other people at work and with our managers, our differential privileges and entitlements, and our degree of happiness.

But we do not describe these things with accuracy. The *de jure* situation is different from the *de facto* situation. Our managers are not really managers. The decisions which vitally affect us are made by people to whom we have no access. Failing clear right of appeal against what they feel is injustice, employees resort to the use of power. Lip-service is paid to the idea of participation by employees in the development of the policies that affect them. But it is only lip-service, so that resort to the use of power or threats follows. Without a realistic analysis of their total real position managers assume authority they have not got, attempt to force through change, and find themselves strike-bound. Employees, unaware of their true power position, believe themselves to be threatened by over-powerful managers and take up defensive positions. In this atmosphere of suspicion and hostility, the power of groups of representatives to disrupt the organization can overtake and overwhelm their sense of responsibility. The lack of any real analysis of the nature of people's feelings about pay leads to payment policies that rapidly increase the

general level of wages without solving the crucial problem of inequitable differentials. Lack of insight into the essentially decision-making
nature of work causes a confused allocation of accountability and
authority between high-level managers and between different divisions of the same institutions. The result is confusion in the making
of policy and delay in the making of decisions.

The comment of the Robbins' Report on the Universities on the
role of the Vice-Chancellor was: 'His is a role which probably *fortu-
nately* [my italics] is seldom precisely spelt out in the constitutions'.
Commenting on university constitutions the report says:

> Universities are no exception to the general rule that a great
> gulf lies between the constitutions on paper and government in
> practice. A description of the functions and composition of the
> statutory bodies is not necessarily an analysis of the real sources of
> initiative and power; these depend partly on the imponderables
> of specific circumstances and individual personalities and are
> almost impossible to determine.

The effects on university life are manifold. For example, a high
premium is placed on research as a means by which staff can obtain
promotion and a low premium is placed on good teaching. The allocation of resources within universities between different branches of
learning is influenced too much by internal politics and too little by a
response to the needs of students and of society itself. University research is influenced too much by the personal leanings of the staff and
too little by the existence of acute social, scientific, and industrial
problems that need urgent study. Many universities fail to devote
enough study to the effectiveness of current educational methods, to
the current content of curricula, and to the appropriateness of the
methods in use for assessing the progress of students.[1] Many teachers
at universities are acutely aware of these things. There is no lack of
will to put them right. But confused organization gets in the way.

Wage problems are largely problems of differentials between one
group and another that are felt to be unfair. Many people know this.

---

[1] 'Mr A. B. Clegg, Chief Education Officer of the West Riding, said
yesterday that the headmaster of Otley Grammar School entered 28
pupils for the English Language 'O' Level examinations under two
different boards. In one case 27 passed and one failed; in the other,
three passed and 25 failed. . . . Two candidates only out of the 28 were
placed in the same grade by both boards and one candidate was
placed in the top grade by one board and the bottom by the other
Mr Clegg said.'—*The Guardian*, February 1965

But the structure of industrial companies, the structure of trade unions, the inadequacy of the institution within which they meet and negotiate, and a lack of insight on the part of the Government, has led to unhelpful and abortive attempts to solve these problems by unsuitable methods. 'Productivity deals' are a fair example of this lack of insight.

There are no means in use for measuring a mixed output of work. Even if there were it would be impossible to identify the particular contribution made by labour to an increase of output. The contribution made by labour cannot be separated from other contributions, arising from increased investment or change in production techniques. In return for increased wages negotiated in this way employers have often received little more than the giving up of a restrictive agreement or, worse, the manufacture of new restrictive agreements as a bargaining counter. The definition of productivity agreements has, in any case, often been so vague as to make it difficult to determine later whether the agreement to give up some restrictive practice has been kept.

Even if it had been possible both to measure output and to decide the source of increased output, those who had held back in the past would have been in a position to do better than those whose effort had been good in the past and could not be improved upon. Governments, employers, and trade unions could not possibly have agreed such methods of bargaining over pay if they had had a disciplined insight into the factors they were handling. We would seem to be at about the same stage of thinking about such matters as the alchemists were in relation to chemistry in the fourteenth century.

People persistently voice the view that trade-union leaders ought to lead, and to see to it that their members do not breach agreements. But the public fail to realize that these union officials are elected and paid by their members to voice the view of those members and to bargain on their behalf. People accuse trade-union leaders of being two-faced because they say one thing in private and another in public, but there must be a difference between their representative and their personal view. One might as well accuse a barrister of dishonesty because he did his best in court for a client who had a dubious defence.

Current conventional wisdom, voiced increasingly by leaders of business, maintains that today's great industrial problem is 'lack of communication'. Great conferences discuss it solemnly. But we live in an age where there are more and better means of communicating than ever before. There is the press, radio, television, tape, typewriters, loud-speaker systems, rapid printing methods, and films. Can it be that in an era of the greatest-ever advances in communication techniques, communication has become one of our major problems? Of course, people often do not really mean 'communication'. It is a dangerous and empty cliché because it seems to relieve those who utter it from the hard work of analysing the sources of the trouble. Undoubtedly the causes of unrest and dissatisfaction at work lie much deeper and are much more complex than is generally assumed, and we ought to be spending major resources on investigating them.

If a company builds a great and complex mechanism like a steel-rolling mill, a chemical plant or a town centre, the plans for their construction and operation must be accurate. But if we want to construct a social mechanism such as an administrative system, then we seem to consider that accurate description is unnecessary. Yet, in terms of human satisfaction, a good administrative system is more important than the steel mill, the chemical plant or the town centre. The basic trouble is that we are not sufficiently concerned to construct an accurate language in which we can discuss social issues and social institutions. There are the terms which have more than one meaning that are seriously used as though this was not so. For example, a distinguished member of a business school, in a recent conversation, criticized what he described as my 'obsession' with precise language. He was by training an economist, and so I asked him to define what the term 'marginal cost' meant, firstly to an economist and secondly to a cost-accountant. In fact, they mean two quite different things.[1] But he seemed quite unconcerned when I protested at the folly of continuing to use one term to refer to two distinct and different concepts. Social and economic life is full of such examples.

There are many terms which are simply misused. Many companies, for example, are changing their methods of paying production

---

[1] The language used by economists and accountants is often imprecise. 'Opportunity cost', 'alternative-use cost', and 'marginal cost' all seem to be used by some as referring to the same thing. But the accountants' 'marginal cost' usually refers to the additional cost of increasing output by a small amount, say, one unit. Some economists regard the cost of acquiring goods as the need to forego the enjoyment of other goods. If resources are used to produce one thing they cannot be used to produce others; therefore, the cost of the one is the value of the alternatives foregone. (See *Dictionary of Economics* by A. Sheldon and F. G. Pennance, published by J. M. Dent & Sons Ltd.)

workers from direct-incentive bonus methods and are adopting what is called 'measured daywork', but in fact there is no measurement in 'measured daywork'; it is simply based on judgement.

Transferred epithets, again, cause confusion. For example, people talk about 'boring work' when they mean 'work which causes boredom in the person doing it'. At first sight it may seem a harmless mistake but, in fact, it leads to the active assumption by many members of the public that 'boring work' is of a nature that will cause anybody who does it to be bored. This is nonsense, because the feeling of boredom is a product of many things, one of the most important being the match between the level of capacity of the person doing the work and the level of the work itself. But many people have not thought this one out, and so they worry about society because they think that an ever-growing proportion of the population is having to do boring work when, in fact, the opposite trend is observable. The fact is that even in the areas of highest unemployment there is a shortage of people capable of doing work at the higher levels.

People talk of 'routine work', which they assume does not involve the making of any decisions. But nobody in full possession of his faculties does such work, because work done by human beings normally calls for the use of some judgement. The use of the term 'routine work' leads to a contemptuous attitude by managers and bitterness by those doing so-called 'routine work', which, in fact, usually involves a great deal of skilled judgement.

All this undisciplined use of language about social affairs (and the false ideas to which it leads) is to be contrasted with the fact that most sixth-form schoolboys would pick you up immediately if you confused velocity with acceleration, atom with molecule, or atomic fusion with atomic fission.

But does it really matter if we hang on to social descriptions which we know intuitively to be inaccurate or incomplete? Some people are anxious about what would happen if we tried to describe ourselves and our social environment more clearly. They ask whether we need, after all, to be precise in our descriptions of and our statements about organization, policy, authority, accountability and individual behaviour. Are we not, they say, in danger of becoming too formal? My reply is that the healthy progress of humanity depends on our getting away from all unrealistic mental images of the world in which we live. The alternative to the possession and use of defined concepts and mental models which are based on careful analysis is not that of having no models at all. The real, and harmful, alternative is the use of formulations that are based upon biased conventions and unchecked assumptions. The distorted models which result are horribly important. Once thought of and expressed they influence our own outlook and actions and the outlook and the actions of others. They impede our actions or, worse, cause us to act in ways that preclude the resolution of the problems we wish to settle.

There are those who are convinced that formalization means a loss of freedom. Their cry is, 'Let's leave it vague so that individual creativeness can have a greater chance.' But there is plenty of evidence that vague and confused organization is the great enemy of creativeness. There are those who claim that disciplined observation, concept formation, and precise language, cannot be used as tools in social situations involving human beings. It is the object of this book to demonstrate that this is untrue.

People comment frequently nowadays on the enormous discrepancy between our ability to solve scientific and technological problems and our ability to solve social ones. I would like to re-phrase the problem and to draw attention to the fact that we are able to describe our physical environment in increasingly precise detail, whereas our lack of precision in describing our social environment is frightening. Our inability to describe our social institutions and situations in disciplined terms has meant that most people are unaware of the source of many social problems. Most people are also unaware of the connection between this unawareness and the social, industrial and administrative problems it has caused and is causing.

I think we are at a decisive stage of history in relation to these social problems. They are becoming almost terrifying in their complexity, and the resulting anxiety about them will, I hope, drive us to the study necessary to produce solutions. Twenty-five years ago people did not go to the dentist until the pain they were suffering was greater than their expectations of pain at the hands of the dentist. As the pain of social problems increases it will no doubt provide the motivation for the necessary study.

We look back to the Elizabethan age as one of dynamic advance. But one of the most important features of that age is often overlooked. It was the time of Francis Bacon and many other scientists of his kind. He and his contemporaries turned the tide of thinking about the study of nature.[1]

---

[1] The Bacon school of thinking led directly to the setting up of the Royal Society in 1662. But what was significant about the early days of that society was that no subject was considered beyond the scope of study by its members. John Evelyn studied and protested against the smoke which fouled the air of London; Sir William Petty (a professor

Many people, even today, do not realize that by changing the mode of thinking of his day he was laying the foundation of that great advance which has now provided society with such a high potential standard of material living. It would have looked an absurd claim, in Bacon's day, to suggest that by discarding the mode of thinking of Aristotle and by adopting a new mode of thinking it would be possible to achieve such results. Nevertheless, there is a direct connection between that change in thinking and our modern scientific achievements.

In relation to social issues we are at the same stage of thinking as that which preceded Francis Bacon in relation to natural science. I believe that a change of our mode of thinking about social issues could lead to the same order of advance that he started by his passionate call to his fellows, expressed thus:

> Nor let any weight be given to the fact that in his [Aristotle's] books on animals and his problems, and other of his treatises, there is frequent dealing with experiments. For he had come to his conclusions before; he did not consult experience, as he should have done, for the purpose of framing his decisions and axioms, but having first determined the question according to his will, he then resorts to experience, and bending her into conformity with his placets, leads her about like a captive in a procession.[1]

In another passage Bacon says:

> Now what the sciences stand in need of is a form of induction which shall analyse experience and take it to pieces, and by a due process of exclusion and rejection lead to an inevitable conclusion. And if that ordinary mode of judgment practised by the logicians was so laborious and found exercise for such great wits, how much more labour must we be prepared to bestow upon this other which

---

of anatomy) published a treatise on Taxes and Contributions; statistics collected by John Graunt became the basis of the first life-insurance tables. And about this time was established the office of Inspector General of Imports and Exports—the first special statistical department successfully created by any European State. It has been estimated that nearly 60 per cent of the problems handled by the Royal Society in its first thirty years were prompted by the practical needs of public use. (See *The Western Intellectual Tradition*, J. Bronowski and Bruce Mazlish, Hutchinson, London, 1960.)

[1] From *The New Organon*, Liberal Arts Press, New York Edition. Originally published in Latin in 1620. (Other quotations from Bacon from the same source.)

is extracted not merely out of the depths of the mind, but out of the very bowels of nature.

Francis Bacon's comment on Aristotle boils down to the accusation that he selected his evidence to support his preconceived ideas. This is what we so often continue to do today in our thinking about social institutions.

If anybody has doubts as to whether this is the current mode of thinking and discussion about many economic and social issues, then let him listen to the speeches of the politicians during a general election or the protagonists in an industrial dispute, or even to the conversations we have with our friends when we turn to what we regard as serious issues.

We are all wont, in argument, to describe what is the same situation in terms which could only apply to entirely different situations. This is a recipe for continued strife not only in politics but in every walk of life.

Many great men of the past have fully realized the discrepancy between the advance of natural science and the halting pace of sociology. Thomas Hobbes, a contemporary of Francis Bacon, spent his long life (1588–1679) studying man's institutions and behaviour. He knew the importance of language. Here is just one of his many comments on the subject, which we ought to take more account of even today.

The first cause of Absurd conclusions I ascribe to the want of Method; in that they begin not their Ratiocination from Definitions; that is, from settled significations of their words: as if they could cast account, without knowing the value of the numerall words, *one*, *two*, and *three*.—*Leviathan*.

John Locke (1632–1704), David Hume (1711–76), and Jeremy Bentham (1748–1832), to name just a few of the most eminent, were all concerned with our institutions and with the use of accurate language to describe them. Locke was one of the first to demonstrate that *power* rested with the people and that governments must be elected to protect collective rights. Hume convinced men of his time that the laws of cause and effect, in sociological matters, were much more complex than had been assumed. Bentham railed against the ambiguity of language and wanted a science of language, to break through all the confusion it caused in social matters. According to John Stuart Mill, Bentham introduced precision of thought into moral and political philosophy.

One may well ask what has happened to all this striving. Clearly, if these great minds were alive today, they would be puzzled by the contrast between the advances of the natural sciences and the lack of advance in the directions which absorbed their interests.

I do not think time is on our side. The need for disciplined thinking and shared language about social issues is urgent. If we fail to make progress then crime, industrial unrest, social schism, resort to the use of power and individual greed, will increasingly disrupt society.

But few are convinced that improved language, more accurate mental models of situations and disciplined building of hypotheses will help these social problems. That is why I draw the parallel with the seventeenth century. Bacon knew that he was starting a long and hard battle. Listen to the closing sentences of the Preface to *The New Organon*.

> Lastly, I would address one general admonishment to all—that they consider what are the true ends of knowledge, and that they seek it not either for pleasure of the mind, or for contention, or for superiority to others, or for profit, or fame, or power, or any of these inferior things, but for the benefit and use of life, and that they perfect and govern it in charity. . . . The requests I have to make are these. Of myself I say nothing; but in behalf of the business which is in hand, I entreat men to believe that it is not an opinion to be held, but a work to be done; and to be well assured that I am labouring to lay the foundations, not of any sect or doctrine, but of human utility and power.

CHAPTER THREE

Concept Formation

'. . . and all depends on keeping the eye steadily fixed upon the facts of nature and so receiving their images simply as they are'.—FRANCIS BACON, *The New Organon*

WE NEED A series of boundary-defined concepts. By this I mean that a person who knows the area with which the concept is concerned ought to be able to identify what falls within its ambit. Thus, for example, the Society of British Aircraft Constructors once defined the term 'manager' as 'a person with executive responsibility for a *substantial* department or *major* function in relation to which he makes a *direct* and *significant* contribution in the formulation of *policy*'. Anybody trying to use this definition to discover whether a particular position was a managerial one or not would have trouble in giving a precise value to the words 'substantial', 'major', 'direct', 'significant' and 'policy'. In short, this is not a boundary-defined concept. It is almost meaningless.

Boundary definition involves identifying the particular features of an institution that make it different from all other institutions. I shall not define 'manager' at this point because such a definition would be lengthy, but give, as an immediate example, a term that can be defined briefly. 'A committee is a body of people possessing corporate responsibility for making decisions and who thus, in the last analysis, make their decisions by majority vote.'

If this be accepted as a definition, then the House of Commons, a Board of Directors, or a meeting of shop-stewards is a committee. But an inter-departmental meeting in the Civil Service, whose members can reserve the position of their departments (and the body is not regarded as having made a recommendation so long as some of its members do so reserve their position), is not a 'committee' according to this definition. Neither is a meeting of a manager with his immediate subordinates.

Again if, for example, we agree that 'there are people who speak the views of others' it is simply a random perception or observation, but if we agree that 'there are persons who are charged by groups of other people to voice the views of the group on its behalf' then the inference is that they must have been elected by the group to do so. We then have a boundary-defined concept of 'representative', i.e. 'A person who is elected by a group to speak its views on its behalf.'[1]

Before moving on to other examples I want to delve a little deeper into the nature of the word 'concept'. It is widely used simply to refer to an idea which has been the subject of a general but not definitive description. I think this is a pity, for science uses it in a much more precise sense. It is because of this imprecision in the use of the term that I talk of 'boundary-defined' concepts, to make it clear that I am using the term in the rigorous sense rather than as a mere reference to a description of something. It is quite difficult to find the word 'concept' itself *defined* in the writings of scientists and philosophers. Some years ago I conducted a search and found what I sought in *The Grammar of Science* by Karl Pearson.[2] I quote:

> In order that a conception may have scientific validity it must be self-consistent and deducible from the perceptions of the normal human being. For instance, a centaur is not a self-consistent conception; as soon as our knowledge of human and equine anatomy became sufficiently developed the centaur became an unthinkable thing—a self-negating idea.

To me the important aspect of what Pearson says is the link he establishes between 'perception' and 'conception' (or concept). It means that if we are to share the use of conceptions we must first agree that our perceptions coincide and, furthermore, we must agree that the conception is deducible from those shared perceptions.[3]

---

[1] It is to be noted that somebody who is elected is not necessarily a representative, for he might, for example, be elected to the role of chairman of a committee or he might be elected a member of a profession, and so on. Nor is a person who speaks the views of others necessarily a representative, for he might simply feel that he is so familiar with those views as to be entitled to do so.

[2] First published in 1892. Now No. 939 in Everyman's Library, J. M. Dent & Sons Ltd, London.

[3] Or as Hobbes put it in the opening sentences of *Leviathan* 'The Original of them all [Man thoughts] is that which we call SENSE; (For there is no conception in a man's mind, which hath not at first, totally, or by parts, been begotten upon the organs of sense.) The rest are derived from that original.'

At this point some may wonder what this has to do with social institutions and organization: but we are unable to discuss such matters without shared concepts. In order to think about social institutions we have to be able to create mental models of them, and we need concepts to do this. If our concepts are not consistent with those used by others then we shall assume that we are each discussing the same situation when, in fact, we are not. If our concepts are not deducible from our perceptions (as in the example of the centaur which Pearson uses), then we may be attempting to discuss something that does not exist. If our concepts are not stated in boundary-defined form then it is not possible to determine whether the thing exists or not. For example, what is Industrial Democracy?

The perceptions upon which we must agree are those that are unique to the thing we wish to define, because it is these distinguishing features that separate it from other things. For example, the distinguishing perception leading to the formation of the concept of 'committee' is the existence of bodies that arrive at decisions by majority vote. The distinguishing perception leading to the formation of the concept of 'representative' is that some people are authorized by others to voice their views for them.

The act of defining the meaning of a term implies separating its meaning from the meaning given to another term. 'Acceleration' is defined as the rate of increase of velocity. The concept of acceleration is thus defined in terms of its relationship to velocity. 'Representative' is defined in terms of its relationship to electors, after sharing the perceptions that elections manifest the choices of electors and that the representative speaks on behalf of those who have elected him.

The foregoing may appear to labour the obvious, but it is seldom set out in explicit form.

I move now to a discussion of the very important concept of 'manager'. In a company employing 1000 people there are, or should be, 999 manager–subordinate relationships if every person in it, except the chief executive, is to be responsible to a manager. As far as I am aware there is only one company, out of all the various institutions in Britain employing people, which has defined these relationships and regularly makes use of the concept of 'manager' in boundary-defined form. It seems to me extraordinary that neither the British Institute of Management[1] nor the American Management

---

[1] In 1970 the British Institute of Management published a study entitled *The Experienced Manager* by Alistair Mant. I was attracted into ordering a copy because it contained a 'Definition of the Experienced

Association,[1] nor most of the business schools or university departments concerned use such a defined concept in their teaching.

I define the concept of 'manager' like this:
The perceptions which we need (and which I have found nearly all people in employment with whom I have discussed the subject agree) are as follows:

(a) In organizations which employ people there are roles to which more work is allotted than the single occupant of the role can personally perform. Let us assume that Mr Smith occupies one of these roles.

(b) Smith, perforce, must arrange for some of his work to be carried out by others.

(c) Although Smith does not personally do all the work allotted to his role he is, nevertheless, accountable to higher authority for the manner in which all of it is carried out.

Those are the unique perceptions about a specific type of role. I have pointed them out to many hundreds of managers in the past and

---

Manager'. I was filled with anticipation: at last a definition of 'manager' from the BIM. But alas, this is the 'definition':

> The definition adopted is an attempt to condense a variety of company definitions of the experienced manager, in so far as he seems to them to represent a problem.

> The description 'experienced manager' was chosen to suggest a man who has probably had at least five years in management and has reached his position largely through success in jobs below his current one. His success has arisen from a mixture of experience, intuition and knowledge, built up by dealing with situations.

[1] The USA Taft-Hartley Act provides the following definition of 'supervisor':

> The term supervisor means any individual having authority in the interests of the employer to hire, transfer, suspend, lay off, recall, promote, discharge, assign, reward or discipline other employees, or responsibility to direct them, or to adjust their grievances, or effectively to recommend such action if, in connection with the foregoing, the exercise of such authority is not of a mere routine or clerical nature but requires use of independent judgement.

It is not however, satisfactory. Was a supervisor intended, for example, to hire anybody he chose, regardless of existing company policies? Could a supervisor reward a subordinate as he saw fit? How could a supervisor transfer an employee to another command without the agreement of another supervisor?

have always found that they are shared perceptions. In order to be able to proceed and deduce the concept from those perceptions I must assume that my readers also share them. These are my deductions.

(1) Smith must be authorized to veto the appointment of persons available to him to carry out some of this work. If some person with authority over Smith insists that a person be appointed who in Smith's view will be incapable of discharging that part of Smith's work which he will have to allocate to such a person, then Smith cannot logically be held accountable for the way in which that part of his work is done.

(2) Smith must be authorized to assess the differential competence of those appointed to do parts of his work on his behalf. If higher authority insists that Smith allocates specific work to subordinate Jones rather than to subordinate Brown, when Smith does not regard Jones as being capable of doing that work, then Smith cannot be held accountable for the results. (Smith's authority to assess the competence of subordinates suggests at least that Smith should have authority for determining some of the *differential* payment of his subordinates.)

(3) Smith must be authorized to decide whether or not a subordinate be retained in his role. If Smith is ordered to retain a subordinate who is not, in his opinion, capable of discharging the work that Smith decides to allocate to him, then Smith cannot be held accountable for the results that follow.

(The subordinate must have a right of appeal to higher authority in order to ensure that Smith has based his decision to have the subordinate removed from his role exclusively on the subordinate's work and not on extraneous matters, otherwise Smith would be assuming authority over his subordinate for matters other than the discharge of work. Smith's accountability for his subordinates' work is the only reason why Smith has this authority over them.)

We now have a boundary definition of a managerial role: a role from which some work has to be delegated to subordinate roles. The occupant of the managerial role is accountable for his subordinates' work and must at least have authority to veto the appointment of persons to the subordinate roles, to insist that they be removed from those roles if they are unsatisfactory, and to determine which portions of his own work shall be carried out by each subordinate.

Using this definition anybody can now discover, by asking a few questions, whether a person is or is not a manager within the terms of the definition. Such a discovery, or the ability to make the discovery, is more important than it looks.

Managers have been described as people who 'hire and fire' and I have heard the definition I have given referred to loosely in these terms. But there are important differences. 'Hire' means 'taking into the employment of the company', whereas vetoing the appointment of a person means no more than 'I cannot accept that person as one of my subordinates'. 'Fire' usually means 'discharging a person from a company', whereas the authority to insist on the removal of a person from a subordinate role, with the prospect of his being found acceptable by some other manager, is a different matter.

As long as we fail to use the term 'manager' in a defined sense then our listeners will attribute to the word a variety of different ideas, and this inhibits communication. But another thing hindering communication is the lack of terms to use as labels for ideas. Thus, there are many social institutions that exist and have functions, but which are neither defined nor labelled, and this makes discussion halting and uncertain.

Here are two linked examples. Their obviousness and simplicity does not detract from their usefulness.

Consider an organization composed of three ranks. Sixteen people at Rank C are at the base of the hierarchy, four at Rank B and one at Rank A, as in Fig. 1.

We can define the four roles at Rank B as being the 'Immediate Command' of A. But A is also responsible for Rank C. I have no doubt people would talk of 'A's whole department', but it may not be a single department. Or they may refer to 'all of A's people', but this is very vague. Is it not better to build a concept and label it? We could refer to A's 'Extended Command' and define it as 'All the employees under the control of A'.

This may seem an unnecessary refinement, but suppose, instead of an organization with three ranks employing twenty-one people, we have one of seven ranks employing 20 000 people, then it will contain hundreds of extended commands. It will become very necessary to be able to refer to them and to discuss them in clear terms.

There are other social institutions which are too little used and whose usefulness is not appreciated because they have not been described, defined and labelled. Here is an example.

Suppose some complicated change in the work of the organization arises and A decides that he ought to explain it personally to all in Rank C. There is, in fact, no word for this act, which is (or at least

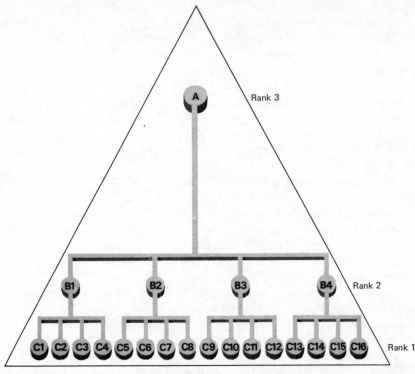

Figure 1

ought to be) a common occurrence. A could be said to be 'contract-ing'[1] the employment hierarchy.

We can set up the concept of 'contraction' and define it as 'the act of a manager when he establishes communication with some or all of the members of his extended command who are not his immediate subordinates'.

Again, this might be considered over-refinement, but, in larger companies, it can be very important to be able to talk about this contraction relationship in very specific terms. For example, it may

---

[1] It may strike readers as a poor word to use because 'contract' has other distinct meanings, but I have been unable so far to find a better one. The only alternative would have been to create an entirely new word, but the production of jargon is never popular. The concept is a familiar one in the Royal Navy under another name. When a com-manding officer needs to communicate something to his ship's company which is so important that on no account must the message be mis-understood, he 'clears the lower deck' and talks to the men directly.

become urgently necessary, when the possibility of misunderstanding (which might lead, say, to a stoppage of work) arises, for the chief executive to instruct one of his factory managers to 'contract' at once and discuss matters with his extended command. Indeed, I would go further and suggest that the non-existence of the concept of contraction leads to a failure to contract in many situations where it would seem to be commonsense to do so. Because many managers have never considered contraction as being an ordinary tool of management they fail to use it when the need arises.[1]

My fourth example is more general, and I give it because it is basic to the ideas contained in this book. Institutions which employ large numbers of people find it necessary to describe their own organization and structure to help individuals understand their place within it, and so that all employees have a common view of it. Thus, charts and descriptions in words of the organization, its policies and its major routines, may be provided. It is common to find situations where a senior person in such an organization, having exhibited an organization chart, goes on to say that in fact the institution is not organized as shown, or that the chart is out of date, or that some of the written routines he has produced are not actually in operation. He is thus displaying what I would like to refer to as the Manifest Organization, which I would define as: 'The organization as formally described and displayed.'

The senior person may then proceed to describe the organization as he believes it to be. Thus, we can refer to Assumed Organization and define it as 'organization as it is assumed to be by the person concerned'. But systematic analysis of the organization may disclose something else again. This we can call Extant Organization, defined as 'organization as revealed by systematic exploration and analysis'. Sometimes, to say the least, the extant organization—the real thing—does not fulfil its purpose well. This is not surprising if the work to be done has changed without adaptation of the system. Once the real nature of the organization has been discovered, changes will often suggest themselves. The prospective new pattern can be labelled 'Requisite Organization', defined as 'organization as it would have to be to accord with the real properties of the field in which it exists'.

If Manifest, Assumed, Extant and Requisite organization coincide, then we are in the ideal position. But I doubt if such a situation has ever arisen, and I believe that in most organizations the differences

[1] I am aware that in many concerns there would be resistance on the part of trade-union representatives to a manager contracting. I have discussed these difficulties in chapter eighteen.

between description and reality are great. If we could pull them together it would affect our lives beneficially in many ways.

I have given these examples simply to illustrate the process of concept formation. In the course of describing other aspects of organization in the following chapters, I will define additional concepts. But I shall not go through, in every case, the process of stating perceptions and deducing conceptions from them, because in most cases, once stated, they are obvious, and such treatment is therefore unnecessary.

My readers may question the usefulness of stating the obvious. But I am using 'obvious' in a particular sense. The concepts are obvious *once stated*. This is the natural result of making an early attack on an ill-trodden field of study. But the further we try to advance, the more difficult fresh concepts become and the greater the need for rigorous description of the basis upon which they have been formed. Some of those I describe later are of this nature, and where this is so I have referred readers to writings that deal with them in greater detail.

In a glossary that appears in chapter thirty-two I have set out all the definitions I have used, except when they are already in common use.

CHAPTER FOUR

Scientific Method and Social Issues

'It is often said that experiments must be made without a preconceived idea. That is impossible. Not only would it make all experiment barren, but that would be attempted which could not be done. Everyone carries in his mind his own conception of the world, of which he cannot so easily rid himself. We must, for instance, use language; and our language is made up only of preconceived ideas and cannot be otherwise. Only these are unconscious preconceived ideas, a thousand times more dangerous than the others.'—H. POINCARÉ, *The Foundation of Science*, New York

I have no use for those people who say that there is a region of science and that you can travel through that region and come to the boundary; that when you have gone through that region labelled science, you come to a region labelled something else—it might be religion, art or anything you will. . . . Some people say that science is a study of those things which are reproducible. This is not true. Perhaps the most significant scientific theory in the whole of the biological order is the theory of evolution, and that is not reproducible. Some people say that science is the study of those things that can be verified. That is not true either. Nobody can ever make exactly the same experiment that somebody else has made.'—
C. A. COULSON, Professor of Applied Mathematics, Oxford University, *The Manager*, January 1956

THIS CHAPTER IS about the further mental tools that we require for the study of social institutions. Perceptions and observation which lead to the creation of boundary-defined concepts enable people to build and to share each other's mental models of situations. But we need more mental tools than this if we want to predict what will happen in a situation when change is introduced into it.

If we can make a prediction (and even if it turns out to be inaccurate) that as a result of changing one factor in a situation certain results will follow, then we are establishing an hypothesis. Many people believe that hypotheses are generated and used only by scientists and technologists. As Professor Coulson implies, they believe that this form of scientific thinking is not applicable to happenings in our social environment. People who believe that are, I think, wrong.

The mental tool I want to discuss is that of scientific method. What the phrase means to me is a number of linked processes.

(1) The building of a mental model of a situation by the use of observation and concepts that are already available.

(2) Observation and collection of data or, at times, the cautious examination and acceptance of the observation of others about events taking place within that situation.

(3) The induction from these observations of an hypothesis that explains the observed events. (Induction is not a prescribed logical process; it involves the imaginative choice of an explanation of the events observed from an array of possibilities.)

(4) The subsequent deduction, using the hypothesis, of the events that must occur in a prescribed set of circumstances to lend support to the hypothesis.

(5) The planning of an experiment to produce the prescribed circumstances, and the observation of whether the predictions of the hypothesis are fulfilled or not.

(6) The reorientation of the hypothesis, if the deduced results do not occur, i.e. if you have got it wrong, start again.

The inductive process and the deductive one often take place simultaneously. That is to say that when someone starts inducing a hypothesis from his observations, no sooner does one occur to him than he starts checking its possible validity by making deductions and imagining the possible results of experiments.

This mode of thinking is endemic in humans. But many people are unaware that they are using it, and probably use it in an undisciplined way. We proceed on a basis of a 'hunch', which is a sort of undisciplined hypothesis.

A child experimentally behaves in a certain way and its mother reacts unfavourably. It gets a hunch that that form of behaviour produces anger. It repeats the behaviour and gets the same result. Its hunch is strengthened. We look at the sky and say it is going to rain. We have made a prediction based on the hypothesis that certain cloud-formations eventually produce rain.

During the last war when the company I managed received a contract for some accurate parts, I was told that these would be delayed in delivery because such parts could only be made on a certain type of machine tool, of which we had too few. We had available production capacity on a battery of machines of a different type. But I was assured that they could not produce with the required accuracy. I had heard that hypothesis before and decided to have it tested by arranging an attempt to make a trial batch of the accurate parts on those machines. The parts were duly produced and passed inspection. I had invalidated a hypothesis.

It would be possible to quote thousands of similar examples. We all use either our own private unstated and often sub-conscious hunches or more widely accepted explicit hypotheses many times each day. I have worked with engineers and scientists for over thirty years. In dealing with mechanical, chemical, metallurgical or electrical problems, their thinking is (predictably) very disciplined. If, in an attempt to correct the metallurgical composition of a product that is the end result of a complex process, they change a single one of the variable conditions of the process and obtain the required change in composition, then they want to be quite certain that the change they *deliberately* introduced was not accompanied by other changes, which might have been *inadvertently* introduced by lack of control. They are reluctant to accept that change X in the process resulted in change Y in the product without repeated experiment.

What is remarkable, however, is that these same people, faced with a social, commercial, managerial or personnel problem, will often throw their own stern discipline to the winds. They will produce hunches that link specific changes with specific results while overlooking other variables, which have been fluctuating in an uncontrolled manner and which may have affected the results as much as or more than the specific changes upon which they have focused their attention. These ill-disciplined conclusions are often the result of a semi or sub-conscious process of selection of evidence, which is itself due to bias, based on emotional experiences in the past.

One can detect in the minds of many people an unformulated anxiety, which seems to run like this. A precious part of our freedom is the right to think as we choose and to come to our own personal conclusions about cause and effect in any manner that suits us. But in fact this is a freedom to believe that because we think something, then it must be so—'What I say three times is true;' Lewis Carroll lives in all of us. In the main, however, we yield to the discipline of the scientist in discussing our *physical* world. It is in our social world where we allow this denial of scientific method and the desertion of the use of logic to run riot.

We see it at its worst when we argue on political themes, where we constantly use grossly oversimplified hypotheses based on selection of evidence, or sometimes on fantasy evidence about cause and effect. Many parliamentarians are guilty of this and insist that the art of debate is the embarrassment of opponents rather than the attempt to reason. To me the salutary feature of spending five years as a member of the Government has been to observe the consistent attempt by civil servants to put emotion to one side and to deal with matters on the basis of reason. (I would admire them still more if they would use their strong logical instincts more adventurously. The two attitudes are not inconsistent.)

Every day we all face situations that require urgent action. Often we have little choice or none at all. If the lights go out in part of the house the first thing to do is to see if a fuse has blown. We have a well-tested hypothesis, shared with millions of others, that the most frequent cause of the lights going out is the melting of a fuse. But, in many other situations, choices present themselves to our minds that mean that we have to make decisions. We make the best decisions we can by selecting the appropriate concepts, building a mental model of the situation and considering various courses of action, based on the predictions we make concerning the results that might flow from each. These predictions are based on hunches. What we are saying is: 'In these circumstances if I take a particular action I expect that result to arise.'

The scientist dealing with physical things has available a vast range of boundary-defined concepts, which have often been in general use in his world for many years. With these he constructs mental models which have a high degree of precision as analogies of the situation external to his mind on which he is working. He has available a range of hypotheses constructed for him by others and repeatedly tested over the years. If he has to produce a new hypothesis he is able to make use of a range of sophisticated measuring instruments with which he can accurately plot the change in the variables while he is experimenting.

When we come to make decisions about our social environment the circumstances are very different. Nevertheless we *can*, if we choose, do much more in the direction of constructing defined concepts, which means that we ought to be able to construct much better mental models too.

Though we can only rarely achieve the degree of sophistication attained by scientists in the creation of hypotheses, we can do much to improve those we use. We can start by discarding some of the obvious absurdities. As the Rev. J. H. Blackham once put it in a sermon in the Ethical Church, Queen's Road, London, *circa* 1938—'Ought we not to dip every idea which we hold dear into the acid tank of scepticism, retaining only those which emerge uncorroded?'

Here are a few hypotheses which I do not think will stand the test:

(*a*) That in some employment-roles people do responsible work and have to think and make decisions, whereas in many lower-paid positions only routine work is called for, which does not require the individual to make decisions.

(*b*) That if, in an institution employing people, there is an established right of appeal by individual employees against the decisions of their immediate managers, then the status and authority of those managers will be undermined whenever, on appeal, their decisions are reversed in favour of a subordinate.

(*c*) That the best means by which the management of a company should convey details of its planned changes to employees in general is through their elected representatives.

(*d*) That ideally the immediate command of a manager should not exceed seven subordinates.

(*e*) Perhaps the commonest reason for confused thinking is the assumption that there must be a single cause of every problem. Halliday[1] recounts a scene in which there is a baby, in a pram, in a street, crying, surrounded by four children. A motherly passer-by stops and says: 'Why is the child crying?' One child says: 'because he wants his mother'. A second says 'he wants to get out of the pram'. A third says 'he is hungry', and the fourth says petulantly, 'because he is a baby'. Many people might say 'you can't all be right'; but, in fact, they could be.

We cannot validate social hypotheses as though we were dealing with physical phenomena, but we can try to make them explicit instead of being unaware of our own thought-processes. We can be vigilant to see if the predictions we derive from them are, on the whole, borne out or not in the uncontrolled situations with which we have to deal. This is not validation, but the testing by explicit scrutiny of results flowing from frequent use. Every decision and the action that follows is, in one sense, an experiment, albeit one in an uncontrolled situation. Nevertheless, explicit awareness of the hunches and hypotheses we are using, explicit awareness that our decisions are based on them and explicit awareness that each decision

---

[1] J. Halliday, *Psychosocial Medicine*, Norton, New York, 1960.

puts them to the test of usefulness would, I believe, demonstrate to each of us that many of them are not tenable and that we ought to think of something else.

The third mental tool that we use is the idea of 'properties', such as length, colour, weight and sound. Bridgeman[1] introduced the notion of operational definition of properties, and illustrates what he means by taking the property of length as an example. He points out that we know what we mean if we can discover what the length of various objects is, and that to find the length of an object we have to perform certain physical *operations*. He says, therefore,

> The property of length is fixed when the *operation* by which length is measured is fixed; that is the property of length involves as much as and nothing more than the set of operations by which length is determined. In general, we mean by any property nothing more than the set of operations; the property is synonymous with the corresponding set of operations.

We talk of length, weight, density, volume, temperature, velocity, voltage and many other physical properties, with assurance and familiarity because since they are measurable we know what they are. But if we want to study human and role relationships in employment hierarchies there are four classes of 'properties' that we shall have to consider.

Firstly, there are innate psychological 'properties' of people—skill, intelligence, responsibility, ambition, integrity, happiness, kindness and so on—which we cannot yet measure. Perhaps one day somebody will establish a correlation between the measured output of a particular form of electrical pulse from the brain and the agreed feelings of large numbers of people about the degree of 'skill' which others seem to possess. This is not as far-fetched as it seems. The establishment of a correlation between varying feelings of heat and cold and the length of a column of alcohol is the basis of measurement of heat. It took nearly a hundred years for people finally to accept that correlation and leave behind them arguments to the effect that though the thermometer might show A to be hotter than B they were sure, on the evidence of their senses, that B was hotter than A. We would not argue like that today, and would put aside the evidence of our senses in favour of the thermometer.

The second group of properties is concerned with psychological

---

[1] *The Logic of Modern Physics*, MacMillan, New York, 1927. Bridgeman actually wrote about 'operational definition of *concepts*'; but from the text it is clear that he is referring to properties.

relations of one person to another, such as love, jealousy, hate, persuasiveness, etc. Measurement of these in the natural-science sense seems a much more remote possibility. It might be possible, however, to define them (rather than measure) in terms of the observable effects they produce in the relationship between one person and another.

Thirdly, there are the 'properties' of a role or a system of roles. For example, a role has a position in an employment hierarchy, perhaps that of colonel, or under-secretary or managing director. Such a role has a specific size of immediate and extended command.[1] It has a certain level of pay, defined work conditions, and it demands a specific level of work. Professor Jaques has established a means of *measuring* the level of work in terms of the maximum period of *time* over which the occupant of the role makes decisions without their being subjected to assessment by higher authority. All these properties can be stated in finite terms, or can be measured, and seem to have the nature of true properties.

Role *systems* have properties too. For example, an employment hierarchy contains a given number of people, has a given number of levels of subordinate–manager relationships, is sub-divided in specifically describable ways, exists to carry out describable types of work, and so on. Systems of representatives who negotiate on behalf of employees have a given number of constituencies, representatives and committees. I think that we ought to try to gain a much better understanding of this particular group of properties, and I shall try to describe them in greater detail later on.

The fourth type of 'property' of social phenomena is concerned with the relationship between roles and the relationship between role-systems. They are crucial to the study of social institutions. Two examples of the fourth class of property are authority and accountability. These are references to the relationship between roles. They can be defined as follows:

Authority is the quality of a role (or a group of roles) that sanctions the incumbent to act within defined limits. The limits can be stated in terms of the rules that the occupants of the roles must observe. One can state, for example, as I have done in defining the role of manager earlier, that the occupant has the authority to veto appointments to subordinate roles. But this is not measurement.

Accountability is the quality of a role (or a group of roles) that determines that the incumbent shall be answerable for the consequences,

---

[1] See Glossary, page 387.

direct or otherwise, of his use of authority. But again, this is not measurement.

Summarizing, therefore, we have:

(a) Characteristics of people, which might one day with research become measurable, and would then warrant the term 'properties'.
(b) Relations between people, which can probably be defined but will probably never be measurable. These would not appear to warrant the term 'properties', but rather that of 'relationships'.
(c) Characteristics of roles and role-systems, which can either be stated in finite terms or are measurable. These would appear to warrant the term 'properties'.
(d) Relationships between roles, which are not measurable but which can be stated in finite terms.

Natural scientists criticize hypotheses about social phenomena because experiments to test them are not always repeatable. Many natural scientists also criticize attempts to study social and psychological phenomena systematically because of absence of precise measurement. These two criticisms have held back the study of social institutions very seriously, and this has deprived us of the means of bettering the quality of our lives. I believe that even though the approach to social institutions has to be different, this is no reason for so many disciplined minds in our universities and elsewhere to shun the subject. It is becoming desperately important that many more of the resources of science should be turned to the study of social institutions.

Perhaps this sounds inhuman. I realize that formal organization, logic and the invasion by science of the social world are repugnant to many. But unreason, lack of logic, superstition, a love of vagueness and imagining things to be as we want them to be, are not really helpful to us.[1] They breed jealousy, greed and unrest. These unintelli-

---

[1] 'By the same token, whoever contributed the right new conceptual scheme makes a great contribution to progress by making it possible for others to do more useful work. Einstein's theory of relativity clearly illustrates this point.

'Also the particular conceptual scheme commonly used has a great bearing on decisions and actions. Witness the differing roles of government in economic activities before and after the impact of Keynes, and how the treatment of alcoholism has varied depending on whether it is thought to be a moral problem or a disease. . . . New developments in exploring the decision-making process and in describing more

gent emotions are the enemies of justice, of provision for the needy, of efficiency, of satisfaction at work, of sound social services and of good government.

In the next chapters I shall try to describe the results of studies over the last twenty years (in which I and my colleague Professor Jaques have been involved, along with many others) which show that social problems *can* be studied objectively, and that there is urgent need to do so.

---

accurately the inter-relationships in business organisations also point up the same lesson.' James W. Culliton, 'The Age of Synthesis', *Harvard Business Review*, October 1962.

CHAPTER FIVE

What is Work?

'. . . and a well made language is no indifferent thing; not to go beyond physics, the unknown man who invented the word heat *devoted many generations to error. Heat has been treated as a substance, simply because it was designated by a substantive, and it has been thought indestructible.'*—H. POINCARÉ *The Foundations of Science,* New York

THE FOLLOWING ADVERTISEMENT appeared in a leading Sunday newspaper:

> Shop Superintendent. Competent and experienced man required to take complete charge of sheet metal and machine shop engaged on commercial work. The aim is expansion particularly in the stainless steel field and applicants must be up to date in methods. . . .

Hundreds of advertisements like this appear each Sunday but only about 20 per cent make any attempt to describe the work required to be done. And in those 20 per cent the description leaves much to be desired, as it does in the quotation above. A closer look makes it clear that:

(a) *The advertisement is incorrect.* For example, the term 'complete charge of' implies that nobody else in the company has any accountability for the 'sheet metal and machine shop'.

(b) *Nobody reading the description can gain any real knowledge of the work involved except through inference.* If the reader already has considerable knowledge of the sort of work done by superintendents of machine shops, he can make some reasonable guesses, but these may prove erroneous if the hiring company uses the word 'superintendent' in an unusual way.

The fact that particular advertisements for personnel are vaguely worded is not vital. But advertisements like this are symptomatic of a more serious problem.

Many of our attempts to describe work consist of a reference to the state of mind of a person doing that work, or some characteristic of that person. For example, we talk about interesting work, boring work or skilled work. But skill is an attribute of a person—not of work—and interest or boredom is an attitude of mind, and not a quality possessed by the work done, for work which bores one person may interest another.

Nor are we any better off if we move one step closer to a specific definition. Suppose we say, as many companies do, that Mr X is responsible for manufacture or for sales. Are we not still mis-stating the facts? It is the Board of Directors which is actually accountable for seeing that these functions are adequately performed at the many levels of the company. Separate individuals, subordinate to the managing director, work exclusively in the area of product development, manufacture or sales.

But as one descends the hierarchy of organization, it is clear that every person in the enterprise is responsible for some sort of work that is connected with these basic functions. To say that Mr X is accountable for sales, or Mr Y for manufacture, tells one nothing about the work either of them does. The real question is: What distinctive part of production work does Mr Y do, and in what terms is it to be described so as to distinguish it from the work done on manufacture by other people in the company?

We can consider two aspects of work: physical effort and mental effort. Many people who watch a craftsman at work assume that they are observing physical work, albeit carried out with considerable manual dexterity. At the same time they may realize that much experience lies behind and contributes to the movements of his hands and his 'manual' performance. In fact, they are watching an activity which is largely mental, for, as soon as the physical endeavour begins to absorb even a low fraction of his total physical potential, he will call for power tools of some kind. Craftsmen are employed because they are constantly able to make wise decisions. A craftsman's deftness, his feel and touch, are dictated by decisions made in his mind. His decisions maintain a balance between such things as quantity of output and material used, quality of output, aesthetic aspects, and perhaps many other things as well.

It ought to be easy to appreciate the constant decision-making required in a craft job. Most of us have spent time carrying out craft jobs. Cooking is a craft job and so is gardening. Nor is it difficult to appreciate that managerial, administrative and technological work largely involve decision-making. Sometimes, however, the decision-making goes unrecognized. Thus I found that there was a kind of myth current among civil servants to the effect that 'we do not take decisions because so many of our activities are involved with the making of recommendations'. But persons making recommendations must *take a decision as to what to recommend*. Many members of the public believe this myth. I think that one reason for the myth is the fact that decisions made in the Civil Service, by their very nature, often set precedents which may apply to millions of citizens. Even *apparently* trivial decisions become important when seen in this context. So civil servants tend to reserve their position until the issue has been thoroughly discussed with colleagues. Even then the joint decision may take the form of a recommendation to a minister.

I have been watching out for roles which contain little or no decisions for many years. The nearest I got to a 'no decision' role was an attendant operating an automatic lift. He had to push buttons to close the door and select the floor he wanted to go to. When the attendant was removed the speed of the work done by the lift was faster, owing to the fact that when the attendant was on duty he did not remain in the lift when no one wanted to use it. There was a short time-lapse between his noting the signal and entering the lift to take it to the floor required. But even in that unusual case of wastage of human intellect, the attendant had introduced an element of low level decision-making. He often decided to give advice to his passengers on the quickest means of finding the office which they sought, and so on. I doubt if anybody could survive for long in a role where no discretion whatever was required.

Many people now believe that industrial workers are simply 'button-pushers' who make no decisions, and that the number of roles that contain responsible decision-taking work is diminishing. There is ample evidence that this is untrue. Anybody who analyses the average 'button-pusher's' role will usually be surprised to discover how much judgement the operator has to use. His acts of judgement will involve assessing whether the machine is functioning correctly and stopping it if it is not, adjusting it, changing tools, watching and deciding on the quality of the output, watching the quality of the material being fed to the machine, and deciding when to call up more supplies of material.

The number of *operators* per unit of output is dropping as capital investment provides faster machines. But the number of people designing, making, adjusting and repairing machines and tools is rising in proportion to the number of machine operators. This is shown by the rising ratio of overhead expense of industry, which is usually expressed as the ratio of direct labour to all other types of expense (except materials). There is a continuously unfilled demand for 'skilled people' even in areas of high unemployment.

All employers try to take judgement out of work at the lower levels of the hierarchies by introducing routines, data-processing, mechanization and automation so as to *reduce* the numbers employed at this level, in order to increase productivity. But this process eliminates the simplest types of job, not the complex ones.

The degree of discretion which a person is expected and permitted to exercise is controlled by the 'prescribed limits of discretion', which can be defined as the real rules in the form of laws, policies, instructions, controls, rules, regulations, and other types of control (both written and unwritten) that he has to obey. Failure to obey constitutes negligence or insubordination.

The existence of these prescribed limits is frequently questioned on the grounds that while in some areas of decision limits clearly do exist, in other areas they do not, and that therefore a subordinate must come to his own conclusions as to how far he can go in such areas. My own experience, which is shared by other managers with whom I have discussed the issue, is that limits, though not always obvious or explicit, are discoverable in all areas. If, as a manager, one discovers that one of one's subordinates has almost unlimited discretion to spend money, or to grant concessions to others, or to engage personnel, or to absent himself from work, or to make alterations to equipment, or to demand services from others, then one immediately sets about establishing reasonable limits. One does not allow unlimited discretion in any direction to continue simply because of one's confidence that a subordinate can be trusted to act reasonably and will voluntarily restrict his decisions.

If policies remain unwritten, as is so often the case, or if the manifest policies differ from assumed or extant policies, then a newcomer to a role will be in difficulty. He may have to discover the limitations on his use of discretion by questioning. He may have to act very cautiously in the early part of his career in the role; he may even learn the rules and policies by overstepping the bounds and then having them explained by his manager. Despite these situations, however, the limits on discretion can always be discovered, because they do exist.

There are two other aspects of limits on discretion which must be mentioned. Frequently they are contained in the details of a task. For example, 'prepare a summary of the negotiations to date and present a report within one month'. The subordinate in this case is not allowed to decide how long he may take before rendering a report, but he does decide what to put in it. If a time-limit is not explicitly put upon a task or is not understood by both manager and subordinate, then in reality no task has been allotted to the subordinate. If the understanding is that it may be completed at any time in the future according to the choice of the subordinate, then it may never be completed. In fact, though target dates for completion are very frequently not mentioned, there is almost invariably an understanding between manager and subordinate of how long it is to take. This can be demonstrated by taking a task on which both claim no knowledge of the completion date required and, by a process of successive approximation, a completion date is arrived at. This has been much used by Jaques, who describes it in the following way:

Successive approximation. One means of helping a manager to structure his intuitive experience about the work he allocates and to make his standards of quality and pace explicit in quantitative terms, is to approach the analysis by successive·approximation. Thus, for example, if you ask a manager when he expects a subordinate to have completed the development of a design, he may reply that he could not give any exact date; he expects the subordinate to get on with it as quickly as he can and to get it done along with a number of other tasks that he has been allocated. If you then ask whether it would be all right if the subordinate completed it within the next ten years, the manager will probably laugh and say, 'Oh no! He doesn't have that much time'. Does the manager expect it to be completed within the next few hours? No, it would be quite impossible for the subordinate to do so; he would need at least some months to do it along with the rest of the work that he has to do. You might then ask the manager if he would allow the subordinate, say, a year to complete it, to which the manager might reply: 'No, not that long—possibly something more like six months.' You can then refine the questions and help the manager to converge upon the maximum number of months that would constitute the longest target completion time that he wanted to allow the subordinate when he allocated the task.

What seems to happen when the method of successive approximation is used, is that the moment the manager has realised that he would not allow, say, ten years for his subordinate to complete the task, he realises also that he must have some target completion time in mind. There begins to form more consciously the longest target completion time that he intuitively assumed when he allocated the task under consideration to his subordinate.

The other means of setting limits to the use of discretion is to award a general responsibility to a subordinate to take specific action as soon as specified circumstances arise. For example, a civil servant might be instructed that some reply, even if it is only an acknowledgement, must be sent to a letter from a Member of Parliament within forty-eight hours of receipt. This deprives the subordinate of the decision to delay a reply longer than that, though it leaves discretion to decide the content of the reply. Another example might be an instruction to a factory manager that whenever an accident occurs which *in his view* is serious he must cause an investigation to start within two hours of its having happened. In this case the factory manager must use discretion to decide what constitutes a serious accident, but, once having decided that it is serious, he has no discretion to postpone an investigation beyond two hours. Thus I use the term 'Prescribed Limits' on the use of discretion to refer not only to general policies but also to those aspects of tasks which can be stated in precise or quantitative terms.

I have so far attempted to establish that employed people are paid for making decisions; they are not paid for obeying rules. The area over which they are expected to make use of discretion is bounded by policies, instructions, routines, tasks, etc. The degree of importance of the role is a function of the length of time that a subordinate is expected to continue to use discretion without the results being scrutinized or becoming available for scrutiny by higher authority. I can now define Employment Work as follows:

Employment Work is the application of knowledge and the exercise of discretion within limits prescribed by the immediate manager and by higher policies towards an objective set by the immediate manager; the whole being carried out within an employment contract. This can be diagrammatically represented as in Fig. 2.

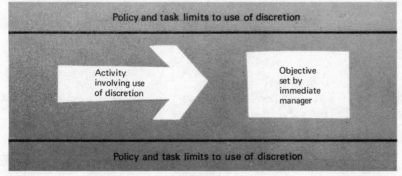

Policy and task limits to use of discretion

Activity involving use of discretion

Objective set by immediate manager

Policy and task limits to use of discretion

Figure 2

The manner in which roles at different levels in the executive hierarchy have their use of discretion bounded by policies, etc., is illustrated in Fig. 3.

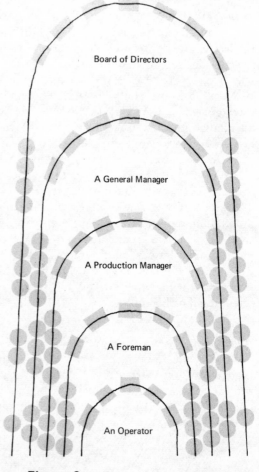

A series of instructions or policies set by one Manager which prescribe the work of an immediate subordinate or of the whole of his immediate command.

A series of instructions or policies decided by a Manager (or the Board) which prescribe the work of subordinates at lower levels than his immediate command.

Board of Directors

A General Manager

A Production Manager

A Foreman

An Operator

Figure 3

I will now return to the original advertisement for the job of superintendent which I quoted at the beginning of this chapter. What is to be done about advertising such roles? My proposal is an advertisement reading as follows:

The company employs X people in total and produces sheet-metal products. It aims to expand the production of those made of stainless steel. It operates one manufacturing department which employs Y people and uses metal-forming and machining processes. A superintendent is required to manage this department. The salary range is £A to £B per year. Please write for a specification of the role and an application form.

This advertisement, by naming the numbers of people employed (both in the company and the department) and by stating a salary bracket, will provide potential applicants with a first approximation of the level of the work to be done. The provision of a detailed job-specification to applicants gives the company proper opportunity for giving the information which potential candidates really need before deciding whether or not to apply.[1]

I do not know the full terms of the job referred to in the advertisement, but I am taking a cock-shy at the likely prescribed and discretionary content of the job, which would be written into the specification that the advertisement said would be sent to interested persons.

Prescribed Elements

(1) The shop superintendent is *immediately* responsible to the plant general manager and has an immediate command of nine subordinates (six foremen managers, a production engineer, a tool-designer and a production-control officer) and 200 machine-operators.

(2) With this team he will be responsible for the management of a department consisting of X sq. ft of factory space, with machinery and tools for the manufacture of a work programme.

(3) He is allotted a group of tasks by the general manager, to be achieved at weekly intervals, with the requirements that products be delivered to stores on the dates named and that they meet specified quality standards. The department is to be operated at the lowest level of expense commensurate with the foregoing.

(4) He must work within the range of *company* policies covering such matters as rates of pay, holidays, relations with trade unions, manufacturing techniques to be used, quality standards and records to be kept. In addition, he must adhere to the more specific policies established by the general manager relating to

---

[1] I do not want to discuss selection procedures too far at this stage because it interrupts the chain of thought about work. In chapter thirty I have said a good deal more about procedures in a section concerned with the work of personnel specialists.

overtime, nightshifts, pay, provision of services, maintenance of plant, purchases, analysis of expense, and so on. Since these company and plant policies have been set down in writing, the superintendent must know them and either conform to them or immediately report any inability to do so.

Discretionary Elements

Within these policies, the superintendent will carry the duty of making a wide range of decisions, of which the following are examples:

(1) How to allot work among his foremen and judge the effectiveness with which it is carried out. If he is not satisfied he must decide how to correct the situation; by criticism, training, advice, reallocation of work, or by seeking removal of the subordinate from his role.

(2) In the light of the tasks that he is given, what jigs and tools to order, what supplies to requisition, what level of overtime to allow, how best to use the service of his production engineer and production-control specialists, and what priorities to set on the work to be done.

(3) What recommendations to make to the plant general manager, if his resources are, in his opinion, insufficient for the programme of work he is given to do.

(4) Whether the rate of expense in his department is the lowest possible and, if not, how it can be reduced.

(5) Whether the expense created by his subordinates is appropriate and, if not, how it can be reduced.

(6) Whether the various analyses of expense provided to him are sufficient for his purpose, and what changes to recommend if they are not.

(7) What changes (within policies set by the general manager) in manufacturing methods should be explored in order to improve output, quality, shorten throughput time, reduce expense, save material, and so on.

(8) What changes in the policies set by the company and the general manager he should recommend if any of these are inconsistent, in his opinion, with the efficiency of his department.

(9) Lastly, and very importantly, he is responsible for *recommending* to his manager any changes that he thinks necessary where he has not got personal authority to decide.

I know that some managers have difficulty in discerning the decision-making content of the simpler type of work. So, to assist them, I will analyse the role of a filing clerk.

Such a person probably has to decide how to establish priorities in dealing with demands for the production of files. He must decide what to do about demands coming at the same time from different sources, whether to go to his supervisor to ask for assistance to meet a temporary flood of work or to allow himself to get temporarily into arrears. He must decide when to open new specific files for correspondence previously filed under the alphabet system; whether particular documents are or are not intended for filing in his centre, when and how to 'chase' the return of files which have not been returned after a reasonable lapse of time, how to develop original work-methods to improve efficiency, and when to recommend their adoption, and so on. If he fails to do these things then, in spite of the fact that his work may be regarded as routine and not calling for decision-making, he will be accused of failing 'to use common sense' or 'to make proper judgements'.

People doing employment work do acquire knowledge of what is expected of them. They get to know the details of a host of unwritten policies, they acquire a sense which tells them which decisions they must make and which belong to others, but they still live in a considerable degree of uncertainty. In ill-defined situations some decisions fall between two stools and do not get made. In other cases uncertainty results in two persons both claiming the right to make the decision, and ill feeling arises. Perhaps the chief disadvantage of uncertainty about where the authority to make decisions lies, is delay. Delay in delivery of goods, delay in giving information, or in saying yes or no to proposals, delay in dealing with grievances, delay in opening negotiations with representatives, delay in implementing investment in new equipment, delay in introducing better techniques for doing work. The examples I have so far given are of an industrial or commercial nature, and I have not commented on decision-making in Government, either local or national. I now wish to do so.

In an open letter to *The Times*[1] Clive de Paula, who was co-ordinator of Industrial Advisers to the Labour Government, commented on his experience of the Civil Service in what I think are very realistic terms except on one major issue. He wrote:

> In the higher levels of administrative class, officials are mainly concerned with advising on the development of policy. They are

---

[1] Tuesday, 4 August 1970.

not so much engaged as are many of their counterparts in industry and commerce in the inevitable taking of all the decisions that are needed to get things done from day to day.

Their time is more often taken up with putting together a departmental view on which the minister can be advised regarding the decision which he should take. It seems to me that as a result they tend not to develop into decision-makers.

I disagree. There is a strong case for suggesting that if, as a civil servant, you are advising on policy or legislation you may, in deciding what exploration of the facts to carry out, whom to consult, whether to risk putting in your minute now or to wait for further facts, and what advice to give, be taking decisions which are going to affect society more seriously than what look like more important decisions in other types of work.

I was often frustrated when I first joined the Board of Trade by the length of time it took for officials to react to some suggestion I wanted to pursue, or to give me advice for which I had asked. The subject-matter frequently seemed fairly trivial to me and I felt that it ought to be possible to investigate it rapidly. Later I began to realize that any decision had to be put into its proper context. In business a decision might affect some thousands of people; in Government a decision that *looked* of the same order of importance on the basis of content might affect up to 50 million people.

Mr de Paula remarks in his letter that the secret of success of many businessmen lies less in what they initiate or innovate than in their ability to cut their losses. This seems sound to me, but what does not seem to be fully realized is that business decisions are not public; often losses can be cut without comment, and this makes it much easier for businessmen to cut losses. In Government this is infinitely more difficult, with an eager mass media and Parliament waiting for mistakes. Because it is so difficult and so upsetting to the public for Government to retrace its steps decisions must, therefore, be taken with the greatest possible care. This is the burden of officials in the Civil Service; to make sure that their decisions on what to advise their minister to do are highly competent. The other aspect that is overlooked is that officials' work extends into many fields of endeavour apart from that of advising ministers. They are constantly in negotiations with officials of other governments, local authorities, nationalized industries, trade associations and individual companies. They have much regulatory work; they administer a tremendous range of national services.

I have not written the foregoing to attack Mr de Paula, who is a wise man, nor do I wish to write a eulogy of civil servants. I simply want to support the general thesis that in employment hierarchies, whatever their nature, the work for which people are paid is decision-taking.

It is idle to try to discuss social institutions and their organization without being able to discuss, in explicit terms, the work that they are set up to perform. I am not suggesting that it is necessary for every organization to start writing up every policy and routine and specifying the work content of every role in Prescribed and Discretionary terms. The work of all organizations changes. Therefore the organization itself has to be dynamic. Policies and roles constantly undergo change all the time. But I do suggest that we must get this concept of employment work into our minds, so that when we build mental models of work situations we build accurate models. If the models are accurate, not only can we think and plan more clearly, but we can communicate with others.

CHAPTER SIX

Associations and Employment Hierarchies

'Sometimes we do not even state the problem in a wholly realistic way. We fear that organisation in a modern society is growing too big and too complex and that we are establishing management controls that are too massive. We describe complex organisation as an Orwellian nightmare. But it is possible that exactly the reverse is the case, that some of our gravest problems in society arose not from over-management but out of under-management, that democracy can become non-participating precisely to the degree that organic and hierarchical management breaks down.'—ROBERT S. MCNAMARA, *The Times,* 31 August, 1968

THIS CHAPTER IS about employment hierarchies. I must start, however, by a comment on how they come to be set up.

An employment hierarchy does not simply emerge: it has to be set up. This is almost always done by people forming an association. There is the case of a single entrepreneur setting up an executive hierarchy, but even in that case the Companies Act insists, if it is to be a limited liability company, that he is joined by others. Such associations may be of various kinds—industrial, governmental, educational, religious, social service, sport, medical, legal, scientific, etc. A group of shareholders with a board of directors, a partnership, a trade union, a football club, a learned society, or even a government, are examples of associations. Associations are people coming together for a purpose. The purpose is either agreed tacitly or expressed in a written document. A trading company has 'articles of association'. A university has its 'charter'. If people who want to form a trade union wish to benefit from the special position that they hold at law, then they must draw up the terms of their association in a prescribed legal form. In other cases there may be no written document at first, as, for example, in the case of a small football club. But they may later be caused to describe their association in written terms as a result, for example, of having to deal with questions of tax or in order to be able, as an association, to buy property. A partnership can sometimes get its work done without employing people, as can a football team, but the majority of associations have to do so. Initially, as in the case of a partnership or a charitable body, or even a trade union, they may not employ anybody, but as their operations increase then we see the emergence of employment hierarchies consisting of people employed to do work in execution of the objectives of the associations.

An employment hierarchy can be defined as 'that network of employment roles set up by an association of people to carry out work required to achieve the objectives of the association. Work is delegated by the chief executive down through one or more strata of subordinate roles.'

This is not a description of a work organization, but simply some thinking based on observation (which I think we all share), in order to establish the meaning of the phrase 'employment hierarchy', so that I shall be understood when I use it. It is surprising (when we consider that nearly all of us are, or have at some time worked within employment hierarchies) that no consistent language is used to describe this very common institution. People who wish to refer to an industrial employment hierarchy will often refer to 'the company'. But, in the first place, legally 'the company' is the 'company of shareholders', i.e. the association. Secondly, the term 'the company' can be taken to mean not only the employment hierarchy but also the shareholders and their board of directors, and the constituencies, voters, representatives, and representative committees forming the representative system that exists alongside every employment hierarchy without being part of it. It is useful to have separate definitions and names for the component parts of an association, its employment hierarchy and its representative system. This is sometimes essential to avoid confusion. Failure to distinguish between representative systems and employment hierarchies has resulted in gross inattention to the importance of the former, with some very unfortunate consequences.

Employment hierarchies have two distinctive features. They are nearly always shaped like a pyramid and they are sub-divided into a series of horizontal strata, each stratum performing different levels of work. The pyramid shape, which implies the few managing the many, has been the subject of much philosophic and political comment during the last 100 years. Some have even claimed that no man should be in command, in any sense, of the work of another. In the late nineteenth century syndicalism, a system of co-operative work under which managers would not exist and production was controlled by workers, was much discussed and experiments were carried out. In the early years of the Russian revolution 'artels' composed of co-operative work-groups trading on their own account but forbidden to employ others were used. Few of these experiments to achieve equality of status in working groups have survived. If one couples with these observations the fact that employment hierarchies have existed throughout the ages and have nearly always been pyramid-shaped, it is worth asking why the pyramids work, or seemed to work, and the syndicates do not.

The answer is obvious if you accept the validity of two observations. The first is that the incidence of the capacity to make decisions is not equal among people. The second is that the distribution of this differential capacity is Gaussian with a left-hand skew, as in Fig. 4.

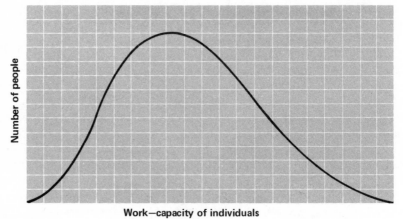

Work—capacity of individuals

Figure 4

Gauss, a German mathematician, who discovered a good deal about magnetism, also perceived that most human characteristics, when plotted against populations, produce a curve which looks like a gently sloping round-topped mountain. Fig. 4 shows (as we move to the right along the horizontal co-ordinate) that only very few people are incapable of doing any useful employment work at all, that a great many people are capable of doing useful work, and that as the level of complexity of the work rises, the number of people capable of doing it diminishes. He who can make only the simplest decisions, concerned, for example, with transporting material from one place to another in a wheelbarrow, is represented at the left-hand end of the curve. The President of General Motors is at the extreme right. But these two extremes of capacity for work are not equally scarce. There are more wheelbarrow-pushers than potential presidents of General Motors.

This is the way in which other human characteristics tend to be distributed in large populations. My description will be plainer if we stand this distribution curve on its end, split it in half, and show it as distributed on either side of a vertical axis (Fig. 5). This diagram is no different in principle from Fig. 4, but it does give us a picture that approximates to a picture of the typical pyramidal structure of industry.

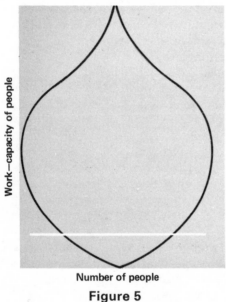

Figure 5

The horizontal line towards the bottom indicates the level of capacity below which people are unlikely to be employable in any way in large hierarchies.

Higher up the curve begins to bulge out, showing that at the very bottom levels we are not dealing with the largest section of the working population. The largest section of the working population represented by the mode of the curve (the widest part of the bulge) is at about the level commonly described as semi-skilled worker or clerk. From that point on, as we go to increasingly higher levels of capacity, the number of members in the population decreases steadily. With this decrease in the numbers of those capable of being employed in higher levels in executive organization, goes a corresponding decrease in the number of employment roles at these levels. This shows why executive hierarchies are pyramid-shaped. *Given full employment* they tend to provide for the employment of all the employable members of the population at a level consistent with their individual capacity. Obviously if they possess such properties then they have survival characteristics.

The second feature of executive hierarchies is that they are built up of horizontal strata. The top stratum is one man, the chief executive; the stratum subordinate to him contains more than one person. Each person in the second stratum has two or more subordinates of his own, and so on down to the base of the pyramid. This creates a series of manager–subordinate relationships. The chief executive is accountable for the total work of the hierarchy. Each manager subordinate to him at descending levels in the hierarchy is accountable for the work of his extended command.[1]

The sequence 'apple–fruit–horticultural products–food' is an example of a series starting at a low level and ending at a high level of abstraction. Each class of thing in the ascending sequence includes in its ambit the previous class, for example, apples are one type of fruit, fruit is one type of horticultural product, horticultural products are one type of food. In the same way, in an employment hierarchy, each ascending stratum includes in its degree of accountability for work, the work of the subordinate stratum below it, until finally the chief executive is accountable for the entire work of the hierarchy. This leads to the notion of considering an executive hierarchy as a series of ascending orders of abstraction concerned with work.

Jaques, in his essay 'Speculation concerning level of capacity'[2] discusses ideas about the nature of the relationship between a person and his work in terms of this relationship being at different levels of abstraction. I paraphrase him thus:

The first level of abstraction: 'perceptual-concrete'. The object of the task must be physically present in order for work to be done. At this level the task is set in terms of 'machine these *castings*', 'assemble these *components*', 'file these *documents*', 'enter up these *forms*', 'stack

---

[1] All those subordinate to him down to the base of the pyramid. See page 384 for definition of 'extended command.'

[2] Wilfred Brown and Elliott Jaques, *Glacier Project Papers*, Heinemann Educational Books, London, 1965.

these *packages* in storage bins', and so on. The notion is that in the absence of perceptual contact, with the physical object, the individual would have great difficulty in thinking about his work in objective terms. He would feel out of contact with his work and unable instead to think about it in terms of mental models.

The second level of abstraction: 'imaginal-concrete'. At this level physical or visual contact with the object of the work is not necessary so long as there has been sufficient contact in the past for an imagined picture of the work to be carried in the mind as a model. It thus becomes possible for the person working at this level to direct, allocate, set quality standards, programme and progress work and to issue instructions to those working at level one so that they give effect to his plans, although he is not in physical touch with all of the objects. But stratum two is uneasy if separated from the physical scene of work for too long by, for instance, having to work in an office some distance from the workshop. The stratum-two man constantly needs to refresh his imagined picture of the work by moving around among it.

The third level of abstraction: 'conceptual-concrete'. Those working at this level are able to deal with future work in terms of mental models and to think up new techniques for execution of probable future work and the tactics necessary to deal with the unexpected. But the picture of tasks and work still however remains tied to models of tasks in physical terms. The level of abstraction is thus still tied to the concrete, though the individual can comfortably make decisions on the basis of what is in his mind without constant recourse to the physical scene of the work.

The fourth level of abstraction: 'abstract modelling'. At this level people show the capacity to detach themselves from the concrete physical things with which their past experience has associated them. This capacity to discard past experience and to think entirely afresh by starting from analysis of the basic data available entails a pronounced capacity for creative thinking. The attachment to what one has handled or seen in concrete form is a restriction on the frame of reference in which one thinks. The ability to drop this frame of reference and start afresh widens the bounds of thinking and results in invention. For instance, somebody tied to the concrete who was asked to design a vehicle would have thought of railways, ships, road vehicles, aircraft, and so on, but not of hovercraft. The fourth level of abstraction is the first level at which the 'break-through' occurs. It is literally a break-away from concrete thinking. Things that have not yet existed have to be imagined and modelled in the mind. Such ideas are not all important new inventions, but frequently appear simply as very intelligent-looking suggestions. But they feel intelligent because they arise from the pulling together, in relation to each other, of things that have not been related before. When a manager thinks in this way and first exposes his ideas to his subordinates he probably evokes initial alarm, because their reaction is 'here comes another hair-brained idea'.

The jump from the third stratum to the fourth requires the ability to start thinking from the basic data, instead of starting off from what others have said or written, or from the individual's own past experience.

The fifth level of abstraction and above: 'theory construction'. The person thinking at this level is a strategist because he has a series of tested models of complex situations in his mind, covering a wide field of work. The simplest example is that of a chief executive, bombarded with conflicting demands from his separate subordinates about the respective emphases which he ought to give to more research and development, or to more investment in new machinery, or to more resources for marketing. This gives him a field of very different types of interacting situations with which to deal. Stratum-five thinking enables him to pick out the basic data from his subordinates' comments and reports and, using his own experience assembled in the form of theories, to work out strategies and plans that deal with the situation.

The Civil Service custom is to ask a principal (the lowest grade but one in the Administrative class) to have first cut at a problem by writing his views in a minute. Then the assistant secretary makes his comment. Then the under-secretary makes his. Finally, if the issue is of great importance, the deputy secretary says something. I have seen the comments of each in one file. Sometimes they make fascinating reading as one notes the changing level of abstraction of each minute. What is notable is the capacity at times of the under-secretary or, more often, the deputy secretary, to put the whole problem into an entirely new context by bringing to bear on it considerations that exist in his mind but which are not present in the minds of the others. His theory will use no data that has not already been considered by his subordinates, but he will take account of all of it, and fit it together into a different pattern that spells out a viable strategy. This is what Jaques means by 'theory construction'.

This ascending order of levels of abstraction can be summarized as follows. At stratum 1 the mind is dealing with work in terms of the restricted evidence of what the eye can see. At stratum 2 a person will have to deal with a considerable increase in the quantity of data in order to come to decisions; he is forced to deal with some of it at the 'image level'. At stratum 3 it is not possible to cope with the expanding field of data in terms even of images of concrete things. The stratum-3 man has to move into classes of things, i.e. concepts; he has to begin building models of the situations he is dealing with. At stratum 4 he is able to cast off his previous attachment to the images of situations and things he has seen and think of relationships, structures, techniques and processes which, as far as he is concerned, have not so far existed. He is able to cast off the old frame of reference and create a new one.

The industrial chief executive is dealing with the interaction of products, investment, markets, labour problems, Government industrial policy, extension of manufacturing capacity, technological problems, competition and profits, raw-material supply and other large matters that require the ability to imagine the relationship of one system to other systems. The senior civil servant at the stratum-5 level is dealing with his problems in an environment built of complex pressures on him: ministers' wishes, Government policy, departmental interaction, the effect on the public, international reactions, pressure groups, and Parliament. All these different kinds of situations and pressures in the minds of people working at stratum 5 and above have to be balanced against one another and integrated to produce a strategy.

The different levels of abstraction can be tabulated as follows:[1]

---

[1] My attention has been drawn to B. S. Bloom's *Taxonomy of Educational Objectives*, Longman, London, 1956, which categorizes the abilities to be developed and assessed in education as follows:

(a) Ability to remember useful information.
(b) Ability to apply given information to a familiar situation.
(c) Ability to apply given information to an unfamiliar situation.
(d) Ability to start, without given information, and construct a method or methods, of tackling an unfamiliar situation.

These are widely accepted by educationalists as being useful, and seem to have quite an elegant match with Jaques's different levels of abstraction.

Stratum 1   Perceptual-concrete
Stratum 2   Imaginal-concrete
Stratum 3   Conceptual-concrete
Stratum 4   Conceptual-modelling
Stratum 5
and above   Theory and strategy construction

I have now sketched out how associations of people form executive hierarchies. I have tried to suggest why they are nearly always pyramid-shaped. I have drawn attention to the fact that such hierarchies contain strata of roles concerned with different levels of abstraction of thinking and decision-making, and I have given a description of the type of thinking that work involves at each level. This sets the scene for a detailed description of employment hierarchies at work.

An employment hierarchy is a social institution consisting of a network of positions, to each of which work is assigned. We can call these 'employment roles', and can say that people are in their employment roles only when they are carrying out work assigned to them, since people can take up other roles associated with employment hierarchies (such as those in the representative system, or in other forms of association like clubs and societies formed by members of the employment hierarchy). The nature and function of each role and the relationship of one role to another can be described and regulated.

Employment hierarchies exist independently of people. An individual position can be vacant because the person who occupied it has resigned and has not yet been replaced; but the position does not disappear. Change in the work to be done can bring about change in the work-content of particular roles. The level of work in roles can decrease or increase. New roles are added to the hierarchy or existing roles can be deleted to cater for change in the work to be done.

This social structure exists as an entity in itself. It can be analysed and altered, though that is not to say that it can be designed without reference to people. I have already, for example, suggested that its pyramid shape is a function of the distribution of capacity to work at different levels of abstraction among large populations. Thus, a structure that called for a very large number of people of very high capacity either might be uneconomic or there might not be the people to fill the roles. Equally, it would at least theoretically be possible to design a hierarchy that sought more people of very low capacity than were available. Such hierarchies are, therefore, designed to take account of the distribution of capacity in the society in which they are to exist. It would be foolish to set up an employment hierarchy in an under-developed country that contained 30 per cent of roles to which there was to be allotted a level of work requiring execution by the equivalent of honours graduates from universities. On the other hand, I know of a factory in India where machines are operated by two men, which in a British factory are operated by one man. This is justified by the fact that licences for the import of machinery into India are scarce while people are plentiful. The employment of an extra operator to man these machines would not be economic in Britain, but it is economic in India because the extra man yields up to 15 per cent more output.

Thus the structure of an employment hierarchy is a function of its social and economic environment, of the volume and nature of the work, and of the techniques available to do it. Changes in the nature of work and of the techniques required to do it are the factors that have always held the attention of managements. The need to adjust rapidly to these factors is usually recognized. But adjustment of organization to broader social, economic and market factors is much slower. There are many examples of this tardiness.

It should have been clear to the managements of companies since 1946 that international trade would play an ever more important part in business. This implies serious adaptation of organization. Yet hundreds of companies have regarded entry into overseas markets, not as something that was essential in the interests of their own future success, but as a patriotic gesture for which they ought to be rewarded by special privileges. Many of these companies attempted to move into overseas trading without the necessary adaptation of their employment hierarchies. The results were often disastrous, and they blamed the losses that arose on anything but their own failure to adapt their own organizations.

Release of people in society from the sharp edge of fear of want has led to fresh aspirations for a higher degree of fairness, justice and participation in policy-making at work. The pressures generated by these aspirations have been vociferously expressed, but have led to very little adaptation of organization. The results have been instability, loss of authority, and tension.

A change in any of the factors that constitute the environment of organization sets up pressures for, and justifies, a change in the structure. But because this relationship between the structure and the factors that bear upon it is frequently not acknowledged, people often make invalid assumptions. For example, it may be held that an optimum organization is that which contains roles that are tailor-made for specific individuals; or that an organization is the best possible because it suits the personal style of the chief executive, or that the choice between, say, centralized and de-centralized organization is a matter of taste.

It is essential to distinguish between hierarchies themselves and the people who fill its roles. People working in hierarchies are aware that they are working within a social structure, but few have an accurate model of its shape in their minds. Sometimes this is because they assume it to be different from what it really is; sometimes it is because there is a conscious effort to prevent the shape of the structure from becoming explicit and describable. Those who approve of this type of situation believe in the desirability of 'informal organization', which, to me, is a contradiction in terms. 'Informal' implies the lack of a structure, whereas 'organization' implies the existence of one.[1]

There is, particularly in America, a widely held view that formality in the organization of employment hierarchies deprives people of the right to make decisions and to be creative. This theory is a false one. I list two of the assumptions used to support the idea of 'informal organization', and I state why they are false.

It is held that informal organization gives to some people who would otherwise have to perform 'routine' jobs the opportunity to make decisions on their own.

This is false, because the *raison d'être* of formal organization is to use human decision-making ability to its fullest possible extent. Any failure of organization to achieve this situation calls for better organization—not its abolition.

The false assumption of the 'informal organization' school of thinking arises from its failure to realize that human work inevitably concerns 'decision-making'. If work does not require decisions to be made there should be no need to employ human beings to do it.

It is held that informal organization begets 'healthy competition' between people to take on additional responsibility. It is held that this creates 'natural selection' of those who should be promoted because the more able take on more work and the less able lose it.

This is false. The implication of such an idea is as follows: If A is the manager of B1 and B2, and if B1 is the most able of the three, he

---

[1] Chambers's English Dictionary says that the word 'informal' means 'not in proper form' or 'irregular'. It also says that the verb 'to organise' means 'to form several parts into an organised whole' or 'to arrange'.

should somehow contrive to do some of the work of B2 or of his own manager A.

Protagonists of 'informal organization' may protest at my interpretation of their views, but I cannot see what else they intend, unless it be that they expect the most able people to take upon themselves work that has not been formally allotted to any role! But that would be an example of bad formal organization. There should not be a bank of unallotted accountability waiting to be informally assumed by rising young men. Such a situation could be potentially disastrous.

The fact is that the 'informal organization' thinkers tend to regard formal organization as a structure of roles down which specific work-tasks are delegated. They do not think of roles as containing precisely defined areas over which the occupant has to make all the decisions. As a result the idea of informality is essential to them, in order to provide the opportunity for somebody to spot the need for a decision to be taken and have the courage to take it. But if instead a role is defined by delineating an area over which the occupant of the role has, as a duty, to exercise discretion and take the necessary decisions, then there is no need to think in terms of informality as a mechanism for filling the gaps left by inadequate formal organization.[1]

---

[1] I have provided a fuller statement of my views on informal organization in *Glacier Project Papers* by Wilfred Brown and Elliott Jaques, Heinemann Educational Books, 1965.

CHAPTER SEVEN

Operational Work

EMPLOYMENT HIERARCHIES EXIST to develop, produce and sell goods or services. Where services are provided free or at uneconomic prices, then the selling operation is (or ought to be) replaced by a system for constantly obtaining, by some means, the reaction of the consumer to the services. This generalization needs to be supported by taking different types of hierarchies and considering whether the generalization is an acceptable description of each. Few would want to question its validity as a generalization about industrial companies dealing with goods, or commercial firms offering such services as retailing, wholesaling, transport or personal services such as hair-dressing, automobile maintenance, house decoration, laundry work, and so on. In each of these cases the success of the business will depend on the maintenance of the correct balance of investment of physical or mental resources in the development, the production and the marketing of the goods or services.

The small retail shop-owner has to consider what he will sell. When he is thinking about that and about making arrangements to extend the range of the goods or services he is offering, he is attending to the development of his range of services. He is doing for his retail business what a large industrial corporation does when it spends resources on developing new products. When the retailer considers re-arranging the layout of his shop so that he can give service more quickly to his customers, he is attending to the producing function of his business. He is setting about the provision of a more efficient service. His effort is analogous to that of the industrial company that builds a new work-shop and installs more modern machinery in order to expand capacity and manufacture its products more efficiently. When the retailer decides to brighten up his frontage, to spend more time on the display of the goods he seeks to sell, or to spend more time on getting on friendly terms with his customers, he is selling. His act is analogous to the marketing operations of much larger companies.

It is more difficult to think in these terms about other types of employment hierarchies. It is not obvious that the hierarchies established by the professions exist 'to develop, produce and offer for sale or free of charge, some goods or services'. Lawyers and accountants used to adhere tightly to the provision of the precise type of service that custom and practice would cause people to expect of them. But even then accountants had to decide whether, as well as auditing accounts, they would look after the personal taxation problems of individual clients; or whether they would become secretaries to trade associations or serve a board of directors in a professional capacity. Today accountants have many more possible types of service to consider, including the diverse one of business consultant. Lawyers have to choose between the different aspects of the law. Decisions on the type of service to offer will have a major effect on their business; the difficult question is whether they offer such services for sale.

Most professions, and certainly the two I have mentioned, forbid explicit selling efforts. This does not mean, however, that lawyers and accountants make no effort to sell the services they offer. They gain their clients both by the reputation of their firm and by personal reputation. Professional men are particularly careful about reputation. They mix with people by joining clubs and by taking up public appointments. They seek recommendations by an existing client to a potential one. I think it is quite clear that professional employment hierarchies do in fact, develop, produce and sell their services. Professionals who do not devote time to this are unlikely to get rich.

Perhaps this is all rather obvious. But what I want to emphasize is that these firms develop and sell. Conversations with a professional man that begin: 'How do you go about the decisions relating to the development or the sale of the services which you offer?' do not get far. But it is important to make the real and essential operations of any employment hierarchy explicit. An explicit examination of all these operational functions by professional firms might result in substantial improvements.

In the social services the development function is usually quite clear, and is maintained by public, civic and parliamentary pressure. The sales function is not so clear. Selling means offering goods or services at a price, and most social services are free. When services are free there is no profit-making incentive to cause activity that will lead to a rise in consumption of the service. As budgets are limited it might be assumed that an effort would be made to reduce consumption. Nevertheless, activities analogous to a selling effort obviously do take place. The existence of new places where the service can be obtained and the existence of new developments are advertised. Stands are taken at exhibitions and are advertised. Television is used occasionally; press conferences are much used. Criticism of the services by the public and Parliament cause a sort of jealous and defensive reaction similar to that known in the attacked professions. Relations with the public are the subject of active consideration and planning within the employment hierarchies of most social services. Many people clearly believe that more resources put into such activity and more feedback from the public would improve such services, but that is another matter.

I do not think the Civil Service would question the idea that its work is to develop, produce and offer services. It is difficult to discuss its work because it is so highly varied, and those to whom its services are offered come from almost every sector of society. In my experience civil servants are extremely sensitive to public, industrial, commercial, educational and parliamentary reaction. Indeed, I have observed occasions when reaction to these pressures is over-warm.

One of the main purposes of this book is to examine the relationships within employment hierarchies. I shall often have to refer to the functions of developing, producing or manufacturing, and selling or marketing. I shall use 'D' to mean Product or Service development; 'M' to mean Production or Manufacturing, and 'Mk' to mean Marketing or Selling (or Offering).

D, M and Mk comprise the operational work of employment hierarchies. The term 'operational work' needs explaining. People in employment hierarchies carry out many kinds of work. Some develop, make or market products. Others keep accounts, type letters, make tools, maintain buildings or buy supplies. There is an endless succession of categories of work, but the object for which the original association of people set up the hierarchy was not to do these things. It was to do D, M and Mk work. When I use the term 'operational work' I mean D, M and Mk work. The other types of work are either specialist work concerned with some dimension of operational work, or work in giving services to support either operational or specialist work.

Having defined what I mean by operational work I can now try to give precise meaning to the term 'Chief Executive' which I shall also use frequently. It is a generic term in that it may be at times variously labelled as chairman, managing director, general manager, permanent secretary, branch manager, divisional manager, and so on.

When I use the term Chief Executive I mean a manager accountable for the development, production and marketing of a discrete group of products or services. Such accountability for D, M and Mk puts him into a situation where he has the authority to take the decisions necessary to exploit and meet the needs of a market. If any of these three functions lies outside his field of authority, then he cannot alone be held accountable for the results. A manager who holds the title of managing director or even chairman of a subsidiary company in a group may or may not (in the terms of my definition) be the chief executive of that subsidiary company, though I think that most people would assume that he is.

In some industrial groups the subsidiary companies may exercise the D and M functions, while Mk is provided (for all the subsidiaries) by a central marketing organization directly accountable to the group chief executive. On the face of it this would take away chief-executive accountability from each of the subsidiary company managing directors. But this is not the case if the central marketing organization is charged with the accountability of providing marketing services to the managers of the subsidiary companies. So long as the managers can specify the services they require and so long as the central marketing manager is accountable for providing, up to specified limits, the services required by the subsidiaries, then the managers of those subsidiaries can be said to carry the accountability of chief executives.

It is useful to define the concept of chief executive in this way because the wide variety of dual roles now held, such as chairman and managing director, director and general manager, chairman with the role of chief executive, implied or stated, makes the discussion of top management organization confused and difficult. The use of the concept in the defined sense that I have suggested draws repeated attention to the following important matters.

(1) *The need to keep, if possible, the co-ordination of D, M and Mk in one manager's hands.* It became very clear to me, when I was carrying a special responsibility for export at the Board of Trade, that when overseas customers were dissatisfied this was often due not to the incapacity of exporting companies but to lack of co-ordination of D, M and Mk. Timing of deliveries depends on M–Mk co-ordination, specification of the product on D–Mk co-ordination, and control of quality on the co-ordination of all three. It was clear from even a superficial survey that several of the problems were due to the lack of co-ordination, and that this in turn was due to vagueness in the allocation of accountability and authority.

(2) *The need to place chief-executive accountability as low in the hierarchy*

as possible. I have seen very large companies organized on what is sometimes called a 'functional' basis. In one case a chief executive had four subordinate factory managers each making different products, two distinct marketing organizations serving different types of markets, and product development was 'dispersed'. It would not have been difficult to organize the company with four chief executives each with D and M, and a central marketing organization providing marketing services. As it was, the chief executive was apparently swamped with work, co-ordination was lacking, and the company's performance (which might otherwise have been good because their manufacturing seemed to be very efficient) was in continual trouble over delivery and design.

(3) *The advisability of a chief executive having subordinates responsible separately for D, M and Mk, immediately accountable to him.* The persons in these roles should be roughly of the same rank, pay and status. The relations between people in these roles ought to be very close. If one is markedly senior to the others co-ordination is more difficult, and the more senior manager tends to get his way when perhaps he should not. If the chief executive does not think that D, M and Mk warrant roles of the same rank then I would suspect that he was confused in his thinking. Designing products that are needed in the market, making them to the required quality at the right price and delivering them according to promises given, and marketing in a manner that sells the products available in the quantities that balance against manufacturing capacity, are all activities calling for the same level of abstraction of thinking, decision and action.

(4) *The need to adjust the balance of resources invested separately in D, M and Mk in accordance with changing requirements.* For example, if tastes or technological requirements are changing rapidly, more will have to be invested in D. If labour costs are rising, more will have to be invested in M. If manufacturing capacity has outstripped the volume of sales, more will have to be invested in Mk.

These are the types of key decisions that will affect the entire future of a business. Often, in order to invest more resources in one area there will have to be a cut of resources in another. If the co-ordination of D, M and Mk is not in the hands of one manager, such compensatory adjustment to keep expense within bounds is rendered extremely difficult.

In discussing these issues I have not referred to examples of service-providing companies or, say, to the Civil Service. Organization in these areas is seldom based on the separate categories of D, M and Mk, and yet I am quite certain that such activities would benefit very greatly from such sub-division. It gives separate high-level managers clear personal accountability for separate initiatives that will safeguard the future. The thinking has to be done and the decisions have to be made in any case. The choice is between a system which entails a great deal of overlapping of accountability and authority (with some necessary activities falling between two stools), and the splitting up of all the operational work that has to be done separately between people in D, M and Mk roles.

I can quote one example of re-organization in the Board of Trade in relation to the provision of services to exporters. For several years the development of new services had been slow. New ideas simply got bogged down in paper. Re-organization took place, and I had to be very insistent in order to get the development responsibility focused on to one senior official with the necessary extended command to assist him. The effect over a short period of six months was dramatic. Ideas which heretofore had seemed impossible suddenly sprang to life. The feeling of achievement among a wide range of officials was very noticeable. The same re-organization introduced to the many officials concerned in the Board's Regional Offices the notion that it was their duty not only to provide services, but to 'market' them by bringing their existence to the attention of exporting industry. This in turn involved the idea of specific officials being given personal 'client responsibility' for a list of existing and potential exporters. I gained a strong impression, when I visited all the Regional Offices and discussed these 'new' ideas with officials, that they had generated some anxiety, some puzzlement but, most important, enthusiasm, because their tasks were now more clear-cut.

CHAPTER EIGHT

Manager–
Subordinate
Relations

*'Managers have to learn that de-selection is made necessary by a bad match between the person and the role, not because a person is "no good".
Nobody is "no good". Nearly everybody can do some work well if the right match can be established. The whole procedure must be de-emotionalised.'*
—WILFRED BROWN

SO FAR I have been trying to emphasize the importance of our employment environment. I have defined Association; Employment Hierarchy; Operational Work and its three subdivisions D, M and Mk; Manager, Immediate Command and Extended Command. I have already said (boldly) that the manager–subordinate relation is the most frequent role-relationship in society (apart from family relationships), and I now want to discuss this in greater detail.

A chief executive is usually responsible to the association[1] for all the operational work it seeks to have done.[2] It is the chief executive's

---

[1] I am using the word 'association' rather than referring to a 'board of directors' or a 'group of partners' because 'association' is the general term I use to cover the many types of bodies that set up employment hierarchies.

[2] There have been many examples of so-called 'functional boards'. These have been composed of some non-working directors and some who work in the organization. The latter are accountable for specific functions such as production, marketing, manpower and technology, to the board itself, not to a chief executive. Manifestly such functional boards have no chief executive. But I believe that in most cases the chairman of the board is regarded by the functional directors as their manager and is a disguised chief executive.

I think that analysis would show that this has not been a very

accountability that makes it necessary to endow him with authority over his subordinates. I have already defined the term 'manager' by describing the three minimum degrees of authority that he must exercise in relation to those occupying immediately subordinate roles. He must be authorized to veto appointments, to assess his subordinates, and to insist that an immediate subordinate be removed from a particular role because he cannot successfully perform the work. These three degrees of authority, if clear both to the manager and to the subordinate, make up the basic environment of the manager–subordinate relationship.

The manager's authority to veto appointments to subordinate roles. It is common for personnel departments, establishment branches of the Civil Service, or high-level managers to choose individuals who are then 'posted' to the immediate command of some lower-level manager.[1] But if the lower-level 'manager' has to accept as a subordinate a person chosen by others whom he finds unacceptable, then a true manager–subordinate relationship does not exist. The essential relationship has been undermined. Let us call the appointee 'C' and the person whose 'subordinate' he becomes 'B'. There is also B's manager, whom we will call A. Wasteful tensions between A, B and C can arise. If A imposes C on B then C will feel that because A has chosen him for the role that he will have to continue to satisfy A and need not try too hard to satisfy B. I have had the experience of having been so appointed, and have felt embarrassed and noted the embarrassment of my 'manager' when I was presented to him. I continued to feel, for a considerable time, that my performance was being reported by my 'manager' to the person who chose me though this, in fact, was not so. My 'manager' certainly behaved at the start of our relationship in a manner that conveyed to me the feeling: 'Well, you are not my choice, but I have to make the best of the situation'; or perhaps I simply felt this myself and projected the feeling on to him. Whatever the cause, it was an unsatisfactory start.

In the absence of knowing positively, there is doubt in the mind of

successful form of organization. The National Coal Board is an example. It started its life as a functional board and this caused inefficiency. Today there is no doubt that it has a chief executive.

[1] In the Civil Service the term 'superior' is used rather than manager. Superior–subordinate relationships are not identical with manager–subordinate relationships, but they are not so different as many civil servants assume.

the appointee (C) as to who he is to satisfy—his 'manager' (B) or the person who appointed him (A). With whom is C to discuss any dissatisfaction he feels at an early stage? A described all the conditions of work to him. If they are breached A seems the obvious person to approach, but there is doubt. If C goes straight to A, B may be very annoyed. If C goes to B, B may say: 'Don't complain to me. I didn't take you on, I made no promises. I don't know what A told you, but I can't give you privileges that don't apply to others in the department.' There are many variants of this rebuff.

This may sound like an argument for allowing a manager to appoint anybody he chooses to his immediate command, but that is an untenable extreme. Hierarchies depend on the accumulating experience of those employed within them. The managers more than once removed from a subordinate role must also have some control over the type of people appointed to that role if the future of the hierarchy is to be safeguarded and if agreed policies are to be put into practice. Here are some examples of policies that a chief executive might regard as necessary, and that require him to exercise control over appointments at levels lower than his immediate command.

He may have agreed with the trade union that all persons in a particular department must be members of that union. He may feel that not enough people at a particular level in the hierarchy have had university training in some particular discipline, and therefore insists that some specified percentage of future appointees must have had this education. He may seek to safeguard the future with conditions about the age of appointees. He may have set up policies that insist on certain types of prior experience in appointees. Many types of personnel selection policies will be required and the matching of such policies may, in a number of cases, be a matter of judgement rather than of meeting precise criteria. For example, a person is or is not a university graduate, but whether his experience matches up to the policy set is a matter of judgement.

Thus, a senior manager or a chief executive responsible for implementing the general policies felt to be necessary for his extended command, will probably want to have a personnel officer taking part in the process of selection. The personnel officer's interpretation of personnel policies will set limits on the freedom of choice of the manager. The manager cannot say to the personnel officer: 'I am having that man whether you agree or not.' Nor can the personnel officer say to B, the manager: 'I have done my best. You don't like any of the candidates that I find acceptable according to existing policies, but you must take one of them.'

The solution is to give the manager (B) the power to veto appointments to his immediate command. In practice the managers (or their staff officers acting on their authority) above B also possess the power of vetoing appointments. There sometimes has to be a compromise agreement. This is not a revolutionary new appointments policy. It is a description of what happens in reasonably well-regulated employment hierarchies.

In many cases, however, there is an uncertain in-between situation. Many managers, particularly at shop-floor level in industry, will claim that they have to accept appointees who are sent to them. But if you ask: 'What happens if the personnel office sends you somebody whom you feel, or perhaps know from previous experience, is incapable of doing the work of the role?' The manager will reply: 'Well, if I *strongly* object they will send me somebody else.' What he is saying is that he has some right to veto appointees if he has the courage to protest. This means that B feels he can object in extreme cases but often has to accept people against his judgement because he feels he cannot object too often. This lack of clarity can lead to trouble. B accepts C because he dare not object too often. C later makes a serious error of judgement, which drastically reduces the output of B's department. A sees B and is very critical of B, whom he holds responsible for the department. What does B do? He can say to A: 'It isn't my fault, it's yours. You chose C as one of my immediate command. I knew he couldn't do the work.' Probably B will not risk being as outspoken as that. In any case, A might reply: 'Then why did you accept him?' If they are reasonable men, then after such an event, the necessity of giving B an explicit right of veto will become clear to them both, but this agreement on the need for clarity is not usual in employment situations. On the contrary, many would regard such explicit statements of B's authority as undesirably formal. But the lack of some such formal statement gives rise to a whole series of tensions, which are blamed on human personality.

If one asks about the arrangements for making appointments in a well-organized hierarchy, one often finds it described as follows. A personnel officer, representing the company's general employment policies, plus the manager once-removed, plus the immediate manager, form an appointments 'committee' which sees the candidates and makes the decision. But this is not a true committee, as can be demonstrated by asking 'can the manager once-removed and the personnel officer out-vote the immediate manager?'. The answer is almost invariably 'No'. If one analyses the situation one finds that all three have the power of veto, though when this is pointed out to those involved it often surprises them. It is important to recognize that such an appointments body is not a real committee. (A committee, I would again state, is a body carrying corporate responsibility, which makes its decisions by majority vote. Phantom committees are another and fascinating subject, to which I will return.)

The Manager's authority to make differential assessments of the work of members of his immediate command. This is the second degree of minimal authority required of a role if it is to fall within the definition of the term 'manager'.

It is important to note that I am talking about *differential* assessments, not absolute assessments. If B is to be given minimum managerial authority then it must be he, and he alone, who decides the order of merit of his immediate subordinates in terms of the work that they carry out for him. He must be able to comment to higher authority in terms that will be taken into account in deciding their differential wages. He must decide how his work is split up between C_1, C_2 and C_3, and he alone must be the person who tells C_1, C_2 and C_3 how well it has been carried out.

Many people might ask why A, for example, should not judge the performance of C_1, C_2 and C_3 and comment to them about it. But A has instructed B to carry out certain tasks. In order to carry them out B has to break down his task and give portions of it to C_1, C_2 and C_3. A does not know the details, as distinct from the outline, of this delegation. He does not know how much guidance B has given to his immediate subordinates. C_1 may apparently have done an excellent job but, in fact, it may be that B has set up the plan and has taken most of the important decisions himself, and that a good result has emerged *in spite* of C_1's mistakes.

If A makes value-judgements of the work of B's subordinates it implies a far more penetrating understanding of the relationship between B and his subordinates than can reasonably be acquired. I have been in a situation where A, my manager, has complimented C_1, my subordinate, and I have had to say to A later: 'You praised the wrong man because C_2 and I did most of the real thinking. C_1 simply wrote up the results. In any case, I signed the report, and I am accountable for it; if you feel satisfied then I am the man to compliment. If it had gone wrong you would not have blamed C_1, you would have blamed me. I am the man to judge whether compliments to or criticism of my subordinates are justified.'

If B has had the explicit right to veto appointments to roles C_1, C_2 and C_3 then, on their appointment, he has already put himself in a position of accountability for the work that they do. If A feels critical of C1 his proper course perhaps is to say to B: 'You should not have accepted that person.' Likewise if C1 does well then B is due for praise, because B accepted C1, trained him, decided what work to give him, and determined on the guidance he needed. Though subordinates appreciate having their work recognized, not only by their own manager but by higher managers, the process can introduce tension between the subordinate and his manager. The implied or explicit terms of C's contract were to carry out the policies of the organization and the instructions of B, his manager. C voluntarily accepted that position, and he can resign if he finds it unsatisfactory. His contract is to establish the soundest possible relationship with his manager and carry out the tasks assigned to him in the best possible manner. If he invites the managerial attentions of A, or if A imposes his managerial attentions on C, trouble will ensue.

Some may think this too absolute. They will wonder what happens if B makes judgements of C that are not based on C's work, or if B fails to carry out the policy of the organization and therefore treats C unjustly, or behaves unfairly in other ways. There must be a means of correcting such mistakes, but it should be in the formal setting of an appeals system. I will return to this subject, but I refer to it at this stage to prevent misunderstanding. Equally I must, at this stage, make a preliminary comment on the question of the differential pay of a manager's subordinates, though I intend to deal with this issue at much greater length later.

B's immediate subordinates ought not to be working at levels that are very different from each other. The best situation is one where they feel like colleagues and can discuss matters together on reasonably equal terms. Inevitably there will be wide differences in age and experience, but their pay should fall within the same bracket. They may be classified in different grades[1] for the purpose of pay, pensions, etc. but they should be of the same rank and should be capable of work of not too dissimilar levels.

B's assessment of his immediate subordinates ought to be decisive in deciding, not the pay-bracket itself, but where those subordinates are positioned within the bracket. B cannot be the arbiter in any way

---

[1] I differentiate between 'Grade' and 'Rank'. The number of ranks in a company is the number of required managerial levels plus one. If you have a managing director, factory manager, production superintendent, a foreman and machine operators, that is five ranks. Within each rank there may be sub-divisions for the purpose of regulating pay, pensions, holidays, etc. I call these grades. I explore the issue in detail later.

of the level or width of the bracket of pay attached to the level of work in his immediate command, because similar levels of work are being carried out in many other commands. But his opinion should be decisive about the differential pay of C_1, C_2 and C_3 within the bracket.

The manager's authority to de-select people from immediately subordinate roles. 'De-selection' is, as I define it, the start of the process of transferring a person to another role, or, if the person proves unacceptable in another role, out of the employment hierarchy.

The authority to do this must be subject to a right of appeal. The reason for the right of appeal is not that higher managers ought to be asked to judge whether or not the subordinate has performed his work satisfactorily. Nobody is in a position to do that as effectively as the immediate manager. Nobody except his manager really knows how a subordinate has done his work, for nobody else knows precisely what work the subordinate has been given in terms of the decisions he is required to make, the length of time in which he was expected to do the work, the *cumulative record* of sound or sub-standard decisions he has taken, the degree of guidance provided, the help or lack of help he has been given. It is the very essence of the managerial–subordinate relationship that the manager is responsible for these assessments. If others intervene or are asked to intervene, they will base their judgements not on the *fullness of the subordinate's total performance over time* but on a few examples of excellent or poor judgement.

Appeal mechanisms are essential. There has to be a check on whether the manager, in coming to a decision to de-select a subordinate, has based his decision entirely on work performance and not on personal characteristics unconnected with work performance. And there has to be a check on whether the manager has adhered to the policy of the organization in coming to his decision.

For example, some older men who choose to take advantage of a policy that permits them because of age to work shorter hours may make their manager's task more difficult. He may, in assessing his subordinates, decide that one of these older men should be de-selected. But he must not count it against that man that he is working shorter hours. That was brought about by the policy of the company, and the man who chooses to benefit from that policy must not be penalized for doing so. He needs a right of appeal if he thinks that his manager has penalized him on that account.

Thirdly, the right of appeal is also necessary in order to ensure that the decision to de-select has been arrived at after due processes have been gone through in accordance with any policies laid down by the company. Such policies might insist that, at a given time before the de-selection decision, the subordinate be formally warned that his performance is unsatisfactory to a degree that will cause de-selection unless it improves. The right of appeal is not therefore a process of asking A to assess whether B's assessment of C is sound, because A is certainly unable to make that assessment. It is a process of making sure that B, in arriving at his decision about C, has carried out the policies of the organization, or, in other words, has kept within the limits that prescribe his use of discretion.

Appeal mechanisms are important for several reasons. One reason is that without them it is difficult to justify the endowment of managers with the third degree of authority that they have to have— the authority to de-select immediate subordinates. In the absence of an appeals system the authority of a manager to insist that a subordinate be removed, probably to another role in the hierarchy, could give him enough authority to enable him to behave unjustly.

Anybody who has worked both in industry and among civil servants will have become aware of two interesting and contradictory myths. Civil servants believe that the 'firing' of individuals is a frequent happening in industrial and commercial employment hierarchies. Industrial and commercial people believe that nobody is ever 'fired' in the Civil Service. These impressions are both gross oversimplifications. The Civil Service is a series of large departmental employment hierarchies. Failing gross misbehaviour, continuity of employment without demotion is guaranteed once a civil servant is 'established'. Such a situation is made possible by three existing conditions:

(a) The Civil Service in toto is very large.
(b) Cross-transference of people between roles in different hierarchies is practised.
(c) The Civil Service is grant-supported, that is to say, its continued existence at its current size is not threatened by loss of income as, for instance, happens in industry as a result of the collapse of a market.

Given such a situation there is no need to 'fire' civil servants by dismissing them from the Service. The inevitable cases of bad initial selection or mistakes in promotion can be dealt with reasonably effectively by blocking further promotion; and if there is no role in one department that they can fill tolerably well, the Service is so large that there is reasonable hope of finding some suitable role by transference.

The unsolved problem of the Service seems to be that of the over-promoted person who cannot be demoted to a lower level and who must continue to receive any increase of salary that is awarded to the grade which he holds. If the Service were allowed to freeze an over-promoted official at the salary he was receiving when the fact of his over-promotion became obvious, then the march of inflation of money values would, in effect, drop his differential salary until it equated with his work capacity. But 'firing' people would achieve nothing in the Service and would produce damaging tensions. If one talks about de-selection as I have defined the term, then a great deal of it does happen in the Civil Service. In my view there is probably, in proportion to size, more de-selection in the Service than in industry. Most officials would deny that a superior has authority to have a subordinate removed, but many agree, in discussion, that if a subordinate is sufficiently unsatisfactory to cause them to put pressure on the establishment division, then that subordinate will be transferred to some other role faster than would otherwise be the case. Though being part of a very large service covering all departments of state gives security of employment, it has the disadvantage to the individual that wherever a person goes his whole record of employment since he entered the Service goes with him. Any adverse report resulting in early transfer can affect his subsequent career. Critical comment on one's records is a serious matter in the Service, and is perhaps the reason why pressure to have inadequate subordinates transferred is not exercised more frequently. As in the Royal Navy, one's entire career may be spoilt by a single seriously adverse report.

In industry the situation is very different. There can be no guarantee of continued employment because company income is not secure. It can fade away, and when it does redundancy follows as night follows day. Compared with the Civil Service the size of employment hierarchies is, on average, very small. Transfer within a company is thus more difficult than transfer in the Service because the number of alternative opportunities for a de-selected person is much smaller. Looked at from one angle, a transfer from one department to another in the Civil Service without loss of employment is equivalent in industry to loss of employment in one company followed by fresh employment in another. But de-selection in industry is in fact called 'dismissal', and has connotations of ejection from the company (and may, indeed, result in this). Because of this, and contrary, I think, to the popular view, managers in industry are reluctant to use their de-selection authority. Equally, in the eyes of workers' representatives in industry dismissal is regarded as the ultimate penalty (though, indeed, in areas of full employment it may prove to be very little like a penalty). This brings very great pressures on managers not to inflict this 'penalty'. The result is that even if people fill roles very inadequately they too often remain in such roles long after their inadequacy has become obvious. In the Civil Service, on the other hand, an all-over pattern of frequent transfer from role to role seems to have made the matching of persons to roles more satisfactory than it is in industry. In other words, my perception is the opposite of that which I believe is generally held.

To complete the picture one must look at the universities, which, like the Civil Service, are grant-supported. They not only offer security of employment to their established staff but also offer *security of tenure in their individual roles*, excepting only cases of gross misconduct. Thus every sub-standard appointment is permanent, unless the incumbent of the role voluntarily resigns. Such a situation would seem to call for the most meticulous appointments procedures, although they do not seem to be meticulous at all. Were it not for the very rapid growth in size of universities and in the number of new universities, security of role would have had the effect of freezing the hierarchy of universities to a very unfortunate extent. Even now some universities carry many 'passengers'. Inadequate selection and assessment procedures, coupled with role security, contain the seeds of substantial future problems for the universities.

We have got to learn to turn a more objective eye on to procedures that initiate transfers from one role to another, and to stop talking in terms of 'firing', 'sacking', and 'dismissing'. They are all emotive words. De-select may be a clumsy word, but it is etymologically very accurate, for the manager is reversing the process of selection. It also implies that he is correcting his own error, which is again accurate. The manager might say to his subordinate: 'I'm sorry, but I made a mistake in appointing you to your present role; your abilities aren't well fitted to the work. I'm going to hand you over to the personnel department; I've already made enquiries and there are several jobs open that don't involve demotion and which might suit you better. It's no good keeping you in my team. You know I'm not satisfied and you can't have had a happy time recently when I frequently had to find fault with your work. It's much better for both of us that you transfer to different duties. I'm sorry that I made the initial mistake in assuming that your skills fitted the job.'

Perhaps all that sounds idealistic, but does it not define what is frequently the real situation? The trouble arises when managers allow dissatisfaction to exist for too long before taking such action, possibly because of uncertainty on the part of the 'manager' about what his authority is, and real doubt as to whether his de-selected subordinate will be properly considered for other roles.

A subordinate confronted with a statement like that for the first time would probably think his manager had been reading some of the 'cynical-funny' books about management which have come to us from the USA, and that he was up against the latest managerial technique for manipulating subordinates. But if, on the other hand, de-selection, in the terms I have described, had come to be accepted as the counterpart to selection and recognized as a means of keeping the entire hierarchy of roles manned with people whose capacity was a reasonable match to their authority and accountability, then the reaction might well be very different. Most people in employment roles tend to be so anxious about their security of tenure that they are reluctant to see the power of de-selection given to their managers; but they overlook the fact that in the absence of mechanisms that make transfers possible they can be stuck for years with an immediate manager who is inadequate. To find oneself responsible to an inadequate manager is a very unfortunate experience.

Managers have to learn that de-selection is made necessary by a bad match between the person and role, not because the person is 'no good'. Nobody is 'no good'. Nearly everybody can do some work well if the right match can be established. The whole procedure must be de-emotionalized.

Some de-selections will result in demotion to a lower-level role, but if it is established policy to maintain the de-selected person's salary at the previous level, then much of the sting is taken out of the event. The person does not have to go home and tell his wife that he has been demoted if his salary level remains as it was. In due course, if increases of salary arising out of inflation are withheld, he can assume his appropriate level of salary. Many companies, in the event, treat people extremely well. But half the value of good practice is lost if the practice is not seen to exist by all. Unless people know that there is a sound process for dealing with these problems the fear of dismissal hangs over relations between managers and subordinates like a spectre.

As long as the whole process of de-selection continues to possess the aura of retribution, people will be very reluctant to set up full managerial roles with proper authority to deal with the discrepancy between subordinate and work. In such cases the authority to de-select, which must reside somewhere, will probably be found at two levels removed from the person concerned. This really does breed trouble. If the foreman who is *apparently* the manager of the machine-operator has not got this authority, which, in fact, resides in the factory manager, then, when de-selection becomes necessary, the situation becomes very difficult indeed. The factory manager who has the authority to make the decision about de-selection is not in a position to assess the work done by the subject of his decision. The foreman, who can make the work assessment, has not got the authority to make the decision. Such a situation will certainly breed feelings of guilt in the foreman and factory manager and anger in the subordinates.

Some of the reluctance to establish managerial roles at all appropriate levels arises from the assumption (on the part of those who could make the decision to do this) that many of those occupying quasi-managerial roles could not be trusted with managerial authority or would not use such authority if it were given to them. I believe that there is a good deal of substance in such assumptions. For example, many foremen in industry lack the psychological capacity that would enable them to manage others. But that is not a good reason for failing to structure foremen roles as managerial roles. Foremen roles should be given full managerial authority, and if their occupants cannot carry the role then industry must set about filling those roles with people of higher capacity. This will be very difficult to accomplish, but if the task is necessary the sooner it is started the better. The filling of these roles adequately can produce some remarkable results in terms of efficiency and increased satisfaction on the shop floor.

I have written at considerable length about this third dimension of managerial authority, because it is very important. There are too many roles in employment hierarchies occupied by people who are poorly matched to the work which has to be done. More transferring of people between roles would lead not only to greater efficiency but also to a higher general degree of satisfaction for employees. But it will not happen until we set up real managerial roles in such a way that everybody has an immediate manager to whom he has access, and until we get explicit and widely understood appeals systems to safeguard people from the misuse of managerial authority.

CHAPTER NINE

Judging the Performance of Subordinates

'*Men are neither good nor bad but only good or bad in this or that position.*'—CHESTER BARNARD, *The Functions of the Executive*

IN DISCUSSING THE nature of employment work earlier I have, I hope, established that while some people do physical work everybody does mental work, and that the main basis on which they are assessed is how they use experience, knowledge and judgement to make decisions.

It is easy to read the foregoing statement, and to accept it intellectually and then to act as though we had not accepted the idea. We tend to be conditioned to assess the work of others too much on the *apparent* results of their use of judgement. We too readily agree that chief executives should be assessed solely on the basis of the *profit-and-loss account*, that the factory manager should be solely assessed on the *volume of output of goods*, or the civil servant on the *speed* with which he can introduce arrangements that put into practice a change in Government policy. But these achievements—profit, volume of output, and speed—are the end-results of processes that involve not only the quality of the decisions made by the chief executive, the factory manager or the civil servant, but also a host of other variables outside their control. It would be very convenient if these were objective parameters of the performance of people; but they are not. Many find this so distressing that they sometimes fail to face up to it and go on trying to assess the work done by subordinates or others on a quite unreal basis. The reason for their distress is that instead of the relatively easy task of looking, for example, at the output volume achieved by the factory manager and accepting the figures as an index of his performance they must, instead, take their whole experience of his performance over a period of time into account and use their own judgement in coming to a decision as to whether his performance is good, bad or indifferent.

Judging the performance of subordinates is, in a very real sense, hard work. It is a very important part of the work of all managers. If assessment work is not done properly excellent subordinates fail to get increases of pay or promotion, inadequate subordinates stay in their roles too long, subordinates are left in a state of anxiety, people in the manager's extended command are left to work under an in-adequate manager, efficiency falls and, in one way and another, a great deal of tension, anxiety and even conflict is generated.

Take the fallacy that the work of a chief executive of a company should be assessed solely on the basis of the annual profit made. The profit-and-loss account is the result of a range of factors, which in-clude the state of the market, the changing cost of raw materials, changes in Government policy, nationally agreed changes in wage levels, the decisions of the board of directors about such things as capital investment, the basis of valuation of stocks, reserves, the pro-ducts or markets on which the chief executive is instructed to concen-trate, and so on. It is difficult to enumerate all the variables in the situation that lie outside his control. The existence of these variables is obvious. Yet the *manifest* basis of judging the chief executive's per-formance is often stated to be the financial results alone. This is an important example of fantasy thinking. (I say that it is the *manifest* basis of assessment because, whatever people say, the actual basis of assessment is often much more realistic.) This particular fantasy can lead to companies setting up 'profit centres' so that they have what they think is a basis of assessment. Quantitative indices such as profit, output, volume of sales, are very important, but in using them in assessment it is essential to consider the other variables that have affected them, and to assess how far they are a function of a manager's performance.

Some years ago an automobile-manufacturing company an-nounced the splitting of their company into four profit centres. None of the four centres manufactured complete automobiles because two were manufacturing units, one was an assembly unit and the fourth looked after spares and servicing. All were interdependent, and com-ponents and parts flowed between them. The prices at which these interchanges took place were an immensely important variable in the differential profit made by each of the four centres, and these interchange prices were fixed by a central accounting division. But because there was no objective basis for fixing interchange prices the decisions about them may have exercised more effect on the individual profits of the four groups than the decisions of the four managers in charge of them.

If one introduces the time element, the fallacy is compounded. To the extent that profits are affected by decisions of the chief executive the effects virtually never show up during the year in which the decisions were made and for which the profit-and-loss account is struck. The chief executive takes decisions in year one. The results will not appear until years later. The larger the company the longer the time-span of the chief executive's discretion. For example, the chief executive may decide to develop a new product, but it may be four years before sales in volume result. In the intervening years the profit-and-loss account will include all the costs of a plan that is producing no revenue. How can it then be said that the chief executive's efforts can be assessed in terms of the profit in the intervening years?[1]

Fallacious perceptions like this about how to assess an individual's work exist at all levels in employment hierarchies and are widespread in society. Factual results are very important, but they must be used intelligently. Their crude use as sole criteria of success not only results in injustice to individuals but also can bring about decisions that damage the future of companies.

Civil servants often told me that one of the great advantages possessed by commerce and industry was that people could be judged on measured results, whereas this was not possible in the Civil Service. I tried hard to correct this false notion but I never felt that I had succeeded. The notion is very deep-rooted. I used to explain the presence of all the variables affecting any quantitative indices, and

[1] Stephen Laner and E. R. F. W. Crossman of the University of California, Berkeley, published in September 1970 the results of a study carried out for the Office of Naval Research on 'The current status of the Jaquesian time-span of discretion concept'. The authors refer to the work of Professor Dearden of the Harvard Business School who, on the basis of his research, criticizes the practice of evaluating the performance of all units of a firm over the same (one-year) period of time. Dearden's interest is in the shortest period of time elapsing before the cost performance of a manager can be validly assessed.

I agree with Dearden. *The length of time* over which the cost/performance parameter of a manager's work should be measured seems likely to me to be as short as months for foremen managers, rising to some years for senior managers. Equally it seems likely to correlate with maximum time-span of the work in the role of those managers.

then point out that even if it were true that profit, for example, were the sole measure of performance it would be a measure only of the chief executive's performance and not of the performance of the thousands of others in his extended command. The civil servants would then call attention to other factors, which they assumed to be parameters of performance of subordinate people, such as volume of output, volume of sales, number of machine operations completed, speed of assembly, etc. But it always proved very difficult to make them realize that every quantitative parameter they mentioned was affected by the decisions of many other people and by many external factors and that it was never possible to isolate, in terms of such factors, the effect of a single person's decisions.

The Civil Service tries very hard to operate good assessment-procedures. Because of their anxiety about the absence of quantitative data they have been driven to pay a great deal of attention to methods of judging the performance of individuals. There are repeated assessment boards, assessment reports, and so on. I am not suggesting that these methods are objective. The opinion of the immediate superior about the performance of his subordinate is often swamped by the opinions of many others who have no day-to-day accumulated experience of the person who is being assessed. But, at least, the Civil Service has not been bemused into assuming that assessment can be based solely on selected quantitative results and requires no act of judgement.

The attempt to base assessment solely on quantitative results derives from false perceptions about the nature of employment work. If we assume that a manager is employed to run a factory, then it is an easy step to make the next assumption, that it is right to measure his performance solely on the output of the factory or on the ratio of expense to the value of the output. (I am almost taken in myself by the apparent logic of that statement as I write it, because I slip back so easily into the wrong frame of reference in thinking about work.)

But if we accept that we want our subordinates to discharge the tasks we give them by constantly using their brains in deciding how to distribute work to their subordinates, how to surmount the daily problems that appear, how to devise ways of getting results when normal methods have failed, how to keep things on schedule, how to deal with personnel difficulties, how to train others to do the job, how to match changes in the environment in which they work that no one foresaw, with initiatives that nobody told them to take, how to use 'nous', then we will not fall into this trap. If we realize that we have to judge subordinates on the way they use their judgement then we will realize that *our* judgements of *their* work are based on experience over time and on *our* use of intuition and judgement. There is no easy formula.

It is only by considering a subordinate's work in the way I have outlined that a manager can help him. It is no help to him to say: 'Your output has fallen, there must, therefore, be something wrong about your approach to running the factory and you must do better.' You can help him only by pointing to examples of errors or marginal errors of judgement, and to do that you must have a pretty extensive knowledge of the type of decisions that his work involves.

The manager who says to his subordinate: 'The way you go about your work looks reasonable to me, but the fact is that your output is down and therefore you cannot remain in the role' is not doing his own work as a manager properly, and is likely to appoint a replacement who will do no better than his previous subordinate (unless the replacement is lucky because of changed circumstances, which result in an improvement of output for which he will unjustifiably get the credit).

'Cost/benefit' studies are very fashionable, particularly in government today. It is obviously sound to make a disciplined attempt to state the measurable results and consider them in relation to measurable costs. But such analyses often seem to go off the rails. It is often quite impossible to quantify all the results and all the costs. The danger is that only those that can be quantified are compared, with the result that very important factors of both input and result are ignored. The only viable course is to take all factors into account by making the best possible intuitive judgements about those which are not measurable. If we fail to do this we will make bad decisions. Trying to assess the work of subordinates solely on selected quantifiable parameters contains analogous errors.

There are psychological barriers that sometimes deter managers from taking stock of their subordinates' work, sifting it, thinking about it, deciding when to teach, when to advise, when to instruct, when to praise, when to criticize, when to check up on what they are doing, when to extend their responsibility and when to restrict it. This presents itself to some managers as the act of 'passing judgement on others'. Many people, perhaps most people, have a deep-rooted objection to the idea of judging others. Most of us are ready to do so in the abstract or to judge those at a distance from us. We do not mind judging politicians, trade-union leaders, tycoons. But we shrink from passing judgement face to face on people we know, and often from passing judgement, though not face to face, on our subordinates. This reluctance is socially acceptable, whereas people in authority are held to be fair game.

The barrier is, I think, simply concerned with the feeling 'who am I to set myself up as a judge of people'. But managers are not given their authority in order to judge *people* as *people*. They have taken on the responsibility of judging *the work* of subordinates, which is quite a different matter.

Subordinates often react to criticism of their decisions as though it was a personal criticism of their character. Managers often criticize work in such a way as to give this impression. This is unfortunate, because it reinforces the false idea that managers wield authority over the lives of people. They do not; they wield authority over their employment and the work that goes with it.

The test case for me on this issue of judging the work of subordinates arose during the war. Information reached us from the police that one of our employees was an active spare-time criminal. My own first reaction was that we should have to discharge this man from our employment. But I then reflected that his criminal activity was not necessarily anything to do with his work. I asked about his performance and was told that it was excellent. We took no action, but a few months later he left and the law eventually dealt with him. I think many managers would have discharged this man on the basis of proof of his criminal activity outside the company's time, but I think they would have been wrong to do so. We must remember that in the eyes of the State it is not a company's job to try to punish a man for criminal activity.

If managers abdicate from their responsibilities for making assessments then the results can be very unfortunate. The manager who retains in his immediate command a managerial subordinate who is incapable of discharging properly the work of his role, probably takes upon himself a large part of that work. Because he becomes involved in doing work which could be delegated to his subordinates (if they had sufficient competence) he may well fail to do his own work competently. His own superior will be doing his subordinate's work. The pattern of distribution of work between roles will be distorted. If in this way undermanning of roles becomes widespread, it will result in the chief executive himself becoming pre-occupied with work that should properly be carried out by his subordinates. If this happens, proper attention will not be given to decisions about development, and long-term strategy and the future of the company will be threatened.

The chief executive who keeps an ineffective managerial subordinate may fail to realize that the inadequacy of that subordinate will affect the performance of the whole of the latter's extended command. Few situations have such a depressing effect on a man's morale as those in which he has to work for a manager who is not fully competent. The manager's inadequacies are reflected downwards and affect every phase of his subordinates' performance. The subordinates cannot perform in a manner that is satisfactory to themselves, and are deprived of the basis of good morale—creative work efficiently performed. The retention of an inadequate managerial subordinate may cause the best people in his command to leave.

If a manager A has a subordinate B whose performance is inadequate, mistakes will be made and inefficiencies will occur. It is likely, in these circumstances, that the performance of B's subordinates, C_1, C_2, C_3, will appear inadequate to A. (This has certainly been my experience.) If, however, B leaves the company or is transferred to another post and replaced by somebody more competent, then the performance of C_1, C_2, C_3, etc. may take on a new aspect. In short, if manager A retains inadequate manager B in his command, then A will probably form an unjustifiably low opinion of the competence of B's subordinates C_1, C_2, C_3. This, obviously, can have unfortunate consequences.

There are plenty of people in employment hierarchies who perform their managerial roles quite inadequately in respect of the treatment given to their subordinates. They are perhaps unjustifiably censorious, they play favourites, they overlook talent, they are indecisive and blame the results on subordinates, they are impatient of advice, they are devious in their ways. Because such behaviour does exist, many people doubt the wisdom of giving managers the degree of authority that I advocate. But somebody must wield this authority. Somebody must be able to veto appointments, make differential assessments and de-select people from roles, if employment hierarchies are to exist. If we shift this authority to the 'manager' once removed from the subordinate then this simply creates a situation where the detailed knowledge that is the essential basis of decision-making is missing. This situation is not uncommon, and is much more dangerous than the risk that some managers will misuse their authority, because if the structure of management is functioning properly, then inadequate managers themselves will be removed.

Firstly, if B is unsatisfactory and is inflicting injustice on his subordinates C_1, C_2 and C_3, it is A's job to spot what is happening. It may take time but it cannot go unnoticed for long if there is an explicit appeals system in use. I have had many years of experience as chief executive of a company in watching an appeals system in operation. Such systems give managers a great deal of insight into the way in which their subordinates handle their own teams.

Secondly, if internal promotion and transfer procedures are freely used then one gets a sort of migration out of the command of B which cannot pass unnoticed.

Thirdly, it is the task of a personnel department to watch people as they change jobs or are promoted. The personnel department is the custodian of knowledge about the total performance-history of people in all the roles they have occupied in a company. If B is overlooking talent among his subordinates the personnel department can organize transfers to the immediate commands of other managers. I am not suggesting that another manager should be able to poach bright subordinates from the command of B. What I do say is that it is the task of a personnel department to initiate the making of such transfers, and that when they do it it should not count as poaching. Admittedly I am relying on a degree of sophistication as a safeguard against the unjust behaviour of managers which is too often not yet present in employment hierarchies.

Human work capacity and experience varies very widely, and so does the work-content of roles. Matching one to the other remains an art and has not become a science. It is a very difficult art indeed. If we get confused and begin to think critically about personalities when what we are really criticizing is a failure to achieve a good match between ability and work, then all sorts of damage can be done to sound relations at work. If we can become more objective we will be better managers. We will find ourselves with better subordinates and work will be better done. Everybody in the employment hierarchy will get more satisfaction from their employment.

CHAPTER TEN

Committees, Boards and Directors

A COMMITTEE IS a body of people who are collectively accountable and are authorized to come to decisions by majority vote. In short, a committee carries corporate accountability.

Committees can be elected or appointed by others with authority to do so, such as local authorities, government departments, teaching institutions or associations of shareholders. Some committees are mixtures of elected people, appointed people and people appointed *ex officio* (that is, as long as they hold some other role that entitles them to membership of the committee). The authority that appoints a committee sometimes also appoints the chairman. Other committees elect their chairmen. At law, corporate accountability involves the notion that if a committee decides by a majority to take some illegal action, the minority who voted against the action are, nevertheless, accountable with the majority unless they make public their disagreement, or resign and thus dissociate themselves from the action.

It is easy to get agreement about all the points I have made, and yet there is a great deal of confusion about committees. Some seem to think that whenever a few people come together to discuss some common interest then they are entitled to call themselves a committee and proceed to settle controversy by majority voting. People working in employment hierarchies show a strong tendency to do this, oblivious of the fact that apart from boards of directors (many of which are committees) and committees of representatives, there are no committees within employment hierarchies. Such committees would run counter to the properties of employment hierarchies, which are based on *individual* accountability.

The Civil Service has a strong tendency to form non-committees. Inter-departmental 'committees' abound, but none of them can decide by majority vote. Universities are prolific breeding-grounds of committees and non-committees. One vice-chancellor complained recently that he was a member of over 200 committees.

There is a great deal of cynicism about committees, summed up in the comment: 'Committees are composed of people who individually can do nothing but who collectively decide that nothing can be done.' Some of this cynicism springs from the existence of fantasy committees and some from lack of insight into the difficult relationships that can exist between members of committees.

In many instances committees are referred to by other names, such as boards of directors, authorities, councils, or associations. In other cases bodies are given similar labels such as 'divisional boards'— boards of wholly owned subsidiary companies—which cause them to assume that they are committees when they are not.

Some people believe that committee control is 'democratic' and any other form of control is not; perhaps this is the underlying motive for our tendency to proliferate real committees and their fantasy versions.

I want to take a look at some forms of committees and non-committees, because in spite of the confusion associated with them, and the cynicism it breeds, committees and other meetings are very important institutions.

Boards of Privately-owned Companies

These often consist of an entrepreneur who owns virtually the whole capital of the company but who, in order to achieve limited liability status, must have (according to the law) at least two directors. Therefore a board has to be set up. The entrepreneur often invites his wife to be a co-director, and possibly appoints a person as secretary to the board who is also a director. In the eyes of the law this board carries corporate responsibility. But *de facto* the entrepreneur is the owner of all or the majority of the shares. He exercises power and, in the last analysis, is in a position to ignore the views of his co-directors (and never mind the marriage vows).

There is often a similar situation in a family business where the chairman, or perhaps the managing director himself, owns a substantial holding of shares, the rest being owned by close relatives. As a result he exercises *de facto* power over the board through his control of their election to that board, by virtue of his own or his family shareholding. In this situation corporate responsibility is something of a legal fiction brought about by the Companies Acts. But there are also many privately-owned companies where a small association of shareholders elects a board that is corporately involved in determining policy and is a real committee.

Boards of Directors of Public Companies and the Role of Directors

At law, boards of directors are elected committees representing the association of shareholders. They are obviously of the greatest importance to their companies, to the company's employees and to the economy of the country. I don't think that the way they work receives enough study, or that some of the problems which arise in the role of director are sufficiently understood.

It is not possible to generalize about the role of directors of companies, because this is governed by the articles of association of companies, and these articles vary from company to company. It is however possible to see what the general intentions of the law are by reading Table A of the first schedule to the Companies Act 1948. This table sets out the 'Regulations for management of a company limited by shares'. Any company that does not register its own special articles is deemed to be bound by Table A. I therefore propose to discuss the roles of director, managing director, and chairman as they would be if the articles of association of the company that had elected them as directors were in accordance with Table A.

The directors are elected by shareholders at general meetings. They must resign every third year, and if they want to continue to be directors, offer themselves for re-election. The chairman of the board is not excluded from this necessity. But the managing director, who can be appointed by the board for any term of years that they decide, continues as a director as long as he continues to be managing director.

The chairman of the board is elected by majority vote of the other directors. Apart from the possession of a casting vote at board meetings, he has no special authority at law except those necessary to conduct a meeting of the board or a meeting of shareholders. Indeed, if he fails to turn up at a board meeting within five minutes of its scheduled starting-time the directors may elect another director to chair the meeting. The same is true of meetings of the shareholders, except that in that case he is given fifteen instead of five minutes' grace. Thus the chairman at law, is first among equals. The board can depose him from the chair by majority vote at any time. The managing director is also appointed by majority vote of the board—but often for a stated period of time, under contract. The managing director thus has two roles—that of director, to which he is elected by shareholders—and that of chief executive, to which he is appointed by the board. In short, he is both a director and an employee. As an employee the managing director's work has to be assessed. That is one of the most important duties of the board.

Briefly, then, the directors elect a chairman and can depose him at will (unless there are special provisions in the articles of association). They ought to do so if, in their estimation, he fails to behave properly. The directors appoint a chief executive (managing director) and are accountable to the shareholders for assessing his work continuously. The directors are accountable to the shareholders for deposing the chief executive (subject to the terms of his contract) if he fails to perform satisfactorily.

Judging by what happens in a good many companies one would assume that many directors are confused about their own roles. Many chief executives seem to want to become chairman of the board of directors. But if the articles of association are more or less in line with Table A (as many are), the chairman, at law, has no greater authority between meetings of the board than any other director. He is not even in an advantageous position to call meetings of the board, for any one director can do this (Para 98 of Table A). If it became law that a managing director could not also be appointed to the role of chairman without relinquishing the role of managing director then I suspect that we would see many changes in the occupants of the role of chairman in British Public companies.

Directors fall into two categories: those who hold no other role associated with the company, and those who do. They are commonly referred to as external directors and executive directors. The latter have two roles: one as elected directors, and the other as employees of the company. It is common to find the Sales Manager, the Production Manager or the Chief Engineer also holding position of director. The prevalent habit of referring to them as Sales *Director*, Production *Director* or Engineering *Director* blurs the distinction between the two different roles that each holds.

I want to examine the difficulties in which executive directors sometimes find themselves. They are employees as well as directors. In the former role they are subordinates of the chief executive, who may variously be managing director or chairman of the board, or he may hold both roles. In the role of directors they must vote as members of the board in the election of the chairman or in the appointment of the managing director. (In addition they also exercise their

vote in deciding which persons should be recommended to the shareholders for election by them as directors.)

These two roles of employee and director clash at times. It is
clearly very difficult for an employee-director to vote against the re-
appointment of his own manager as managing director. It could well
finish his career with the company. The same difficulty arises when
employee-directors have to use their vote in the election of chairman.[1]

Sometimes people fail to recognize that the executive directors
occupy two roles. When this happens the executive directors cannot
be clear about the role in which they are contributing to discussions
at a board meeting. In their employed role, as subordinates of the
managing director, they would carry the responsibility for saying
which policies they would favour so far as their own executive commands were concerned. But to say this at a board meeting would be
inappropriate. The board would expect its managing director to
speak about the effects of any policy they were discussing on the
whole of the company. He alone can deal with the wider frame of
reference and consider the whole company; and he alone will be held
responsible by the board for making recommendations on the policies it should follow.

In his second role, as a director, each executive who sits on the
board is responsible for speaking in the same wide frame of reference
as the managing director himself, and without any special regard for
the particular segment of the company's operations for which he is
responsible in his executive role. If, however, he speaks up bravely in
his board role as a director, he may come up against the managerial
authority of the chairman or managing director. In these circumstances executive directors often simply try to be helpful but non-
committal. They try to help the board to reach optimum decisions
but, at the same time, to avoid argument with the managing director.
The meeting will then be less useful as an instrument for setting
company policy.

To say all this is to expose a difficulty without putting forward a
constructive solution. I do not wish it to be inferred that I am against
the presence of any executive directors on the board. Their presence

---

[1] There is evidence that in some of our very largest companies, executive directors do in fact exercise control over the election of chairman
and appointment of the managing director. This seems to arise when
the employee-directors are not fully employed as managers but spend
a high proportion of their time in the role of director. Companies
such as Du Pont in the USA and I.C.I. and Lever Bros in the UK
would, on the face of it, seem to be examples.

can be very valuable, not only in making experienced comment available but also in allowing external directors to get to know possible successors to the managing director. Nor do I suggest that the board should consist of the chief executive plus a number of external directors. This would put the chief executive in too powerful a position. He alone among the directors would have continuous daily contact with the affairs of the company. The other directors would be dependent upon him to an extent which would restrict their capacity to criticize.

What needs to be done instead is to raise the level of insight into the nature of the situation. All must be made to take into account more fully the fact that executive directors carry at least two roles. The managing director occupies the roles of chief executive (in which position he is the manager of some people who have seats on the board) and of a director (in which position he is a member of a committee that carries corporate responsibility to the shareholders). It would be salutary for all concerned to realize the difficult position of the executive directors. In their directorial role they must take part corporately in the formation of the policy that the managing director has to carry out. In their executive roles they are responsible to the managing director for carrying out parts of that policy. They will thus have special difficulties in taking part in board discussions on policy. All the executive directors have to try to keep within their directorial roles and to exclude their executive roles in discussion at board meetings. Likewise, they must move out of directorial roles into executive roles in between board meetings.

The fact that a manager in charge of the company's manufacturing activities is also a director should add nothing to his executive authority. This authority is derived not from the board but from his manager (probably the managing director). The manager who flings his weight about because he is also a director is not only a nuisance, but confused about his own roles. A desire for prestige probably causes him to sign his letters 'Production Director'. But this is wrong, because he is elected to the board by the shareholders, and they did not elect a 'Production Director'. He should sign his letters Production Manager and Director if it is necessary (as it often is) for his membership of the board to be known.

What, then, is the role of the external director? A hundred years ago many companies which had sold shares to a widespread public retained nevertheless the character of a private company. Family interests held large blocks of shares and exercised a direct influence on the directors. The directors themselves often held substantial blocks of shares and their personal incomes were affected by the efficiency with which the company was managed. Often, from past experience, they knew a great deal about the type of business in which the company was engaged and held strong opinions on how it ought to be managed. They elected one of their number to be chairman and he acted on their behalf between meetings of the board. The chairman kept an eye on the managing director. The managing director used the chairman as a sounding-board for his ideas.

With the growth in size of companies and the spread of shareholdings we have reached a situation today where often there is no shareholder who holds more than a small fraction of the total share capital. 'Institutional shareholders', who are more interested in the value of their shares in the market than on the detailed way in which the company is managed, have emerged in the form of banks, insurance companies, trusts, pension funds, etc. Shareholders have ceased to know the directors personally. Directors frequently have no personal experience of the type of work in which the company is engaged, nor are their shareholdings large. The work of external directors has gradually become more of a professional role, as family and personal financial ties have diminished.

The growing tendency for the role of chairman and managing director to be held by one man is another important change. The surveillance of the chief executive's work between board meetings ceases when this happens. As long as the roles of chairman and managing director were occupied by different people there was at least one external director who knew something of the detailed operations of the company because of his contact with it between meetings of the board. But when both roles are occupied by one man then all the external directors may lack this knowledge.

I held the roles of managing director and chairman of a public company continuously for twenty years. I was aware of the shortcomings of this situation but was ambivalent about it. Prompted by me, the board of directors, at one stage, made a serious attempt to find a suitable person, from outside the company, to appoint as chairman of the board. They were, however, not very enthusiastic about changing the situation, and failing to find a suitable person quickly, they gave up the attempt. I continued to be chairman. I was both glad and sorry.

There is a strong temptation for every chief executive to hold the two roles of managing director and chairman. It gives the chief executive more authority and prestige; it eliminates the potential danger (experienced by some chief executives) of interruption of plans by a chairman who has little detailed knowledge of the company, but is able to sway the board.

On the other hand the holding of both positions by the chief executive puts him in a lonely and exposed position. The 'chairman plus managing director' rather than the whole board, tends to be the object of criticism by the shareholders and the financial press when the company's results are poor. There is no separate chairman with whom the managing director can sound out his ideas before presentation to the board. The chief executives' immediate subordinates (some of whom may also be directors) are not necessarily a good source of advice—because they are in a 'role-biased' position. Each of the chief executive's immediate subordinates is separately accountable for some particular function in the company. Each, in giving advice to the chief executive, will tend to 'load' his advice from the point of view of the function for which he is accountable.

The external directors on the board often do not know enough about the operations of the company to be a helpful source of advice to the chief executive. I think therefore that it is best to have two people, one chairman of the board and the other managing director, who are regularly available to each other between board meetings to debate the major decisions which have to be made.

The holding of the roles of both chairman and managing director by the chief executive introduces yet another serious problem. If the chairman is a separate person he can play a large part in helping the board to maintain a running assessment of the manner in which the managing director is doing his job. But where both roles are held by the chief executive then this assessment does not always take place. The result can be disastrous if a chief executive whose powers are failing, or who is losing interest in the job, is allowed to carry on too long.

Formally, it would be the task of the board, as a group, to assess the performance of their chief executive. But they cannot discuss their 'chairman plus managing director' at board meetings in his presence. To do the job properly the board would require to meet for this special purpose without him. I have never heard of a board holding such meetings, except in crisis conditions. On more than one occasion I suggested that it was the duty of the board that I chaired and on which I also served as managing director to hold at least one such meeting each year. But they thought that I was being too 'theoretical' in making the suggestion and that it would feel wrong to meet in this way.

Directors of companies often feel that informal chats with each other will suffice to share opinions about their chief executive, and I know that views both critical and otherwise are often exchanged in this way. But this is not satisfactory. It is common experience that members of boards of directors (or indeed of many other types of committees) who in fact share strong critical opinions of their 'chairman plus managing director', in the absence of the focus of a separate chairman fail to take concerted action until crisis conditions prevail. By then much damage has been done to the institution. This might all have been avoided by proper formulation of constructive criticism conveyed to the chief executive by the chairman of the board at a much earlier stage.

In extreme situations boards of directors can thus become bodies composed of employed directors who have difficulty (because of their double roles) in criticizing the chief executive, and external directors who, because they know too little about the company's operations, are unable to do so. If the chief executive is capable, all may be well. But if he is not, or if his capacity deteriorates, then companies can slowly become less and less efficient, which is bad for the shareholders, the employees and the national economy.

The effectiveness of the chief executives of our companies can never be of a uniformly high standard. There are at times difficulties in finding men equal to the task. Mistakes can be made in the selection and appointment of managing directors. The effectiveness of chief executives who have performed well can decline. Companies that expand rapidly because of market growth can outgrow the managerial capacity of those in charge of them. These situations are simply natural hazards but, in the absence of a natural process of correction, they menace the efficiency and continued existence of companies. They menace the continued satisfactory employment of those who work in such companies, and if the company is large they menace a valuable national asset.

The need is to strengthen corporate interest and to make scrutiny by the board more effective. Amendments to the Companies Act that prevented chief executives also holding the role of chairman might help. (Though it would also be necessary to insist that the chairman's role was not also a full-time executive post, otherwise managing directors would simply give up their existing title, allot it to another, and take for themselves the title of chairman; nothing would have been gained.)

A second step would be to say that public companies in excess of a specified size must have at least a stated number of external directors. The board would be required to propose to the annual general meeting that three of these external directors be appointed as special directors. The special directors would have the authority to insist, when they saw fit, that an efficiency audit of the employment hierarchy be carried out by external management consultants. The special directors would display their qualifications to the annual general meeting, would be paid higher fees than other directors, would be expected to spend more time achieving familiarity with the company's affairs, and generally would be in a position of special accountability to the shareholders. If the company was performing poorly and they had not insisted on a special audit, no doubt shareholders would express their discontent.

These are examples of the sort of measures that are becoming necessary to stimulate the directors of some companies to perform properly the functions for which they were elected. Directors must, in the interests of shareholders and employees, maintain a proper scrutiny of the work of their chief executive and be prepared to act when the situation warrants it.

I know that many people will object to such measures because they fear constant and detailed interference with the chief executive's plans. But it is always possible to object to any new administrative proposal if stupid behaviour on the part of those who operate it is postulated. To those who do not wish to see a closer scrutiny of the effectiveness of chief executives, I say this.

In the last few years there have been many examples of substantial companies getting into serious trouble through ineffective executive management. (I do not suggest that this is the only cause of failure, because some companies fail even though they are *well* managed.) Employees, suppliers, customers and the City have known of the existence of these situations well before disaster has struck. But all are powerless if the directors lack the courage to act.

There will be those who believe that the capacity of the average external director is not high enough to warrant trusting him with the task of assessing the chief executive. No doubt that is a valid criticism of the boards of a minority of large companies, but if there is any general validity in the criticism then that is another problem to which attention must be turned. Perhaps more cross-fertilization between companies would help. If active executives from one company were permitted to join the boards of other companies operating in different markets, then the supply of experienced high-capacity directors could be increased. Such appointments would bring into boards of directors management experience that is often lacking at present.

What has to be done is to amend the constitution of the board to enable it to exercise the function for which it was originally intended. The chief executive would be in the presence of an informed small group who would be continuously watching the progress of the company, and who would have effective authority. That is the missing element in some large companies. It would re-institute a situation which has been eroded by environmental change and the passage of time since the idea of controlling companies by corporate authority first arose.

The foregoing comments are not, however, to be read as supporting the opposite view that shareholders have virtually lost control of the companies they own. Many commentators say that owing to the divorce of ownership from management, shareholders are today virtually powerless. This view derives support from the very limited attendance at annual general meetings and the fact that at such meetings the board's own nominees for election as directors are nearly always voted into office; and because nominations for a seat on the board are very seldom made by shareholders themselves.

What the commentators overlook is the small but significant number of occasions on which shareholders actually do exercise their prerogatives and insist on changes of policy or changes of directors. But shareholders seldom do this until after the company is in serious trouble. The remedies upon which they insist may be suggested too late, or they may be ill-informed and wrong-headed. There is no substitute for a continuous and active scrutiny by the board and a readiness on the part of the board either to insist that the chief executive changes the policies he is pursuing or that he be replaced by another.

Boards of Subsidiary Companies

Subsidiary companies are defined in the Companies Acts as those in which the holding company owns a minimum of 51 per cent of the shares. Most subsidiary companies are wholly owned by the holding company. (A common form of partially owned subsidiary companies is the overseas company, where local interests own the balance of shares and take a very active part in management because they are on site, so to speak, whereas the majority holding company is not.[1])

---

[1] For completeness it should be mentioned that associated companies are defined as those in which the holding company has less than 51 per cent shareholding but which is not simply an investment of surplus funds.

Because of the vertical and horizontal integration of British industry (through the extensive series of mergers and takeover bids which have characterized our industrial society since the war) many companies now have a large number of wholly owned subsidiary companies. The subsidiaries can, if the holding board so decides, be wound up as separate minor entities and be merged into the holding company. But, because of the goodwill that their names carry and the need to continue the feeling of a separate trading existence (in order to satisfy the managers of the company they have purchased) it is customary to continue running the company that has been taken over as a subsidiary. This, in accordance with the Companies Act, involves the appointment of a board of directors of that subsidiary.

In the eyes of the law this board is a corporate body carrying responsibility for the operation of the company to its shareholders; but its shareholders are not a series of persons. They are another corporate body, the holding company. *De jure* it would be the responsibility of the subsidiary board to appoint the chief executive and elect the chairman. *De facto* the holding company will do this almost invariably. The holding company will certainly appoint all the directors of the subsidiary. It would, in these circumstances, appear inevitable that the chairman and chief executive of the subsidiary would feel, and would, in fact, *be* accountable to the board of the holding company, or perhaps to the chief executive of the holding company. The chairman and chief executive of the subsidiary could not abide by a majority vote of the subsidiary board if this ran counter to an instruction from the holding company. It seems clear, therefore, that the subsidiary board cannot and does not carry corporate responsibility for the affairs of the company.

It is unusual for the board of a subsidiary company to contain external directors. Usually they contain employee-directors of the subsidiary company, plus other employee-directors from the holding company board, or people holding employee directorships in other subsidiary companies in the same group. A board meeting of a subsidiary company is sometimes difficult to distinguish from a meeting of the chief executive with his own immediate command.

This description of subsidiary boards of directors, if accepted, might help the directors of some of these companies to visualize their own role of 'director' more clearly, and might thus prevent confusion.

What is happening is that the Companies Act is failing to differentiate between directors of subsidiary companies and those of other companies, and is legislating for two different roles as though they were the same. It grants limited liability to a subsidiary company and holds its board accountable, though the direction of the subsidiaries' affairs lies in the hands of the holding company. Thus, at law, a subsidiary company can go bankrupt (with liabilities in excess of assets) because of plans imposed upon it by the holding company; and yet the creditors have no recourse to the assets of the holding company to recover their debts. The law in fact holds the wrong body accountable.

Divisional Boards

There is a third type of institution, which is termed a 'board of directors' but legally is not a board. Such institutions are sometimes set up by very large companies. They sub-divide the company into divisions. In each there is a chief executive and his immediate subordinates. In order to provide status, or perhaps through confused thinking, they call the chief executive 'chairman' and his immediate command (or most of it) directors, and regard the whole as a board of directors.

I can understand the motivation towards setting up these divisional 'boards'. A single division of such a company may be much larger and more important than many of the legally constituted companies with which it competes. Many of the senior managers of these smaller companies sport the title of 'director'. In the home market this gives prestige in dealings with other companies. Overseas it is not uncommon to find customers (governments, public corporations and large corporations) who insist on dealing with a 'director of the company'.

The large concern, therefore, has a problem. It could turn its divisions into legally constituted, wholly owned subsidiaries. But this is a most wasteful step to take. It yields little benefit and results in more complex, inter-subsidiary accounting. It involves complete returns each year to Companies' House. But if it does not take this step it then has the problem of how to confer prestige titles on its chief executive and on its senior managers. So a divisional 'board' is set up.

The danger is that they try and behave as though the 'board' carried corporate responsibility. This can lead to interference with the work of the chief executive who is, in fact, an immediate subordinate of the chief executive of the total company. Or it can lead to a chief executive who is titled 'divisional chairman' trying to *behave* like a chairman and abdicating from his full accountability by trying to share this accountability with the 'board'. I know that this actually happened in one large company and that an analysis of the situation led to its rectification. I do not see harm in divisional 'boards' so long as the 'chairmen' and each of the 'directors' are fully aware of their real role.

In the United States complexities of the type I have described in relation to 'divisional boards' are often avoided by the provision of the titles 'president' for the chief executive, and 'vice-president' for some of his immediate subordinates. Such positions carry high prestige, but do not become confused with the terms 'chairman' or 'director'.

Management Committees

When I was first a chief executive in industry I tried to treat the regular meeting I had with my immediate subordinates as a committee. I called it a committee. I took informal votes by looking round the table to see who was or was not in agreement. If there were too many in disagreement I re-started the discussion in order to win over more adherents. It was a long time before I realized that I had got to take the decisions, whether or not the others agreed. It would have been impossible for me to go back to the board and say: 'Yes, the wrong decision has been taken. I did not agree, but I could not take the right decision because so many of my subordinates were in disagreement.' That is a nonsense. I do not intend to infer that it is a chief executive's role to take the decisions that seem right to him without regard to the views of his subordinates, or without regard to the reaction of his entire extended command. That would equally be a nonsense. A chief executive who fails to consider the views of his subordinates very carefully is on a slippery slope (equally he must take very seriously criticisms from representatives of all strata of his extended command). The task of a manager is to gain real insight into the detailed effects of any change he is considering, by explaining these changes very thoroughly to his subordinates, by giving them an opportunity to discuss the effects with *their* subordinates, and then by listening to their interpretations of the probable results. Having done all this he must make up his own mind, and be decisive.[1]

The manager is working at a higher level of abstraction than his subordinates and has to take into account not only what each of them feels about the effect on the particular part of the operation for which each is accountable, but also what he feels about the total overall

---

[1] I am leaving out of consideration at this stage the question of what representatives of employees feel. I shall discuss this fully later. I am now discussing reactions of subordinates only.

effect, for which they are not accountable, and with which they are much less concerned than with their own particular part of the company.

A chief executive may find, for example, that a particular change will result in more expense, without tangible gain in most of the commands of his immediate subordinates, who will therefore object to the change. But the chief executive may yet be convinced that the total result for the company over the years ahead will be highly beneficial. He must then decide to go ahead. But if he is trying to behave like a committee chairman he cannot, because he is in a minority. If he shrinks from such a decision he is abdicating from personal accountability and taking shelter among his subordinates.

I quote just one example of such a decision. A company is losing business to a competitor because the competitor has developed products that are technologically better. If, over the years ahead, the situation is to be retrieved there has to be a large increase in the resources deployed on product development. This means diverting investment away from other parts of the company. And it means an increase of overhead charges, which will raise the apparent cost of production. It may mean smaller total profits for some years to come. The chances are that people in other parts of the company facing the demise of some of their pet projects through diversion of investment, and facing the inevitable call for economies to offset the increased expense of the product-development project, will try to reduce the size of the proposed product-development programme. But a decision in favour of the programme could well save the company from eventual bankruptcy.

In short, when managers meet their immediate commands they are not a committee in session. Behaviour based on a misunderstanding of this, the reality of the situation, is counter-productive. A manager's subordinates, in spite of their detailed objections, would probably regard too much compromise over a programme as proposed by their manager himself as abdication of responsibility by him. On the whole subordinates welcome firm, decisive behaviour from their boss—even if they do not agree the detail. The source of many unsatisfactory compromises on the part of managers is the wish to behave 'democratically' and to win the support of their subordinates. But the manager, not the group composed of himself and his subordinates, is responsible. They are each doing some of his work for him. That manager must, within the policies set by his own manager, or, in the case of a managing director, within the policies set by the board of directors, make his own decisions.

Co-ordinating 'Committees'

Theoretically it is possible for a chief executive or the manager of a large extended command to set his policies in such a manner that the decision made by individual members of his command cannot affect each other. If, for example, a chief executive is operating a business which owns a number of retail shops widely dispersed geographically, then the likelihood of interaction is small. If, on the other hand, he is in charge of a shipbuilding yard, then it is impossible to determine policies that will avoid a great deal of interaction.

I saw, for example, during my time in the Board of Trade, a very high degree of interaction between the decisions of officials in many parts of the Board. As soon as one division tentatively advised others in a minute of their intention to act in a particular way, one would see other minutes, sometimes from unexpected sources, calling attention to the fact that such a decision would affect some other aspect of the Board's work in a manner often quite unexpected.

These interactions have to be mediated. Most are dealt with by personal interaction in face-to-face meetings, telephone calls, etc. But many of them are too complex to be dealt with in this way. When they become burdensome then somebody suggests the formation of a committee, a co-ordinating committee. But these bodies again are not real committees because they do not carry corporate responsibility. The members of such a 'committee' cannot by majority vote commit the various departments or divisions of the organization 'represented' on the co-ordinating 'committee'. There is an important set of relationships, arising in every employment hierarchy, which have not been defined and labelled and which are not much discussed. I give such relationships the name *collateral relationships*, and will discuss them in the next chapter.

CHAPTER ELEVEN

Collateral Relationships

MANY YEARS AGO those departments of engineering companies that manufactured their own jigs and tools were frequently organized on the following basis.

The manager of the tool-room had a number of skilled craftsmen immediately subordinate to him. Each craftsman could operate the full range of machines in the tool-room—lathes, drills, grinders, screw-cutting machines, milling machines, etc. The manager gave to a tool-maker the task of producing a complete tool or jig from a drawing. The interaction upon each other of the decisions of each of these tool-makers as they pursued their different tasks was very limited.

A tool-room today is different. Here one finds groups of 'specialists'. There are those who do nothing but turn parts of tools on lathes. There are those who do nothing but grinding. There is a specialist group for each type of operation. During its manufacture a single tool is thus worked upon by a number of craftsmen. The way in which one craftsman does his part of the task will affect the others in terms of dimensional accuracy, finish, time taken, etc.

In the tool-room of days gone by, collateral relationships were at a low level. In the modern tool-room they are at a very high level. These greatly increased collateral relationships have changed the organizational structure. The early tool-room may well have had a manager or foreman in charge of up to fifty tool-makers. In the modern tool-room the manager has much more co-ordination work to do. The manager often has a 'foreman' or 'supervisor' (both rather vague terms) subordinate to him in charge of each of the several specialized sections. Another stratum has been introduced into the hierarchy to accommodate the increase in collateral relationships.

This is an example of increased collateral relationships brought about by the need to employ people on more specialized tasks. But there are many other pressures working in the same direction. Industrial products, to an ever-increasing extent, are becoming complex assemblies of electrical, mechanical, hydraulic, and other types of sub-assemblies. Each sub-assembly may itself be composed of hundreds of parts. Each part may have to be processed by many specialized manufacturing sections.

Urban authorities now include departments concerned with sanitation, roads, housing, welfare services, town-planning and others. This degree of complexity used not to exist. Government departments are responsible, for example, for the introduction of the Kennedy Round on tariffs, for changes in health and welfare services, for national research and development investment, or for entry into the Common Market. They find themselves proposing changes that impinge on half the other departments of Government, and on many external interests too.

The greatest single cause of increased collateral relationships is growth in the size of employment hierarchies, because the larger they are, the higher the level of abstraction at the top and the greater the ambit of the considerations that have to be taken into account. A manager who seeks to reduce the degree of interaction between his subordinates can only do so by limiting the amount of discretion he allows each to exercise. Theoretically a manager can prescribe the area over which a subordinate uses judgement so as to prevent the subordinate from doing anything that affects the tasks of his colleagues. But, by so doing, the manager will increase the volume of his own work. At the same time, he will lower the level of work he gives to his subordinates. In practice, therefore, it is usually counter-productive to make the attempt unless one is forced to because the managers' team of immediate subordinates cannot cope with the level of work that one wishes to load on to them.

The mediation or settlement of these interactions in a hierarchy nearly always takes place between people of the same rank. The marketing manager, facing difficulties about late delivery of products, sees the production manager himself and does not ask one of his subordinates to do so. The foreman of one department, faced with a flow of inaccurate parts from another department, does not send one of his supervisors to see the foreman of the other department at fault. He goes himself.

Collateral relationships can, therefore, be simply defined as the relationship between people of the same rank when the authority delegated to them can impinge on the effectiveness of each other's activity. Some might well ask at this juncture: 'Why delve in this detailed way into such a natural and well-understood issue as inter-dependent relationships at work? It is a question of good teamwork among people who are trying to help the organization employing them to produce the required results.' This is true, but even if people do often face the need for mutual adjustment in the common cause, it does not always take place. Large organizations could help them-selves by teaching their staff quite explicitly that staff members are accountable to higher authority either for agreeing mutual adjust-ments or for taking up difficulty with the manager at the cross-over point.[1]

People at work must be persuaded that this is not a matter of doing personal favours for colleagues, but a serious question of account-ability, which is essential if sound total results are to be achieved. When an inquest is being held on some mishap many conversations run like this:

Manager: Why did you not see X and explain the need for him to help you out of the difficulty?

Subordinate: I suppose I ought to have done so, but he is usually so damned awkward and unco-operative that I didn't think he would play.

Delivery and, sometimes, the quality of exports often suffer in a big way from that type of situation.

But perhaps the most important result arising out of an explicit statement about collateral relationships is to get rid of a widely accepted series of ideas which in fact have no validity.

It is widely believed, for example:

(*a*) That the higher you go as a manager in the hierarchy the smaller the size of your extended command should be.

(*b*) That no manager should have an immediate command exceeding about seven in number.

(*c*) That you cannot give foreman roles managerial authority because necessarily they are often in immediate control of too many for a *managerial* command.

These notions arise from thinking done many years ago and attribu-ted to Graicunas, which has since been supported by many writers on the subject of organization. Such thinking was based on the idea that

---

[1] Cross-over point is defined, in relation to any two or more roles, as the most junior manager whose command comprises these roles.

in a Group of A and B only one relationship is possible, AB. But in a group of A, B and C there are three relationships, AB, AC, BC. In a group of A, B, C, D there are six: AB, AC, AD, BC, BD, CD. In a group of eight there are twenty-eight relationships. It was felt that as the manager of that group had responsibility for all those relationships then the number of subordinates must be limited to about seven, with twenty-one relationships.

But this thinking took too little account of the *nature* of these work relationships between employees immediately responsible to the same manager. If a manager is accountable for seven small retail shops situated in different towns, the work of his seven subordinates, each in charge of one shop, might not interact at all. A collateral relationship might not exist. If this were so the manager could control a much larger number of shops.

Thus, in my view, the number of people in a manager's immediate command is not a function of the number of *potential* relationships, but of the complexity of the collateral relationships that really do exist. This complexity in turn is a function of the nature of the work that the manager has to delegate to his subordinates, and the degree of discretion he allows to them in doing that work.

I think that it is important to get rid of Graicunas' idea, because it has in the past caused some counter-productive organizational structuring. For example, a company has a sales manager with a number of subordinates, each accountable for a different geographically defined market. The company extends the number of markets rapidly and the sales manager finds himself with two or three times as many immediate subordinates as he had before. Without examination of the degree of collateral relationship that exists, the decision is taken that the situation has to be reorganized. What happens is set out in Fig. 6.

An extra level of manager has now been squeezed into the hierarchy. But though the sales manager in fact requires to be in direct touch with the area sales managers to get his task carried out appropriately, he has to deal with them at one removed. The level of work being done by the area sales manager remains unchanged, as does that of the sales manager. The two new sub-sales managers are only a half rank removed from their subordinates and will be unable to assume full managerial control of them. Everybody will be dissatisfied in this reorganized situation. There are other ways of dealing with this situation, such as reducing the level of collateral relations between the area sales managers, increasing the size of the areas and reducing the number of area sales managers, or providing the sales

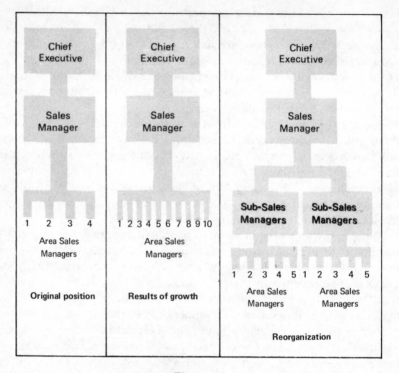

Figure 6

manager with a staff officer to help him to manage his enlarged command. But I shall not explore the example further. All that I want to demonstrate is the danger of the Graicunas theory in biasing decisions towards unfortunate distortion of organization.

Co-ordinating Committees

I return now to what are called co-ordinating 'committees'. They are concerned with collateral relationships but are not really committees. Such 'committees' meet regularly to resolve interaction between a number of managers or departments. They are not committees for the following reasons.

Consider the position of a member, B, of such a 'co-ordinating committee'. He is executively accountable to his manager A for running his own command. He meets a number of colleagues at his own level who are accountable to other managers. Each is concerned about the executive management of his own command. The function of the meeting is to sort out difficulties arising in areas where various interests overlap and require co-ordination.

In what role is B to speak at such a meeting? If he behaves as a member of a committee he must try to rise above his own executive role and to take corporate decisions, which will inevitably include some sort of compromise with each of the other committee members. Now comes the rub. What will his own manager A think about these decisions, which now set the policy within which B himself will work? Will the decisions fit in with the policies that A has already set? Or should B refer the matter back to A before committing himself further?

Consideration of such questions makes it clear that if B rises above his own work-role and behaves as though he were a member of a committee setting policies for the work of himself and his colleagues, he finds himself in direct conflict with his responsibility to his own manager and the policies his manager has set. If B treats the 'committee' as though it really were a committee, and if his manager allows him to do so, then for the time being B has taken over his own manager's role.

If, on the other hand, B accepts the fact that he can take part in the deliberations of a 'committee' only so long as he stays within the policies set by his manager, then it becomes immediately apparent that he is not a member of a committee. It is a committee in name only since it cannot take decisions by majority vote which are binding on all. The actual (as against the assumed) situation is that each member is trying to find means of getting his own work done so that his needs can be satisfactorily co-ordinated with the needs of others, but only within the policy limits set by his manager. What is needed is a collateral meeting. Each member can express his own views as to what is required. Mutual adjustments and compromises can be expressed and decisions taken; but every decision has to be consistent with the different policies within which each member of the meeting is working.

If adjustments within these different policies cannot be made then each member of the collateral meeting must return to his own manager for further terms of reference, perhaps explaining to his manager recommendations that have been agreed as reasonable by the collateral meeting. Where the members are subordinates of the same immediate manager, then the various points of view must be taken to him so that he may consider the various possibilities and conform or modify his policies.

By these means, the subordinates are free to act so long as they can find solutions consistent with the policies within which they are bound. Moreover, their managers can be assured that their policies are being implemented. But compromises and adjustments which, even though they may be based upon a majority vote, nevertheless break or 'bend' the policies within which any of the subordinates is working have to be disallowed or precluded.

CHAPTER TWELVE

Specialist Roles

*'When William Knudsen, top production man at General Motors, went to Washington to organise production for World War II and was asked about the difference between line and staff, he is reported to have said: "Well, you know, at General Motors we say that line people are the fellows who bring in material, put it together, and ship it out. And the staff people are the fellows who are trying to prevent the line from doing the job".'—*Quoted by Ernest Dale in his book *Management: Theory and Practise*

ARMIES ARE THE largest employment hierarchies that have existed over a long period. Their role has always been vital. The organizational forms that have developed within them under pressure, through the years (and which, in their case, are somewhat akin to the processes of natural selection) ought to be viable and to contain lessons for other organizations. Some lessons can certainly be learned in the area of specialist support for operational managers.

The army has three branches of specialists called Administrative, Quartermaster, and General. The terminology is, however, misleading and its vagueness is perhaps one of the reasons why army experience has not been absorbed and made more use of elsewhere.

A—Administrative is concerned with special knowledge of manning, training, posting, pay, administration, organization, etc. This is roughly equivalent to personnel work in industry and to the work of Establishment Divisions in Government Departments.

Q—Quartermaster is an historical but deceptive term. Q work is today concerned with special knowledge of the provision, movement and timing of all forms of supplies. It is roughly equivalent to industrial work concerned with buying, storing, supplying and moving materials and the progressing and timing of programmes of work. There does not seem to be an equivalent specialist branch in the

Civil Service, where the work appears to be done without the assistance of specialists.

G—General. This is the most deceptive title of the three. It is a contradiction in terms. It is difficult to conceive of a 'general specialist'. Some writers on organization assume that G staff officers are the senior specialist branch of the army, with authority over the other specialist branches. In fact, they are concerned with special knowledge of the techniques of fighting and therefore with tactics, strategy, weapon systems, etc. The equivalents in industry are the techniques of doing operational work. G staff officers' industrial opposite numbers are production engineers, metallurgists, chemists, jig and tool designers—anyone concerned with devising better ways of manufacturing. In the Civil Service the equivalent would seem to be part of the work of the Organization and Methods (O & M) divisions, the 'organization' component being properly part of the Establishment Division, while the 'methods' component would seem to be equivalent to G in the army and work techniques in industry. Fig. 7 sums it up:

Army		Industry		Civil Service	
A	Administration	P	Personnel	E	Establishments
Q	Quartermaster	Pr	Programming	?	
G	General	T	Techniques	O	of Organization & Methods (O & M)

Figure 7

I have added symbols for industrial specialist branches—P for Personnel, Pr for Programming and T for Techniques. In the analyses of specialist work that follow I shall use the same symbols and will base my remarks on industry, which contains many specialist roles. It is difficult to embrace commerce or the Civil Service in the description because, in these areas, the development of specialist roles has not yet proceeded very far, and operational managers are not provided (at least explicitly) with much specialist support.

(I have made no mention so far of accountants, auditors, company secretaries, and so on. I will devote a chapter to these roles later. I do not consider them to be part of the employment hierarchy proper. I will argue the case for that statement later.)

Is there a general reason for the gradual emergence of the same three types of specialist branches in three quite different areas? I think there is, and I would somewhat tentatively state the reason as follows. Human work (as I have pointed out) is decision-making. In arriving at decisions people require knowledge, and I think there are natural sub-divisions into which this knowledge falls.

When one observes employment work being carried out one is looking at:

(a) People in roles in employment hierarchies   (P)
(b) People using *techniques* on tasks   (T)
(c) People undertaking quantified and timed programmes of
    work   (Pr)

All this has to be done in an environment that is subject to economic pressures and considerations.

It would seem therefore that every person in an employment role, however far down the hierarchy, has to have knowledge in order to make decisions, and that this knowledge falls into three discrete categories, P, Pr and T. The higher up the hierarchy the position of the role, the wider is the field of knowledge required in each category, until eventually the occupant of the role must have help in one or all of them. He cannot keep up with the rate of growth of knowledge required, so he is given specialists to help him. It is as though each role had three dimensions as in Fig. 8:

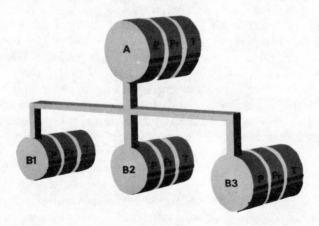

Figure 8

A and his subordinates B1, B2 and B3 are operational managers, each carrying out the full range of P, Pr and T work of their roles unaided by specialists. But pressures arise. First A needs help in the personnel field. Later B1 is in trouble with the very advanced production techniques that are coming into use in his area. B2 is constantly in trouble because he manages an assembly department and co-ordination of a large flow of components from external sources is taxing him. So specialist roles are introduced and the new organization takes the shape depicted in Fig. 9.

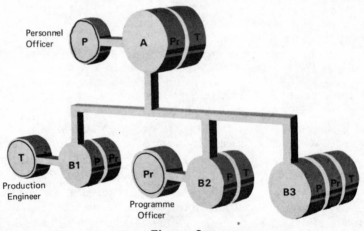

Figure 9

In Fig. 9 specialist roles are shown with a double ring round them to distinguish them from operational roles.

I know that this is an oversimplified picture of the position in industry, but I shall continue to deal with the problem in these terms in order to get certain conceptions about the role of specialists established.

Once specialist roles begin emerging in a hierarchy then it becomes obvious that they can conveniently manage quite a large range of the services that have to be available. For example, the P specialist may become accountable for the canteen manager, the training department, factory security, factory cleanliness, etc. The T specialist may become accountable for departments concerned with work study, jig and tool design, tool-making, machine maintenance, etc. The Pr specialist, besides being responsible for his planning and progress staff, may carry accountability for stores containing raw materials, consumable supplies, work in progress and finished goods. In short, a strong tendency develops to make specialists responsible for operating many of the services required by operational managers.

Accountability, Authority, and relation of Specialists to Operational Managers

I have been putting a double ring round a role to indicate that it contains a specialist immediately accountable to an operational manager. I want to establish another convention to help description. I wish to denote specialists responsible to A as AS, and specialists responsible to B as BS.

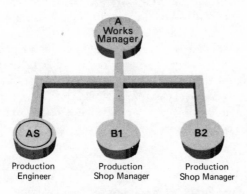

A
Works
Manager

AS
Production
Engineer

B1
Production
Shop Manager

B2
Production
Shop Manager

Figure 10

If AS is regarded simply as a colleague of B1 and B2 then many questions are left unresolved. I have presided at meetings embracing all the four roles in Fig. 10 in an attempt to solve problems. The production managers claimed that the manufacturing methods devised by AS were too complex and involved too much expensive tooling. They claimed that if they had had discretion to alter these methods they would have been able to avoid scrap and increase output. AS complained, on the other hand, that he and his staff were responsible for ensuring that fast mechanized methods of production were used and that lack of co-operation on the part of B1 and B2 was sabotaging their efforts.

If one assumes that the relation of AS to B1 and B2 is analogous to the relation of B1 to B2 then it is simply a case of mutual adjustment or reference back to A. But to say this is merely to state the problem. In principle, the discussion was concerned with a dilemma that can be described as follows. B1 and B2 are accountable to A for all the decisions required to optimize output and keep expense to the minimum possible. But, at the same time, AS is accountable to A for introducing modern methods of production, which will attempt to lead to the same results. There are bound to be differences of opinion on such matters. Whose viewpoint prevails? If AS's responsibility is simply to give 'advice', which can be rejected by B1 and B2, then he cannot be held accountable for the long-term development of sound modern methods, and his knowledge and experience is being wasted. If, on the other hand, AS is in a position to insist that his methods are adopted, then B1 and B2 cannot be held accountable for what happens in their workshops.

This kind of problem is very common. Many managers have found it almost insoluble and resort to vague comment about the need for goodwill and co-operation. Some writers on organization have suggested that what is needed is very careful selection of specially mature and tactful people for appointment to specialist roles. In fact, however, the problem has been dealt with effectively not only in the army but in many industrial companies. The problem continues to exist elsewhere because a conceptual description of the solution has not been provided and understood.

If AS is regarded as an Extension of the Role of A Himself then Solutions begin to Emerge

I suggest that the real role of AS fits into the situation in the following manner.

(1) AS is responsible for advising A in some field of knowledge.
(2) A considers the advice of AS; he may discuss it with B1, B2, B3, etc., and he then decides on his policy.
(3) A holds AS accountable for seeing that his (A's) policy is implemented by B1, B2, etc.
(4) AS, in order to carry such accountability, is granted authority by A to give instructions to B1, B2, etc., so long as those instructions are clearly within the policy established by A. AS becomes now what the army has for a century called a staff officer, and the authority to instruct B1, B2, etc. is staff authority. *It is not managerial authority.* AS has no control whatever over the appointment, assessment or de-selection of B1, B2, etc.

As I see it, one of the reasons why this resolution of the relationship between specialists and operational managers has not generally emerged is because of the widely held belief that you cannot give instructions to another employee without being his manager.

This structuring of the role of AS deals with the problem of the arguments I described between the production engineer and the production superintendents, because giving the production engineer the position of a staff officer means that he must get sanction from the works manager for the new technical policies that he wishes to see introduced. But once he has the works manager's assent the production engineer is armed with staff authority to instruct the superintendents, although the latter are entitled to question the appropriateness of the staff instructions received with the works manager whenever they choose. If the shop superintendents now believe that new methods are reducing output and increasing expense, then these feelings are criticisms not of AS but of A, their manager. They are, in effect, saying to A: 'You insist on our using certain production methods and, of course, as our manager you are entitled to do so, but be it on your own head—the results will be yours.' This is the every-day stuff of manager–subordinate relationships and is well under-stood. The implied requirement on the part both of the specialist and of the shop superintendents that they should somehow 'co-operate' with each other, and stop arguing, has been removed because the accountability and authority of both parties has been defined. This does not necessarily bring about agreement, but it does take the tension and personal feelings out of the situation.

As hierarchies grow in size similar types of specialist assistance have to be provided for managers at different levels. Staff officers AS and BS, and even CS, begin to become necessary at the senior levels of large employment hierarchies, as in Fig. 11. (In this diagram A is the operational manager of B. B is the operational manager of C.)

We now have to consider the relationship of AS to BS and of BS to CS, for it is obviously counter-productive if BS advises his manager B along lines that take no account of the higher level of thinking of AS in advising A. If AS is held accountable for seeing to it that BS is sufficiently knowledgeable in the specialist field in which they are both engaged, and also for seeing to it that BS understands the policies on which AS is basing his advice for A, then advice being given by AS and BS to their respective managers will be consistent.

If, however, AS is to be held accountable in this way for the *quality* of the advice BS gives to B, then AS must have some authority over BS, which will enable him to ensure that BS is technically competent.

We now have what at first sight looks like a complex set of relation-ships surrounding BS. B is BS's manager, in the sense that B holds BS

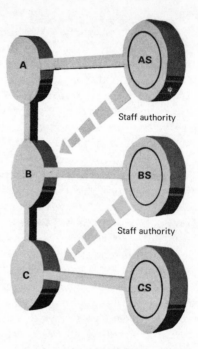

Figure 11

responsible for advising him, for working on problems that B specifies, for seeing to it that C carries out B's technical policies (based on BS's advice). On the other hand, AS also has authority over BS to ensure that his work is of the necessary technical quality.

But the situation is simpler than it looks. B is BS's operational manager; AS is BS's specialist manager. Thus B and AS are *co-managers* of BS. B specifies the range of tasks on which he wishes BS to work, and uses BS full time. AS instructs BS on the right way of fulfilling the tasks specified by B. This role-structure is not an invention, but a description based on observation of how these complex relations do successfully work in practice. Though the description I have given may at first sight be rejected on the grounds that co-managership is unacceptable, in fact the practice is widespread, and works (though it is seldom explicitly stated).

This is another case of the manifest and the assumed being different from the actual relationship. For example, suppose a company has established a role at position BS and that the role falls vacant; who then would take part in choosing a candidate to fill it? B certainly would, A might well do so, but if both A and B are not themselves knowledgeable in the area of specialized work to be done by BS they may well want AS to play a leading part in that choice. He alone would be capable of testing the knowledge and the potential ability of candidates seeking to fill the role of BS, because he is himself a product of the same branch of learning. If AS, who is not B's manager is to take a leading part in the choice of BS then clearly there is a special relationship between AS and BS. If both A and B wisely insist that (as neither of them is technically qualified) AS, who is, should be asked to keep an eye on the technical quality of the on-going work of BS, then this further extends the special relationship between AS and BS. The formal expression of this relationship is that AS is the co-manager of BS.

If a company actually has such relationships between its higher and lower specialists and yet fails to make them explicit (by a detailed exposition of the authority and accountability involved) then the company will make the relationship unnecessarily difficult for those in such situations. Whenever role-relationships at work remain un-structured, undefined and hazy, then personal difficulties creep in. These can be avoided by describing organization explicitly. That is why explicit descriptions are important.

In a previous book I devoted some chapters to a description of specialist roles and (owing to unclear writing) gave the impression that I was advocating the appointment of specialists in the P, Pr and T phases at most levels of management in the hierarchy. I must therefore make it clear that the decision as to whether or not particu-lar dimensions of a manager's work should be 'externalized' into specialist supporting roles must depend upon the particular circum-stance of each employment hierarchy and on the work which it has to do. I am suggesting only that where specialists exist it is necessary to describe clearly the relationships between each of them and also the relationships between them and operational managers. Otherwise optimum performance will not be achieved. Having said that I can risk a diagram which might otherwise be open to the misunderstand-ing to which I have referred.

Fig. 12 is a model of a specialist division as it might appear if all managers two ranks down from the chief executive required and were provided with one type of staff officer.

Managers in industry often used to object to this particular con-vention for positioning staff officers in organization diagrams. The objection is that by placing them in a 'higher' position than the manager's operational subordinates the chart makes it appear that

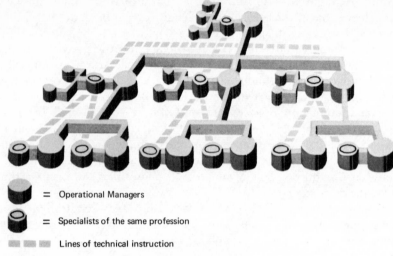

= Operational Managers

= Specialists of the same profession

Lines of technical instruction

Figure 12

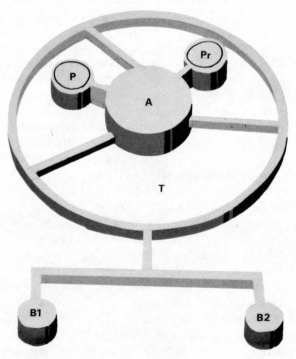

Figure 13

they are of higher status than their operational colleagues. But the staff officers are, in a very real sense, a part of the manager's role, albeit in one dimension only. It has been suggested that they could be depicted as in Fig. 13.

This would signify that A has staff officers in the P and Pr dimensions but no staff officers in the T dimension. The diagram is clumsy but helps to explain the real situation.

I would add, however, that unless staff officers and operational managers in the same immediate command are of the same rank then the staff concept will not work. If staff officers are clearly of lower rank (and lower capacity) they cannot give *staff* instruction to the operational managers. If they are of clearly higher rank the operational managers will *feel* that they have several managers in command of their operations, which is just as bad.

Grouping all Specialists into one of three Categories, P, Pr and T

I have tried to show that the aspects of knowledge that people at work must explore before making decisions fall naturally into three dimensions, which I have labelled P, Pr and T. I have not yet explored the content of these fields. This can be done by stating an example of a possible job specification for the person in charge of each of these specialist divisions in a large employment hierarchy.

Responsibilities of the Personnel Division Manager (P)

He is generally accountable for advising the managing director on those policies for the structuring, manning and operation of the organization of the company that (in the light of its product development, manufacturing and marketing activities) will make an optimum contribution to the managing director's total plan of operations. To discharge this general responsibility, he will need to advise the managing director continuously on the following matters:

(a) Whether the current organization and its manning are actually helping to achieve the current planned programme of activity.

(b) Changes that ought to be made to ensure that the structure of the employment hierarchy stays matched to the requirements of a changing company work-load, and of its forward planning.

(c) Policies for the manning of roles in the hierarchy that take account not only of current but also of future requirements.

The foregoing responsibilities require:

(1) Analysis of work content and the level of work in roles;
(2) Development of systematic payment techniques that take account of the level of work in roles and the developing capacity of individuals;
(3) Constant review of techniques for recruitment, selection, training and progression of people that will lead to optimum filling of roles;
(4) Planning for future manpower needs by maintaining a continuous scrutiny of the personnel employed, and by consideration of what people are available externally;
(5) Arranging for a constant feedback of information (through such institutions as assessment boards) on the effectiveness of:

  (i) current organization,
  (ii) allocation of work between roles,
  (iii) performance of individuals in roles.

(d) Changes in personnel policy made necessary by changing programmes of work, changing production techniques, legal requirements, etc.
(e) Changes in conditions of work arising out of national agreements and contact with managers, representatives, trade-union officers, etc. This will involve assisting the managing director to take part in discussions with representatives of employees, implementing new policy arising out of such discussions, keeping written company policy up to date, drafting new standing orders, etc.
(f) Following up personnel policies (including welfare policies) that the managing director sets for his subordinates, discussing difficulties as they arise, reporting back to the managing director if necessary, and co-ordinating the implementation of these policies.
(g) Attaching personnel specialists to managers, maintaining the necessary flow of technical instructions to the specialists, assessing their technical effectiveness, and ensuring that the personnel division, as a whole, maintains a clear perspective of its specialist duties.

Service provision: the PDM may command and be accountable for a range of services such as canteens, medical services, works police, training, recreation facilities.

Responsibilities of Programming Division Manager (Pr)

He is generally accountable for working out and presenting to the managing director the timing, quantification and balancing of a pattern of product development, manufacture and sale, which will make an optimum contribution to the managing director's general plan of operations.

(*a*) He will need to take continuous account of at least four main sets of interconnected variables, and must base his advice on his observations. The variables are:

(1) *The company's target of manufacturing activity*. He must, from this statement of activity, derive the product-development and selling programmes that he considers necessary to maintain manufacturing activity at an optimum economic level.

(2) *The company's total target sales*. He must work out policies on product-mix and selling prices which, within the terms of target manufacturing activity, will maximize profitability.

(3) *The company's target on minimum investment*. He must continuously advise the managing director on the changing policies required to minimize the level of investment in plant, buildings, raw materials, work in progress, finished goods, etc. in a manner consistent with targets of manufacturing activity and total sales.

(4) *Company continuity of business into the future*. He must continuously advise the managing director about the levels of production capacity, total sales and stock levels that will best safeguard the future and allow a profitable programme to continue.

(*b*) In brief, the Programming Divisional Manager is responsible for advising the managing director how to achieve an optimally balanced level of activities, a mixture of work that will keep the company's manufacturing capacity continuously loaded at a level at which optimum sales can be obtained, optimum stocks held and optimum continuity of business achieved.

(*c*) The Programming Divisional Manager is responsible for developing techniques that help to control the balance of operations. Examples are:

Operations research, which is concerned with the modelling of multiple-factor situations, predicting the effects of altering controllable factors and indicating those changes most likely to result in the optimum.

Routines control, which is concerned with designing, refining, altering and simplifying the routines that handle the flow of enquiries, orders, materials, work in progress, finished goods, etc., from outside the company, through it and out again.

Service provision: the PDM may command and be accountable for a range of services such as purchasing, sub-contracting, storage of materials and goods, inter-department transport, packing and despatch of finished goods.

Responsibilities of the Technical Divisional Manager (T)

In the most general terms he is responsible for working out, and for presenting to the managing director, those policies for the development, modification and exploitation of manufacturing techniques which, in the light of the company's product development, manufacturing and selling operations, will make an optimum contribution to the managing director's total plan of operations. These responsibilities will involve the Technical Divisional Manager in constantly advising the managing director on the following matters:

(*a*) The production methods required to optimize volume of output and minimize cost, at given standards of quality, accuracy, finish, etc.

(*b*) The manner in which available capital resources ought to be used to optimize production techniques.

(*c*) The specification of materials most suited to given techniques to optimize volume and minimize cost of output at given standards of quality.

(*d*) The production techniques in which members of the company have to be trained in order that optimum output at minimal cost may be achieved.

(*e*) The desirability of developing one new technique as against another, in the light of the economic results which will be obtained.

(*f*) The optimum standards of quality, accuracy, finish, etc. that are attainable with a given level of equipment and organization. The techniques and equipment required if standards of quality are to be raised.

(*g*) The range of products that can be manufactured with the equipment and resources available in the company, and what further techniques or equipment are needed to produce new products when they are required.

(*h*) The Technical Divisional Manager is also responsible for co-ordinating the managing director's subordinates in the execution of his production-technique policy, and for maintaining the technical competence of his division of the company.

Service provision: the TDM may command and be accountable for providing a range of services such as machine-building, maintenance, work-study, jig and tool design, chemical analysis, physical testing, and estimating.

I do not wish to leave the impression that industrial specialists are, in fact, usually organized in the groups P, Pr and T. There are many departures from such forms of organization. One may find works managers of large plants who have responsible to them a chief production engineer (T), a manager of a tool drawing office (T), the head of a work-study department (T), perhaps a metallurgist in charge of material analysis and testing (T), a personnel manager (P), a chief production programmer (Pr), the manager of a buying office (Pr), and others and these are in addition to his subordinate operational managers. In this example I have named four specialists in the T dimension, one in the P dimension and two in the Pr field, making a total of seven specialists within the factory manager's immediate command. Such a situation not only calls for much co-ordination but, more important, *it makes it well-nigh impossible to give each of them the specialist staff authority I have described.* It would be equally difficult to give one of them such authority without giving it also to the others in the same dimension. The grouping of specialists into these three dimensions of P, Pr and T is probably, in most cases, a pre-condition of the full operation of the concepts of staff authority and the co-managership of attached specialists at subsidiary levels of the hierarchy.

It may appear to be very difficult to group all these different specialists under one of only three dimensions, but there are great gains in doing so. Take the example I have used above of the works manager of a large plant who has subordinate to him:

(*a*) a chief production engineer and staff concerned with methods;
(*b*) a manager of a tool drawing office;
(*c*) a manager of a work-study and rate-fixing department;
(*d*) a manager of a metallurgical team.

The collateral relationships between these departments are very extensive. All of them are concerned with speed, technical methods, quality and quantity of output. In my experience the works manager will have much more time to do his job if these specialists are organized as in Fig. 14 to provide the works manager with a single T staff officer:

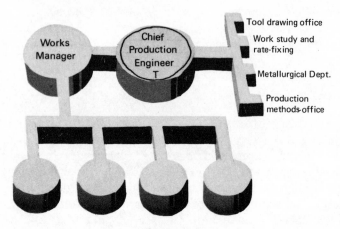

Figure 14

Many types of employment hierarchies *apparently* do not set up any specialist staff roles to assist operational managers. Frequently, however, there exist roles entitled 'deputy managing director', 'assistant works manager', 'personal assistant to the sales manager', and so on. At other times, one finds in the immediate command of a manager, or of a senior civil servant, roles which though they appear to imply supervision over others have, in fact, few or no real subordinates. If one digs deeper into the actual duties being performed by people in such roles, they often appear to be staff officers in disguise. The work pressures in the situation have forced such roles into existence in order to relieve the load on a manager. But, because the organization has no experience of the use of specialists in this way and no defined conception of the existence of such roles, they are regarded as assistants to or deputies of the manager. They are simply managers' helpers. Analysis of their work and relationships with the manager's other immediate subordinates might help people in such roles to perform very much more effectively.

The following is a summary of the ideas used in this chapter.

Operational manager—a manager in charge of the whole or part of the work which an employment hierarchy is set up to discharge.

Specialist role—one in which the occupant is accountable for assisting a manager in a specific dimension of his work by the discharge of one or more of the following responsibilities:

(*a*) *Advisory responsibility* for giving technical advice or assistance to his manager.

(*b*) *Service-providing responsibility*—that of providing services to his manager and to his extended command.

(*c*) *Staff responsibility*—that of assisting a manager in the co-ordination of the work of that manager's immediate subordinates in a dimension of his work by exercising authority and issuing instructions on his (the manager's) behalf.

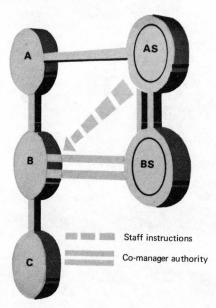

Figure 15

In Fig. 15,

(*a*) A is B's manager.

(*b*) AS is accountable for advising A on a dimension of his work.

(*c*) AS is accountable for giving staff instructions to B so long as they are in execution of policies agreed by A.

(*d*) AS is accountable for the education in technical policy of BS.

(*e*) AS is technical co-manager of BS.

(*f*) AS is responsible, in conjunction with B, for the appointment and assessment of the work of BS.

(*g*) B is the operational co-manager of BS and relies on BS to advise him and to help him form his policy in a specific dimension of his work.

(*h*) BS advises B and helps B to ensure that C is carrying out B's policy in a specific dimension of B's work.

These ideas may seem quite new to some managers, yet I believe that if they themselves have specialist subordinates and will carefully examine how these specialists get their work done they will, in most cases, discover that the practice is very similar to what I have described.

Take, as an example, a factory manager (A) who has a subordinate specialist (AS) who manages for him a production engineering department, as in Fig. 16.

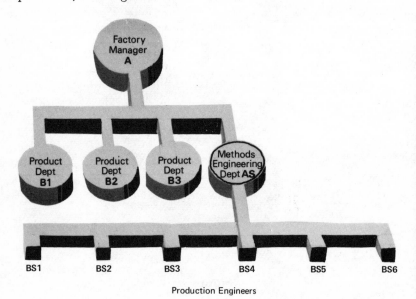

Figure 16

A may well find on examination that BS1 works almost permanently on the problems of B1. BS2 works on the problems of B2, and BS3 on the problems of B3. A may also discover that BS1, BS2 and BS3 work on the priorities set respectively by B1, B2 and B3. But what is missing is a clear-cut statement of the authority relationship of AS to B1, B2 and B3, and of BS1, BS2 and BS3 to the subordinates of B1, B2 and B3.

I have heard much comment from managers in manufacturing industry, both in Britain and overseas, to the effect that specialists have to have particularly tactful and persuasive dispositions to get their work accomplished satisfactorily. The personal relationships between specialists and 'line' managers are regarded by many in industry as particularly difficult to handle successfully. But in fact I believe that sensitivity and difficulty are always symptoms of un-structured or non-explicit accountability and authority.

On paper, the explicit specialist–manager and specialist–specialist relationships that I have set out in detail may sound complex and difficult. But my experience of presiding over their introduction was that they came as a great relief to all concerned and proved easy to operate.

One of the substantial gains from this explicit structuring was that it enabled some specialists to be moved out of central offices and to be physically housed within production departments. In Fig. 17 I have re-drawn Fig. 16 to show this re-arrangement.

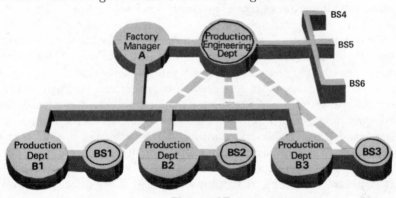

Figure 17

I was keenly aware of the absence of the idea of attachment of specialists to senior officials in the Civil Service. Each major govern-ment department has its own Establishment Division (P). Most government departments employ many thousands of officials and have hierarchies containing up to fifteen or more grades. But the establishment divisions do not attach establishment officers to the sub-divisions of the departments.

Virtually the only assets of a government department are its em-ployees. Thus, personnel work concerned with transfer, promotions, filling vacancies, re-structuring of departments, and recruitment are of more than usual importance to the Civil Service. But the operations of establishment divisions are painfully slow and laborious. They seem to have continous trouble in getting their work done. Civil servants are not given to criticizing other departments within the Service, but they certainly do criticize the establishment divisions.

I believe that attachment of specialists 'down the line' would be of material assistance to all. It would bring establishment officers into much closer contact with all the personnel involved. The real problems of establishment divisions would be seen more clearly by 'operational' officials, and establishment divisions would receive more sympathy and help. It would certainly speed up manning work because many of the problems could be solved within sub-departments at a junior level, without cluttering up the central establishment division with detail. Most important of all it would, I believe, result in officials being much bolder in initiating the transfer of people from one role to another. This would have the result of getting square pegs out of round holes. It might also result in getting surplus staff shifted more quickly into areas where there was shortage of staff, and in the allocation of more work and more responsible work on to some of the younger people.

There is no area of employment hierarchies in which there is less explicitly structured authority and accountability than in the levels where specialists are extensively employed. I believe that if an opinion survey were conducted among specialists concerned with production methods, programmes of work and personnel policies, there would be widespread agreement that much of their specialized knowledge and experience is at a discount. Similarly, I would expect that many operational managers would agree they are often confused and their work rendered less effective because the precise authority of specialists is never clear. This is certainly an area of organization which would repay study and clear structuring.

CHAPTER THIRTEEN

Organization of Services

I REFERRED RATHER briefly in the last chapter to the possibility that staff officers might conveniently be held responsible for the command of a wide range of services, and to the fact that this often happens already.

Service provision is exceedingly important. The resources spent are huge, and grow greater as hierarchies increase in size. But I still think that insufficient thought has been given to the authority and accountability of those in charge of maintenance, tool design, tool manufacture, transport, cleaning, typing pools, filing of documents, stores, buying offices, printing departments, canteens, security, first aid, and many other activities.

In small hierarchies people often provide for themselves. Managers organize filing, typing, cleaning, for their own departments. As concerns get larger it becomes economically necessary to concentrate the provision of services in the hands of people who have the necessary experience. But when concentration takes place it sometimes causes a great deal of dissatisfaction among those who use the services. Buying offices reduce variety in order to buy economically, so that managers are refused the precise article they want. The same thing happens in stores. Maintenance departments draw up timed work-schedules and managers cannot always get services at the time they want them, and so on.

These frustrations throw up the whole issue of precisely what a person in charge of a service is accountable for supplying. Clearly he cannot be held accountable for supplying anything required on demand, for if he were ready and able to do this it would involve unlimited expense.

Equally clearly a service-provider cannot be given authority to decide what to provide and when. Nor do I think that in large companies these issues can simply be left to be decided by 'common sense'. This approach produces situations in which, for example, an entire contract is held up because a storekeeper has decided that it was unnecessary to continue to keep certain items in stock, or because the manager of the typing pool decided that all the girls must leave at 5.30 sharp, and as a result the chief executive did not get his brief in time.

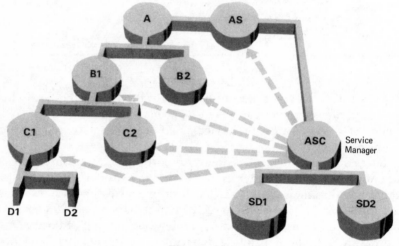

Figure 18

Fig. 18 shows a typical situation. I have shown A's staff officer in command of ASC, the service-provider, but it would have been as typical to show the service-provider as being responsible, say, to B2 (though it should be noted that if B2 were in command of the service manager and B2 himself made demands on the service, then it is likely that he would receive undue priority as against similar demands from his colleague B1).

ASC is allotted certain resources in terms of subordinate personnel, investment in stock, budgets of expense, etc., by AS. These are probably approved by A. In an explicitly structured situation, ASC is held accountable for providing a specific and prescribed range of services to A, to B1 and B2, to C1 and C2 but not to D1 and D2. If D1 and D2 require services they will have to get C1 to requisition them. The following principles are implicit.

(1) The service manager's use of discretion in providing services is prescribed in terms of expense, quality, quantity, and to whom service is to be rendered.

(2) Those authorized to requisition the services must be informed by A of the limits beyond which service cannot be provided without reference to higher authority.

(3) Such services are essential if operational managers are to be able to complete their tasks in terms of time, quality, cost, etc. Thus, operational managers, not the service manager, must be the judge of what service they need. The service manager must give such services as he is asked to provide up to the limits of his own terms of reference. He is not entitled to refuse a service requested that he is able to give, and which is within his terms of reference to provide, on the grounds that in his judgement the service is unnecessary.

(4) If a service manager is unable to provide service that he is authorized to give, because total demand exceeds his capacity, then he must report the facts to AS and suggest that the operational manager raises the matter with his own manager if the operational manager's work is seriously affected by the shortage.

(5) If a service manager is unable to organize his priorities as between demands from differing departments in a way which is at least tolerated by operational managers, then he must report such difficulties to AS.

Suppose, for example, that ASC (the service manager) is in charge of a factory tool-supply department, and that AS is technical staff officer to A, who is a factory manager. It will be clear that AS, who carries accountability to A for production technology in the factory, is able to bring pressures to bear on problems of priority over the supply of tooling, which will enable decisions to be more satisfactory all round than if the decision had rested with ASC.

It will be seen that P, Pr and T staff officers are often better able to mediate the problems arising out of the provision of services than operational managers. Moreover, their discharge of accountability for services takes them into very close contact with the day-to-day problems of their operational colleagues, and this helps to diminish 'distance' between them.

Concentration of services will increase as sophistication increases. Machine-shops in industry used to grind their own tools. But, as knowledge about cutting materials and cutting angles advances the work has had to be concentrated in specialized hands. Data-processing is forcing concentration in a number of directions. Filing and records will yield to random-access electronic memories. Containerization and air-freighting call for experts to handle transportation.

Stores and warehouses become more mechanized and reliant on computerized records. Tape-recorders reduce the need for shorthand typists and create more typing pools. These trends transfer work from operational managers on to service-providing centres. But they also increase the need to understand the authority and accountability that these changes imply for service-provision. For unless these are well understood there will be irritation and waste.

CHAPTER FOURTEEN

Accounting Systems

I HAVE DISCUSSED specialist roles, staff roles and service-providing roles at some length, without direct reference to accountant roles and accounting systems. I must now turn to the accountants themselves. Though they are widely regarded as simply another and very important type of specialist, I would argue that the system of roles within which they work is distinct and separate from the employment hierarchy proper, and that it is not part of the extended command of the chief executive. I start with a discussion of the role of the company secretary, and let it be noted that he is, *de jure, secretary to the board of directors.*

The secretary's unique position arises from the manner of growth of trading companies. Historically the members of a company banded together in an association, appointed a manager (he was frequently the captain of a ship, which the association had decided to build and send on trading expeditions overseas) who, in turn, established an employment hierarchy. But they also needed an official to organize meetings of the association and later of the board of directors, and to carry the legal and financial responsibility for safeguarding them from dishonest conduct on the part of their manager. This official had to prepare financial reports on the operations of the manager. The official was given authority by the board of directors that enabled him to require the manager and his subordinates to provide any details of their operations that he required, and he had complete access to all details of the venture.

The main point is that he has always been immediately responsible to the association itself, or to the directors whom they appointed. He was not and is not accountable to the chief executive of the employment hierarchy. This principle is enshrined in the various Companies Acts, which place him in a different position from any other official of the company. He is *personally* responsible at law and subject to penalties if he infringes the provisions of the Acts.

Thus, in principle, the modern company secretary reports to the board on the results of the chief executive's management of the affairs of the association. It is not for him, the secretary, to pass value-judgements on whether the chief executive has done his job well or poorly. The secretary's job is to establish the *results* in terms of the balance sheet, profit-and-loss accounts, and the detailed accounts, and to draw the attention of the board to any infractions of the law of which he believes the chief executive and his officials may be guilty. If he fails to carry out such tasks he may find himself in trouble.

The secretary is thus the servant of the board and the shareholders, accountable not only for reporting accurately the financial state of affairs but also for ensuring either that they are managed with integrity or for reporting any failure in this respect. He thus carries an auditing responsibility.

This is not an exhaustive account of the role of the secretary. Since he holds this position and has been trained in finance and the law, it has been natural for a secretary to be given many additional responsibilities concerned with taxation, the raising of capital, the relations of the board of directors with shareholders, the flow of funds, or investment policy.

So that he can produce all the information required by members of the company and its board of directors and by the taxation authorities, the secretary is provided with the resources necessary to build a hierarchy of accountants and clerical staff, who are given authority to insist that the proper statistical discipline and routines (necessary to provide the data on which the financial accounts are built) are maintained by managers and others throughout the company. Because of the requirements of the law, of the Inland Revenue and of the board of directors, the authority of the secretary reaches far down into the operations of the company.

A second and now most important function of the accounts became apparent as companies grew in size. Authority for expenditure had to be delegated to managers in all functions of the company. To control such expenditure within limits set by top management, budgets for various items of expense had to be established. Working within these budgets, managers wanted to know the details of the resources under their control that they had expended. They also wanted accurate, rapid and frequent feedback of financial information about many phases of their operations. At the same time, unit-costing systems were being introduced in an attempt to be able to state the differential profitability of products. In some forms of costing this led to the distribution of all expense on to manufacturing centres, and to complex procedures for establishing differential overhead rates for separate departments and processes.

The task of the secretary[1] can now be sub-divided into four different aspects:

(a) Work connected with cash flow, investment, taxation, relation, with shareholders, purchase of other companies, insurance and the law.

(b) Preparation of the financial accounts for presentation to the board at frequent intervals, and to the annual general meeting. This phase of the secretary's work embraces the auditing function[2] through which, on behalf of the board, he keeps a grip on the whole of the company's activities to ensure that the law and policies of the board are not breached and that resources are expended with integrity. This phase will also embrace all the functions arising from the responsibility of preparing the accounts.

(c) Feedback of operating data to managers at many levels in the executive system. This phase will involve him and his hierarchy of subordinates in the giving of much advice and explanation of the data to managers. This phase will embrace also calculation and payment of wages, wage deductions, pensions, etc.

(d) Prediction of future expense in analysed form, the distribution of expense to manufacturing centres, recommendation of budgets for decision by the chief executive, unit-costing systems, etc.

It can now be seen that the secretary's task falls into two main divisions; (a), which is not accounting work and (b), (c) and (d), all of which broadly conform to the accepted meaning of the term. I propose to refer to all the roles involved in the work of (b), (c) and (d) as the 'accounting hierarchy'. But (b), the preparation of the financial accounts and all that it involves, is again different from (c) and (d) because, in the case of (b) the secretary or chief accountant is responsible to the board for such work. The managing director cannot order the accounts to be altered, and he is not normally in a situation (for example) to decide that a new method of valuing stocks

---

[1] The role of secretary, as duties multiply, may be altered to 'secretary and chief accountant' or there may be a secretary with a chief accountant subordinate to him, or some of the work of the secretary will be taken over by a finance director, etc.

[2] 'The auditors' are a firm of accountants appointed with the approval of the shareholders to examine the accounts of the company and certify that they are correct. But the secretary also carries an auditing function.

be introduced, which might increase or decrease their value substantially and thus alter the profit or loss figure.

(c) and (d) are concerned with the provision of services to executive management, e.g. wages and pensions, the provision of advice on budgets, and of a feedback of information to managers that will enable them to maintain a proper relationship between input of resources and output. The accounting system is thus, in these latter respects, serving managers, and cannot be considered as being responsible to the board.

The organizational situation therefore is that the secretary–chief accountant is in charge of the accounting system and is responsible to the board of directors. In respect of service-provision the secretary–chief accountant must be accountable to the chief executive for providing a wide range of services to him and his subordinate managers.

Many managing directors might regard the repeated statement that the secretary is responsible to the board as too strong. However, one has only to discuss the work of an accounting system with the person in charge of it to realize that this is a reasonable description of the normal situation. Suppose one addresses the following questions to a managing director:

Do you control the technique of accounting employed? Can you override the secretary's statement of what the profits for the period are by insisting on adjustments which the secretary does not agree are correct?

Can you instruct the secretary on the rate of depreciation to be applied to plant valuation for the purpose of the accounts?

Can you unilaterally decide the percentage reserves to be applied to the value of stock?

Can you alter the details of the returns and reports that the secretary wishes to deposit with Company House?

If the assets of the company are found to be missing, or of lower value than appear in the accounts, can you instruct the secretary not to disclose the facts to the board?

If the board of directors are carrying their proper responsibilities, then the answer to all of these questions must be 'no'. The managing director is thus clearly not executively in charge of the secretary and his accounting hierarchy.

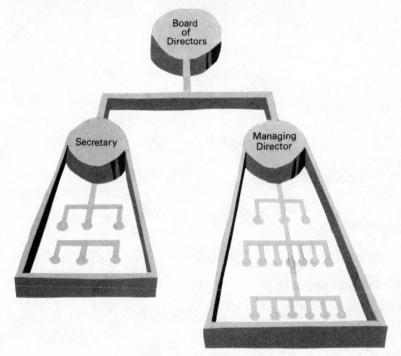

Figure 19

Fig. 19 shows the accounting system as being outside and separate from the employment hierarchy. It is accountable to the board for the work it does, apart from its service-provision to the employment hierarchy.

I would define the accounting system as follows. It is that hierarchy of roles that is accountable:

(a) for providing economic and financial data about the operation of the employment hierarchy to the association's representatives;
(b) for reporting to the association's representatives any deviation by the chief executive or his subordinates from the law or from the policies established by the association;
(c) for providing any services required by the association's representatives (e.g. the board of directors in the case of a commercial company);
(d) for providing a range of data-processing and other specified services to the chief executive and to his managers.

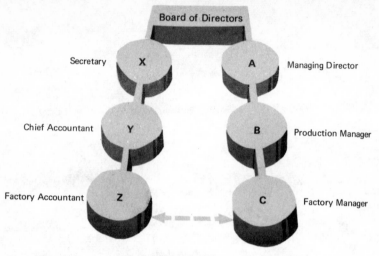

Figure 20

I will now examine the relationship of members of the accounting system to operational managers.

Fig. 20 is a selection of roles in the employment hierarchy and the accounting system. (It is a random selection in the sense that many different titles for such roles are in current use.) I will examine the relationship between Z and C. It is a fairly typical relationship, because most chief executives will want the services of an accountant for each factory that the company operates. The organizational chart will often be drawn as in Fig. 21.

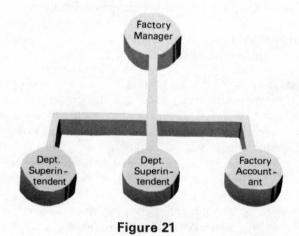

Figure 21

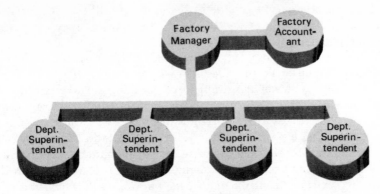

Figure 22

Or it might be drawn like Fig. 22.

Both Fig. 21 and Fig. 22 depict the factory accountant as a subordinate of the factory manager, but the relationship of the whole accounting system to the board and to the law means that such a link does not function as it is depicted.

The relationship of Z to C in Fig. 20 is simple. Z is not a subordinate of C. All the work he does in building up the financial accounts of the company, and on taxation, valuation of stocks, maintenance of statistical discipline in handling of data, plant register and depreciation, etc., have to be carried out in accordance with the direction of the head of the accounting system.

Z is also responsible for providing a data-processing service to C, the factory manager. C can, within the resources available to Z, demand what he requires to help him to do his job. But this does not make Z a subordinate of C. If Z fails to provide an efficient service it is up to the head of the accounting system to investigate and put things right.

I believe that clear thinking about the organization and the position of accounting systems is very important. Human nature being what it is, critical scrutiny and audit (from a financial point of view), of the working of the executive system is necessary. When the accounting staff intervenes to inform managers that better records must be kept or that greater control over stores of materials must be instituted, the result can be tension, and often is. If those carrying out the operational work of the company wrongly assume that accountants are (like themselves) responsible to the chief executive, then the accountants' conduct in insisting that 'colleagues' conform to financial disciplines will look like bossy interference. If, however, their role is clear, tension can be avoided. Accountants will be able to carry out their responsibilities without being hesitant, as they sometimes are, and efficiency will be all the greater.

The use of electronic data-processing equipment, the casting-off of some of the historic shibboleths in which accountancy is involved, and the emergence of more objective thinking to take account of disciplines like statistics or operational research is, I believe, bound to alter substantially the techniques and the role of accountants in the future. These potential future changes will add substantially to the need for clear thinking about the role of accountants. If there are doubts about the necessity for change in accounting techniques the following extract[1] from an article by one of my former industrial colleagues may help to support my contention.

From the earliest days managers have been 'numerate', i.e. have had some familiarity with and aptitude in the use of numbers. Archimedes, the manager of the Greek army, was notably numerate as no doubt were the managers who built the Pyramids. Computers have increased the numerate facility to, if not beyond, the limit of our imagination.

By this means I mean that capability of processing data has outstripped the understanding of most managers of the significance of numbers. This was true to some extent even before the advent of computers. For example, the consolidated balance sheet of one large company displays the sum of £56 583 304 as a measurement of the total assets. This is equivalent to saying that the distance from London to Glasgow is 394 miles 732 yards 2 feet and 5 inches give or take ¼ inch.

One can find reputable chartered accountants certify the former figure but no chartered engineer would certify the potentially much more precise measurement of the distance from London to Glasgow in correspondingly significant terms. . . .

Because numbers can be expressed with unlimited quantitative precision the real state which is modelled is often attributed with the same absolute property. The certification that the assets of a company amount to £56 583 304 is harmless in itself but when an important real factor is assessed by means of the arithmetical process of subtraction of one number modelling input to within a tolerable degree of accuracy from another number modelling output within a tolerable degree of accuracy the difference

---

[1] P. P. Love, Chairman, The Glacier Metal Co Ltd, 'Keeping the model in line with reality', *The Times*, 4 May 1970.

cannot be assumed to model the extant difference in the real situation.

Thus an input of £1m with an accuracy of plus/minus $\frac{1}{2}$ per cent taken from an output of £1.1m with an accuracy of plus/minus $\frac{1}{2}$ per cent can only be stated as £100 000 plus/minus $10\frac{1}{2}$ per cent. In accounting practice generally the percentage deviations from reality are not displayed if indeed they are even admitted. As shareholders rely on numerical models for assessing the state of affairs and the activities (balance sheet and profit and loss account) of their company there is great scope for the concealment wittingly or otherwise of substantial errors.

In the way that annual accounts constitute the numerical model upon which shareholders assess the progress or otherwise of their company, so also can internal accounts be the numerical model upon which managers may make some of their decisions. The extent to which the numerical model fails to display the possible differences between the data in the model and reality determines the possible quantitative errors in these decisions.

Since the model does not normally display the extent of possible errors the errors in reality are also not displayed. It is for this reason, whether or not recognised, that the numerate manager of today does not by and large place a great deal of confidence in management accounts. And it is in this field that accountants should take a lead. They are professional numerates in the business world.

What would the effect of scientific data processing have in management if even fairly elementary statistical laws were brought into play? The time a manager spends upon understanding and 'interpreting' the mass of accounting data which are pushed in front of him could be cut by 95 per cent if presented as changes in terms of standard deviations. With the advent of the computer the processing of data to this end is child's play and a manager need then make decisions about issues which are shown in the numerical model as deviating significantly from the planned course.

But this requires a confidence to be engendered in both management and accountant in the validity of the statistical processes having a counterpart in the influence of random factors in the real operations and an understanding that if a change is greater than the standard deviation, then it is probable that an uncontrolled non-random factor is operating which has to be identified and brought into control.

As the ratio of standard deviation to mean falls it can be assumed that control is becoming more effective. If the ratio of standard deviation rises then the means of control requires attention. These techniques have been used extensively in the actuarial field and the whole of risk underwriting as a successful business depends upon such models in which the data is processed by mathematical statistical methods. The numerate manager can also use these to advantage.

CHAPTER FIFTEEN

Delegation of Accountability

ONE OF THE curses of our era is the way we waste the energies and the creativeness of younger people. It arises because our employment hierarchies are growing larger and because our understanding of the process of delegation is insufficient. There are countless examples in industry and commerce of training schemes which take the cream of our youth from universities and other places of higher education and which—for a period of one or sometimes two years—provide these people with work that could be adequately performed by much less intelligent individuals. Our apprenticeship schemes are too long. Men of 25 are regarded as too young and too inexperienced to be given responsibility that deploys their talents. Boredom sets in. This situation also prevails in the Civil Service, where standards of selection are high and the pay is good. But, because the quality of and quantity of work allotted to young people is inadequate, boredom is a common complaint. There are many causes of this. One is lack of insight into the nature of work, and the ways in which tasks are split up and delegated down the employment hierarchy.

In chapter five I defined work as the application of knowledge and the exercise of discretion within limits prescribed by the immediate manager and by higher policies towards an objective set by the immediate manager, the whole being carried out within an employment contract. It is worth analysing further the process by which the boundary round the area in which a manager exercises discretion is drawn. An analysis of this process gives greater insight into what is meant when people talk about centralizing or decentralizing administration, and illuminates the feelings of people at work about 'participation in the making of policy'.

When the committee of an association, the council of a university, or the board of directors of a business take decisions, they are extending, reducing or altering in detail the area over which their chief executive officer exercises judgement. If a board decides to invest more funds, enter new markets or close down a subsidiary it is, in effect, instructing the chief executive to arrange for the activities that will put their decisions into practice. The directors thereby authorize the chief executive to take any decisions of his own that are reasonably necessary to implement theirs. The decision to invest a million pounds, in order to increase the manufacturing capacity for a given product, authorizes the chief executive to make a range of decisions concerned with the spending of the million.

The chief executive may in turn delegate the spending of parts of the one million pounds to his subordinates, within a policy stating the results to be achieved by that spending. Those subordinates give instructions to *their* subordinates, which set in train studies of how best to spend the additional capital. The original policy decision results in a series of decisions extending down into the hierarchy. The lower down the hierarchy they travel, the more detailed and circumscribed the decisions become.

It will be easier to consider this hierarchical process of decision-making if, instead of referring to a line of managers as A, B, C, and so on, I talk about different ranks of employees and managers. At the base of the hierarchy we have Rank 1, the first level of manager being Rank 2, and so on. An employment hierarchy can thus be referred to as a six-rank or a five-rank hierarchy, and so on, down to a two-rank hierarchy. (There is no hierarchy if there is only one rank.)

Fig. 23 attempts to depict graphically the idea that the decisions of Rank 4 prescribe the area of decision-making of Rank 3, and the decisions of Rank 3 in turn prescribe the discretion area of Rank 2, and so on to the base of the hierarchy. Rank 1 personnel will not know what decisions Rank 4 takes, but because Rank 3's decisions must take account of Rank 4 decisions, and Rank 2 in turn takes account of Rank 3's decisions, Rank 1 personnel are working within an environment contributed to by the decisions of all managers in the direct line of command above them.

The diagram shows only one subordinate for each manager, in the interests of simplicity, but it is to be understood that each of several subordinates of a manager may have a different area of discretion in accordance with the different work he is given to do.

Fig. 24 does not show the relations of Rank 3 to Rank 2 or of Rank 2 to Rank 1. It is designed to illustrate the different types of decision that a Rank 4 manager can make. The 4/3 decisions are to his im-

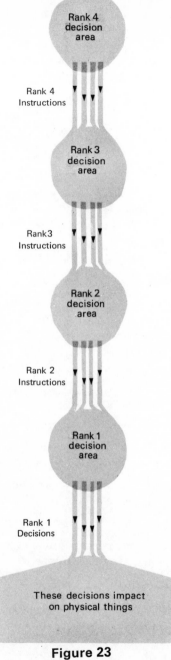

Figure 23

mediate subordinates at Rank 3 and to nobody else. Rank 3 will deal with these as I have illustrated in Fig. 24. Decisions of type 4/3 and 2 are those given directly both to Rank 3 and Rank 2. Decisions of type 4/3, 2 and 1 are given directly to Rank 3, Rank 2 and Rank 1, and perhaps, sometimes, to the whole of Rank 4's extended command.

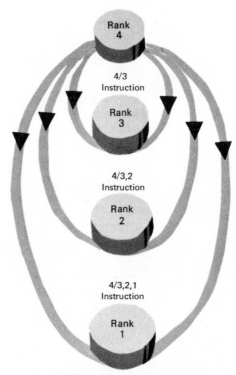

Types of Rank 4 Instruction

Figure 24

I am going to refer to instructions given by a manager to more ranks than his immediate subordinates as 'contraction instructions'. I am afraid that this is another clumsy term, but it already has limited currency and it is difficult to find a better one. It conveys the idea of contracting the hierarchy when a manager 'reaches down' to a point several ranks below him.

It is often argued that a manager should not give instructions to people other than his immediate subordinates, but observation shows that contraction instructions are frequently issued in practice. For example, a chief executive may issue an instruction that in the interests of eye safety all employees must wear protective glasses or goggles when entering a particular workshop. The official head of a government department may issue an instruction to his top three ranks of officials about security of documents, and so on.

It is to be noted that the more ranks that are covered by a single instruction the less important the instruction is likely to be. For example, a 4/3 instruction by a factory manager to his immediate subordinates to increase output by 20 per cent within four weeks is meaningful. But to make such an instruction a 4/3, 2 communication would probably result in puzzlement, because the Rank 2 subordinates (probably foremen) need to have more detailed instructions of the 3/2 type before they can each recognize the particular new tasks that they will have to perform. These instructions would be concerned with detailed production arrangements, which would collectively produce the 20 per cent increase. To give an order 'produce 20 per cent more' as a 4/3, 2, 1 instruction would be meaningless.

Contraction instructions, particularly those of the 6/5, 4, 3, 2, 1 type or even of the 6/5, 4, 3 type are really a chief executive or a senior manager saying to his immediate subordinates: 'Carry out this activity yourselves and see to it that your subordinates in your extended command do so as well. Furthermore, I am not giving you discretion to alter this instruction so I am communicating it directly to all whom it concerns.'

Sometimes contraction instructions are communicated directly to the immediate subordinates of a manager, with the further instruction to pass it down the line. This practice follows from two bad conventions that characterize manager–subordinate relations. The first is: 'managers should give instructions only to their immediate subordinates', and the second is: 'managers passing on an instruction [actually a contraction instruction] from their own manager to their own subordinates should never do so in the name of their manager but in their own name'. (Thus the convention is that a manager does not say to his subordinates: 'The managing director has instructed me to instruct you . . .') The result of these conventions is that a chief executive will issue contraction instructions but they will be made to sound otherwise. Thus a manager at Rank 3 who has received a 4/3, 2 instruction will say to his immediate subordinates at Rank 2: 'I have decided that it is necessary to . . .' This is a lie, because *he* has not decided: Rank 4 has decided. Everybody at Rank 2 knows this, because four or five other Rank 3 managers are each giving the same instruction to their separate immediate commands. Thus is cynicism bred about managers. One can hear shop-stewards and others saying: 'Why doesn't the factory manager come out into the open and give the order himself instead of letting each departmental manager pretend it's his own bright idea?'

We have thus two types of policy: 'that which applies to members of a manager's immediate command, and that which applies to other levels as well. It may well appear unnecessary to delve into this amount of detail and definition. But if we are to achieve precision in some very important matters there is a real need to define.

Consider first the question of 'centralized' or 'de-centralized' management. This is a subject widely discussed in Government itself (with particular relation to the social services), in industry, in commerce, and elsewhere. But without definitions and concepts, 'centralization' and 'de-centralization' are little more than aspirations.

One word used in connection with de-centralization is 'autonomy'. People in high positions talk of having established 'local autonomy' for subsidiary companies or branches, or departments of great undertakings, without realizing that autonomy means 'self-government' or 'independence'. If a company gives a subsidiary independence then it has renounced the use of authority over it and has ceased to hold it accountable to itself (which, incidentally, would be in defiance of the Companies Acts).

No doubt some of my readers will object because they mean no such thing when they use the word. But what matters is the meaning attached to it generally. I want to make accurate communication and discussion of these matters possible by achieving a situation analogous to that existing in the natural sciences, where, by and large, a common defined language exists. Consider the following extract from the *Times* leader of 15 August 1970 on the Prices and Incomes Board recommendation that there should be further centralization of management control of the National Coal Board.

... it is held that the amount of control exercised from the centre of top management should be strengthened, with the special aim of exercising close and continual supervision over the 17 area directors.

This would be a fundamental change of policy. The Coal Board has stoutly insisted on maintaining the *autonomy* [my italics] of area directors in running colliery operations in the belief that local characteristics, work forces, and special problems are best handled close to the pits than the London boardroom.

Until recently the devolution of control over area operations has been remarkably effective. Facts and figures for annual improvements in the miners' productivity bear favourable comparison with those for many newer and less labour-intensive industries. The suggestion that a new deputy chairman, or a single board member, ought to take on day by day responsibilities for productive operations, co-ordinating area directors, ought to be treated with some caution. There is some evidence that a lack of a focal point for management control has not given the board, which believes in collective decision taking, the full benefits of central planning. What the PIB leaves out are the advantages that might be lost if on-the-spot area directors, paid to get results, became subject to more interference from the centre and to a further stretching of line management. . . .

It seems to me that the PIB is in no position to advise a huge undertaking like the National Coal Board unless it has some clear language in which to communicate precisely what it intends, and this seems to be lacking.

There is no state of centralized organization or de-centralized organization. We are dealing with a continuum stretching from one extreme to the other. A higher degree of de-centralization arises when managers:

(*a*) Ask subordinates to make decisions that heretofore managers have made themselves.

(*b*) Increase the resources that subordinates can commit to their work. For example, if heretofore a subordinate could requisition supplies in any one period up to a total of $£x$, and this maximum is changed to $£2x$, then a move towards de-centralization has taken place.

(*c*) Withdraw contraction policies. For example, if heretofore compassionate absence from work was allowed only by the decision of the personnel manager, and the chief executive decides that such decisions are better taken by a person's immediate manager, then a move towards de-centralization has taken place.

(*d*) Give longer time-span tasks to subordinates than heretofore. For example, a chief executive wants a subordinate to examine the possibility of exporting to Ruritania. He might tell the subordinate to obtain all facts about consumption, competitor products, taxation, tariff barriers, local potential customers, etc. and present a report to him within three months, for discussion before proceeding further. Or he might ask the subordinate to make a thorough reconnaissance of the Ruritanian market, including visiting the country, and recommend whether or not the company should enter that market, all to be completed within six months.

In principle, a manager can either give a complete task to be finished in $3x$ months or he can split the task up into, say, three parts. He gives out the first part, which he expects to be completed in x months; he reviews the result and allots the next part of the task, and so on. Such managerial decisions about giving work to subordinates are usually made quite intuitively. Managers are not explicitly aware of reducing or increasing time-spans. They do what they do on the basis of varying degrees of confidence in the ability of subordinates. When they lengthen time-spans they are moving towards de-centralization.

Later in this book I shall discuss participation in the making of policy by representatives, and explore the extent to which this is viable. Some of the current discussion about 'participation' arises from a felt need for the limits on the discretion of people in hierarchies to be widened, so that employees can carry greater accountability in their respective roles. This is often justified. Many of the younger men and women in particular are under-employed in the sense that the level of their work is too low. But it is difficult to respond to this need unless we have a common language in which to discuss practical action.

Many years ago the company of which I was chief executive was experiencing a shortage of cash. Examination showed that the rise in the total of our debtors was disproportionate to the rise in turnover, and that if we could return to the former ratio we could release a large amount of finance for other uses. Our first reaction was to blame the persons responsible for control of credit for doing a poor job. But investigation showed that a situation had grown up which allowed too many people at different levels to make decisions about curtailing or extending credit. There were countless arguments. The sales manager and the company secretary jointly made the main customer decisions. People further down the line, in the commands of both, knew a great deal about the past performance of the thousands of companies with whom we were trading, but they felt that their knowledge was being ignored. They said that the results would be much better if they were allowed '*more participation*' in policies for controlling credit, and if fewer overriding decisions were made by senior managers who were often unaware of the past records of our customers. There were many clear instances, they said, of credit being given on a generous scale without benefit to the company, and other instances of failure to grant quite limited credit that had resulted in unnecessary loss of customers. By extending the boundaries of the discretion exercised by area sales managers on the one hand, and by the accountant responsible for the sales ledgers on the other, and by emphasizing the collateral relations that existed between them, the company succeeded in substantially reducing the ratio of debtors to sales and removed much detailed decision-making from the desk of senior managers. This series of moves was described to me as a 'de-centralization' of credit control by enabling people to '*participate*' in determining credit policy.

If every manager appreciated that every time he decides on some policy, sets a task for a subordinate or sets up routines for control of his subordinates, he is weaving the pattern of delegation within which his people work, then he would delegate more. Each decision he makes in the daily course of his work is an opportunity either gained or lost to employ his subordinates more effectively. Each contraction instruction that he issues is a move towards centralization of authority, and vice versa.

More de-centralized management is not something that can be decided on as a policy and implemented by a few well-chosen decisions. It can be achieved only by understanding that whether an employment hierarchy moves towards de-centralization or towards centralized administration is being decided every day in the acts of all its managers.

Part Two

Power Groups, Participation and Wage Differentials

An Analysis of the Power Situation[1]

EMPLOYMENT HIERARCHIES EXIST in an environment of groups able to exert power upon them. A body of shareholders can inhibit change by voting against a resolution at a meeting of a company. A body of consumers or customers can do the same by threatening withdrawal of custom. A body of employees can do so by threatening strike action. People in our society are frightened of power (rightly so, I think), but this should not allow us to hide our heads in the sand and pretend that the growing problems caused by the activities of employee power-groups do not exist. We assume too easily that better communication, more consultation, and improved leadership will cope with the situation. I hope to show that, important as such things are, they alone will not deal effectively with the problems of employee power, and that we require instead to set up new institutions, through which the power of various groups can be effectively canalized and used constructively, instead of being used destructively in supporting feelings of hostility, envy and frustration.

People often confuse power with authority. I hope I have made it

[1] In describing the operation of employment hierarchies it is almost inevitable that I have given the impression that I have overlooked all the many problems concerning the sources of authority of managers, the need for people to take part in the formation of the policies that govern their work, the use of power by representatives to effect change, etc. These are extremely important issues in the world of employment work today, but it is not possible to discuss such issues objectively without first establishing the concept of the employment hierarchy and its role relationships.

I have not finished discussing the way in which the employment hierarchies work, but I shall delay doing so until I have explored the representative systems and policy-forming institutions that inevitably accompany work hierarchies.

clear already that authority is a property that attaches to a role, not to a person. The Prime Minister's role has authority, and so long as he is in the role he exercises the authority belonging to it. When he loses the role he ceases to possess the authority that he previously exercised. This is so of all roles in an employment hierarchy.

I define *authority* as that quality of a role (or group of roles) that sanctions the incumbent to make decisions and act within defined limits.

I define *power* as those qualities of a person or associated persons that enable him or them to cause other persons to act.

A person in a role that has authority will possess some degree of personal power, based on his status as a person in the eyes of others.

Power used intensively enables a group to inhibit change or even, at times, to force other groups with less power, or people with authority, to accept change that is unwelcome to them.

There is a strong interaction between power and authority, which is insufficiently understood because people dislike even discussing power, and because of confusion about the two concepts. I have examined the authority of a chief executive and other managerial roles in previous chapters without commenting on the sources of their authority. But it is clear that in the last analysis authority is derived from the personality of individuals and from the power of groups.

The associations of shareholders formed to set up trading ventures are power-groups. These power-groups set up employment hierarchies to carry out manufacturing, trading and other activities. It is the association power-group that originally vests authority in the role of the chief executive. As time has passed the degree of shareholders' power has been contained by law. But, despite what the Government or the employees or the consumers feel, the shareholders can still close down the employment hierarchy and disband themselves, the association and the employment hierarchy at will. Thus one very important source of managerial authority is the association of shareholders, wielding their power through their elected representatives on the board of directors.

At this point, some of my readers may protest that as directors of companies today are virtually self-selecting, the power of the association of shareholders is a myth. This is not correct. Power is a potentiality, and it is not diminished, nor does it cease to exist, simply because it is not used for long periods. Shareholders do not use their power frequently, but it is always there as a factor in the situation. Whenever the performance of the board becomes intolerable to them they move in and use their voting power to make changes. Perhaps the most frequent example of the use of power by shareholders is when, defying the advice of the board, they accept a take-over bid.

It would be wrong to leave the impression that shareholders' power has no effect except when something stirs them to use it. Those who have been directors of companies know that the deliberations of the board and the kinds of policy decisions that the board takes are constantly affected by the assumed future reactions of shareholders. Thus the chief executive's authority is partially based on the power of shareholders.

The second source of authority in the employment hierarchy is derived from the consumer or customer. Customer groups are amorphous in the sense that they do not get together as a group, except under pressure generated by feelings of exploitation.[1]

The prevailing assumption in society is that the customer is in a very weak position. This is true of monopoly or oligopoly[2] situations, but in most situations the customer has the power to stop buying. If enough customers do this they can close down a company. This is obvious, but I tediously commit the obvious to paper in order to make a point that is not obvious—the connection between the power of the consumer and the authority of managers and others in the employment hierarchy.

The shareholder power-group may demand that the directors increase prices so that profits rise and dividends begin to flow. The employee representatives may demand higher wages, and perhaps these can only be paid if prices rise. But neither group can endow the chief executive with the necessary degree of authority to maintain the same volume of sales at higher prices if the customers decide otherwise. If this fact is ignored the company will, in the long run, cease to exist. A sales organization can be looked upon as an institution

---

[1] The formation of the co-operative retail societies in the nineteenth century is a notable example of organization of the consumer. Another example is the move, after the last war, of certain automobile manufacturing companies who, as buyers of certain supplies, became concerned at the growing concentration of those supplies in the hands of one company. They bought and supported a second supplier. I think research would disclose other such cases.

Groups of buyers, such as retail shops, who form associations to buy on behalf of their members in bulk (instead of buying individually) now have to register the nature of their activities with the Registrar of Restrictive Practices. The Registrar may disallow them.

[2] 'A market situation where each of several producers is able to influence the market but not able to ignore his competitors' reactions'—*Penguin English Dictionary*.

continuously employed on the task of obtaining customer sanction for the managers' authority to make decisions about price, quality, specification and delivery time.

The third power-group that forms part of the environment within which employment hierarchies operate is the representative system.

In a two-level employment hierarchy, with one manager in charge of a group of employees, any employee will usually find it reasonably easy to speak to his manager (who is also chief executive). If there are two levels of management, communication with the chief executive, or even with a manager once-removed, becomes more difficult. Group views have to be expressed by representatives. These may be formally elected—shop-stewards in industry, Whitley Council members in the Civil Service, or elected members of senates in universities. But frequently part of the representative system is informal. This happens most often in the higher echelons of the hierarchy, where the tendency is for non-elected people who feel that they express the views of the majority to approach management on an informal basis.

Representative systems with their constituencies, electors, representatives and committees, are power-groups. They can close down the work of the employment hierarchy and they can do so unilaterally.

From time to time other power-groups may appear on the scene, but they are transient and often illegal. For example, a supplier to an industrial company who holds a monopoly position could starve it of raw material. But for the purpose of making a general analysis, transient power-groups can be ignored, because the employment hierarchy can take steps to negate that power.

The employment hierarchy and the three power-groups operate together within limits prescribed by the law—company law, tax law, the Trade Descriptions Act, merchandising laws, trade-union law, the Factory Acts, etc. The interaction of the three power-groups with the employment hierarchy and its chief executive produces a second series of 'laws', which take the form of policies agreed with the chief executive or forced upon him.

Fig. 25 is not a new scheme of organization, but an attempt to display the role of the power-groups.

AA is the existing body of law affecting employment hierarchies in all their forms.
BB is the range of policy generated by interaction between the employment hierarchy and the power-groups.

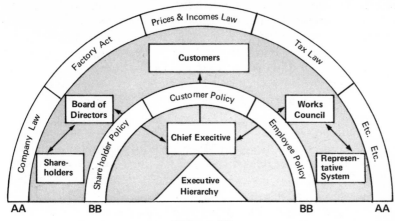

Figure 25

The area within which the chief executive can exercise discretion is thus bounded by the law and by this inner circle of policies that arise from the existence of these power-groups. Their power waxes and wanes with changes in the total environment. For example, a rise in unemployment weakens the power of the representative system, a drop in demand for goods strengthens the position of the customer, and the wider dispersal of share ownership weakens the power of the shareholder system. In the last analysis, nevertheless, these systems always are capable of inhibiting change if the feelings of their members are sufficiently aroused and they become sufficiently resolute. It is demonstrable that they possess the power to stop any action to which they object strongly enough.

Even if these three systems are not explicitly institutionalized or understood, their existence can be deduced from analytic observation of any company's operations. While each system is concerned with the continued existence, growth and future prosperity of the organization and with the national interest, each also has its own special interest, which it seeks to promote. The shareholder system is specially concerned with dividends, financial stability, capital appreciation, and the like. The customer system is specially concerned with the product or service produced by the company: its price, quality, reliability, availability, design, etc. The employee-representative system is specially concerned with the maintenance of continued employment, wages, work conditions, hours of work, and a range of psychological factors affecting the individual at work.

The organization itself, led by the chief executive, is specially

concerned to ensure that the interaction of the power systems produces optimum satisfaction for employees, customers and shareholders, combined with efficiency at work. But again, while the shareholder, customer and employee-representative systems possess power,
the chief executive and his managers exercise authority—an authority
derived from the various policies sanctioned by the power-groups,
which set limits to the use of discretion by the chief executive and his
managers.

The shareholder, customer and employee systems all use their
power to defend, and to extend, their own differential entitlements.
The entitlements of each power system interact one with another.
Higher dividends may mean less money for investment in new plant,
and, therefore, higher prices to customers. The consumer's claim for
lower product-prices may, in the long run, mean lower wages to
employees. Employees' successful claims for higher wages may mean
higher prices to consumers. The policies that emerge are, therefore,
in one sense, a means of holding the balance of advantage between
the interests of the three systems.

The three power systems interact, but they do not normally meet.
Boards of directors seldom meet customers or shop-stewards. The
mechanism of interaction is in the employment hierarchy. The chief
executive takes much of the responsibility for this interaction. His
presence at meetings of the board of directors will ensure that the
policies upon which the board decide will take into account the
differential entitlements of the customer and employee systems. When
the sales organization negotiates with customers it does so within
policies set by the chief executive; the chief executive's policies take
into account and try to safeguard the interests of the other two systems. When the representative system meets the chief executive, his
presence ensures that before any agreement is reached with the
representative system its effects on the customer system and the shareholding system have been fully considered.

Because, in the last analysis, each of the shareholding, customer
and employee-representative systems can close down the company,
the chief executive can take no action that is not at least tolerated by
a consensus of opinion in each of the three systems. Any act taken by
the executive system that does not result in the closing down of the
company is evidence of the toleration of that act by each of the three
systems.

National legislation, plus the quasi-legislative outcome of the interaction of the four systems associated with the company, constitute the
source of the authority of the chief executive and of the hierarchical

employment system subordinate to him. Any group in the environment of a company that has the power to inhibit change in the policies governing its operation, plays its part willy-nilly in setting up the
framework of local 'legislation' within which that company does its
work. We know from experience what happens when an attempt is
made to introduce policies that take insufficient account of the
strengths and interests of one of the power-groups. Here are some
familiar examples:

(a) In response to pressure from the customers a board of directors,
interacting with the chief executive, decides to invest a higher
proportion of profits earned in a new product, and temporarily
to pay no dividend. The decision may be reversed, or some directors may lose their place on the board at the extraordinary meeting of shareholders that is called to object to the policy.
(b) A chief executive, interacting with the representative system,
decides to increase wage rates and then has to announce an increase of prices to the customer system. Some customers will withdraw their orders and there will be a redundancy.
(c) A chief executive, attempting to increase the volume of work being
placed by the customer system, lowers prices, but the profits of the
company decline. Later he is unable to meet demands for higher
wages, which are regarded as legitimate by the representative
system, and as a consequence a strike takes place. A wage increase
is then agreed and prices have to be raised.

These are industrial examples, but the same holds good for employment hierarchies in the Civil Service, in universities or in nationalized
industries. The power-groups are the same in principle: for example
in the case of the nationalized industries read government instead of
the shareholder. In the case of the universities, for 'shareholders' read
a combination of the Privy Council, the University Grants Com-
mission and the Government. And there are always consumers and
employees.

If those who manage an employment hierarchy are not aware of the
existence and strengths of these power systems, then the policies that
emerge from the complex interactions that take place will not have
been fully sanctioned, because the forces at work will not have been
sufficiently understood. If this has happened, the policies will be dis-
rupted later by the use of power by the group whose interests have
been too little taken into account.

These power and authority interactions are sufficiently analogous
to legislation to be given the title 'quasi-legislative system'. It permits

the statement that there is need for explicit 'quasi-legislative' institutions, within which the hierarchy can interact with the representative power system.

'Quasi-legislative' institutions already exist for two of the power systems. The company secretary is responsible for the one that concerns shareholders. This is formal, and governed by provisions of the Companies' Act in the case of industry and commerce, and by charter in the case of the universities. Parliamentary legislation governs the interaction between ownership and the employment hierarchy in the nationalized industries. Company annual general meetings and extraordinary meetings are not usually described as 'quasi-legislative' gatherings, but in one sense that is certainly what they are.

In relation with the customer power-groups very sophisticated sales departments exist, largely to obtain customer sanction for change. To regard the interaction of a sales department and a group of consumers or customers as a 'quasi-legislative' institution may seem bizarre. On the other hand, this interaction produces thousands of agreements every year, which have a vital effect on the working of the employment hierarchy. Here again, resources are devoted to getting sanction for policies, and in a highly sophisticated way. There is no such sophistication in the relation between the chief executive and employee power-groups. Representative systems have immense power, but the attempts to construct institutions are puny, lack resources, and seem to avoid facing real issues.

I have often talked to groups of chief executives who are concerned about industrial unrest. I always point out how important it is that the representative system should be well organized and that it should be operated with integrity and that, to this end, the convener of shop-stewards in a large factory should be released from work for his period of office (with pay), and provided with an office, telephones and secretarial help. This proposition usually causes astonishment. Many chief executives seem to think that by starving a representative system of the resources that are essential to efficient operation they will be able to ignore it or to reduce its power. They fail to understand that representatives are essential feedback systems. Without them managers would be unable to discover in advance which change will be tolerated and which will not. A convener of shop-stewards who has to continue with his employment work and try to carry out his duties as convener effectively has a very difficult life. He is disapproved of by his manager (for the good reason that he cannot do the work of his employment role effectively) and he has equal difficulty in fulfilling the demands of his convener role.

Many honest men of goodwill would refuse such a position. A 'highly charged' individual might find it attractive (I am not saying that all conveners are 'highly charged') but one is scarcely likely to find men who are really interested in their work role agreeing to be elected to the role of convener if they have to try to do both jobs at once. Managers often say that the views held by the generality of employees differ from those of the employees' representatives. This may or may not be true. But if it is, one reason would be the denial of reasonable facilities to representatives.

Most attempts to set up institutions within which communication, consultation, negotiation and all the other processes of discussion between power on the one hand, and management authority on the other, have been quite inadequate. For example, what is the meaning of a joint consultation body composed of equal numbers of managers and representatives, whose terms of reference exclude the discussion of wages and salaries? That was the original form of joint consultation bodies, and still continues in some companies. The 'sides' are balanced because majority voting is implied. But everybody realizes that if six managers and one representative outvoted five representatives, the decision could have no real meaning.

Then there are the arrangements for discussion and negotiation (which exist in many employment hierarchies) whereby official representatives of the lower strata are recognized, but representatives of other strata are not, because they are regarded as 'part of management'. This particular confusion is due to a failure to recognize that every person in an employment hierarchy has another role in a representative system, either as a voter or as a representative. Talking as a manager, a specialist, a clerk or a technologist, he will hold one set of views. Talking as a member of one stratum of a representative system, he will express another. By attempting to deny the existence of representative roles in the middle and upper strata of hierarchies, management is depriving itself of the means of discovering the consensus of opinion in these strata. This leaves behind feelings of frustration caused by lack of participation. Deprived of feedback about opinion, managements embark on changes that are not acceptable and tensions build up. Middle or even senior management personnel who are *chosen* by the chief executive to sit on joint consultation bodies as 'representatives' of *middle* management are not real representatives. They cannot speak freely but must adhere strictly to the policy of the chief executive. They serve no clear function at all.

The essential need is for institutions that show clearly that employees in their representative roles have real power to inhibit policies to which they object, and to influence change. (They can *inhibit* change proposed by others but they cannot necessarily enforce change on others, because this brings them face to face with other power-groups.)

De jure, shareholders can inhibit change and force change. *De facto* they can only inhibit change, because the attempt to force change brings them up against customer and employee power and they may not achieve their aims. But all the processes through which share-holders set about putting their power to work have been considered over hundreds of years. The institutions they use are defined in law and in articles of association (see, for example, the precise rules under which the chairman at a meeting of shareholders is empowered to take a vote first but must move to a poll, which takes account of the weight of individual shareholdings, if a single shareholder calls for one). The company secretary is one of the more highly paid members of the company. The resources of the company lawyers, accountants, and his own staff are at his disposal.

The decisions made at shareholders' meetings must, by law, be very carefully minuted and available to all shareholders. If a change in the articles of association is agreed, then the new articles must be printed and registered with Company House. It is a very sophisti-cated process.

Compared to this the arrangement for sealing an agreement with the employee power-group is makeshift. Agreements are often sketchily and vaguely recorded and employees seldom have access to them. The research resources used to discover the facts and present them are limited. The representatives often have to do all their work in their spare time or steal time during working hours. And, as I have already pointed out, the secretary of the central committee of repre-sentatives seldom has even an office from which to work.

This failure to institutionalize the interaction of the employment hierarchy with the representative system in a rational way results in muddle and confusion within the company. There is resentment by managers of representative activities, and vice versa. There are negotiations that take place in an atmosphere of unreasoning hos-tility: each system fears dominance by the other. There is polariza-tion of all views on any topic into two factions of 'for' or 'against'— and representatives sometimes resort to the use of power on the slightest pretext. Shareholders behave quite differently because there are time-honoured institutions, routines and procedures for dealing with every contingency.

Explicit institutions are not a cure-all, but they constitute an essential step towards the generation of an atmosphere that allows reason to take the place of hostility.

In the next chapter I shall discuss the nature of representative systems, and in chapter nineteen I shall attempt to describe the type of institution that is required if hostility and unreason are to be lessened at the management–representative interface.

CHAPTER SEVENTEEN

The Representative System

From *The Economist*, 26 November 1853

'*Sir—Some fifteen years ago I was involved in a strike of four months'*
duration and I suffered so much in pocket and in mind, that I directed my
attentions to the feelings by which the factory workers of Lancashire
were actuated. The result of my study and investigation resulted in a plan
which I have invariably adopted from that time to the present with perfect
success. . . . In each of our works I selected two of the steadiest and
most intelligent of the workers, as a medium of communication with the
hands and the firm, stating to them our willingness at all times to receive
any communication from the hands through them. . . . By having a
sort of tribunal to resort to, conducted on rational principles, we have
been . . . free from the injurious influence of paid dictators, and our hands
have had the full benefit of their own industry. Now you will see sir, that
the above plan presents many advantages. One is, there can be no angry
contentions going on without a speedy adjustment. Another is, that
any person employed knows that any reasonable requirement will be laid
before the employers, and receive due consideration. . . .

Yours most respectfully

A Cotton Spinner'

IN OUR LIVES we all inhabit many roles and there is never a time
when we do not inhabit several at the same time—father, uncle,
citizen, employee, member of some social or leisure committee. But
always, if we are employed, we are also a member of the representative system, that exists side by side with the employment hierarchy
in which we have a work role.

A representative system comprises constituents, constituencies,
representatives, and elected committees. These systems exist, whether
they are recognized or not, wherever some people take on the task of
voicing the views of others. Any experienced manager can detect the

activity of informal systems in operation. People will approach him and tell him that there is feeling about this or that issue. There are nearly always such unofficial spokesmen wherever informality rules.

There is a contrast between the relationship of a person to his manager (or to the manager of his extended command) in his role as an employee, and in his role as a representative.

When he states an opinion in his employee role he is held accountable for that opinion. If he makes the same statement in his representative role he cannot be held accountable, for it cannot be assumed that the opinion is his own. Supposing he says that his manager is untruthful. In his employee role he is in trouble. In his representative role he is conveying to his manager information of importance. The fact that some members of a manager's extended command believe this of their manager is a serious matter, and calls for a discussion to clear the air.

A person can be de-selected from his employment role by his manager. A manager cannot, however, tell a group of constituents that they must elect someone else to represent them because he (the manager) is taking action that will oblige their representative to have to look for work elsewhere in the hierarchy or even outside the company.[1] A manager can criticize or praise a person in his employee role but not in his representative role. That is the responsibility of his constituents.

A manager may learn from a representative that militant action is being planned by members of his extended command which, in the manager's view, is based on a misunderstanding. The manager may explain this to the representative, but he cannot instruct him to tell his constituents of what he (the manager) regards as the facts of the situation. It is the manager's responsibility to explain to people, in their employee roles, the nature of his plans and intentions.

When a manager is negotiating with representatives he must bear in mind that the views they express are not necessarily their personal views. The representatives may indeed be voicing attitudes that seem foolish to them personally, because their task is to voice the views of

---

[1] 'The management have been urging the men to appoint new representatives and shop-stewards—(only five of the original 29 shop-stewards have got their jobs back) but in some cases the men have refused to do so as their elected representatives have not been re-employed. In one instance the press operators were told by their foreman . . . to select a representative. . . . The men reaffirmed that their elected representative Mr X, one of those not re-employed, was still in office as far as they were concerned.'—*The Observer*, 17 December 1961.

their constituents. In such circumstances, if a representative is personally criticized for what he says, he will be understandably angry. The representative speaks on behalf of an unnamed person or persons. All that the manager knows is that what the representatives says is the opinion of the whole or part of his command. The anonymity of all communications reaching managers through the representative system contrasts with the openness of communications from the employment hierarchy. The manager can insist on knowing the individual source of these latter. He would be unable to do his job without knowing this. The representative, on the other hand, would be unable to do *his* job if he had to disclose the names of those of his constituents who had expressed views.

A manager will sometimes feel that the views expressed by a representative are inconsistent with what he believes to be the consensus of opinion in his command. If the manager's assessment is correct then the representative is failing his constituents. But a manager who tells a representative that he is failing to observe the terms of his election is usurping the function of those who elected the representative. Suppose, for example, that representatives have made proposals for some change that is not only unacceptable to a manager but also runs counter to his strong intuition (based possibly on the comments of individuals) that this particular change is not wanted by most of the people in his extended command; what is the manager's proper course? I suggest that if the issue is important enough he should meet his extended command *en masse*[1] and make the following type of statement.

'You seek the following change in working conditions. . . . I have called you together to state why I find this change unacceptable, as follows. . . .' It is possible that some members of his command may say: 'You say that we want such and such a change; that is not so; we are pressing for something different.' The manager's appropriate reply would be: 'If you feel that your representatives are not presenting your views accurately, that is a matter between you and them, it is not my business.' Such a discussion may well result in constituents calling their representative to account. I know of instances where this has happened.

This rather formal language is necessary because the discussion must be precise. The language may sound unrealistic. Many may feel that in the hurly-burly of the discussion between a factory manager and shop-stewards, there is often much tension, and little

---

[1] I realize the current difficulties of doing so, but I shall discuss the resolution of these difficulties in the next chapter.

time for thinking in such terms, and that if a manager talks like this no one will understand him. This is not necessarily so. Representatives know their roles much better than most managers realize. Many managers have never been representatives themselves and they lack the 'feel' of the job. I have spoken to a meeting of my extended command and have said: 'You believe so and so to be the case. . . .' The words were scarcely out of my mouth before a few people protested that this was not so. I rejoined: 'Your representatives have stated that those are your views; do you want me to disbelieve them? If I do so how am I to learn what views you hold? . . . If what they have told me is incorrect then that is a matter between you and your representatives and I must leave you to sort the matter out, but I am going to accept what they say as being correct until they alter it. Do you want it otherwise?'[1] There is not, I think, anything unrealistic about that.

There is a real need for managers, and particularly chief executives, to realize that the activities of representatives are not unavoidable manifestations of the unruly spirit of modern man. Managers must comprehend and accept that these are essential social mechanisms whose existence is vital if anarchy is to be avoided. If outlets do not exist through which the views of masses of people can be expressed (and on the basis of which discussion and negotiation with managers can take place), then rising feelings of frustration and anger will lead to explosive use of power. Indiscipline and strikes are not usually caused by representatives (as so many assume) but by the absence of satisfactory institutions through which the power–authority relation between representative systems and management can be mediated. Formalized representative systems are essential to the setting up of satisfactory institutions. (I shall describe the form they could take in a later chapter.)

Certainly some representative systems exist that permit corruption

---

[1] The actual occasion was in a subsidiary factory, which was in a development area. There was much unemployment in the area. Representatives came to assume that the company planned to close the factory in due course. (The opposite was the case.) I do not know of any precise result flowing from my comments to the factory, though I did notice that there were some new faces among those elected as representatives at the next election.

The value of managers commenting in the way I have described is to reinforce the idea that it is the job of *constituents* to make sure that their representative voice *their* views, and not views that are personal to the representative.

in their election processes,[1] whose members do not understand their responsibilities, which fail to maintain appropriate contact with constituents, and which are obsessed with the idea that the only way to resolve difficulties is by the use of power. Such systems exist because there has been too little study of the nature of social institutions. In the absence of realistic concepts and a common language, too few people at all levels within employment hierarchies consider it necessary to spend time and resources in considering the essential properties of sound representative systems.

People in employment ought to study their representative systems, to understand them, to insist on written constitutions, to adopt rules for elections and to learn how to use them. People will only gain confidence in their system by understanding its potentialities and its limitations and thus prevent anarchic behaviour by the few.

Managers can help this process forward by respecting representative systems as the important social mechanisms which they are. Many employers are very helpful to employees who take up roles in town councils and other external bodies. Yet the same hierarchies sometimes fail to treat representatives of their own employees with similar respect.

Shop-stewards and staff representatives must be allowed time to carry out their tasks. What they have to do on behalf of constituents must be regarded as equal in importance to their employment roles. People who are elected as representatives have taken on unpaid work on behalf of others that is often onerous and thankless; if managers add to this burden by showing misunderstanding and lack of respect,

---

[1] Though people do not seem to realize the enormous improvements in behaviour which have taken place. Contrast present moves with those exemplified in this extract from a letter written by a certain Antony Henley to his constituents, which appeared in *The Shrewsbury Chronicle* of 12 November 1774. The letter was a reply by Mr Henley to a request from his constituents to oppose the Excise Bill, which was before Parliament:

'Gentlemen—I received yours and am surprised at your insolence in troubling me about the Excise. You know what I very well know, that I bought you, and by G. . . . I am determined to sell you.

And I know what perhaps you think I do not know, you are now selling yourselves to somebody else. And I know what you do not know, that I am buying another borough.

May G. . . .'s curse light upon you all. May your houses be as open and common to all Excise officers as your wives and daughters were to me, when I stood for your rascally corporation.'

then small wonder, at times, if only 'hotheads' are prepared to become elected representatives.

I often told the whole of my extended command that the representative system was vitally important to the company; that representatives were to be treated with dignity and courtesy; that (under procedures that had been worked out) managers were obliged to give them contact with their constituents; that the use of canteens for representatives to meet their constituents was to be permitted; that if feelings were running high over some problem it was much better to stop work for a brief period so that representatives could meet constituents and managers could meet representatives. More strikes are prevented by representatives than were ever started by them.

Such statements caused much shaking of heads among some of the older managers, but these rules led to a responsible, well-informed body of representatives and to discussions between them and managers which were governed by reason and not by emotion.

In British history the Crown or the Executive has often treated members of Parliament with contempt. This always led to strife. The situation of representatives in employment hierarchies is not precisely analogous, but the parallel is close enough to illustrate the stupidity of some of the attitudes to representative systems that now exist in employment hierarchies.

There are representatives and trade-union officials who are obsessed by power, and they represent a grave problem to the managements of some companies. But despair will not solve the problems. The demagogues are supported and maintained in the power positions that they achieve by masses of employees who give support to them out of ignorance, confusion and (sometimes) out of despair. The industrial demagogues' progress would be much more difficult if companies devoted a quarter of the resources they now give (for example) to marketing, to the study of social institutions such as the representative system; to helping trade unions to organize such systems more efficiently within the factory; to helping representatives to do their jobs competently; and to educating their own employees in the nature of the representative system of which they are a part. The constitution of the Representative System at Glacier, which was adopted by the representatives, is a good example of the kind of approach that I feel is needed.

Constitution of a Representative System

Conditions governing the Election of Representatives

(1) Each member who is eligible to vote shall vote only for those members standing for election in his own constituency or electoral unit.

  1.1 Each factory shall be divided into electoral units, and each electoral unit shall have a representative committee. The boundaries of the electoral units of a factory shall be defined or approved by the Works Council of that factory.

  1.2 Each electoral unit may be divided into constituencies according to administrative convenience, for the purpose of electing representatives to the representative committee. The boundaries of any constituency shall be defined by the representative committee of the electoral unit within which the constituency is created.

  1.3 Where constituencies are sufficiently large, they may be divided into sub-constituencies, each of which will elect representatives to a constituency representative committee.

  1.4 Any sector of the Operating Organizations not below unit status may have its own legislative body. The definition of electoral units and constituencies shall be a matter for decision by the members of the sector.

(2) The members of each electoral unit shall have the right to determine the conditions of franchise in the constituencies comprising the electoral unit, subject to the following conditions:

  2.1 Conditions governing the franchise shall be determined by a referendum of all those within the electoral unit who are eligible to vote, provided that not less than two-thirds of the valid votes are in favour of the conditions.

  2.2 No member shall be disfranchised unless he has a reasonable opportunity to enfranchise himself should he wish to do so.

  2.3 Where a constituency contains disfranchised members, the elected representatives of that unit shall, in acting for the constituency, act also on behalf of the disfranchised members.

  2.4 Because the structure of representative committees is of vital importance to the efficient running of the Operating Organizations, any proposal for the amendment of conditions of election or constitution of a representative body should, wherever possible, be the subject of discussion between the responsible manager and the representative body.

Rights and Responsibilities of Constituents

(3) Each in his role as constituent:

3.1 Has rights to participate in the election of his representatives in accordance with the regulations laid down in each electoral unit.

3.2 Should co-operate with his representative and the other members of his constituency in deciding the general lines to be followed by his representative when discussing policy.

3.3 Should, as far as possible, vest representative authority in his elected representative.

3.4 Must accept the consequences of not keeping himself informed about those aspects of policy which are likely to affect him.

3.5 Must accept the executive actions arising out of and consistent with the policies which his representative agrees on his behalf.

3.6 Should pass to his representative any information which will enable his representative to be aware of the main interests of his constituents, including special interests such as Trade Union interests where these exist.

3.7 May seek advice on an executive matter from his representative at any time, but may only seek action through his representative if he has first taken the matter up with the member concerned and has been unable, after a reasonable time, to obtain satisfaction.

Responsibilities of Elected Representatives

(4) A representative is accountable to that constituent group or electoral unit which elects him; and it is his responsibility:

4.1 To make himself aware of the main interests of all in his constituency.

4.2 To represent the point of view of his constituents in committees and Councils, even where this may mean presenting a point of view contrary to his own personal opinion or his view in his executive role.

4.3   To allow Councils or committees to work with the greatest possible realism by judging when to state any views held by minorities within his constituency or committee.

4.4   To judge when reference to constituents is necessary, and when to accept responsibility for acting without such reference.

4.5   To initiate proposals for change which would be in the best interests of his constituents.

4.6   To take appropriate steps when in his judgement executive actions or the actions of his constituents are inconsistent with policy.

4.7   To assist his constituents to understand the executive implications of the agreements he has accepted on their behalf.

4.8   To familiarize himself with the Constitution and Standing Orders of those bodies of which he is a member and with established rules of procedure.

4.9   To know policy, and in particular to understand those aspects of policy which are of most immediate concern to his constituents.

4.10 To ensure, before taking up an appeal with and on behalf of a constituent, that the constituent has in the first instance taken the matter up with the manager concerned.

4.11 To act as adviser to any of his constituents in cases of appeal when requested to do so.

Responsibilities of Committees

5.1   To serve the best interests of their constituents by arriving at conclusions which take account of the facts of the case and possible implications for the future.

5.2   To decide when reference to their constituents is necessary, and the means by which this reference should be made.

5.3   To meet as soon as reasonably possible at the request of their constituents or of the manager accountable for their constituents.

5.4   To determine, when questioning Management's implementation of policy or when taking up some difference of viewpoint, whether they are questioning the manner in which the policy is being interpreted or the policy itself.

5.5   To frame constitutions for regulating their conduct.

Subsequent to the adoption of this general constitution the various strata of employees drew up and recorded constitutions governing the committees of which representatives became members upon election. I quote also the constitution of the shop-stewards' committee of one factory.

(1) TITLE   The Committee shall be known as 'The Glacier (London Factories) Works Committee'.

(2) SCOPE   The scope of discussions shall cover any reasonable subject.

(3) FUNCTIONS   The functions of the Committee shall be:

(*a*) to provide a channel of communication between Shop Committees and the factory council,

(*b*) to provide a direct channel of communication between Company members and the Management,

(*c*) to provide machinery for the joint consideration of such matters affecting members and the Company as may be suitable for joint discussion.

(*d*) to provide the means for constructive co-operation in obtaining efficiency and the comfort of those employed by the Company.

(4) COMPOSITION   The Committee shall consist of:

Shop Stewards from each Shop Committee of the London Factories elected by each Committee in meeting.

(5) MEMBERS TO RETIRE ANNUALLY   Those who serve on the Works Committee shall be members of the Committee by virtue of their election as Shop Stewards to Shop Committees and by virtue of their election by Shop Committees to the Works Committee. Because of these annual elections, all members of the Works Committee shall therefore retire annually each January, with the exception of the Secretary and the Chairman elect.

(6) FAILURE TO ATTEND MEETINGS   Should a member without reasonable excuse fail to attend three consecutive meetings of the Works Committee, he shall be deemed to have retired.

(7) VOTE OF NO CONFIDENCE IN COMMITTEE   Shoud 75% of the Union Group of a Department which elected as a Shop Steward a member serving on the Works Committee present a petition calling on that member to resign, and provided that such petition clearly discloses the reason for such a request, and

provided that the Works Committee, after investigation find that the reasons put forward are substantial, then such a member shall resign his seat on the works committee. Such a member shall be at liberty to stand for re-election, provided that in the opinion of the Works Committee he is not guilty of such conduct such as to cause them to veto his nomination, by a majority of 75% of Works Committee members in meetings.

(8) ARREARS IN UNION SUBSCRIPTION   Should a member of the Committee be found to be in arrears with Union subscriptions, provided that he is in arrears within the meaning of the barring clause of his particular Union rules, he shall resign from the Committee.

(9) QUORUM   A majority of the members of the Committee shall form a Quorum at any meeting.

(10) OFFICERS   *Chairman.* The Chairman shall be elected by the Committee from members of the Works Committee at the first meeting to be held after the 31st August in each year. He shall hold office for twelve months from 1st January in each year, and shall be eligible for re-election. He shall be ex-officio a member of Works Committee for his period of office.

Vice-Chairman. A Vice-Chairman shall be elected from amongst members of the Works Committee by that Committee at its first meeting in February and shall retire annually, being eligible for re-election. The retiring Vice-Chairman shall continue to hold office whether or not re-elected to Works Committee until the new Vice Chairman takes office.

Secretary (see Appendix)

Steering Committee. The Secretary, Chairman and Vice-Chairman shall form the Steering Committee of the Works Committee. Their responsibility will be to co-ordinate the work of the Works Committee and of any sub-committee which it sets up, and to take such action on behalf of the Committee as shall be necessary between meetings. Any action taken shall be subject to ratification by the Committee at its next meeting.

(11) MEMBERSHIP OF WORKS COUNCIL   The Chairman, Vice-Chairman and Secretary shall, by virtue of their office, be members of the London Factories Works Council, together with four other members of the Works Committee, who shall be elected by the Committee at the first meeting in January of each year. Included in the total of seven members there shall be at least one representative of each of the following Trade Unions.

Transport and General Workers' Union

Electrical, Electronics & Telecommunications—Plumbers Trade Union

Amalgamated Union of Engineering & Foundry Workers

Draughtsmen and Allied Technicians Association

(12) ELECTION PROCEDURES All elections of Shop Stewards to Shop Committees shall be organized by the Works Committee, who shall appoint a Returning Officer and Scrutineers for this purpose. The Committee may ask the Management to lend such assistance in this task as circumstances dictate. The validity of voting papers shall be decided by the Returning Officer, whose decision concerning all matters in connection with the election shall be final.

The Works Committee shall have power to fix from time to time the basis upon which the hourly-rated personnel of the Company shall be grouped for the purpose of election of Shop Committees, and shall be generally responsible through their Secretary for maintaining the work, numbers and activities of such Shop Committees, in accordance with the Constitution of Shop Committees.

(13) MEETINGS The Committee shall normally meet at least once in every month of the year, and more often as may be deemed necessary.

(14) EXTRAORDINARY MEETINGS The Chairman and/or the Secretary shall have power to convene or cause to be convened Extraordinary Meetings should such meetings be considered necessary.

(15) AGENDA All items for discussion at Works Committee shall be sent to the Secretary in writing at least three working days prior to a meeting, in order to enable him to compile an Agenda for circulation to members.

(16) VOTING Questions that arise in meetings of the Committee shall be decided by a simple majority of votes. The Chairman shall have a vote and a casting vote in the event of a tie.

(17) MINUTES Minutes shall be kept of all proceedings. Minutes of meetings that have by agreement of the Committee been signed by the Chairman shall be final and unalterable.

(18) PAYMENT TO MEMBERS Payment to members shall be made in accordance with the Report of the General Purposes Committee adopted by the Works Council at the 112th Meeting, or as subsequently amended by Council. Members of the Works Committee who work on night shift are permitted, by

arrangement with Management, to leave the factory before the end of the shift and will be compensated for any loss of earnings arising.

(19) AMENDMENTS TO THE CONSTITUTION Proposed amendments to the Constitution, so long as the Union/Management Agreement of which this Constitution is a part is not infringed, must be given in the form of a written notice to the Secretary, and be handed to him not less than seven clear days before the meeting at which the amendment is to be discussed. Such an amendment must receive a 75% vote of the Works Committee members in meeting, in order to be passed.

WORKS COMMITTEE SECRETARY

(1) ELIGIBILITY Any Trade Union member of the factories is eligible for election.

(2) NOMINATIONS Any Trade Union member of the factories may nominate candidates for the position. Such nominations, after having received the endorsement of the appropriate Trade Union, must reach the Steering Committee of the Works Committee 14 days prior to the meeting at which election is to take place. The Steering Committee to forward these nominations to Management for their comments.

(3) ELECTION Election shall be by the members of the Works Committee in duly constituted meeting.

(4) TERM OF OFFICE The Secretary shall hold office for two years from the date of his election.

(5) CONDITIONS OF OFFICE
(a) The position shall be a full-time position.
(b) The Secretary shall be accountable to the Works Committee during his term of office, subject at all times to rules and policies governing the members of the London Factories.
(c) Works Committee shall determine his activities. He shall make himself reasonably available for discussions with Management. If on any specific occasion there are conflicting demand from Management and from Works Committee upon his time, the Secretary shall decide which of those demands shall on that occasion take precedence. If either the Managing Director or the Works Committee consider that the Secretary is not giving the correct precedence, or if the Secretary finds himself in difficulty over deciding precedences a meeting shall be arranged between the Managing Director

(or his nominee) and the Works Committee Steering Committee to discuss the difficulties and to work out appropriate terms of reference.

(*d*) Payment shall be made by the Company, on a staff basis, commencing at a rate which will provide the Secretary with an income equivalent to that which he was earning at the time of his election.

(*e*) The Secretary shall receive National and Glacier awards, and shall be not less favourably treated in relation to other wage reviews taking place within the Company.

(*f*) The executive position of the Secretary shall be administered by the Personnel Divisional Manager for the Management Member of Council for items payable out of Management's account, and for purposes of payment of salary, notification of sickness and absence, and maintenance of premises.

(6) REINSTATEMENT ON VACATING OFFICE

(*a*) The Secretary, on vacating office, shall be given employment by the Company at a salary and in a status commensurate with his position at the time of vacating office.

(*b*) Reinstatement in an executive role shall if necessary be accompanied by a training period of not less than three months and not more than one year, during which the member's rate of pay shall be maintained.

(7) RETIREMENT

(*a*) The Secretary may resign from his position prior to the full term of office by giving one month's notice in writing to the Works Committee Chairman.

(*b*) The Secretary shall vacate his position at any time on the passing of a vote of 'No confidence' by a 75% majority in favour by Works Committee members in meeting.

(*c*) On vacating his position, whether by resignation or at the completion of his term of office, the Secretary shall, at the behest of the Committee, be prepared to carry on the duties of the office in concert with the newly-elected Secretary for the first month of office of the new Secretary, being paid by the Company during this period of one month.

Those constitutions, along with much else to which I shall refer later, are included in a handbook of which each representative has a copy. A copy is available in every department. The salient points contained within this handbook are explained to every new employee.

There is, of course, no guarantee that constitutions will be observed. But unless they exist there is no standard of behaviour to which anybody who wants to contribute to a well-ordered system can conform; without a constitution there is no standard against which even the grossest of deviations can be compared. Everybody is at the mercy of the whims of others. These are the circumstances which cause people to lose trust in those whom they have elected. This creates situations where the opportunist can step in and cause confusion and strife.

I have seen the effects of building a representative system. It engendered a technical interest in form and procedure and pride in something achieved. People value constitutions that they have helped to build. They are jealous of those who attempt to ride rough-shod through their provisions. It is important to stimulate such feelings by encouraging the building of explicit social institutions, for these are the basis of order and justice.

Representative systems are incomplete unless they include the higher levels of the hierarchy. In small employment hierarchies managers, specialists, accountants, or even clerical workers, feel close to the chief executive and often identify themselves with 'the management'. To them the idea of electing representatives seems unnecessary or even repugnant. As hierarchies grow, however, various strata and, indeed, groups within strata, grow their own identities and begin to think about their own position as a group distinct from others. This is a modern phenomenon. The evidence for it is the emergence of militant representatives of many of our professions. Many trade unions are now recruiting members in strata of hierarchies where thirty years ago the idea would have been rejected.

In the light of these changes (and of all that I have said about representative systems) the ideal must be to formalize the representation of all strata. Everybody in a hierarchy will then have the experience of taking part formally in the election of their representative. This means that management has an assured feedback of information about the feelings of all strata and it promotes the expression of views which, if suppressed, are liable to fester. But there are even stronger reasons for the completion of a formalized representative system. The institution that is required to mediate the power–authority relations between the representative system and the employment hierarchy must be all-embracing. It is impossible to leave out of such an institution representatives of some employees, whoever they are. They cannot appear as 'management representatives' (as is so often the case in 'joint consultation' arrangements). It is possible to reach an agreement about changes with part of a representative system, but this partial agreement does not necessarily endow management with the necessary authority to implement the changes. (I shall pursue these arguments in a later chapter.)

In Britain (at any rate) managers or personnel specialists of large employment hierarchies usually discuss contentious matters with trade-union officers on the assumption that the officers' views represent the views of the employees. But the truth is that problems are sometimes discussed in artificial terms and agreements are reached that do not satisfy the wishes of those affected. This is a serious problem and can lead to the rejection of agreements between union officials and managers that have been settled and signed. When these agreements are later breached by the man in the plant, the managers will criticize them bitterly. This is another example of the results of confused thinking. The only people who can choose representatives are constituents. Discussions between managers and union officers should take place only at the request of plant representatives. Union officers are the servants of trade-union members, not their masters. Meetings between union officials and managers that have not been prompted and promoted by plant representatives can appear to men on the shop floor as a sort of unholy collusion. This practice alone can sometimes cause an unofficial strike.

Many very large companies make a practice of negotiating changes in conditions of work not with representatives elected directly by their own employees, but with national trade-union officials. Some national agreements laying down procedures for the settlements of disputes tend to suggest this course of action. The companies that do this do not always appreciate that the procedure they use can be construed as a sort of 'slap in the face' for their own employees' representatives. It is possible for this to lead to attitudes such as: 'What's the use of electing representatives if the negotiation is always done by others?' 'Why take a lot of trouble to select the right representatives if, at the vital stage of decision, they are not "in the picture"?' or, 'Why take all the kicks and criticism that fall on a representative if one is consistently left out of the picture when the crunch comes?' People who are elected carry great responsibility and are exposed to much criticism for no economic gain. Unless they gain status and a sense of taking a full part in an important democratic process they will have no feeling of achievement.

It seems to me that managers who are thinking of making changes ought to insist on meeting those persons elected by the employees who would be affected by the changes, unless—but only unless— those representatives specifically request that a union officer should negotiate on their behalf. This is not to suggest that general discussions should not take place between trade-union officers and managers at any time at the request of either. But the elected representatives of groups of employed people have rights to negotiate on behalf of their constituents, which must not be flouted.

CHAPTER EIGHTEEN

Communication by Contraction

I HAVE ALREADY described 'contraction' as a communication issued by a manager that is applicable not only to his immediate command but also to members of his extended command. I may have caused some of my managerial readers to feel that I am unrealistic in even envisaging a manager meeting a mass of employees because of the objections that would immediately be raised by the employees' representatives. There are certainly difficulties, but I believe they can be overcome by a rational analysis of what managerial contraction really implies.

Let me describe first a typical industrial situation. I shall hope to show how contraction might have helped to resolve it; and I shall describe how one company overcame the objections to contraction by forging, with representatives, certain policies that were able to govern and regulate such managerial action.

The company is nearing the completion of some large contracts. New ones for somewhat different types of work have been negotiated and this new work is about to be put into production. These changes in work-load entail alterations in plant, tooling, reorganization of departments, switching of men from one department to another, change of type of work for a proportion of the work force, etc. Details of the way in which the changes are to take place begin filtering down the employment hierarchy. Considerable anxiety is already beginning to build up, and this is exacerbated by the usual rumours that there will be a pay-off and that wage rates will be affected.

Representatives of those affected ask to see the Plant Manager, and a meeting takes place. The Plant Manager explains in detail the changes that are planned and their effect on jobs, pay and conditions. The representatives refuse to accept some of the changes and propose others. A state of disagreement emerges.

The meeting closes and the representatives go back to their constituents, discuss the situation and, in the light of their discussions about what the Plant Manager has told them, formulate a series of demands. The Plant Manager, concerned about the apparent resistance to changes that he feels are reasonable and necessary, reconsiders the whole situation, sees the General Manager in charge of manufacturing and decides, with his concurrence, to put forward a modified plan in an attempt to reach an amicable settlement.

A second meeting of Management and Representatives is arranged and the Plant Manager puts forward his compromise plan in precise terms. The representatives say they will consider it and sound out their people about it.

At a third meeting the representatives state that even the compromise plan is quite unacceptable, and threaten strike action unless their original demands are met. These, to the Plant Manager, seem quite unrealistic. He also feels that to accept them would seriously weaken the authority of management, because if he gives way in the face of threats of strike action, the threat to use force will be used again and again in the future. The next day there is a strike and the plant stops.

A number of significant characteristics (which seem to be fairly common to most strike situations) now begin to emerge:

(a) There is considerable reluctance among many operatives to walk out.

(b) Many operatives have no clear idea about the purpose of the strike. They would have stayed at work had it not been for the fact that, whereas stopping work would have merely meant loss of pay, staying at work as a minority might have meant catastrophe for them.

(c) They know that there have been discussions with management but know little of the compromise offered. In view of the rumours about pay-offs or transfer to less acceptable work, they rationalize their doubts about the situation by assuming that because their representatives have called for strike action, management must be trying to put something over which is not to their advantage.

Eventually, higher management, in meetings with trade-union officers, works out some further modification to the original plan. The strike ends, but everybody has lost a week's wages or more, and the company has lost a lot of output.

There are many reasons for this sort of sequence of events—the previous labour-relations history in the plant, the personalities of managers and representatives, the actual details of the plans and of the proposals made about them, etc. There is, however, one source of the trouble that is seldom seriously considered, and this involves the notion of contraction. Why did the chief executive not speak to all the employees?

In strike situations like this managers often say:

'The Company's proposals are thoroughly reasonable—nobody is going to have a raw deal. The trouble is that you can't rely on shop-stewards to present them accurately or fairly to the labour force. Every time there is a strike in this plant it is because people have a completely unrealistic picture of Management's intentions. We need representatives who will convey proposals accurately to the rest, instead of these fellows with chips on their shoulders who distort everything we say.'

Let us go back to the second meeting, where the Plant Manager presented his compromise proposal. This proposal was a contraction communication. It was addressed to an entire stratum of his extended command at a level separated from him by his superintendents and foremen. There were two courses open to him. He could have made his proposals clear to his immediate command (his superintendents) and instructed them to see that they were communicated equally clearly *in his name* to each operator whom they affected. Or, he could have stopped the plant for half an hour and presented his proposals in person. This would have given every operator an opportunity to ask questions and thus to clarify the proposal. But the Plant Manager did neither of these things; *he relied on representatives to convey his message for him.*

I believe that thousands of situations occur each year in major employment hierarchies that are mishandled in this way. In each case there is a strong argument for the manager (whose command embraces the entire sector of the hierarchy affected) to 'contract' and to speak personally to the members of his extended command in their role as employees.

Industry relies largely on the ability of representatives to be impartial reporters and, in doing so, industry usually makes a mistake. It is uncommon for managers of large extended commands even to consider calling a meeting of their command to explain what is or is not going to happen. Talking directly to workers appears to be an approach to real problems that is not even considered or, if considered, is dismissed. There are a few dramatic examples of chief executives establishing contact with the rank and file (to the very great advantage of relations in general)[1] but such examples do not seem to have had much effect in persuading others to follow suit.

I am interested in the reasons for this unrealistic behaviour. One, I think, is the extent to which we unconsciously model our industrial behaviour on the democratic nature of our social life. If a government wants its proposals to be discussed and commented upon, it submits them to representatives of the people—members of Parliament, county councils, town councils, and others. Government proposals are routed through representative systems. This is appropriate. But what managers overlook is that our social life is different from our working life. We are born into the role of citizen or constituent, with the eventual right and responsibility to choose a government and to elect representatives who form a legislature. This legislature and government not only make laws but appoint and control the executive systems that put the laws into practice. But governments are not the employers of citizens, and managers are. That is the difference and that is why managers must behave differently in this respect from government.

Industry is very different. We decide individually to contract into an employee role. We undertake to carry out the instructions of a manager and the policy of the company in return for specified pay and conditions. Having assumed an employee role we take on another role as a constituent and also, perhaps, as a representative, but we lose these latter roles when we lose our executive position. There is an important distinction between social and industrial situations. All I want to make clear is that they are not analogous and that therefore industrial democracy (if the term means anything) is not another form of political democracy, but a completely different thing. Personally I think that the use of the term 'industrial democracy" should be dropped, because it can only lead to confusion. It implies that the mechanisms of association in political and industrial life are the same, and they are not.

The second reason for not talking directly to employees is compounded of fear and confusion. The fear is often simply that

---

[1] The late Sir Charles Bartlett, Chairman of Vauxhall Motors, and Lord Robens, Chairman of the National Coal Board, are just two examples that come to mind. Field-Marshal Montgomery and the late Field-Marshal Slim are two examples of Army Commanders who realized the importance of contraction—though they did not use the word.

engendered by talking straight to a large body of people who may be in a somewhat emotional state. The confusion arises from the lack of a precise idea of the purpose of such a meeting and of anxiety about the prospect of arguing with hundreds of people simultaneously.

It is a great pity that these inhibitions should exist. They are largely unreal. Senior managers in industry are often unpopular figures not because of what they really are as personalities, but because they remain unknown quantities to the rank and file if they never talk to them. If you are an unknown quantity people can project into their image of you all the negative ideas that the ordinary anxieties of life at work generate.

A third reason why managers fail to communicate directly with members of their extended command in stress situations is that union officers and shop-stewards are equally confused about the situation. Most representatives, on being informed by a senior manager that he will call his extended command together to inform them directly of his proposals, would object in vehement terms.

I have had experience of such objections from both shop-stewards and union officers. The conversations that have ensued have been on the following lines:

REPRESENTATIVES: If you talk in person to a general meeting of our members it will be a breach of accepted negotiating procedure. It is utterly illogical to negotiate with us who are elected to speak on behalf of our members and, at the same time, to discuss the issue with our members behind our backs. We are not going to allow it.

MANAGER: I must make certain that those who are responsible to me, and for whose work I am held responsible, will clearly understand the full import of my detailed proposals. There are two possible channels of communication: the first through the representative system, the second by speaking to a mass meeting. If you wish me to use the first, I must have some means of making certain not only that the precise communication I want to make reaches members of my extended command, but also that the answers to any questions about my proposals are the ones I would give myself. Now, to enable me to accomplish this end through the representative system involves certain safeguards. Are you prepared to agree to say to your constituents precisely what I tell you to say, to report back precisely any questions they ask, and to convey my answers to those questions in the form I give them? Furthermore, I must have some means of checking to make sure that you are carrying out my instructions precisely, and therefore I would have to insist that an observer, chosen by me, was present at your discussions to make certain that you reported with accuracy.

REPRESENTATIVES: That is a ridiculous suggestion. Shop-stewards can't take instructions from managers. Their job is to look after the people they represent and to defend them from managers. The idea of someone on the management side super-vising our discussions with our constituents is unthinkable.

MANAGER: Fair enough. I too agree that it is a ridiculous sugges-tion. I only wanted to demonstrate the complete impracticability of asking a manager to rely on representatives as a means of making his proposals clear to his own extended command. Do you, how-ever, agree that a manager must have at his disposal *some* means by which he can make quite certain that his specific proposals are understood by his extended command?

REPRESENTATIVES: Not necessarily. We don't understand what all the fuss is about. It is customary for managers to present pro-posals to representatives, and the extent to which the detail is conveyed to the rank and file is a matter for our judgement.

MANAGER: Well, now the cards are on the table. I am accountable to the Board for the operation of this company. If it is not operated efficiently, I am responsible and my career is at stake. If my poli-cies and plans are not communicated clearly and directly to those they affect, then they become the subject of speculation, rumour and distortion, and efficiency will suffer. I am sure you have all had plenty of experience of that. Yet you defend a situation in which I am to be denied free communication with my subordinates and must leave what is said to them to be the subject of your individual discretion. To be consistent you should equally try to deny me the right to post notices or to instruct my superintendents or foremen to speak directly to their commands.

REPRESENTATIVES: You don't understand our attitude. We are not objecting to a manager talking to his men; we are objecting to two sorts of negotiations going on at the same time: one with us, the men's representatives, and the other between you and all our constituents.

MANAGER: But I have no intention of negotiating with all of my extended command together. That would be impossible in such a large gathering. Negotiation involves two parties coming together, exchanging views, separating to consider what is in their best interests, modifying their attitudes, and coming together again. Such a process, repeated if necessary many times, eventually leads to proposals that are acceptable to both parties. If that is negotiation then it would be rendered impossible if it involved thousands or even hundreds of people. Representative systems are essential in large companies because they make negotiation of changes in conditions of work possible. If I were to attempt to negotiate with all the men at once, I would undermine the status of the representatives, and that would be detrimental to the company.

REPRESENTATIVES: Well, we are glad to know that you have some sense of realism about our function, but we are not yet satisfied. If our members start discussing a settlement of the problem with you when you meet them, then you cannot stop them. There is always an element of stupidity among those in a large meeting. They might well start on a process of negotiation with you along lines which are quite inconsistent with the long-term interests of the majority of our members.

MANAGER: *My* meeting will be with my subordinates in their role as employees, not in their role as your constituents. The meeting will be held in working hours and those present will be paid for the period of attendance. I shall then, as the Cross-over Point Manager,[1] issue a contraction instruction[2] to them to attend. You will also be present, but in your employee roles, not as representatives. The rest will not be there as constituents but as employees. I shall make it clear that the purpose of calling them together is to present my proposals and to have such questions and answers as are required to make them quite clear.

REPRESENTATIVES: But how can we be sure that the whole thing will not turn into one vast confused negotiation?

MANAGER: You will be present and I am prepared to sign an agreement with you which will preclude me from such mass negotiation. You will then be in a position, at such a meeting if things go wrong, to assume the role of representatives and draw attention to the breach of agreement.

This report is not verbatim, but contains the substance of points that were discussed at great length at many meetings. Out of these discussions a set of policies was drafted in a form that enabled them to be taught and understood by managers and representatives. Here is a summary of the policies that emerged.

---

[1] *Cross-over Point Manager* is the lowest-level manager whose extended command embraces all the employee roles involved.

[2] *Contraction instruction* is one issued by a manager to members of his extended command other than his immediate subordinates.

(1) New managerial plans and proposals can be elucidated directly if necessary by managers speaking to their extended commands by contraction.

(2) Negotiation will take place only at meetings between managers and representatives.

(3) The communication of the consensus of opinion of a group or stratum of employees in their role of constituents is the responsibility of representatives, who must pass it on to managers.

(4) A manager who communicates directly with his extended command to elucidate his plans is exceeding his authority if he uses the occasion to attempt to negotiate or to solicit views or information.

I believe that most experienced managers would regard these policies as unexceptional. There is nothing in them that would limit their authority or their use of their discretion, because to exceed the provisions of the policies would obviously be counter-productive. In fact, in most employment hierarchies policy (1) represents an extension of the authority of managers: in most industrial companies (and perhaps in other hierarchies) representatives would use power to prevent contraction by senior managers for the elucidation of their plans to the rank and file. Contraction could become an exceedingly important concept in the context of today's growing industrial unrest.

CHAPTER NINETEEN

Policy-making Works Councils

From *The Economist*, 14 April 1860

'THE CAUSES OF STRIKES

We have before informed our readers that a Committee of the Social Science Association has been for some months vigorously at work on . . . the practical causes and effects of Strikes. . . .

But while the Committee have found their inquiry much easier and smoother than they expected with regard to the men—they have certainly found it much more embarrassed and difficult than they expected with regard to the employers. Here,—with many honourable and praiseworthy exceptions—secret diplomacy had been perhaps the rule. . . . But the questions at issue between the employers of labour, and the combinations of labour, are questions of principle. . . . There is no peace, as yet,— there is only truce between capital and labour in this great country. All true men must wish this uncertain and inconsistant calm to be exchanged for a durable and well-founded peace. What better method can be adopted than to forward in any way the inquiries of such a Committee as that to which we have drawn attention? It belongs to neither party. It contains representatives of both parties, and many who belong to neither, and simply desire to attain the truth. It sincerely desires to bring to light the secret of the chronic strife between those whose interests, moral and material, are really identical. And when the inquiries of such a body are stopped with the traditional answer, 'Least said soonest mended', one inference, and but one, will be drawn by the public at large. They will say with some justice, that there is most real uneasiness where there is most secrecy. . . .'

THERE IS AN imperative need in developed industrial societies for institutions through which employees can participate in the formation of policies that affect them. Governments, employers and trade unions have been wrestling with this problem for a hundred years.

There was the wartime burst of enthusiasm for joint consultation, but this was no solution. Joint consultative 'committees', often containing equal numbers of 'management representatives' and employee representatives, were never viable institutions. Though they were called 'committees' this was not a true description. What would happen if one 'management representative' were to 'defect' and vote with the employee representatives to pass a motion unwelcome to management? Equally, if an employee representative had 'defected' and voted with management, employees would not have accepted the result.

In fact these bodies consisted of two teams. But all the members of each team were normally expected to vote in unison, and usually did. This is a recipe for deadlock. Most joint consultative bodies excluded from their terms of reference the right to discuss matters affecting payment; so that they could never discuss one of the central issues, which required the existence of some viable institution. It is sad that more objective thought was not given to the construction of a realistically based institution during the war, when the general acceptance of the need to co-operate made the introduction of change easier than it is today.

No doubt there are many instances in which advisory bodies of employee representatives have made a real contribution. But there is no institution in general use in employment hierarchies today that takes account of the existence of power-groups (as I have outlined them), or of the fact that managerial authority is derived from this power. It is thus essential to have a means to secure the sanction and backing of representative systems for new plans and policies. This sort of procedure is necessary if the plans are to be effectively carried out and if the authority of managerial roles is to be maintained.

Many of our larger employment hierarchies are now suffering from an increase in the use of aggressive power by representatives and from a progressive erosion of essential managerial authority. This will spread to smaller companies in due course unless more objective thinking is applied to the problem. The present situation is unrealistic These are some of the reasons why:

(1) Employees continue to feel that employment hierarchies are essentially autocratic systems within which managers can impose their will on subordinates.

(2) Though many groups of representatives have successfully used their power to defend the interests of their constituents (or at times to gain unjustified sectional benefits), most groups are still

on the defensive psychologically. They see themselves as defending the workers against exploitation.

Representatives of workers, and trade unions themselves, often seem not to appreciate the great change that has come over their position relative to that of the managements of companies. Instead of managements being able to impose their will upon workers, the reverse is now the case. They do not realize that their position is such that a management cannot take actions which run counter to the wishes of representatives. The result is that managerial authority to operate the employment hierarchy is now dependent upon the sanctioning of their plans and policies by representatives.

There is, for example, growing concern in trade-union circles about low efficiency, lack of investment and absence of initiative by the management of industrial companies. What unions fail to see is that there is a connection between these deficiencies and the erosion of managerial authority caused by the misuse of power by representative groups.

(3) Employees in general often bestow power on their representatives in a quite irresponsible way. They will go on doing this as long as they fail to appreciate that managers cannot, except in very unusual circumstances, force change upon them. Most people never realize how much power they wield when organized into closely co-ordinated representative groups. Too many people believe that the sacrifice they make when they go on strike is necessary to defend their position and, consequently, support their representatives in almost any display of power. It is rather like giving guns to people who do not appreciate that guns can be dangerous.

(4) Constituents in representative systems usually do not realize that when they choose representatives and back them, they are affecting the economic future of the hierarchy that employs them, and that of the economy as a whole.

They do not realize that many closures of companies, redundancies and locally high unemployment levels are partly due to the use of representative power to prevent essential changes.

(5) Thousands of people, who fail to attend trade-union meetings, who are not interested in the activities of their elected representatives in industry, who would refuse opportunities to become representatives themselves, talk about the need for more 'participation' or for more 'industrial democracy'. Repeated and often destructive examples of the use of the power of representative groups to disrupt supplies and services run side by side with a

failure to realize that this power can be used to insist on the 'increased participation' for which so many seem to yearn.

There is a general failure to realize that the ball is at their feet. This is because representative power is so often used to assert 'rights' and so seldom used to take part in the formation of constructive new policies, which help not only the company but also its employees.

(6) The best managerial policy from an administrative or technical point of view may prove much less successful if it arouses the employees' hostility than a policy which is not 'technically perfect' but which gains the support of those who have to implement it. This is an obvious statement. Nevertheless managers who feel that they must attempt what is, in their view 'best', repeat the same mistake again and again. Their repeated failure to discover the state of feeling in advance, leads employees to assume that managers are autocratic. The scene is then set. All managerial plans are questioned and the battle is on.

(7) A great many managers are hostile to representative systems. They fail to regard such systems as an essential element in the operation of employment hierarchies. Representatives feel slighted and undervalued and the scene is set for a trial of strength. If managers fail in taking active steps to make the real position clear to all employees, then nobody else will do it. Chief executives ought to make it clear to employees that, collectively, they have the power to block the plans and changes that are necessary to maintain the company as a going concern. They ought to say continuously, in one way or another, to employees: 'Collectively you have great power over this company; the way in which you use it will decisively affect the company's future and your own careers in it. Be careful how you use that power.' But instead, many chief executives regard representative systems as an unfortunate manifestation of presumption which could well be done without.

(8) The ethos of management is to regard the board of directors as the first source of policies, with the customer a good second. Managers realize that both shareholders and customers must consent to changes. But managers do not always think objectively about the third power-group, the representative system.

(9) There seems to be a sort of sub-conscious collusion between management, employees and representatives, to avoid recognizing and facing up to the real properties of the situation within which they all have to do their daily work. The result is that group

greed, constituent irresponsibility and managerial blindness reign.

My experience is that it is possible to break through to reality by setting up an institution in which management, carrying the sanction of the shareholder and customer power-groups, meets with the representative power-group to 'legislate' on problems and policies.

I have experience of setting up such institutions in the Glacier Metal Co Ltd. Its first form was established in 1941. Though from its inception it was based on unanimous voting, it contained defects, and was modified in 1949.

The 1949 councils were formed as follows:

(a) One was established in each geographical area where the company employed substantial numbers of people.
(b) Each consisted of the senior manager in the area, one representative of the most senior staff, two of middle stratum staff, three of the junior stratum of staff and seven representatives of hourly paid staff.
(c) Among the seven representatives of the hourly paid staff there had to be at least one shop-steward from each trade union with members in the factory.
(d) All representatives of hourly paid staff had to be union approved shop-stewards.

The various works councils of the Company, meeting together, established in writing not only the Council Constitution but also what is known as the Company Policy Document. This has been modified and brought up to date several times during the last twenty years. There are some important passages in this document about councils, which I quote.

> The broad purposes and legal constitution of the Company are laid down in the Memorandum and Articles of Association which govern the activities of the Shareholders and the Board of Directors.
>
> This document sets out the policy on individual duties and entitlements within which the Board of Directors, in consonance with Works Councils, directs that the Operating Organizations of the Company shall be governed. . . .
>
> This policy assumes that shareholders and members [employees] individually and collectively want to go to the very limit in trying to work out policies which are in the best interests of the Company and its members as a whole, and that they are willing to tolerate some shortcomings in policy in order to achieve this end. *These*

assumptions are embodied in the principle that Councils shall pursue their deliberations until they reach unanimous agreement. . . .

It is realized that when, after a serious attempt to reach unanimous agreement has been made, differences of viewpoint proved irreconcilable, action may be forced by the section which has the most power. The use of power by any group at any stage in the procedure is a breaking of the constitution. This statement includes the use of power in place of continued debate in Council. . . .

The desired interaction between the Executive[1] and Representative Systems does not impair the scope either of managers or of representatives. Indeed, great responsibility and authority have to be accepted by managers for the leadership of their subordinates; and elected representatives have to occupy fully their elected role in the sense of knowing policy, of being able to speak responsibly on behalf of their constituents, and of being able to integrate their views with those of representatives of other groups. . . .

The passage entitled 'The Legislative System'[2] reads as follows:

When all the members of a designated area are formed into constituent groups then—if it is the desire of those members as expressed through their representatives—they shall be entitled to form a council.

Subject to the following conditions, a legislative body so formed shall be authorized to determine policies on all matters relating to the duties and entitlements of members in the area, so long as those entitlements do not impinge on the entitlements of members in other areas.

Policies shall be determined by unanimous agreement. Legislative bodies shall accept, pending a unanimous decision, either:

(*a*) the continuation of existing policy, or
(*b*) such immediate decisions as the management member thinks fit, where the matter under consideration is not covered by existing

---

[1] I have used the term 'Employment Hierarchy' throughout this book, because it embraces all forms of employment organizations. In previous writings I used the term 'Executive System' instead, because this is the term used by Glacier.

[2] We used the term 'Legislative' because it was recognized that we were in council meetings producing internal 'laws' which applied to all employees and managers. On reflection however I feel that the use of the term 'Legislative' was a mistake. It should be reserved for national laws. We could have used the term 'policy-making'.

policy or where there is disagreement on the interpretation of existing policy, and where the interests of the Company demand that action shall be taken. The manager concerned shall, where possible, make every endeavour to give representatives prior information on the steps he intends to take, to enable them, if they so wish, to inform him of their views. Acceptance of the decisions shall be without prejudice to the final decision of the appropriate council or councils, and they shall make every effort to reach a unanimous decision without delay.

Legislative bodies shall otherwise conduct their business in conformity with normal committee procedure.

After some years of operation of these councils a difficulty emerged, which had not been foreseen. From time to time the trade unions to which some members of the council belonged called for national strike action by all of their members. These were brief strikes for one or two days in support of national wage negotiations. This put a council in great difficulty. Some members of the council occupied roles that called for conflicting action. As members of the council they did not wish to break its constitution by striking. As members of a national trade union they did not wish to act against their union by failing to carry out its decisions.

They appealed to the other council members to endorse the strike. I, as the management member of the council, pointed out that I could not possibly do so. I could not condone a breach of the individual employees' employment contracts, even to save some members of the council from breaching its constitution.

On the first occasion upon which this situation arose, the council issued a notice to all employees pointing out the clash of loyalties. It stated that the council had recognized the dilemma and that it was unanimously agreed that each employee must take his own decision as a matter of conscience. But it also pointed out that in the light of the difficult situation in which individuals were placed, there must be no subsequent recrimination between those who stayed at work during the strike and those who went on strike.

Subsequently the following guidance note was, by the agreement of all councils, inserted in the Policy Document:

Realism forces the recognition that power may be resorted to from time to time, and the constitution broken. Such use of power does not necessarily, however, destroy the constitution. Part of the value of having a constitution is to be able to recognize clearly when it is being broken, so that due care may be exercised to avoid destroying it by such frequent breaks as would bring it into disrepute.

It is further recognized that some breaks in the constitution may come about through the divided loyalties of sections which are an organic part of outside organizations such as trade unions. Conformance to part or all of actions called for by the outside body may not necessarily be specifically aimed against the Company. For example, Works Committee members are directly represented by the Trade Unions in national wage negotiations. At such times they may be called upon to take part in activities which are a breach of the employment contract. Other sections represented on council are ordinarily not in this position. The difficulty of such situations for Works Committee representatives has to be stated and understood. It is accepted that these divided loyalties exist, but while a constructive understanding of the reasons for a break in the constitution may be arrived at in council, nevertheless, it is agreed to be important to recognize that a break has occurred.

In the final analysis, even when power is used, agreement must eventually be arrived at between the contending groups. The Works Council procedure provides a setting where agreement can be sought before recourse to power, under conditions where those concerned are faced with the fact that if they cannot find a solution, then there is nothing else to be done.

These are excerpts from documents unanimously agreed by management, by the board of directors, and by the representative system (representing everybody in the Company).

All concerned in Glacier today regard it as a *sine qua non* of operating the Company. It has been vital to the Company's success by eliminating industrial stoppages for thirty years (apart from one one-week strike in a rapidly growing factory in Scotland and a few one-day strikes). It has given employees an expressed and powerful sense of participation. It has never yet failed to deal with conflict of policy or aspiration between the parties concerned.[1]

The establishment of unanimous-voting works councils has achieved two very important advances:

(a) It has endowed managers with a degree of authority over subordinates that is consistent with their accountability. This repre-

---

[1] The idea of a council is known to a large number of companies. Unfortunately I do not know how many have set up such councils. Companies in the UK seem reluctant to publish detailed accounts of their negotiating procedures.

sentative-sanctioned authority of managers is of an order that is most uncommon in industry.

(b) The power of representative groups has been explicitly recognized in the constitutions of these works councils. This has resulted in the constructive use of this power in council meetings towards the creation of a series of agreed policies, which form the basis of managerial authority. Power has thus been diverted from destructive fighting into constructive debate and agreement.

Councils have, in discussion, worked out and agreed policies in such vital areas of pay, holidays, pensions—policies which have led to the establishment of agreed differentials between various strata of the hierarchy. It has enabled the Company to introduce a very rapid rate of change in products, production methods and organization. It has taken from managers the continual strain imposed by constant negotiation, resistance to managerial authority and stoppages of work, and has enabled managers to concentrate proper energy on technological advance and extension of markets. It has allowed a small company to grow into a large one and become prosperous. It has facilitated technological change. It has helped a company which had, in 1939, fallen disastrously behind one of its American competitors (and their UK licensee), to recover its position and take a technological lead.

I resigned from the Chairmanship of the Company in 1965 when I joined the Government. Many managers who were interested in the Glacier Project believed that the structure of institutions that it had built up relied on my own continued leadership, and that it would collapse when I left. I understood the reasons why people held this point of view, for there are many examples of companies that have progressed greatly under one chief executive's drive and energy, and regressed when he retired. But those who expected this to happen to the Glacier Metal Company always misunderstood what had been achieved. This was not a personal effort of mine, but the result of hundreds of managers and representatives facing up to reality and building institutions that took account of it. This did not cause the Company to operate in some entirely new way. *There was no unique Glacier system at work.* What had been achieved was the *institutionalization* of the same roles, role-systems, power-groups and relationships that exist in every employment hierarchy. This institutionalization made them explicit and made it possible to describe them in terms which could be understood by any interested employee in the Company. It enabled the Company to teach its own managers how its employment hierarchy actually operated, and the precise policies which the managers must implement with the use of their authority. This institutionalization made employee-participation in the formation of policy not only a reality, but a reality that was felt to exist by most employees. By recognizing the important part played by representatives it greatly reduced their feelings of cynicism, suspicion and hostility, and enabled them to take a highly constructive part in the affairs of the Company.

There could be no question of retreat. If the Glacier Project had simply been composed of a series of new administrative techniques then, no doubt, these could have been dropped and others substituted for them. But instead Glacier had conceptualized and derived principles from a norm that exists throughout all employment hierarchies, but which elsewhere had only been recognized subconsciously or intuitively.

Thus regression at Glacier would have implied the abolition of knowledge, the giving up of insight, and reversion to a situation in which the institutions would continue to exist, but without anybody being clear about them. That type of regression can occur, but it takes a generation of change rather than the exit of one chief executive to bring it about.

In the event the Company has progressed as rapidly under my successor as it did under my command. It has continued its interest in sociological matters and has advanced its thinking in some notable directions. It will I hope continue to make serious contributions to the understanding of industrial organization.

A second objection to the institution of a works council of the type described, which I have had put to me hundreds of times, runs like this:

> 'If you have to get a unanimous vote of all fourteen members of the council then it is clear that on a wide range of issues where a decision is necessary, agreement will never be reached. One individual can inhibit progress and such a body may well contain at least one individual who desires deadlock.'

This objection, like many others, is based on the assumption that people's behaviour remains unaffected by their institutional environment. Because those who make this objection have observed certain behaviour in other situations, they assume that the same behaviour will take place in a unanimous voting council. But in my experience behaviour changes dramatically in the environment I have described. Plenty of objections did arise to proposals laid before the council:

some seemed unreasonable, but they were all sincere. They had to be met by modifications.

As soon as particular representatives saw that the management member of the council was genuinely trying to meet the objections to his proposal they themselves started to modify their own objections. Sometimes it was a lengthy business extending over more than one council meeting, but proposals for some change were *always* eventually agreed.

I cannot recollect objections raised in council for the sake of objection although I can remember cases of apparent stupidity. In such cases it was better to try to obtain the postponement of further discussion until the next meeting. This sometimes meant irritating or perhaps costly delay, but in the interim some of that representative's constituents who had been in the strangers' gallery would argue an alternative course with him; or his fellow representatives would help him to change his mind. Or the management member would come to the conclusion that he was being unnecessarily rigid and would alter his position. Whatever the cause, a change of mind would take place.

What has to be remembered is that the giving to every individual member of a council of the right of veto also places each member in a very exposed position if he uses it (rather like in the Security Council of the United Nations). The minutes of the meeting are available to all, and his objections are stated, as is his use of the veto. People have to have a reasonably strong case if they are to put themselves into such a position. *They cannot*, as in a committee, sink their own individual vote in a nameless majority or minority. The right of veto conferred by the unanimous voting rule involves personal accountability, and this is a heavy pressure towards responsible action.

A third type of objection maintains that if there is no bar to the subjects that representatives can put on the agenda of a council meeting, then some matters that are the prerogative of the board or of management will come under discussion. It will be impossible to hold a useful discussion because it would involve the disclosure of information that should remain confidential.

There are a great many issues that managers try to keep confidential, which would be better brought out into the open. I maintain, for instance, that it would be salutary if salaries became known at least within the hierarchy. Civil servants know what each other's salaries are and it does not appear to create problems.[1]

---

[1] I introduced the 1967 Companies Bill to the House of Lords and had to listen to dire warnings about the future effects of the partial

Nevertheless, there still is much information that cannot be disclosed. For example, the profit cannot be disclosed unless the shareholders have already been informed. The terms of commercial contracts usually have to be confidential. New technological developments cannot be disclosed unless valuable patents are to be sacrificed or advantage given to competitors. But where there is a reason behind a refusal to give information representatives will accept the logic of the situation. For twenty-five years I always found this to be so. Indeed, on a few occasions representatives have questioned the advisability of providing some of the information that had been given to them.

No institution is viable if one postulates unreasonable human conduct. All institutions rest on the ultimate reasonableness of people. This is not to suggest that they break down in the face of any irresponsible conduct, for they must be able to deal with a modicum of it. But unless most of those taking up roles in an institution are able in the last analysis to behave in accordance with reason, then the institution will fail to achieve its purpose. I found works councils to be thoroughly viable in this way.

Some readers may perhaps assume that the representatives who manned these councils were unusual people, but it would be unreal to expect the continued election of specially reasonable representatives over a period of twenty-five years. The fact is that the behaviour of all members of council was unusual only by comparison with what their behaviour would have been had the constitution of the council not been based on the unanimous vote.

The unanimous vote is the key factor. What is missing from most meetings of chief executives and representatives is realism. In one sense unanimous voting is not a new idea at all. Managers and representative systems solve their differences by unanimous vote all the time without realizing it. Take a simple strike situation in a factory involving three or four different trade unions, managers, supervisors, foremen, etc. Suppose the strike is over pay and holidays. It will not be settled until shop-stewards of all the unions involved have agreed. It will need the agreement of supervisors and foremen, who may feel that their differential advantages with regard to pay and holidays

---

disclosure of salaries that its provisions would enact. In the event, however, such disclosure has caused many boards to pension off 'passengers' who were earning high salaries and, in other cases, has caused managements to adjust unjustified differentials in salary. From all that I have heard, the provisions have done a great deal of good.

are being eroded. They may give in tacitly if the advance for others is fairly limited but they, too, will demand an advance in conditions if they feel that they are losing their place in the order of things. The chief executive of the area will have to agree. If representatives of one group of trade-union members or of some particular stratum of the hierarchy disagree, then the strike continues. Wherever there is a series of power-groups and a manager, then it is obvious that wherever change is sought, an arrangement must be worked out that will be at least tolerated by all. We are deceived by not realizing that compromise, reluctant acquiescence, even angry submission, are all essentially forms of agreement.

We all settle our industrial and employment problems on the unanimous principle in the long run; but we tend to want to fight first. The fight takes many forms: 'working to rule', going slow, being generally difficult, strikes, etc. Managers sometimes react to the use of power by representatives by reducing privileges, tightening up discipline, delaying promotions, and in other ways. But these fighting acts simply raise emotions and make eventual agreement much more difficult.

The setting up of a council enables the fight to be a verbal one across the council table. The strike is replaced by a delay in introducing the change, but meanwhile work continues. If unanimity must eventually prevail, then why not make that the rule of the initial negotiation and thus avoid the necessity for a show of power or authority?

It will be very difficult to convince the managers in employment hierarchies that experience a great deal of industrial strife that continuously responsible behaviour can be expected from representatives, even when a council is established. I can understand their feelings. Some recent strikes have been characterized by displays of the arrogant use of power in pursuit of wage increases which differentially are quite unjustified. But if the managers' feelings lead them to refuse to consider means of changing the environment (because the managers refuse to accept that environment is a powerful determinant of behaviour) then they have reached an impasse. I must, therefore, try to convince them by examining the effects on the individual of being a member of a unanimous voting council.

The full implication of the unanimous vote is that argument, discussion and reason take the place of the use of power, either by threats or by block voting (for majorities are the use of the power of numbers). Every member of the council has precisely the same power, that is, the power of veto. He needs no assistance from others.

Any representative can delay or veto a proposal that he feels will be unacceptable to his constituents or to his trade union. The management member of the council can delay or veto a proposal that he feels will be unacceptable to the chief executive of the company, or if he is the chief executive himself, to the board or in its effect on the company's customers. But any objecting member of council will be questioned by other members for his reasons, and these he must give. If he simply remains silent and obdurate the fact will become known after the council meeting to his constituents or, if he is a manager, to his superiors. (I have only once seen a rather unintelligent and new representative behave thus, and within weeks he resigned as a representative.)

If he states his objections then it gives others the opportunity of explaining that they are based on wrong assumptions, or are unreasonable, or of modifying the proposals to meet the objections. In other words the individual finds himself in a position where he will cause himself much embarrassment should he try to avoid reasonable discussion. The existence of a strangers' gallery reinforces this situation.

Representatives' past experience before the existence of the council has usually embraced many negotiations with managers. These may well have been tense affairs. The line of argument to be pursued has generally been agreed beforehand by representatives in committee. The rule has been that you must support your fellow representatives almost willy-nilly, for solidarity is strength. If you fail to support other representatives they may fail to support you and you will have to acquiesce in an arrangement which you know in advance will cause anger among your constituents.

But the constitution of a unanimous voting council changes that. Management cannot, by constitution, try to proceed with their plans regardless. You do not have to rely on fellow representatives to support you in your objections, for you can veto any proposal singlehanded.

Once this change of situation has made its impact on the minds of council members, it becomes obvious that group solidarity is simply not needed. This enables every member of a council to make his individually different contribution to a debate or argument. It is recognized by most psychologists and sociologists that polarization of opinion into two camps, though a very frequent occurrence, does not help reasoned discussion. It usually results in the false dichotomy of 'for or against' a proposal. This shuts out contributions that might produce fresh proposals or modifications of the original.

Most strikes arise because of these false dichotomies, and are resolved by modifications to the original proposal or by entirely new proposals. But settlement after a strike is always difficult because of the emotions which it has aroused. Thus unanimous voting produces, at the original stage of a negotiation, those compromises that would not otherwise be generated until after a period of hostility or actual strike action.

I have watched newly appointed members of council (not all shop-stewards, but including representatives of middle and top strata of the hierarchy) start their contributions in early meetings by displaying the tendency towards a 'for or against' polarization of attitudes. One could almost hear them trying to decide which 'side' to join. Their contributions were initially nearly always in defence of the ideas of the side to which they had allied themselves, or directed against the arguments of the other 'side'. Gradually the attitude shifted. Soon they ventured a point that was neutral and cut across the arguments of others; at that moment one felt they had emotionally accepted the meaning of a unanimous voting council.

These are the psychological and sociological aspects of a council. But what sort of work can it do? I have already commented upon the inner framework of policy within which hierarchies operate (see Fig. 25 in chapter sixteen). One part of this policy framework is enacted by the council.

Each Glacier Metal factory has a 'Policy Handbook' Every word in it, apart from the constitutions of the various representative committees, has been debated and agreed at council meetings. The policy document at the beginning contains the following sections: Definition, Achievement of Purpose of the Company, Structure of the Organization, The Executive System (in this book I have used the more general term Employment Hierarchy), The Representative System, The 'Legislative' System (with which this chapter is concerned), and The Appeals Procedure.

There follows a series of what are called Standing Orders. These are the equivalent of law in the factory. Some of the more important ones deal with such varied subjects as: appointments (this standing order is much concerned with the right of employees to be given first opportunity to be considered for promotion to vacant roles), training for management, apprenticeship, redundancy, staff ranking, the different entitlements and conditions of work of various strata of the hierarchy (including wage and salary brackets), conditions of overseas assignments, sickness benefit, shift-working, overtime, night-shifts, etc. All of these standing orders deal with issues that can be vital to different groups of employees. All have been approved in council. Many of them have been modified several times during the years. Some have remained as they were agreed more than twenty years ago.

I have recited this descriptive detail so as not to give the false impression that the main purpose of a council is to resolve incipient disagreement. The agreement is that all problems that cannot be resolved do become council matters. But a very important part of the work of a council is the production and modification of these standing orders.

It is important firstly because it is the means whereby employees, via their representatives, *participate* in the formation of the policies that affect their working lives, and, secondly, because it is the means by which the representative group uses its power to provide managers with authority and individual employees with rights.

Standing orders, after agreement by a council, are issued as instructions by the chief executive to his extended command. They set up limits to the use of discretion by managers. This may sound as if they are purely restrictive on the use of authority, but this is not true. For so long as a manager keeps within their terms he can in that area take any decision which seems right to him. Let me take a simple example.

London Factories Standing Order No. 13 (issued 10 October 1955 amended 26 May 1964) states among other provisions that thirty hours overtime per month shall be the normal maximum. But although overtime is a contractual requirement, which employees must work if requested to, managers must try to obtain the consent of persons to work overtime. No employee shall be *required* to work weekday overtime unless he has been notified before the end of the previous full working shift. No employee shall be *required* to work weekend overtime unless he has been notified by Thursday night. This is not a complete rendering of the substance of the standing order, but I have quoted enough to show that while managers are endowed with authority to require certain overtime work, employees have rights of refusal if certain conditions and limits are exceeded. This balance is typical of the 'legislative' work of a council. The result is a perhaps surprising combination of increased participation in the formation of policy by employees and an increase in the authority of managers. Because it is explicitly sanctioned it is usable authority instead of 'paper authority', which, if used, would be defeated by threats of the use of power.

For example (and keeping to the terms of the overtime example which I have quoted above), an employee is required by his manager to work overtime on Wednesday evening. He resents the instruction and calls on his shop-steward to intervene. That shop-steward is likely to produce his handbook, turn up the standing order on overtime and say to his constituent: 'Were you notified before the end of the Tuesday working shift? Have you worked less than thirty hours overtime this month? Are you fit medically?' If all the answers are 'yes', he will probably say: 'Your manager is entitled to instruct you to work overtime. What are your objections?' If the constituent then describes, say, a family problem of significance, the shop-steward will probably say: 'Right, I'll see your manager and see if I can persuade him to find somebody else, but I can't guarantee success. Next time explain your problem to him at the time he instructs you. Don't load on to me problems that you may be able to resolve yourself.'

Many large employment hierarchies continue to operate without explicitly sanctioned policies covering working conditions; indeed, many have no written policies on such matters at all, let alone policies explicitly sanctioned by representatives. I do not believe that this is because of a general lack of realization of their value, but because they have no legislative institution. Their negotiating procedures are confined to dealing with problems as they occur. Their procedures are not designed for agreeing policies that will obviate the emergence of more problems in the future.

Many people regard any rule as a curtailment of freedom. In one sense it is, for it curtails the freedom of the individual to do things that lessen the freedom of others. But in another sense it enlarges and does not restrict the freedom of the individual. Without law we should all be at the mercy of each other's whims or power and the powerful would impinge most horribly on the less powerful and the weak. Lawlessness leads to bullying. In large employment hierarchies, which are in themselves 'work societies', people often fail to see the necessity for explicit written internal laws. But without them managers with powerful personalities can impose on weak subordinates. Powerful employees or powerful representatives can deprive managers of authority.

I have heard managers boast that they have no formal arrangements in their company, no red tape and no bureaucracy, because they believe in flexibility. People who think like this will certainly not have got beyond the first chapter of this book. But if they are in charge of large hierarchies I would expect to find them beset with personnel problems.

Some people are afraid of formal arrangements because they believe that formality means inflexibility. To such people I would point out that if you want to change a procedure or an institution you must first have a clear idea of what you are changing. (If you issue instructions to change something on the assumption that it has one form when it actually has another, you will create confusion, and worse.) Many managers have the argument upside down. It is informality that is inflexible, and formality that is the most easily changed.

The provision of explicitly sanctioned managerial authority and explicit policies about working conditions, wages, and the rights of employees in large hierarchies could, I am certain, make a very substantial contribution to efficiency and to satisfaction at work in many of our large employment hierarchies that have so far failed to move in this direction. For example, the existence in the Civil Service of a great deal of written policy is one reason why relations between superior and subordinate are considerably better than those found in many industrial companies. In the absence of written policies, decisions about the treatment of subordinates by hundreds of managers in the same hierarchy will vary very greatly. One group of employees will feel that they are being unfairly treated when they compare the treatment they get with the treatment meted out by a more benign manager in charge of another group. Representatives generate pressure for the highest common denominator of generous treatment. If there is no formality there will be hosts of serious problems arising from the drive by representatives (and by individual employees) for what they think of as fair treatment relative to others.[1]

It would be easy to assume that setting up a unanimous voting council and its use to agree policy would take up a great deal of time. I am quite sure, on the contrary, that it *saves* a great deal of time. Thousands of arguments about regulations that would otherwise take place are settled in advance by the existence of agreed policies. The councils I have described used to meet once a month, with an occasional special meeting. There were many subsidiary meetings of managers and representatives, but most of the problems that arose at

---

[1] The lack of explicitly sanctioned policy seems to me to render abortive much internal company training or managers. If the training is not to be concerned with the detailed policies within which the company operates, then what is the content of training? The current philosophy of so much managerial training—which holds that it is the coming together of managers and the discussions that take place that are the most valuable result—arises because this is the way in which managers, within the same hierarchy, usually try to achieve some consistency of outlook in the absence of explicit policies. But it is more effective to have explicit policies and to make training a course in understanding these policies.

these could be resolved by reference to the policy document or to standing orders. If a problem arrived that could not be solved in this manner then it indicated the need for a new agreed policy. When this had been formulated and agreed then it was possible to resolve future problems of that kind by reference to that new policy.

I have so far deliberately avoided discussing an extremely thorny problem so as to simplify the discussion of unanimous voting councils. First I must state the problem.

I have been describing the work of a council in the context of situations where the management member of a council makes proposals and tries to get the sanction of representatives. But many readers may have become impatient because their experience as managers has been that the most difficult problems arise in connection with pressing proposals *from representatives* for betterment of wages, salaries and various other entitlements. Their objection to a works council might be stated thus: 'We understand that if the management member of a council raises a proposal for change, then it is agreed that the current arrangements carry on until some change has been agreed. Representatives can veto his proposals or insist on modifications as the price of sanctioning them. But if representatives make proposals and insist that they be accepted without modification or else they will down tools, what then?'

The first part of my answer is that in accordance with the constitution the management member of a council, like all the representative members, also has the power of veto, and he can refuse to vote in favour of the proposal. But that is not a good enough answer. The second part of my answer will be lengthy. It goes to the root of the matter.

The setting up of a council is a bargain, the terms of which are:

(*a*) That management will not even attempt to introduce change if the representatives object. It will submit matters to council discussion whenever requested to do so and undertakes that change will not be introduced without unanimous agreement. This means that employees can stop change without threats and without the costly business of the occasional strike to demonstrate their power. This power is explicitly acknowledged by management.

(*b*) That the representative system will not try to force change on management by using threats and strikes, and will submit their suggestions for change to a discussion in the council. In doing so they recognize that management is faced with two other power-groups—the shareholders and the customers—and that the management member of council, in stating his policies, is confined to those for which he has, or believes he can get, sanction from these two other groups.

(c) In return for accepting that threats of strike or actual strike action are breaches of the constitution, representatives are entitled to participate fully in the formulation of any policies, rules, regula-tions, which they choose to make an agenda item, on the single condition that if new policies cannot be agreed then the *status quo* continues.

(d) Representatives are entitled to any information about the com-pany that can be provided, which does not, in the opinion of the management member of council, endanger the company or is *ultra vires*.

I do not suggest that this is an easy bargain to strike nor an easy one to keep. But unless this agreement to proceed by reasoned dis-cussion can be made, then large employment hierarchies face a very troubled future.

The bargain implies a substantial change in outlook by representa-tives and managers. It requires that all strata of the hierarchy are represented in council and are parties to the contract. Management must be prepared to do everything possible to give the council the status it ought to have and must have in the eyes of all employees if representatives are to be permitted by their constituents to keep with-in the constitution. This means using the council on all possible occasions as a policy-making body. If, in its early life, the council produces a flow of policies that are felt to secure the employees from the fear of arbitrary action by managers, then it will gain status. If it is seen to be able, by sensible compromises, to solve problems that would, in previous circumstances, have led to threats or strikes, then confidence in it will grow.

It would, in my view, be useless to set up a council without a pro-longed educative campaign to make clear the basic analysis of the situation on which it is built. This will not be achieved by distributing documents or by a few public speeches. It involves prolonged and repeated discussion,[1] and question-and-answer sessions involving

---

[1] The Glacier Metal Company held many residential working sessions in hotels at weekends, for each factory. Managers, representatives, trade-union officials and other key people were present. The company's ideas were formed with the help of these working conferences.

Every new employee of the company spends a day or more having the Company's institutions explained to him by personnel officers and by

trade-union officers, representatives, key constituents, managers and directors.

The management member of a council and the chief executive must insist that the constitution is observed to the last letter. He must see to it that managers who deliberately breach the policies agreed by council are disciplined, and are seen to have been disciplined.

Managers must help employees to realize that the written policies they are administering are not management edicts but joint policies agreed by *their* representatives as well as by management. When people want managers to 'bend' these policies the answer must always be 'no'. 'The chief executive himself cannot change the policy—only the council can do so.' In my time I have addressed whole departments saying:

> 'You have indicated your intention to down tools unless. . . . I can't stop you. I can't exact penalties if you do so. *You have the power to do so.* But be careful how you use your power. A strike will simply cost you wages and will achieve absolutely nothing that can't be achieved at a council meeting without striking. If you are angry about changes that are to be made, your representative can stop them simply by failing to raise his hand when the motion is put in council. It is much less expensive to you and less damaging to the company to achieve the result that way than by what you propose. In addition, these threats of a strike are a breach of our constitution. If you breach it you weaken it. Do you wish to do so?'

I found that kind of talk to be effective. But it also helped to highlight the place of a council in the scheme of things.

There are tremendous pressures and temptations to use power to achieve higher wages and better conditions. But I found that once the council had established itself then the desire to safeguard its constitution and the realization that use of direct power would endanger something that had come to be regarded as an absolutely essential institution was enough to prevent breaches.

If representatives on a council over a period continuously go on sanctioning policies that fail to satisfy large and growing minorities

---

representatives. This may sound like the spending of a lot of man-hours. But one post-war strike lasting one week cost the Company 40 000 man-hours—more than we spent over many years building works councils and the like. 40 000 man-hours spent on creating a clearer and more realistic institutional environment would in many companies save far more than it cost.

among their constituents, or if the management member continuously vetoes reasonably based claims for higher wages[1] or better conditions, then such acts will bring the use of power and a breach of the constitution near. Council discussions must take account at all times of the pressures that exist, because they are real and do not go away of their own accord.

The vast majority of British people (perhaps all people) want law and order. They want fairness and integrity in management. They want to feel that they can rely on society to give them a reasonably fair deal. They dislike having to watch out all the time in case they are being 'done down' or in case somebody else is getting favoured treatment. They will put up with a great deal of hardship if they feel it is unavoidable, but will object most strenuously if they feel it is avoidable. A unanimous voting council can, if it takes full advantage of the opportunity its constitution provides, go a long way towards the creation of the sort of environment that is desperately wanted by people. If a council succeeds to a reasonable extent in this it becomes something that is, in my experience, very highly valued by all employees. They know that threats and strikes can damage the capacity of the company to provide good employment and are capable of eventually bringing it down in ruins. Given a good council they will hold their fire even if they do not achieve all the advances that they seek.

None of our important national institutions arrived overnight and were immediately successful. The history of the emergence of our parliamentary process or of our judiciary is one of eventual success, achieved by a gradual growth in understanding by citizens of the essentiality and the integrity of such institutions. We could make progress much more quickly in building the necessary institutions for our employment hierarchies if we set out to do so with sufficient resolution and faith in the ultimate reasonableness of individuals. But we will never achieve that faith unless we realize, from the outset, the extent to which behaviour is affected by the institutional environment in which we work.

There is only one way to test the validity of what I have claimed, and that is to try and see. Managers will feel that this is full of risks. But are these risks greater than the risk of trying to struggle vaguely against growing unrest?

---

[1] I know full well that wage claims are the most pressing modern source of conflict. I have not referred to them specifically but talked more generally in terms of 'changes', because I want to explore wages as a special problem in a later chapter.

In some very large industrial companies in recent years, and in some service industries, there has been so much successful use of power by representatives in pursuit of extremely large wage claims, that the mere idea of constitutionally giving up the use of power would be totally unacceptable at the present time. This I realize. But what is to be the future of such companies? Power tactics not only produce wage levels that are inequitable by comparison with those in other parts of society but also maintain the atmosphere of combat, which infects other problems and leads to a whole series of strikes on lesser issues. Many of these could be simply resolved if the wage problem did not inhibit the setting up of a council. Power tactics lead to bankruptcy.

Soon, and the sooner the better, there must be an end to these grosser uses of power, for the companies concerned will fail unless reason prevails or the Government intervenes. It is when one of these two latter situations arises that the opportunity must be seized by such companies, which currently would find it impossible, to set up an institution of the type I have described. Other companies could do it before crisis arrives, given the courage.

The powerful arguments in favour of unanimous voting councils is that they give expression to underlying realities. I do not wish, however, to leave the impression that I think councils could solve the national problems of differential wages and wage inflation. They would not, but they are an essential part of a programme that would. In chapter twenty-one I discuss Wage Differentials and in chapter twenty-two a proposal for setting up a National Council for the Regulation of Differential Entitlements.

Criteria for the use of Unanimous Voting Councils

It has become clear to me that the unanimous voting council is an important type of institution for group decision making which in a non-explicit manner is in more general use than is today realized. The Council of the European Economic Community is an outstanding example of an explicit unanimous voting institution, but there are many examples where those who use the institution are unaware of what they do. For example, when the management of a company and representatives of the various trade union members involved meet to resolve a strike, then all must agree before the strike is concluded.

In fact, whenever a number of different bodies or associations set up an institution within which they agree to negotiate with each other, then implicit in such an institution is the right of each to with-hold their agreement until they are satisfied that their interests have been met. In other words, the representatives of each different body have the right to veto proposals brought before that body. The un-animous voting rule essentially holds for such institutions.

The need to recognize the existence of such institutions in industry is becoming paramount. There is also a need for recognition of the reality of such institutions in other realms of society. Bodies such as universities, hospitals, assemblies of trade unions where a number of powerful interests have to arrive at agreement if necessary changes are, from time to time, to be introduced, are examples. Thus, unani-mous voting councils may turn out to be one of the very important institutions in society which, if explicitly understood and recognized, could do much to assist the mediation of conflict.

But the general tendency is to refer to anybody containing a variety of people representing divergent interests as 'a committee'. It seems, therefore, important to state the criteria which determine when to use the institution of a committee (with its majority voting method of arriving at decisions) and when to use a council (with its unanimous voting decisions). In order to arrive at these criteria I shall now describe a number of different situations by quoting examples of them.

The first type of situation is exemplified by boards of directors, management committees of many types of clubs, meetings of shop-stewards of one trade union or those representing one department of a factory, committees of the learned institutions and, indeed, Parlia-ment itself. These are all examples of true committees where deci-sions are arrived at by majority vote.

The characteristic of each of these bodies which I single out for the purpose of establishing criteria, is that their members are all elected by a single association. Boards of directors are elected by the share-holders, management committees of clubs are elected by members of the clubs, meetings of shop-stewards of a department of a factory are elected by members of the department, committees of learned bodies (such as, for example, the Institution of Mechanical Engineers) by members of that institution and Parliament by citizens of the United Kingdom.

I exemplify the second situation as follows. A board of directors sectionally elected by various types of shareholders, such as those holding ordinary shares, preference shares or debentures, the man-agement committee of a club elected by different sections of the club concerned, say, with tennis, golf, bridge, etc., meetings of shop-stewards elected by different unions within one factory, committees of learned institutions elected by different types of members of the institution, such as, fellows, members and associate members. Here we have committees elected by associations which are sub-divided into sub-groups. The associations have a general overall purpose which unites them but its members have separate sub-interests. Members of a management committee are elected to represent the various sub-interests.

The third situation is exemplified by the following. A chief executive meeting representatives of a number of different trade unions, whose members are employed within a company, representatives of the six countries forming the EEC, a meeting of the chairman of the council of a university, its vice-chancellor and members of the teaching staff, and representatives of the students, a meeting of representatives of several different learned institutions brought together at regular intervals to co-ordinate examination requirements.

In the first situation which I have described all members of a single association take part in the election of all the members of the body whose function it is to make decisions on behalf of the association. I shall refer to this type of association as a simple association. In a simple association the body of representatives will undoubtedly use a majority voting mechanism to make their decisions. This comes about because only the association itself has power and as each representative has been elected by the association, no single representative can exercise power on behalf of the association against other representatives.

Put briefly this means that when there is a simple association, then those they elect will form a committee and take their decisions by majority vote.

In the second situation, where members of the decision-making body are elected separately by different sub-groups or constituencies of one association (which I shall refer to as a complex association) then what is formed I will describe as an 'unstable' committee. It will use the majority voting mechanism up to the point where decisions imposed on a minority of the sub-groups of the total association, find that imposition intolerable. They then may use their power, as sub-groups, to opt out of the association. If the constitution of the association denies their right to opt out, then they may resort to the use of power in an attempt to reverse the majority decision. Examples of unstable committees are political parties which elect representatives from sub-groups within the party. Particular constituencies of such parties sometimes break away and form new political parties. Specific trade unions are examples of complex associations.

The members of the committees which conduct the business of the trade unions are elected from separate branches or areas or regions to conduct their affairs. But committee majority decisions may be unwelcome to some representatives of the sub-groups within the trade union. Often such sub-groups cannot break away without severe risk of economic retribution and, in such a case, a sub-group within the trade union may attempt disruptive action.

It is always possible for representatives of different associations to meet to negotiate with each other, on an *ad hoc* basis. Equally it is possible for those in charge of employment hierarchies or parts of such hierarchies, to meet with the representatives of one or more associations to negotiate. When such people meet each has the right to reject proposals put forward by others. Agreement is reached by all parties to the negotiations continually modifying their proposals in bargaining sessions until all are agreed. That is the nature of negotiation.

If, however, the parties to a negotiation share in common tasks and cannot achieve their objective without all over agreement between the parties to the negotiation, then they will either implicitly or explicitly set up an institution within which negotiations can take place as the need arises. Sometimes this institution will be referred to as 'a committee' but clearly that is a false description. Negotiations cannot be conducted on the basis of majority voting but require assent of each of the parties involved if they represent different associations. It is based on the right of each of the parties to withdraw from the negotiation as and when they choose and, indeed, to use such power as each possesses to pursue their own objectives by trying to impose their will on the other parties involved. I use the term 'negotiating council' to refer to such an institution.

A unanimous voting council is a modified form of a negotiating council. Its members are either *ex-officio* (e.g. a chief executive of a company) or elected by different constituencies of the same association or by different associations. It agrees upon a constitution which provides the following conditions:

(1) That each member shall possess the right of veto over the proposals put forward by others (i.e. unanimous voting on changes).
(2) That it will continue its negotiations until unanimity is achieved.
(3) That threat of or actual use of power by any members or those who elected them is a breach of the constitution.
(4) That the existing situation, whatever it may be, will continue until all members of the council can agree on some change.

(5) That it is unconstitutional for the council to agree on the abolition of any practice until agreement is reached on what shall take its place.

Unstable committees, as I have defined them earlier, could resolve their difficulties by deciding instead to meet within the constitution of a unanimous voting council.

I now suggest that the criteria which determine whether to use a committee constitution or a council constitution, are as follows:

Committee: an institution wherein there is one constituency comprising a single association (simple association) which elects all the members of the decision-making body. In other words, each representative of the body shares the same constituents.

Unstable Committee: an institution in which the members of the committee are each elected by sub-groups who are members of the same association (complex association).

Negotiating Council: an institution comprising representatives or *ex-officio* members from different associations which is set up to provide a formal setting within which *ad hoc* negotiations can take place as the need arises.

Unanimous Voting Council: an institution comprising representatives and/or *ex-officio* members from different associations which agrees to continue negotiations over differences of viewpoint until a unanimous agreement is reached and renounces the use of power against each other.

CHAPTER TWENTY

Appeals Procedures

I CAN NEVER understand why so many commercial and industrial companies do not operate explicit appeals procedures for the benefit of those who feel that their managers' decisions have been unjust to them personally. An appeals procedure exists in Queen's Regulations for the armed forces. Most university charters contain provisions for appeals. There are appeals procedures in the Civil Service. No doubt some companies have appeals procedures, but though I have often asked companies what their arrangements were, I know of only one written procedure agreed with representatives that is public knowledge to the employees.

The press nowadays is for ever reporting the events leading up to a strike. Some descriptions clearly relate to individual personal grievances of a type which, in my experience, should have been capable of resolution if there had been an appeals procedure. It is clear, however, that most of these grievances are taken up by the representative system, and this leads to strike action. The existence and use of an appeals procedure would often have averted strike action.

Appeals procedures, however, should not exist simply to avert strikes. In general society we have a legislature, an executive and a judicial system. The judicial system has to ensure that the decisions of the executive do not exceed the limits of the law. In other words, the judiciary tries to ensure that the executive arm of government does not transgress the boundaries of discretion imposed by law. The judicial system of appeal is available to anybody who thinks that the government has done this. I have tried to show, in chapter nineteen, the need for an explicit internal legislature within employment hierarchies. If there is to be a 'legislature' there must also be a 'judiciary' to police the boundaries of the areas of managerial decision. That is the basic case for appeals procedures.

The probable reason for the absence of such procedures in industrial companies is the absence in most of an internal 'legislature'. If a company that lacked a body of written and agreed policies governing the rights of employees were to set up an appeals procedure it would not achieve very much. Those who had the task of hearing appeals would always be making judgements that would *appear* arbitrary. No doubt managers could base their decisions on the best knowledge available of what the policies of the company were. But, unless the policies were written and available to all, managers would certainly appear to be 'making up the rules of the game' as the appeal proceeded. And, even if explicit written policies existed, but had not been agreed with representatives of all employees, then the policies would not be acceptable as a basis of judgement. The most likely result would be to incite the representative system to use power in support of an unsuccessful appellant. Such action would destroy the procedure.

The foregoing is not entirely based on speculation. I was responsible for the setting up of an appeals procedure at Glacier Metal. At the time a council did exist but it had not, by then, agreed many policies. As soon as appeals started to come in the difficulties caused by the absence of agreed policies became apparent. They began to threaten the status, the usefulness, and the confidence of employees in the appeals procedure. As a result, the management of the Company embarked on a very large programme of writing out the policies on conditions of employment and of putting these policies before the council for agreement. From then onwards, it became easier to hear appeals and make awards. It became possible to convince managers that they had not been entitled to make the decision that was the cause of the appeal because it was in defiance of a particular clause of some agreed policy. It became possible to convince an appellant that his appeal must fail because his manager *was* acting within the bounds of an agreed clause of a policy. In many cases there was dispute as to how the clause should be interpreted, and in such cases the appeal could be re-heard at a higher level in the hierarchy. But these arguments about the proper interpretation of 'laws' are very much less emotive than the wisest of comment from the best of managers who has to decide on an appeal in the absence of explicit 'laws'.

Experienced managers will, I think, be the first to agree that however impartial and logical they try to be in making decisions about the rights of their subordinates, it is very difficult indeed to dispel the subordinate's assumption that 'in the last analysis managers are forced to take the side of the company notwithstanding the clear justice of a subordinate's case'. This attitude is probably endemic in a very large percentage of all employees. I think it is natural, even where managers are indeed acting impartially, so long as there are no internal 'legislative' bodies, agreed policies and appeals procedures. The three go together.

In principle there are two types of individual appeal; firstly those where an appellant claims that a manager has no right to make the decision that is the subject of objection. It is claimed that he has exceeded his authority by stepping beyond the bounds of the area over which he is entitled to exercise judgement. Secondly, there is the appeal that claims that though the manager has, according to agreed policy, the right to make that particular decision, his choice was unfair to the appellant.

Appeals of the first type are easier to adjudicate so long as policy covering the area exists; if policy does not exist there is a case for writing a proposal and getting an additional policy agreed by the council.

The second type of appeal might seem to imply the ability of the manager hearing the appeal to decide whether or not the defendant manager's decision is fair. This presents problems. The classic cases are those where an individual fails to get a pay increase or a promotion that he thinks he deserves, or where he has been de-selected. In such a case the adjudicating manager (who is not, by definition, the immediate manager of the appellant) is being asked to assess the appellant's work performance. Clearly he cannot do so. What he can do, however, is to find out (a) whether the immediate manager's assessment is based on work performance and on nothing else; (b) whether the immediate manager has given explicit warnings of his dissatisfaction, thus giving the appellant an opportunity of improving his performance; (c) whether having given a warning the manager has allowed enough time between the warning and the decision for the subordinate to adjust his performance, and (d) whether the decision not to promote or to de-select is properly based on a long-period assessment of the subordinate's performance rather than on the fact that he has made a few recent errors of judgement.

If the adjudicating manager finds that the immediate manager has failed in any of these respects he may well be able to grant the appeal, but probably, except in case (a), with a warning that the appellant would have lost his case but for these lapses in procedure, and that if his behaviour or performance continue to be unsatisfactory to his manager then he will lose his next appeal.

I have frequently heard this type of appeal. The appellant is thirsting for what he regards as justice, but the plain fact is that he rates *his own* work performance better than does his manager. It is impossible to grant an appeal simply on these grounds, for it would contradict the concept of 'manager'. A manager, according to the definition I have set out in chapter three, is a manager only if he has the authority to assess his immediate subordinates and to de-select them if he is dissatisfied. Granting an appeal on such grounds would leave a manager with an immediate subordinate who was not acceptable to him. It is important, however, to understand that in order to get acceptance by employees in general of such a condition of appeal it is necessary to get the boundary definition of manager accepted by representatives.

This is the appeals standing order adopted by one of the councils of the Glacier Metal Co Ltd, as amended in 1967. It is much used and has become, in the eyes not only of employees but also of managers, an essential part of the structure of the organization.

APPEALS PROCEDURE[1]   (26.9.67)

1. GROUNDS FOR APPEAL

   1.1. Every member of the London Factories shall have the right to appeal when he considers that a manager's exercise of discretion is such that that manager's instruction to the member or decision about him affects him adversely in an unjust manner.[2]

      1.1.1. Exercise of discretion would include the possibility of appeals against:

        (a) a manager's interpretation of the meaning of the wording of a policy;

        (b) a manager's interpretation and evaluation of the evidence concerning a matter which is at issue;

        (c) a manager's judgment that a policy as stated deals fairly with the appellant under special or unusual circumstances.

---

[1] It may be noted that the Appeals Procedure applies only to individuals, and does not itself cover the notion—which was in the previous procedure—of a representative appealing on behalf of a group. That procedure, now no longer called an appeal, is now covered in para. 3 (Procedure for Dealing with Controversial Matters Raised by Representatives, including Disagreement over Interpretation of Policy) of the London Factories Standing Order, 'The Legislative System'.

[2] If a member whose immediate manager is the highest level of appeal feels that a decision of his manager affects him adversely in an unjust manner, he shall, after having notified his manager of his intention, have the right to request his appropriate Steering Committee to take the matter up with his manager (see para. 5 'Steering Committee Representation Procedure').

1.1.2. Should it emerge in the course of an appeal and be agreed by the appellant, that he is seeking to propose a change in existing policy and is not seeking redress for a grievance, then the manager shall discontinue the appeal, and the appellant shall seek to have the matter raised through the Representative System if he wishes to pursue it further. If the appellant does not so agree, the appeal shall continue upwards.

2. GENERAL PROCEDURE

2.1. Before an appeal can be initiated, a member shall discuss the matter with the manager concerned.

2.1.1. If, following the discussion with the manager, the member wishes to appeal, then he shall give notice of appeal by seeing the manager with his adviser. Thereafter, if the appeal is to continue, that manager shall make the necessary arrangements for the appeal to be heard.

2.1.2. If such notice is given by the beginning of the third working day or night following the working day or night within which the decision was made, the appeal shall be heard.

2.1.3. If the notice of appeal is given after this time limit has expired, then it shall be at the discretion of the manager appealed to whether or not the appeal shall be heard.

2.2. At the beginning of the appeal procedure, the manager hearing the appeal shall record in a form agreed by the appellant:

(a) what the appellant is appealing against; and
(b) what he is appealing for.

2.2.1. If at any stage the appellant wants to change what the appeal is for or against, he may do so, but the appeal shall be referred back to any managers who have already heard the appeal in its previous form.

2.2.2. No other written records of appeal proceedings shall have official status in any further stages of appeal.

2.3. The appellant and the manager whose decision is the subject of appeal both have the right to appeal against the decision of the manager hearing the appeal and to take the appeal to the next higher manager, up to and including the Managing Director.

2.4. Before an appeal reaches the level of Rank 4 Command Manager, it may, if both parties agree, be referred by either party to the Personnel Specialists for advice. This advice shall not be binding on either party.

2.5.[1] A member who appeals against dismissal and for reinstatement shall continue to occupy his role pending the hearing of his appeal.

    2.5.1. In the case of summary dismissal, notice of appeal must be given at the time of the dismissal.

    2.5.2. Suspension may be exercised up to a maximum of three days, but if the appeal is upheld and the member reinstated, he may be paid for the suspension period.

3. PROCEDURE AT HEARINGS

3.1. The appellant shall have the right to request any member of the same Council area, except managers in his line of command, to advise him. (Appellants are encouraged, however, to choose as their advisers members who have official representative roles.)

    3.1.1. If the appellant's chosen adviser is not a senior or experienced elected representative, such a representative may be invited to assist at Rank 4 Command Manager or Managing Director level if either party so wishes, especially if there are policy issues involved in the appeal that have to be sorted out and possibly taken into the legislative or negotiating procedure.

3.2. Those present at an appeal shall be the appellant, his advisor, and the manager whose decision is the subject of appeal. The manager hearing the appeal may have his Personnel Specialist with him.

---

[1] Where a member appeals against dismissal to the Managing Director and the Managing Director is absent but has nominated a deputy, that deputy will hear the appeal as the last step in the executive chain; the next stop, if required, would be the Steering Committee procedure. While other kinds of appeal could await the return of the Managing Director, it is not the intention that this shall apply to dismissal appeals.

3.2.1. In higher appeals, the manager originally appealed against shall have the right to be present to state the facts of the issue from his point of view.

3.2.2. If the manager originally appealed against, or any intermediate manager who has heard the appeal, considers that the issue is such that his personal integrity or standing is being questioned, he shall have the right to remain throughout any or all of the hearings.

3.3. Witnesses may be called, but shall be present at the enquiry only long enough to give their testimony and to answer questions arising out of their testimony.

3.4. The appeal decision shall be given in the presence of both parties.

3.5. It is the responsibility of the manager hearing an appeal to decide whether the decision appealed against was based on discretion which he considers satisfactory in the sense of—

(a) having been based upon sufficient information;
(b) due regard having been paid to the facts;
(c) the matter having been given sufficiently serious attention and care.

3.5.1. He shall not adopt a discouraging or unfriendly attitude towards an appellant who might wish to take his case to a higher level.

3.5.2. He shall deal with appeals with the minimum possible delay.

3.5.3. He shall encourage the appellant to have present an officially elected representative as his adviser.

4. INFORMATION ABOUT THE OUTCOME OF APPEALS

4.1. If a manager disallows an appeal against his subordinate manager and no further appeal is forthcoming, then he must decide whether or not he should inform his extended command in general terms about his decision. In deciding this, he shall take into account whether the appeal has to do with a new situation which might recur and which his extended command should therefore be informed about.

4.2. If a subordinate manager has an appeal against him allowed, and decides not to appeal himself, then:

4.2.1. He must work out what implications the appeal decision has for him in terms of any necessary change in his discretionary outlook.

4.2.2. He must inform any immediate managerial subordinates of the change in his discretionary outlook, and of the implications which this change has for his subordinate managers and for any future appeal cases.

5. STEERING COMMITTEE REPRESENTATION PROCEDURE

5.1. If after an appeal is heard by the Managing Director the decision is still not acceptable to both parties, the member shall, if he wishes to pursue the matter further, ask the Steering Committee of his Representative Committee to make representation on his behalf to the Managing Director.

5.1.1. The Steering Committee shall, if they think fit, make such representation.

5.2. If the Steering Committee of an appellant's Representative Committee agrees to his request that representation be made to the Managing Director, the following conditions shall apply.

5.2.1. The purpose of the representation shall be not to take any decision with regard to the appeal, but to explore the issue with the Managing Director so as—

(a) to discover whether the appeal hinges on a point of policy which might be formulated and referred to Works Council for consideration;

(b) to discover whether some obscure factor may be making an agreed decision difficult;

(c) to acquaint the Managing Director with what strength of feeling exists within the constituent group about the matter in question, so that he may test his outlook in relation to the feelings of members of the Company.

5.2.2. The Steering Company may, if it feels that other members of the Representative Committee or of its constituents have special experience or capacities relevant to the case in question, co-opt such other members to stand in in place of one or more of the Steering Committee members.

5.2.3. The appellant and his adviser shall be present.

5.2.4. The Personnel Division Manager shall be present.

5.3. If in the course of these discussions it is agreed by both the Managing Director and the Committee that it would be useful to invite one or more persons to help provide an independent view of the appeal issue, then they may invite such a person or persons from either inside or outside the Company.

  5.3.1. If one person can be agreed upon, then he shall be invited.

  5.3.2. If no one person can be agreed upon, then the Steering Committee and the Managing Director may each invite persons of their own choice.

A long history of experience has been built into this procedure. It was first introduced in 1941 and has been amended several times since. I suggest that it is a valuable example of a sound and well-tried procedure. Its introduction was very difficult. I should like to relate some of these difficulties for the benefit of those who wish to consider introducing something similar.

Foremen, superintendents and other managers were at first anxious on the following grounds:

(a) The great expenditure of time that would result and the large number of appeals that would arise.

(b) That it was higher management's duty to uphold the decisions of their managerial subordinates, not to assess their validity in front of their subordinates.

(c) That the judging manager would be exposed to strike threats and that he would, therefore, be unable to operate in an impartial manner consistent with policy.

Because at that time there was very little Company policy in written form, and current standing orders did not exist, this anxiety was understandable. In retrospect, I can now see that what was being said indirectly was something like this: 'You do not set clear policies within which we can make decisions. In their absence, we have no knowledge as to whether our decisions will or will not be upheld. If a large number of our decisions are deemed by a higher manager to be wrong (because, in fact, we are not aware of the policy which the Company wishes us to operate), then we shall lose status and authority in the eyes of our subordinates'—which was reasonable.

I think that most employees initially distrusted the idea, felt that a higher manager was bound to 'back up his own side' and that therefore they could not hope for impartiality. A few employees, too, have subsequently told me that at that time they regarded the act of appealing as being one that would certainly lead to their being noted by managers as 'troublemakers' and, later, to subtle victimization.

I think there was also a feeling that either one lost (which would not be satisfying) or one won (and got one's manager into trouble and that this was not 'cricket'); and so it was better to try and resolve the difference at a low level in the department, rather than involve senior managers in the matter, with all the unfortunate repercussions that the exposure (that would inevitably occur during an appeal hearing) of practices and customs might produce. Thus the system came into practice only gradually, and fear dissipated slowly. A number of things helped to reassure managers: there was no immediate rush of appeals; written policy began to grow in volume so that the appeals, instead of being wordy recrimination, often turned out to be a search for the real intention behind some statement of policy; frequently, when an appellant won his appeal it was not because his immediate manager had made a foolish decision, but because the Company itself had not sufficiently clarified the policy it wanted him to follow. These and other insights into the operation of the procedure proved reassuring.

Some appellants won appeals; but none of those who had done so was victimized; for I think every manager realized that all eyes were on him to see how he would subsequently treat a subordinate who had appealed. (I was very anxious in the early stages on this point, and used to follow the subsequent careers of some of those who had appeared in appeals at my level; but I never observed or heard of a case that caused me disquiet on this score.) Gradually the system began to operate in a formal and widespread manner. For five years I kept records of every appeal that I heard. These are analysed in the table below. During that period the Company employed 3000–4000 people. The total number of appeals heard was of course much greater than the number that reached me, but I have no record of appeals at subordinate levels.

I have been impressed ever since, in all but a minority of cases, with the sincerity, though not always with the objectivity, of the appellants, and with the fact that nearly all managers have obviously tried to deal impartially with appeal matters.

I have commented on the difficulty that will arise when the policy of the company is not agreed and written. However zealous a company is in this respect there are bound to be areas where a clear policy does not exist. In these cases it will be a waste of time for appeals to be heard by ascending managers in the line that leads up to the chief executive; for none of the in-between managers can safely decide the

Analysis of Appeals Heard by the Managing Director

	Jan. 53/ Dec. 54	1955	1956	1957	1958
Type of appeal					
Individual	16	9	7	8	7
Group	4	—	1	5	1
	20	9	8	13	8
Grade of membership					
Hourly rated	15	6	6	11	5
Staff	5	3	2	2	3
	20	9	8	13	8
Results					
Disallowed	15	5	5	11	7
Allowed	4	1	3	1	1
Compromise	1	3	—	1	—
Subjects dealt with					
Dismissal	5	2	—	2	1
Sick pay	2	1	1	1	2
Wages payment, expenses, etc.	11	2	2	6	—
Time spent on representative work	1	—	—	—	—
Classification of work available to women	—	—	—	1	—
Reduction of overtime	—	—	—	1	—
Appointments (including operation of S/O)	1	—	4	1	—
Alternative holiday	—	1	—	—	—
Upgrading	—	1	1	—	1
Loan	—	1	—	—	—
Demotion	—	1	—	—	—
Dissatisfaction with job	—	—	—	1	—
Retirement	—	—	—	—	3
Salary level	—	—	—	—	1

issue. It saves time if appeals in areas where there is no agreed policy can go straight to, say, the personnel staff officer of the chief executive, who may be able to deal adequately with them.

Appeals must be conducted with due decorum. The procedures of our courts are not immaterial: their main effect is to invest the proceedings with seriousness and integrity. It is therefore essential for managers who have to hear appeals to learn the rules of evidence:

(a) Reject hearsay.
(b) Prevent people not present from being criticized.
(c) Make sure that both appellant and defendant have uninterrupted opportunity for stating their case (while, at the same time, excluding gross irrelevancies).
(d) Intervene at once if abuse or threats of any sort are made.
(e) Adjourn the proceedings if these are not at once withdrawn.
(f) Refrain from criticizing either defendant or appellant (that is the task of their immediate managers).
(g) Treat the representative who appears in the appeal to aid his constituent with respect (his is often a difficult task because it is his responsibility to do his best for his constituent even though he may in many instances feel that there are really no good grounds for appeal).
(h) State decisions clearly in front of both appellant and defendant.
(i) Make clear the right of both to take the matter to a higher manager if they are not satisfied with the decision.

Appeals are time-consuming. They must be heard without delay. It is difficult for managers to fit them into a busy life and the subject-matter often *appears* trivial. It is thus easy to dwell on the difficulties and overlook the benefits that arise from the existence of an appeals procedure. Here are some that might be overlooked.

The hearing of appeals gives insight into the way in which subordinate managers are handling personnel problems, an insight that is difficult to get in any other way. It is intensely interesting and important to see how different managers behave in the various appeal situations that arise. If one is chief executive or a senior manager, the procedure keeps one in touch with people at the lower levels of the hierarchy. The existence of the procedure ensures most effectively that managers down the line know their policy and attempt to implement it with integrity, for they know that if they do not they are liable to have appeals made against them that they will lose. The right of the individual to appeal puts representatives in a much easier

position to deal with grievances that are raised with them by constituents.

When a constituent approaches a representative, the representative can ask: 'Have you appealed?' If the answer is 'No' then the
representative is entitled to ask: 'Why not?' I know of many instances
where shop-stewards have told constituents that if they will not take
the trouble to inform their manager that they wish to appeal then the
grievance cannot be of sufficient importance to warrant the expenditure of the representative's time. In the absence of appeal procedures
personal grievances have to be taken up by representative committees. If the atmosphere is already strained exaggeration is likely,
rumours fly and simple personal issues escalate into major trials of
strength between managers and representatives. Some of the reports
published after independent enquiries into strikes indicate to me that
the strikes would probably never have started if explicit appeal
mechanisms had been available.

Another perhaps unexpected benefit relates to the fact that employment hierarchies constantly have to adapt to changes in their
own environments. Whatever its nature, change seems always to
create anxiety in some group in the hierarchy. One could almost say
that resistance to change is endemic in employment hierarchies. If
one debates some new policy with representatives in a conventional
negotiating situation, hanging over the discussion there is always the
question: 'Where is the catch in this?' If a manager is able to point
out that ill effects that may unexpectedly arise are of course subject
to appeal, then anxiety is reduced and acceptance of proposals becomes easier. In many hundreds of council meetings that I have
attended I had over and over again to face the question: 'Is this
subject to appeal?' As nothing was excluded from the appeal procedure it was a question that need not have been asked. But it *was*
asked, and the answer was always: 'Of course it is'. Had I had to
demur or say 'no' then many essential changes would, I am sure, have
been vetoed by representatives.

There is a final question: 'Is it right that managers should adjudicate appeals? They are a team responsible for managing an employment hierarchy, and are they not therefore biased from the start? Is
there good reason to suppose that they can adjudicate in a disinter-
ested manner? Ought not the appeals to be heard by people who are
independent of the management of the hierarchy?'

Seebohm Rowntree, the practical visionary (who was far ahead of
his time and accomplished so much for Rowntree & Co and the
City of York and set so many splendid examples to British industry)

did, in fact, make a lawyer available to hear grievances. Unfortunately, a report of the results of this procedure has not, so far as I know, been published, so I do not know how the many difficulties of getting appeals heard by independent persons were overcome, if they *were* overcome.

The national judiciary is concerned with issues that are *on average* much more serious than the average situations that give rise to internal appeals within employment hierarchies. Because the issues that come before the civil and criminal courts are serious, a very large profession is engaged in legal procedures. In many types of action taken to the courts a case must first be made out to show that the dispute is worthy of the court's attention, so as to avoid using an expensive social mechanism to settle trivial issues. Moreover cases are based not only on the combined knowledge of the parties in dispute but also on the evidence of witnesses, which is committed to paper. Both the defendant's and the appellant's cases have often been pre-explored (at the cost of substantial expenditure of time) by legal men, who later appear to argue the case.

Thus the independent judge is presented during the hearing with all the relevant facts. This involves substantial preparation and long lapses of time between the lodging of the appeal and its hearing. This is the price of using independent judges.

In the close-knit community of an employment hierarchy, grievances fester if hearings are delayed. In addition, the circumstances can be forgotten in the fast-moving life of industry. Speed in hearing appeals is, therefore, extremely important. The committal of evidence to writing, which would be essential if an independent adjudicator were used, would involve long delay. It would, I think, be essential to limit appeals heard by independent adjudicators to one hearing. This could lead to miscarriages of justice, particularly as the independent adjudicator would be unfamiliar with the policies and practices of the company. In a large employment hierarchy it might well be necessary to have available the services of several independent adjudicators. If many firms instituted appeals procedures using independent adjudicators it is doubtful whether enough legal talent would be available in the country to deal with the mass of work that might result.

Such objections could be overcome if it were possible to provide the large resources in man-hours that would be needed, and obviate the delays that would arise. But there is, in addition, an objection of principle, which was disclosed in the earlier experience of Glacier. Paragraph 5 of the Glacier procedure, which I quoted earlier, says that if a final appeal to the chief executive is turned down by him then the Steering Committee of the Council has the right to approach the Chief Executive to explore the matter. The history of this final part of the procedure is important.

At one time this appeals procedure allowed final appeal to an independent adjudicator of legal standing. It had been part of the procedure for many years *but had never been called into use.* One appeal arose where the calling in of an independent legal person was required. After several weeks of effort no lawyer could be found to accept the task. This led to the re-exploration of the whole final procedure with representatives. The representatives put forward very strong objections to the use of an independent adjudicator.

(*a*) The inevitable delay would be unacceptable.

(*b*) In terms of knowledge of the Company he would be an 'amateur'.

(*c*) The result might be an adjudication which management and representatives both felt to be damaging and yet, by the nature of things, it could hardly be questioned or set aside.

(*d*) What would happen then if employees felt so aggrieved as to take strike action? Management could scarcely fail to back an independent decision, even if they felt it to be wrong. Representatives would have to back the strike. An insoluble situation might arise.

(*e*) They argued that it would be far better for the chief executive to make the final adjudication on cases that reached him. If there was mass feeling against it the matter could still be discussed without prior commitment in council.

There seemed to be much logic in the points put forward. The appeals procedure was amended.

In theory the use of independent adjudicators seems to argue a sound approach, but in practice it would probably cause grave dissatisfaction.[1]

---

[1] This experience is important, because most people who start thinking about systems to ensure justice in industry usually seem to assume that independent adjudicators are essential. For example, as I write the Government has just published the Industrial Relations Bill. This includes extensive provision for employees to appeal against unfair dismissal. But the Bill in its initial form is in my view unsatisfactory on two counts. The right of appeal is confined to cases of alleged unfair dismissal, and this would cover only a small minority of the cases of felt injustice in industry. The second objection is that the appeal has to be made to an independent court, which, as I have already argued, will severely limit

The 'trivial and unimportant' issue that would have to be refused a hearing would not feel trivial to the aggrieved employees. Indeed, the act of refusal might magnify feeling and lead instead to representative action. The setting up of an official external hearing of adjudication might lead managements to feel that as the matter had been taken out of their hands there was no need for them to consider internal processes for dealing with grievances.

In the light of my own experience I believe firmly in the need for legislation that would require every company employing more than a given number of employees to set up an internal appeals mechanism of the type which I have described. Such systems would give rise to pressures to produce a growing volume of agreed and written policy, and this would be very salutary.

If legislation were enacted on these lines I believe that in due course it would be acknowledged that external courts were unnecessary. I say this because (having taken part in operating the Glacier procedures for twenty-four years and having watched subsequent developments) the final adjudication of the chief executive has been challenged by representatives (under the procedure outlined in paragraph 5) only once. Managers elsewhere may find this extraordinary. I am sure that some of them who have read the foregoing will say: 'This company must be quite unusually fortunate in its shop-stewards; they must have been of the non-militant variety.' This suspicion is understandable but invalid. By and large Glacier shop-stewards are intelligent and reasonable in their behaviour because they operate within an explicit representative system of high status, because they participate in all major policy decisions through representation on a unanimous voting council, and because they take part in the development of the appeals procedure itself. They are extremely well-informed and very experienced. In my time the institutional environment in which they carried out their duties certainly did produce behaviour which, compared to the behaviour experienced by many other companies, was unusual. Nobody who knew them however would have questioned their militancy. From time to time

---

the number of cases that can be dealt with and will involve long delay and expense. There is provision in the Bill for the setting up, by agreement, within a company of an appeals system to deal with 'unfair dismissals'. But it is laid down that the Industrial Court may not accept an agreed company appeals procedure unless the procedure includes a right to arbitration by an *independent* adjudicator.

they included individuals who were of influence in both trade-union and political circles.

I believe that soundly built internal appeals procedures could make a great contribution not only to peace in industry but also to human satisfaction at work.

CHAPTER TWENTY-ONE

Wage Differentials

THE TWO MOST damaging and fundamental mistakes in government economic policies in the last twenty-five years have been acceptance of the following two ideas in combination.

(1) That the size of the total national wage-bill can be controlled by budgetary policy concerned with the manipulation of macro-economic factors.[1]

(2) That within such controls the different rates of earnings for different types of occupations can be left to find their own pattern on the basis of the differential demand for various types of experienced and skilled persons.

Throughout these years there has been ambivalence. On the one hand it has been assumed that the scarcer certain types of competence in people are, the higher their earnings will rise because of demand. It has been assumed that if there is a shortage of skilled mechanics then pay for mechanics will rise, that more people will become mechanics because of high pay, and that in this way market demand or lack of demand for labour will control differential earnings. This attitude is based on the assumption that labour is a commodity whose price is controlled by market forces.

On the other hand one government after another has explicitly or tacitly admitted that this or that occupation is underpaid—in other words that the level of pay should be a function of the type of work being done. This is a denial of the market-price idea about differential wages.

The confusion has been compounded by governmental support of free bargaining over wages. Free bargaining is affected by the macro-

[1] The term 'macro-economic factors' is shorthand for a variety of government measures, including increasing or decreasing the level of consumption, money supply, credit, taxation, employment levels and government expenditure.

economic situation, by ideas about paying in accordance with level of work done, and by the relative power of the negotiators.

This confusion about the criteria that ought to be used in attempting to deal with the problems of employee unrest, wage inflation and the level of employment has prevented any viable government policies emerging.

Every manager knows that the capacity of individuals varies; that though at times particular occupations have to be paid at a higher rate because of scarcity of people with the necessary skills and training, in the long run we must pay in accordance with the level of responsibility carried by the occupation or the individual.

If we all deplore a situation where machine-operators earn more than foremen or more than tool-makers, or nurses earn less than female clerks, then we are agreeing that people must be paid in accordance with the 'importance' of the job rather than on the crude basis of supply and demand.

But a third manner of establishing the differential pattern of wages is now taking over from the labour-market basis and from the level-of-work basis. This third method is power-bargaining by trade unions and others. In effect this method, if pursued to its logical end, will result in those who have the best organization, the most power and the most effective position to disrupt the economy, getting the highest earnings, and those in the weakest position getting the lowest earnings. That will be a form of anarchy.

I am one of those who believe that the basic cause of recourse to power-bargaining is not primarily a drive for more absolute pay but a drive to keep up with the pay of others who are felt to be carrying the same level of responsibility: though once power-bargaining has started and people begin to realize just how powerful they are, the original motivation for its use is often supplanted by greed for more without reference to fair differentials. Nevertheless, if a pattern of differential pay existed which was felt to be fair, then the heat would be taken out of power-bargaining.

If resort to power-bargaining receded then government policies to contain the size of the total national wage-bill within the economic limits set by national increase of output would become viable. The economy could then be operated at its full productive capacity, real unemployment could be eliminated and the standard of living would rise. This in turn would further diminish the tendency to resort to power-bargaining. That is why the differential pattern of wages both for occupations and for individuals in the same occupation is so vitally important.

There is a deep wish in the individual to equate earnings to different levels of work and personal capacity. If it were not so why should society be outraged by the grosser forms of what they regard as inequitable differentials? Why should representative power-groups so often seek to justify their claims on the grounds that they are seeking parity in pay with others whom they claim to be performing work of the same level as themselves? No group has yet dared to say in public that their object is to gain the maximum earnings that their power situation enables them to achieve. They know that this would cut across the ethos of society.

I propose simply for convenience to use the term 'equitable differentials' to describe this inner drive to equate level of work and earnings, and 'power wages' to refer to the alternative.

I have little doubt that in the long run the drive for equitable differentials will force into existence the means to achieve them. But unless a much larger proportion of society achieves a clearer understanding of what is happening, the unhappiness and economic problems that will arise before equitable differentials are achieved will be appalling. I want, therefore, to examine some of the attempts to influence pay levels towards a fairer pattern of differentials that have been employed so far.

The first is payment by results. For convenience I shall refer to this as 'piecework' (although this is inaccurate as a description, for piecework refers to the original system whereby employees were paid so much per actual physical work-operation performed: most payment-by-results schemes today are based on 'measuring' the time that a piece of work ought to take and stating work done in terms of numbers of hours).

The underlying theory of piecework is that everybody is given the same opportunity to earn and that the higher a man's ability the higher will be his earnings. It has failed and, in the process of failing, has probably produced more strife and ill feeling in industry than almost any other single factor.

The reasons for failure are manifold, and I have discussed them in detail in my book *Piecework Abandoned*.[1]

The reasons, briefly stated, are:

(a) The fixing of money or time allowances for the performance of given work assumes that the other conditions surrounding that

---

[1] Published by Heinemann Educational Books Ltd, 1962. My first published criticism of 'Piecework' as a means of payment was in *Occupational Psychology*, April 1945, Vol. XIX, No. 2.

work can be held reasonably constant. This is possible in some circumstances, but there are too many situations where this is not so. The result is a variation in performance due not to the employee but to varying circumstances over which he does not exercise control.

(b) It is a method of payment that cannot readily be applied to any work that has not got a physical output. For example, attempts to use it on clerical work usually fail because only part of the output is physical.

(c) It was assumed that the input of worker-hours necessary to produce a given physical output could be measured reasonably accurately. This assumption is wrong. Several closely controlled research projects show a standard deviation between rate-fixers of 18 to 20 per cent. This is roughly equivalent to a variation in measurement of the time required of plus or minus 40 per cent.[1]

These defects have progressively led to very widespread measures on the part of employees who are on piecework. They try to:

(a) Safeguard the continued existence of 'generous' piecework contracts by fixing maximum rates of output for any employee given such work to do.

(b) Counteract the inaccuracy of rate-fixers by various forms of mild corruption and collusion with shop-floor management so as to get rid of the gross variations in earnings from task to task that would otherwise arise.

(c) Safeguard rate-fixing contracts for current techniques of doing work that they feel to be satisfactory by resisting changes to more advanced techniques requiring the setting of new piecework contracts, which may prove less satisfactory.

Piecework has been the source of widespread unrest, friction between management and employees, restriction of output and strikes, though the facts of the situation are being faced at last and the use of piecework is declining. It is being substituted in many instances by what is called 'measured-day work'. The use of the term 'measured' is to be deplored, for we shall continue to get variations as between one 'measurer' and another of around plus or minus 40 per cent. It is necessary, of course, to set up targets of output for individuals. But it would be very much better if these were treated as *targets* based on intuition, and acknowledged to be subject to variables outside the control of the operator.

---

[1] See, for example, Winston Rogers and J. M. L. Hammersley. Reported in *Occupational Psychology*, Vol. 28, No. 2.

The second attempt to establish equitable differentials has been through the use of 'job-evaluation' techniques. American experience (which has been extensive) suggests that most job-evaluation schemes rely on four main criteria: qualifications and specific skill requirements; effort required; responsibility carried; environmental conditions; and special hazards. Each factor under these main headings has a maximum number of points allotted to it. From these the job-rater allots a chosen number of points to each type of job. The total number of points indicates the wage for the job. Research done indicates that the technique has proved useful.[1] The criteria selected, the maximum points allotted to each criterion and the points allotted to specific jobs are entirely subjective. As a management tool for comparing various types of jobs it would certainly bring more formality to the process and add consistency. But the results are judgements—not measurements. No attempt has been made to use it as a means of determining appropriate differentials between, say, teachers, electricians, miners and printers. There would seem to be no hope of its being used in this way—owing to its subjective nature.

There have been other novel approaches to wage-payment methods—'profit-sharing', 'Scanlon plan' and group bonus schemes. None of them attempts to make differential assessment of the performance of individuals or of the level of work in individual roles. They are therefore irrelevant to a discussion of the way to get equitable differentials.

The third approach is that of Professor Jaques's Time-Span theory. Time-span measurement is a technique for discovering the maximum period of time a manager will expect and allow his subordinate to work without reviewing the results.

Every employee is given control over greater or lesser resources. These comprise such things as equipment, materials, the time of his subordinates, services made available to him, and his own time. In his work he is required to use his judgement in expending these resources. The maximum length of time over which different employees will continue to commit the use of resources, without having the soundness of their decisions checked by higher authority, varies. This variation in time-span is a function of the degree of confidence possessed by a manager in the capacity of his immediate subordinates

---

[1] See, for example S. Laner, E. R. F. W. Crossman, and H. T. Baker, *The Human Factors in Technology*, Research Group Report No. 69–10, Berkeley University.

to make wise decisions. The manager's degree of confidence manifests itself in the maximum lapse of time that he will allow to take place between the giving of a task to a subordinate and the targeted completion time of that task.

There are two different ways in which managers assign tasks: one task at a time to be finished before the next is begun—single-task roles; and many tasks at the same time—multiple-task roles.

In single-task roles the procedure is to measure the longest sequence of tasks before any one of those tasks comes under review: by the time of this first review on any task, the subordinate may have completed several tasks without review. In multiple-task roles, the subordinate has to use judgement continuously in deciding his work priorities; if he is marginally too slow, he can borrow against the longest task he has, but will eventually be late in completing the longest one; thus the longest-assigned tasks give the time-span in multiple roles.

Taking these conditions together, the most general definition of time-span that emerges is: the longest period that can elapse before the manager can be sure that his subordinate has not been exercising marginally sub-standard discretion in balancing the pace and quality of his work.

From this brief description the measurement of time-spans may well sound difficult. Readers may, for example, question whether target completion times of tasks are always discoverable. I could not convince my doubting readers without going into these matters in all the detail that Jaques covers, and I must refer them to his works.

I can assure the doubters that measurement of time-spans is not difficult, can be carried out by trained people in periods ranging from five to twenty minutes per role, and is repeatable.

In itself this takes us no further in the search for a method of establishing equitable differentials. But Jaques also discovered a very important correlation between maximum time-span and *the wage that a person felt was fair for the work he was doing*. Jaques called this 'Felt-Fair Pay'. Note, however, that felt-fair pay is not what an employee feels to be fair for his abilities, but fair pay *for the work he is doing*. (He might feel that he is worthy of a role carrying higher-level work at higher pay, but that is a different matter.)

This can be stated in a different way. Ask a thousand people employed at different levels of work in different types of occupation, what is their felt-fair pay. Organize the thousand felt-fair pay figures into sub-groups of similar pay figures. Next measure the maximum time-span of the work of each of the thousand people. Organize the thousand time-spans into sub-groups of similar time-spans. The two sets of sub-groups will contain the same individuals.

This discovery was made in 1956, and much testing has taken place since.[1] For example, the Honeywell Corporation of America, working with two Minnesota University Departments, carried out a two-year research, which involved the discovery of the Felt-Fair Pay of 200 Honeywell employees and the time-span of the work they were doing. The resulting correlation was 0.86.[2]

At first sight this theory sounds impossible. That was certainly my own reaction when I first had it described to me. For the only explanation of this correlation is the existence, in each person doing employment work, of the ability to weigh very accurately the importance of his own work in comparison with the work of others, and to state it in terms of a figure of felt-fair pay. Unchecked intuition alone could not produce such consistency among an unlimited number of people; but if each is, in fact sub-consciously using the yardstick of time-span then such accuracy is explicable. I think there is no doubt that people do use their own knowledge of the maximum time-span of the work they are doing as the basis of their statements of felt-fair pay. People are largely unaware that this is what they are doing, but one is driven to this conclusion because no other explanation explains the phenomenon.

Having been introduced to the idea, and being conscious of it, I

---

[1] Elliott Jaques has described his technique in *Measurement of Responsibility*, Tavistock Publications, and *Equitable Payment* and *Time-Span Handbook*, both Heinemann Educational Books. The Honeywell study referred to above is reported in *Fair Pay and Work* by Roy Richardson, Heinemann Educational Books. A team led by Evans and Krimpas of Brunel University gathered data in ten different UK companies. A preliminary report of their findings appeared in *New Society*, 27 November 1969. Laner and Crossman of the University of California, Berkeley, published their working paper *The Current Status of the Jaquesian Time-Span of Discretion concept: Research and Applications* in September 1970 for the Office of Naval Research. It is an excellent review of research done and current attitudes to the time-span theory in the USA. Many other papers have also been published.

[2] For those unfamiliar with statistical correlations it should be explained that if it is felt that two factors are related and a statistical correlation of, say, 0.3 established then there would be some indication of a relationship. At 0.4 there is moderate evidence; at 0.5 it is strong; at 0.6 it becomes highly significant; at 0.7 the relationship is virtually proved, and so on. Statistical correlations in economic and social issues at the level of 0.86 are unusual.

found personally that this was in fact so. As a manager I found that I had indeed been assessing my degree of confidence in my subordinates in terms of time-span. If I had felt great confidence in one of them I had given him tasks to carry out that would occupy him for longer periods (without my knowing how he was getting on) than I could possibly have brought myself to give to other members of my team, in whom I had less confidence. I naturally arranged salary levels that reflected those varying time-spans. My colleagues had similar feelings and experiences. We became aware of the yardstick we had been using in the past and became convinced. We had, so to speak, transferred the yardstick from a sub-conscious level to a conscious one.

I now have no doubt at all that everybody in employment constantly, but sub-consciously, uses this time-span yardstick not only about the work they delegate to subordinates, but about their own work also.

Through the years I often discussed Jaques's theory with industrial managers in other companies. Here is an example of such a conversation.

Mr A This time-span measurement idea that you are interested in sounds pretty impossible to use.

WB Let's walk through your factory and I may be able to spot some situations that will help me to explain its potential usefulness.

(We enter the jig-and-tool drawing office and I am introduced to CD, the chief draughtsman. At one end of the large office are three small offices.)

WB Who occupies those three offices?

CD Those are the offices of my three senior designers, who tackle all the big complex jobs.

WB Are they all doing the same type of work?

CD Yes.

WB Are they all paid the same?

CD No. One of them is more experienced than the other two and is paid considerably more.

WB Do you pay for experience in this company, or for work done?

CD (embarrassed) Well, we try to pay for work done but, of course we have to recognize experience by higher pay when people are all doing the same work.

WB I am quite sure that they are not doing the same level of work.

CD I assure you that they are.

WB If you will bear with me, I think I can prove to your own satisfaction that they are not. What is the exact nature of the method by which you allocate tasks to these three men?

CD We receive from the machine-shops specifications of the tools they require, with a sample of the components on which there are various machining operations to be completed.

WB Will you please describe precisely what you do when you give one of these jobs to your senior designer?

CD I explain the job to him, and we discuss potential problems that might arise. He takes the specification and the component, and fully designs the tool. He issues an order on the tool-room to manufacture it. He is available to answer queries that arise in the tool-room, and he progresses the job through the tool-room so that it is completed on time. He arranges a trial run in the machine-shop and informs me. I watch it run its trials; sometimes I criticize but usually I approve it after watching it operate, timing it and checking on the dimensional limits of the component.

WB Now what happens when you give a job to one of the two less experienced men?

CD Just the same.

WB Are you quite sure of that? Are you sure that there are no intervening stages when you examine closely how they are going about the job?

CD Well, of course there are. I told you the other two are less experienced and I have to watch them more carefully. I ask one of them to bring his general arrangement drawing back to me before going further, and we discuss it. After that he does a detailed drawing and we discuss that, because mistakes can creep in and they would be expensive. After I've agreed the detailed drawing the designer issues the order on the tool-room and proceeds in the same way as the senior designer.

WB In other words, the length of time during which the senior designer carries on with his work without your checking what he is doing is considerably longer than in the case of the less-experienced designers.

CD Yes, that's so. The work is just the same but I do have to keep an eye on them more closely.

WB If you had the same confidence in the two less experienced designers as you have in the other man, would you treat them any differently?

CD Yes, of course. I would pay them the same and I wouldn't have to keep such a close check on their work. It would relieve me of quite a lot of work!

We make assessments of our own work and of the work of our subordinates in this way whether we are aware of it or not.

Those who come afresh to this description of Jaques's technique will not, I think, be able to accept the statement in the last sentence. They will (if they are like me) have great difficulty on first acquaintance with time-span measurement in coming to terms with it. I think they will find my description inadequate. But my purpose is the limited one of drawing attention to the existence of what I regard as an important break-through. It is so important that I cannot write about organization and its attendant problems of wages without mentioning this break-through. If I stimulate people to read Jaques's writings I shall have succeeded in my limited aim.

It will not be possible to use this method of measurement as an arbiter of differential wages until managers, trade unions and representative groups in employment hierarchies have understood the method and accepted it as valid. But, in the meanwhile, it could provide administrators with much vital information. For example:

(a) When a large number of wage-claims are being put forward simultaneously managers (and sometimes governments) are forced to come to some conclusion as to whether they should be accepted, modified or resisted. These judgements are unavoidable. Time-span measurement would enable those concerned to *know* which claims were justified and which were not, and by how much. In the negotiations that followed, power would no doubt influence the final result but at least the administrator would not be entirely dependent on intuitive judgement as to which claims to resist and which to accept.

(b) The Government has to be continually concerned about the pay differentials within the Civil Service. Questions of comparability arise all the time. Decisions have to be made about the right relationships between the wages and salaries paid to doctors, judges, nurses, teachers, prison officers, police, customs officers, etc. The use of time-span measurement would show the correct relationships, and over a period of years it might be possible to bring about equitable differentials between all these occupations.

(c) Trade-union and representative groups within employment hierarchies also have to make judgements as to where to use their bargaining power and where not to do so. They too could avail themselves of positive knowledge.

These are examples of the use of time-span measurement simply in order to gain knowledge. Ultimately, if accepted, time-span measurement, and its correlation with felt-fair pay, could be substituted for bargaining as a means of arriving at different wages and salary levels for different occupations. This would take a very long time, but the prospect is important. Feelings of injustice about wages generated by comparison with the wages paid to others, coupled with the growing conviction that if you are smart enough (or if your representatives are sufficiently militant) the sky is the limit, are responsible for a great deal of general social unrest. These two factors help to inhibit co-operation at work. They cause strikes. They reduce the efficiency of working at all levels. They cause acute unhappiness in industry. The effects bleed over into society as a whole.

The first industrial country to make full use of this technique as a means of establishing equitable and accepted differential wages will move ahead of other countries.

Jaques's work was first published in 1956. Since then he has simplified the methods of discovering maximum time-span and sharpened his concepts, but the basic approach has remained unchanged. Most people, on having the existence of the correlation explained to them, simply do not understand it and do not therefore believe it. Some understand it but are unable to spare the time to learn how to measure time-spans so that they can make some personal tests of the validity of the method. Without looking at data arising from real work-situations, they convince themselves that the correlation cannot exist. One of the ways in which the sceptics convince themselves that they are right is by speculating about work instead of getting first-hand data from people in specific roles about the work they actually perform. In this way the sceptics can create hypothetical occupations in which the maximum time-span indicates a level of salary they know to be absurd.

I was chief executive of the company where Jaques carried out the work that led to his time-span theory. My colleagues and I originally greeted his ideas with complete disbelief. It became a sort of sport to produce details of work in particular roles that disproved the theory. But the cases which 'disproved' Jaques's theory, on investigation, always proved to be based on false assumptions about the work and the assessment mechanisms applying to it. When the actual details of the assessment mechanisms and the work were obtained from the person doing the work and from his immediate manager, the case against time-span measurement fell to the ground.

It seems irrational to many people that it should be possible to measure level of work by reference to the one parameter of time. This is a very understandable point of view. Work is concerned with decisions that produce profit or loss, waste or sound use of resources, excellent products or failures, satisfaction or dissatisfaction. A theory that purports to measure all these results of work along the dimension of time alone sounds absurd. But Jaques did not set out to measure work. He tried to discover how people came to their conclusions about the level of their work as compared with that of others. He discovered that people were using the time-span criterion without realizing it. The strange thing is that as far as one can see everybody at work uses it internationally. Time-span measurement is not a newly invented technique—it is a discovery. It no longer surprises me that we choose the length of time during which we are allowed to carry on making decisions. We all have feelings about the comparative importance of our work. We have to use some criterion and obviously we could not intuitively adopt something complex like 'job evaluation'. We choose time, but we have not all realized what we have done.

I cannot refrain from comparing our situation with that of Kepler, the great German cosmologist. He had to discard fundamental assumptions about the universe in order to create the conceptual basis of modern cosmology. His predecessors in the field of cosmology showed amazing ingenuity in trying to invent theories that would account for the movements of stars and the planets. But none of them (except Copernicus, who did not conceptualize his ideas) produced a theory that fitted all of their observations. Frustration drove them towards fantasy thinking, involving metaphysical and theological ideas. Arthur Koestler's book *The Sleepwalkers* gives a fascinating account of how Kepler, by sheer force of intellect, shakes off the sub-conscious conditioning of his mind and begins to produce boundary-defined concepts and observation-based hypotheses, and then regresses again into the fantasies of the past. He goes through this cycle of progress and regression several times, to emerge at last with the general theory on which twentieth-century man has based his landing on the moon.

We are at the Kepler stage in our thinking about wage and employment theory. The notions bred in the past keep on rearing up and interfering with more objectively based processes of thought. It is exceedingly difficult to slough off the current frame of reference and move to a new one. We must, however, come to terms with the ideas that labour is not a commodity, that human work is decision-making work, and that speculation about social phenomena is no substitute for disciplined observation. For unless we can get out of the bargaining frame of reference for regulating wages and move to a method of doing it by measuring to obtain equitable differential wages, an increasing degree of anarchy in employment hierarchies is in store for us all.

Before I end this chapter I must add a postscript. It is an extract from an essay written by Jaques,[1] which describes some of the history of the development of the measurement of temperature. This, at first sight, may not sound analogous to the development of means of measuring level of work, but I will leave my readers to judge its relevance for themselves after reading his comments.

Measurement in The Physical World
In order to illustrate *some* of the main points, we shall consider first of all some of the basic features of temperature.

To get at the essentials, let us drop our present scientific sophistication, and have a fresh look at the problem as it appeared to scientists in the fifteenth century, before thermometers had been discovered. In these days the concept of temperature as a potentially measurable quality hardly existed. You will recall that the prevalent theory was that of heat as a fluid calor, which could be transmitted from one substance to another; but whether all heat was the same, or whether heat of combustion, solar heat, and animal heat were different, was a matter of debate.

Imagine then the available data. First and foremost there is the sensation of heat; the sensation of one thing feeling warmer than another, or of things getting hotter and hotter. These sensations are the basic data. It is these sensations which allow us to know about the existence of something we call hot, or cold, or warm, or burning, or freezing. Along with these sensations go our observations of hotter and colder things; flames are hot; so is the sun; ice is cold; fresh water is cooling; boil it and it gets hot; some animals including humans, are warm to the touch, others like snakes are cold. We know that things get hotter and colder, because our senses tell us so.

Let us interject at this moment, an observation on the similarities between that situation and our present day experience of phenomena such as level of responsibility—we can sense when it is higher and when lower; or individual capacity—we can sense our own capacity to be increasing as we mature; or aggression, or love, or envy, or any of a hundred other social and human attributes, which we 'know' to be greater and lesser, and to be changing in amount, but which we do not

[1] 'Time and The Measurement of Human Attributes' from Elliot Jaques, *Work, Creativity, and Social Justice*, Heinemann Educational Books Ltd, 1970.

as yet know how to measure. So the problem of heat and temperature up until the fifteenth century.

One other observation had been made, however, that was to prove of outstanding importance; namely, that as calor was transmitted to air, and the air gets warmer, it increased in volume. We can observe this phenomenon by warming the air trapped in a test-tube by holding it over a dish of water. If we hold the tube in our hand, or otherwise warm it, the level of water in the tube can be observed to go down; if we cool the base, say by holding a piece of ice against it, the water level can be seen to rise in the tube. Clearly, we may conclude, the air is expanding and contracting as it gets warmer and colder.

This observation and its possible significance for measurement, is not, of course, available simply for the taking. We have to be in a proper frame of mind to pay particular attention to it. For it is merely one datum in the midst of a host of other data and pseudo-data and questions which are in many ways emotionally more attractive; for example: what is the nature of calor? How is it transmitted from the sun through space? What are flames? Are there flames inside the human body? What happens when water turns into steam, or into ice? These are the fascinating questions. And surely they are more practical and realistic than bothering with the problem of trying to measure what after all is an insubstantial psychological sensation, namely heat.

But it is happily a characteristic of human scientific endeavour that it does eventually cut through this distraction and obscurity of popular thought to the things that matter. The significance of the column of air in the test-tube gains force, until someone (probably Galileo), thinks to graduate it. He puts a mask in the tube at the level of the water when the tube is held in the hand, and another when the tube is immersed in ice. And so the thermoscope is born! Not much can be done with it, but it is a kind of scientific curiosity which we can use to show what happens to a column of air when it is warmed and cooled.

It remains a scientific curiosity for some hundred years. What would your own view of it be under these circumstances? Who would dare to claim to be able to perceive the thermometer nascent in that test-tube? To do so it would have to occur to you that the column of water was going up and down *at the same rate* that it was getting colder and warmer! Who could make such an assumption? And if you did, how could you prove it?

What data are available? On the one hand we have the column of water going up and down. We can all see that. It is directly observable. On the other hand we have our sensations, our feelings. We can perhaps agree that the test-tube is getting colder and warmer, but who knows by how much and how quickly? And how can we possibly agree?

Here we have the prime dilemma and the prime characteristics of all measurement. *Measurement is the process of ordering the psychological experience of magnitude to an external readily observable scale.* It is a relationship between inner sensations that are not directly shareable and an outer yardstick which we can all observe in common.

Yet someone does break through these emotional and intellectual barriers, does find his way through the clutter of knowledge, half knowledge, undigested facts, and fantasies and falsehoods. He decides to calibrate the thermoscope: to divide the space between the body temperature mark at one end of the scale, and the freezing point mark at the other end into one hundred points. With that one decisive act we have moved from thermo-scope to thermo-meter.

Who took this step is not certain, but it was very likely Newton. For the instrument first appeared in England, in Newton's circle, at the height of Newton's best work. It was no longer in the form of an open ended fuse, but of a tube sealed off at both ends. And the liquid was no longer water only. Coloured alcohol and other non-freezing liquids were used as well.

With the use of these first crude thermometers, the study of temperature was transformed. The movement of columns of various kinds of liquid (including soon after, the liquid metal, mercury could be systematically observed, recorded, and compared as they were moved between different baths of sensibly different temperature.

From then on, the problem of the development of the thermometer became a technical problem, firstly of discovering which liquids expanded and contracted with greatest constancy as they were heated and cooled (water, for example, was ruled out, for it was known that after contracting as it grew colder, it began to expand again just before it began to freeze), and secondly of stating a theoretical basis for the instrument. A major step forward was then taken in the middle of the 19th Century with the formulation of the laws of thermodynamics, and with the development of inert gas thermometers. Then another major step was achieved with the discovery of the behaviour of electric currents at different temperatures and the construction of the thermo-electric couple.

It was now possible to measure changes in temperature by means of changes in liquids, in gases, and in the flow of electricity. It can be fairly well established that equally calibrated distances represent equal changes in temperature. But it has taken some 300 years to get to this point.

Our brief sketch of the development of the thermometer allows us to illustrate several important points in measurement. One we have already mentioned; namely, that measurement has to do with the ordering of sensory impressions to an external scale. In effect, it is incorrect to say that we measure temperature. We do not. We measure the length, say, of a column of mercury, and we assume that this measurement corresponds to a particular sensation of warmth or coldness, as a result of the instruction and calibration of an instrument called a thermometer. We have not yet had the experience of the column of mercury getting observedly shorter as the air gets sensibly warmer. Should such a happening occur but once, we should probably have to throw our thermometers away and start again!

Thus it is, that not only can it not correctly be said that we measure temperature, but as Bridgman has pointed out, it is our thermometers, our measuring instruments that give us our best mode of defining temperature. All qualities of things, like temperature, length, hardness, redness, are most accurately definable in terms of the operations we go through to measure them.

The problem of measurement then can be stated in terms of finding a means of ordering our sensations about the properties of things or of people or of social relationships in terms of the equal interval scales of length, or of mass, or of time. Against this background, let us now consider some problems of the measurement of qualities of social life, and the particular relevance of a time scale for such measurement.

REASSUREMENT IN THE SOCIAL WORLD

Our starting point is the measurement of level of work as developed on the Glacier Project, in terms of time-span of discretion; it has been fully described elsewhere. . . .

The reason for our taking an interest in this time-span of discretion, was that its length was observed to accord with the sensation of level or weight of responsibility. The larger the time-span, the greater the feeling of weight; the smaller the time-span the lighter the feeling of weight; increase the time-span and the feeling of weight increases; decrease the time-span and the feeling of weight decreases.

These relationships were supported by the fact that people at the same time-span feel entitled to by and large the same pay; the larger the time-span, the higher the payment to which they feel entitled. However, there is the familiar phenomena that if a manager finds that the responsibility he has assigned to a subordinate is too heavy, he can reduce it by dividing the larger tasks into two or three parts, giving him the first part, then the second part when he finishes the first, and so on. In effect the manager is involved in progressing the work for his subordinate on a shorter time-scale. Or contrariwise, it will be found that as a manager gains confidence in a new subordinate, he allows him greater freedom by allowing him larger tasks.

We have here the same conditions that we found in the case of the measurement of temperature. There is first of all the sensation, the psychological experience of weight and level of responsibility. And secondly, there is the objectively measurable datum, that seems to vary in correspondence with variations in the sensation. Let us consider each in turn.

The psychological sensation of weight of responsibility is just as 'real' a sensation as the sensation of warmth. We have all experienced it. We know when we feel the weight is too heavy, and we feel worried, oppressed and over-burdened. Equally we know when the weight is becoming lighter, and when it has become too light, oppression and worry turn into relief, which turns into boredom and lack of interest if the weight of responsibility is too light.

That is to say, we are here dealing with an individual experience, sensed in terms of magnitude, of greater and lesser; we can equally sense variations in magnitude, in terms of feelings of weight of responsibility getting lighter and heavier.

The problem of measurement (a definition) of this sensed property of tasks, namely weight or level of responsibility, just as was the case in measuring the sensed heat of liquids or other bodies, is to find some objectively measurable datum that appears to vary, as did the length of a column of liquid, in concert with variations in our sensation. That datum we found in the assigned time-span of discretion.

Time-span of discretion is as objective a datum as mercury in a glass tube. In order to be able to observe it we must get an explicit and definitive statement from the manager of the maximum target completion time for the tasks he has assigned to his subordinate. These target times, and his subordinate is informed of them, are objective facts. They are the facts that then govern the behaviour of the subordinate in planning and carrying through his work.

However, they are measurable data; they can be ordered to a time-scale. We are thus in a position to examine variations in the subjective sense of weight or level of responsibility and concomitant variations in the objectively measurable time-span of discretion of the assigned responsibilities whose weight is experienced. The situation is the same as that of being able to examine variations in the sense of the warmth, say, of liquids, and the thermometric readings of those liquids. Systematic observation can begin.

Measurement of level of work is available. Sufficient testing has been done to enable this statement to be made. But more testing will be required to bring conviction to large numbers of people. Even if it is eventually accepted as a means of helping to establish national wage differentials, a national institution of some kind will be required to enable it to be used effectively.

In the next chapter I describe the form that such an institution could take. If it were possible to establish such an institution now, it could help greatly with the problem of wage inflation even without using measurement. But its staff would very soon realize the value of a means of measuring the level of different types of work. So the establishment of such an institution would bring nearer the day when measuring would be substituted for bargaining, or arguing and compromising.

CHAPTER TWENTY-TWO

A National Council for Regulating Wage Differentials (NCRD)

'*New scientific propositions are eventually accepted not because the original opponents are converted to the new way of thinking but because they died.*'—MAX PLANCK

I WAS CHIEF executive of a company which, after much discussion and negotiating between management and representatives, finally eliminated the use of direct monetary-incentive payment systems. There were about twenty different types of occupation, and a bracket of hourly rates of payment was agreed for each. These rates replaced rate-fixed time targets for doing work.

It was clear that as time moved on the differentials between these brackets of pay would need to be changed as the level of work in some of them changed. At some time in the future there were bound to be demands for change in the bracket of pay, demands which would come from the representative of the group to which the bracket applied. Collectively we worked out an institution to deal with the problem. It was based on the following considerations:

That whenever one sub-group in an employment hierarchy achieved an increase in pay then *relatively* to that sub-group all the other sub-groups had less pay.

That unless representatives of the other sub-groups had agreed that one sub-group's pay should rise, then as soon as one sub-group got more money all the other groups would strive to gain similar increases.

That if the other sub-groups succeeded then the differential relationship between all the sub-groups would have reverted to the *status quo*.

That if this happened and went on happening it would theoretically be impossible ever to adjust the differential wage relationship between the sub-groups.

That this was unacceptable because change in intake of work and changes in technical methods of manufacture were bound to alter the levels of work of at least some of the sub-groups; it was essential to have some means of changing differentials.

It was therefore agreed that when one sub-group felt that their level of work had risen they would formulate a claim for an increase of their bracket of pay and inform management. They would then place the claim on the agenda of the next meeting of the works committee[1] (which consisted of all the shop-stewards).

If the works committee endorsed a claim by one sub-group this constituted an acknowledgement by all the other sub-groups that the claiming sub-group was underpaid in relation to the others. The acceptance of this principle also meant that an increase of pay awarded to one sub-group could not be used as grounds for claiming similar pay increases for other groups. If this had not been an accepted part of the procedure the granting of one agreed claim (which adjusted differential pay) would simply have released pressures which if acceded to, would have forced a return to the *status quo*. In terms of differentials everyone would have been back where they started.

This procedure has been in use for about twenty years. It has produced a situation in which differential pay levels can be continuously adjusted, and are so adjusted. In my time scarcely a month passed in which some adjustment was not agreed by management. In most cases the works committee's recommendation was in support of the original claim, but included one or two other occupations closely allied to the sub-group submitting the claim. Sometimes the additional claims were for lesser amounts.

There were very few cases indeed when management did not accept the claim once it was endorsed. They had good reason to accept, for here were twenty or more shop-stewards agreeing that one sub-group represented at their committee should receive an increase relative to all the others. Finally the wage proposal went before the council (unanimous voting) so that it could also be endorsed by *representatives of various grades of staff*.

I imagine that some eyebrows will go up when they read the last sentence, for the idea of shop-stewards agreeing that a claim had to

---

[1] This is not the works *council*, to which I have referred earlier, but a committee of representatives.

pass through a unanimous voting council containing staff representatives is unusual. But, on the other hand, staff brackets of pay also had to be endorsed by the shop-stewards on the council.

Staff representatives never failed to endorse this sort of claim. But many of the staff constituents assumed that their representatives were simply 'rubber-stamping' such claims. This, however, was not the case. The claims were always reasonable. Had they proved unreasonable I have no doubt at all that staff representatives would have intervened on the grounds that their own differential position was under attack. After I left the company there were prolonged discussions and eventual agreement between management and all representatives on the council about holidays, pensions, hours of work, and so on, as they applied differentially to all strata of employees. Staff representatives were not backward in defending their differential position.

Some people from other companies who examined this procedure contended that in most circumstances it would not be viable. Their reasons were that the possibility existed of representatives 'rigging the procedure'. The method would be for all the sub-groups to queue up in turn with a claim and for the works committee, by agreement, to pass each of them in turn without debate. I could recite a great many arguments as to why this is most unlikely to happen if such a procedure is established, but perhaps the best answer to such doubts is that over a period of nearly twenty years it did not happen at Glacier.

Any *general increase* of wages for all the sub-groups normally arose from National Engineering Wage Awards, although claims for domestic general increases did come from the works committee. On more than one occasion management proposed small general increases to keep the general level of wages on a par with that of other companies in the district.

If all this sounds like conduct that could not be expected from average representatives, I would point out that such a procedure was agreed and operated within a total climate produced by the existence of a unanimous voting works council, appeal procedures, clarity about organization, abandonment of piecework, and much else.

I have given this rather lengthy description of an institution brought into being in one company because it is a microcosm of a missing national council. I think it has been clear, at least since the war, that one 'successful' wage negotiation begets another. Each time a particular occupation successfully achieves a large increase in wages all other occupations feel that they have had a drop in wages relative to the 'successful' one. And so the round of claims by those occupations that feel they have sufficient power continues on its frightening progression. Each year the size of the claims is larger. The position of those without representative power, and who cannot fight a claim, becomes progressively worse as others move up the earnings scale.

Successive governments have encouraged the use by employers of piecework schemes, collective bargaining by whole industries, job evaluation and productivity bargaining. All of these have failed either to contain the national wage-bill within their targets, to equate increase of earnings to increased output, or to limit industrial unrest and strikes. Such measures do not even attempt to achieve a more equitable pattern of wage differentials.

As I write, the present Government is about to introduce a Bill that makes substantial changes to the legal position of trade unions and employers. But none of the measures envisaged seems to take account of the problem of inequitable wage differentials.

There has been, and apparently continues to be, a failure to appreciate that the nation totally lacks effective means of tackling the national differential-wage pattern for all types of occupations. There is a serious danger that this blindness will allow a situation of near-anarchy to come about in the employment zone of society.

Since the last war we have been trying a range of macro-economic recipes for our employment ills. Each has been concerned with different percentages of the same ingredients: to curb wages or to free them, to increase taxation or not to do so, to allow credit to ride or to freeze it, to reduce consumption or to allow it to rise, to increase or decrease the supply of money, and so on.

These macro-economic solutions continue to be used because of two convictions. The first is that labour behaves like a commodity in the market: the higher the demand the higher the price, and vice versa. The second conviction is that there is no possibility of getting agreement between all types of employee as to what are equitable and acceptable differences of pay between them.

The first conviction is false. In some industries where there is a surplus of labour, wages are rising as fast as in those where there is a shortage. Differentials in wages between occupations are increasingly brought about by power today—not by surplus or shortage.

The second conviction, that agreement on differentials is impossible, may or may not be true. The fact is that no national attempt has ever been made to sketch out a pattern of differentials towards which workers in all occupations might agree to aim.

Because such an agreement is regarded as unattainable the

rewards of achieving it are not even considered; and because the rewards of such an agreement are not in the mind's eye of the country the admittedly enormous task of tackling agreement about the national pattern of differentials is not attempted. If ever there was a vicious circle, this is it.

So governments continue to curb production and consumption and give assurances to the country that this will curb wage inflation, while the trade unions continue to press for the curbs to be taken off, giving assurances that somehow this will lead to the wage-inflation problem curing itself. I cannot but think that both government and trade unions must by this time know that neither course will curb wage inflation. The policies of both are based on false premises. Their assurances are the false assurances of despair.

Suppose instead, in order to provide the incentive to tackle the problem of getting agreement on wage differentials, we look at the potential rewards of doing so. Such agreement would enable the country to run the economy at near-maximum output without the risk of wage inflation. Some might argue that this would lead to a high volume of imports, and balance-of-payment problems. This is false, for full production *without* wage inflation has been proved by the experience of other countries to be the best basis for expansion of exports.

But the prevention of balance of payments deficits is a negative gain. The real benefits would be:

(a) Full employment—with much-increased opportunity for everybody to find attractive work that fully utilizes their personal ability.

(b) A rising standard of living for all, in itself an antidote to the anxieties that currently help to generate wage inflation.

(c) A greater ability to tackle the problems of the social services and the environment.

(d) An ability to provide more aid to under-developed countries (and let nobody assume that this is simply benevolent charity, for unless the 'haves' of this world soon get down to helping the 'have-nots' on a much larger scale, then future generations may have to face problems that will make the current problems of our society look trivial).

These are immense gains. They could be achieved by getting agreement on a national pattern of wage differentials.

But we shall not get such agreement simply by hoping that the good sense of people will prevail in the long run. Great social problems are always solved in the long run by changing old institutions or by creating new ones. Examination of the history of this country's approach to health, education or administration of the law, demonstrates that this is so. Unfortunately the larger the problem the more difficult it is to create the necessary institution.

The necessity for an institution to tackle the problem of wage differentials can be seen from an examination of certain aspects of our constitutional history. Pre-parliamentary government was a function of the power of the crown and of other groups. *The growth of parliamentary processes was one of gradually incorporating in a legislature representatives of groups who possessed power.* Those who owned land (with the power that it gave to raise armed forces), and the church (with its power over the minds of people) are two early examples of power-groups. The power of the mercantile classes was challenged by Charles I. They responded with the cry 'No taxation without representation' and established new rights for parliament in the Civil War which followed. The Reform Acts of the eighteenth and nineteenth centuries were responses to the emergence of new power-groups in society. They resulted in the grant to those groups of the right to representation in the law-making machine.

The growth of education and of industry led to the emergence of working-class power-groups. Reform gave them votes and led to the emergence of the Parliamentary Labour Party. Simultaneously, the decline in power of landowners and the Church led to a decline in their hitherto privileged representation in Parliament. The last major changes have been the loss of double votes for university graduates and for property-owners, and the grant of votes to women and 18-year-old people. The latter two changes constituted a recognition that women and young people could exercise power.

Whenever reform has been tardy in promoting change in the distribution of the franchise to accord with changes in the power of different parts of society, we have approached revolutionary conditions. We are approaching them today for precisely this reason.

Over 90 per cent of the income-earning population of Britain are today employees. Less than 5 per cent are either self-employed or employers. But Parliament is based entirely on geographical constituencies. Thus no employee-group, as such, is represented in the legislature. It might be argued that because every person in an employee-group has a geographical constituency vote that these groups are, in fact, represented. The fact is, however, that dockers, engineers, teachers, doctors, miners, council employees, and many others have reached the stage where they do not accept the right of Parliament to legislate on matters that directly affect their earnings and other economic entitlements.[1]

The type of institution required can be deduced from analysis of the problem. Many groups are emerging in society that have the power to disrupt society, and they increasingly use that power to better their material position at the expense of others. *Apparently* there is no countervailing power. This is not in fact true. As long as wages have been regarded as a commodity then bargaining over their price will naturally take place between those who represent the supply (the trade unions) and those who buy them (the employers).

Giving up the notion that labour is a commodity changes the frame of reference of the problem. If the wages of different occupations are to be based on the differential level (or the importance) of their work then bargaining between buyer (employer) and trade union (seller) is irrelevant and illogical. Employers should have no part whatsoever in the process. If they wish to employ labour to perform a given level of work then they must pay wages in accordance with that work —not in accordance with the results of some bargaining procedure.

If we adopt this new frame of reference then the problem takes on a new aspect. It becomes one of getting agreement between different occupations about the relative values of the different levels of work done by each. *The argument is thus shifted from one between relatively powerless employers and powerful bargaining groups of employees to arguments between power-groups. By this shift countervailing power is brought into play.*

But for there to be any hope of such agreement it is essential that representatives of all of these occupational groups meet together in a formal setting to carry out very serious work. No institution exists in which such work can be done. *It never has existed. No discussion between representatives of all occupations to get agreement about differential wages has ever been attempted nationally.* To me this has been a quite staggering thought for some years. That is why I claim that we are missing an important national institution. I shall now describe the main outlines of such an institution.

A National Council for Regulating Differential Wages (NCRD).

A series of occupational constituencies. These would elect representatives to the NCRD. It would be necessary to accept rough justice in the early stages. Every registered trade union containing more than a minimum of members would have the right to representation. This would be on a basis of diminishing proportionality to the number of

---

[1] I define 'entitlements' as referring to earnings, pensions, hours of work, holidays, etc.

each trade union's membership. For example if a trade union has 700 000 members it might get one representative for the first 100 000 members, one for the next 200 000 and one for the next 400 000. I use 'trade union', in the legal sense, which includes many bodies such as the British Medical Association, which are often not so regarded.

Any body of employees in a type of occupation that has not formed a trade union would have, of necessity, to create one in order to be represented.

I do not know what the strength of the council would be, but it would be wise to try and keep the total membership low. If this proved impossible then some of the smaller trade unions might have to share a representative, who would have to look after the interests of more than one union.

The council thus formed would have an independent non-voting chairman appointed by Parliament. The council would be provided with a secretariat of economists, researchers, and those with experience in industry and in trade unions.

The council would be set up by Act of Parliament. Its terms of reference would be along the following lines. It would be given an annual sum by which total wages could be increased. This figure would not be the amount by which GNP is expected to rise. A developed country that today succeeds in equating its increase in total earnings with its rise in GNP would be in such an advantageous position *vis-à-vis* other developed nations that it would have to revalue its currency within quite a short period. Therefore, the amount would have to take into account not only the expected rise in GNP but also the rate of wage inflation in other countries. Failure to proceed along these lines would result in terms of reference for the NCRD that would be unacceptable to its members.

The function of the council would be to make recommendations to Parliament about changes in the national differential pattern of wages, to be made within the total target set for them by Parliament.

In principle the council ought to come to its recommendations by unanimous vote. In practice I believe it would be necessary to modify this, at any rate in the early stages of the life of the institution, to a 95 per cent majority vote.

The principle of unanimous voting is new to most people. The only instances of its use of which I am aware are the United Nations Security Council, the Council of the EEC, and the Glacier Works Councils. I shall argue the need for and the viability of such a principle later. At this stage I merely point out that unanimous voting would bestow on each member of the council the right of veto. Thus each representative would have equal power. The equation of power in this way negates it and forces reasoned debate and compromise in its place. It also makes much less important the issue of the number of people on the council representing each trade union.

I have proposed, in fact, 95 per cent majority voting to allow of the possibility of a small number of representatives combining to wreck the constitution of the NCRD. If the majority required were to be substantially smaller than 95 per cent it would deprive a larger number of representatives of the power of veto, would introduce un-balanced power, and might lead to the exploitation of some of the occupations with few representatives by those with greater numbers of representatives. This would be seen as injustice by society, and the moral basis of this means of determining wage differentials would be undermined.

In year one the council would invite from its members details of all their claims for increased wages for year two. On the basis of these the secretariat would work out a draft proposal for the new national pattern of wage differentials for year two. This would be debated by the council on the following basis.

(1) That in order to make a recommendation to Parliament they must agree by 95 per cent majority,[1] and
(2) That the result of the recommendation must not involve a total rise in wages in excess of the limit pre-set by the Government.

In year one there would have to be, I think, a statutory limit set to any wage increases.

In year two, if Parliament accepted a recommendation for a new pattern of differentials, they would make it statutory by order in council. Thus in year two the only wage increases that would be permitted would be those required to give effect to the agreed new pattern of National Wage Differentials. During year two claims from the representatives of various occupations would be received, studied

---

[1] A method of *objective measurement* of the level of importance of work has been discovered by Professor Jaques and rigorously tested. I have described this in chapter twenty-one. It would be of immense help to our society if it were understood and accepted, by a sufficiently large per-centage of our population, as a means of establishing equitable differen-tial wages. I do not propose to discuss this method of measuring level of work because it would take much too much space and because it is my view that while it would be of immense help to the NCRD, if it were to be accepted, it would not come into use as an arbiter of differen-tial wages without the prior existence of such a body as the NCRD.

and take their effect on the formation of the draft plan for National Wage Differentials for year three, and so on.

The NCRD might well have to make some interim recommendations to Parliament with regard to agreed increases for particular occupations where their annual plan had inadvertently produced real injustice.

The recommendations of the NCRD would be to Parliament—not to the Government. My reason for this suggestion is that if made to the Government there would be an implication that the Government could amend[1] the proposals of the NCRD before presenting them to Parliament. Such a power to amend would undermine the psychological status of the NCRD. The NCRD proposals would be therefore for acceptance or rejection by Parliament. If Parliament rejected them they would be returned to the NCRD for reconsideration.

Employers would play no part in the deliberations of the NCRD though no doubt their advice would be sought by those responsible for preparing the draft plan to be placed before the council for debate.

The council would be set up in the first place by Act of Parliament, and I have little doubt that it would require agreement between political parties to bring it into existence.

The membership of the council would represent employees of all types and levels of work. Each representative would be paid a salary by the State. In other ways their conditions of work would be similar to that of members of Parliament. The burden of work would be such as to require long debate sessions. Recesses would allow its members to keep in close contact with their constituent trade unions.

Either Parliament or the NCRD would have to establish a court that could settle disputes concerning detailed implementation of the National Differential Wage Pattern.

The council would carry accountability to Parliament for the working out and recommendation of all or any of the changes that could affect the national pattern of wage differentials.

I am well aware that these proposals represent one of the most radical and difficult adjustments that our society would ever have

---

[1] Any such amendment—which would by definition run counter to the near-unanimous vote of the NCRD, would deprive it of the sanction of occupational representatives, which the original recommendation would have received in the NCRD. A single occupation, so deprived of a wage benefit that had received the sanction of the NCRD would, I think, unquestionably be regarded as having been unjustly treated by the other occupations and by society as a whole.

been asked to contemplate. But they have to be viewed against the absence of any alternative proposals, the growing menace of the current situation, and the rewards that might accrue from their adoption.

I now set out in question form the objections to these proposals that have already been posed to me, and my answers to those objections.

Assume that Parliament accepted the NCRD annual recommendation and that one or more occupations, who had not benefited under it, organized a strike in an attempt to enforce amendment of the award: what then? This question takes us to the root of the problem. First, let me sketch in the details of the situation in which this strike might take place.

Ninety-five per cent of the representatives of the trade-union constituencies of the NCRD have agreed the recommendation. Parliament has accepted it. It is now law. Employers have taken no part at all in debating the recommendation. The strike is not against them. It is against the NCRD and the law. Such a strike would be against the sympathies of the representatives of the other trade unions on the NCRD. This is a new situation in which to strike. I think that it would deter most other trade unions from backing such a strike. It might deter most individual employees in the disgruntled occupation.

Assume, however, that in spite of this new situation a strike occurred that caused considerable disruption of industry or of services. I think Government would, as part of the process of setting up the NCRD, have had to avail itself of powers to bring sanctions against such strikers.

The first potentially available sanction would be to make it illegal for trade unions or employers to pay any money whatsoever to strikers until they return to work, so that any who did pay would be liable to prosecution. The second more powerful sanction would be the withdrawal of supplementary benefits from the families of strikers.

In present circumstances, where a pay dispute is between employer and employee the use of such sanctions is rightly regarded as immoral. In particular, the withdrawal of supplementary benefits is an attack on the family of strikers. In the new situation brought about by the creation of the NCRD I do not believe that such sanctions would necessarily be regarded by society as immoral. The strike is not a private wage-battle with an employer. It is a challenge to a national decision arrived at by democratic process.

One of the major deterrents to breaches of the law by individuals is the effect it may have on the well-being of their families. *Most* men are (or should be) cautious even about the most *tempting* breaches of the civil or criminal law if it is likely to involve hardship for their families.

All ordinary breaches, such as those which result in fines, payment of damages, loss of tenancy of a house, dismissal from occupation, or imprisonment, do involve hardship for families from which the State does not protect them (except at minimum levels on some occasions). Strikes are rightly the exception in present circumstances, and the State does substantially mitigate the financial effects of strikes on families.

I do not believe that in the new circumstances I have outlined such financial support of the family is justified. Every man whose family is so threatened has the possibility of protecting it from hardship by returning to work.

This is strike-breaking by the State. But if we set up the NCRD the strike is against the State. I have stated the case for what might be regarded as a very reactionary move. Looked at in the present context it would be highly reactionary. Looked at from within a new context I am not at all sure that this would be so.

If Parliament decides that a new airfield is to be built in a new area and local citizens decide to barricade all roads leading to that area in order to prevent it being built, they will be prosecuted and, if necessary, imprisoned. This would happen even if there were widespread public sympathy with the grievances of those citizens.

As a society we make our laws by parliamentary process and we insist that the law must be upheld. Once we accept that the economic problems of the country are so serious that they must be dealt with by law then, in the new circumstances created by the existence of the NCRD, I believe that those laws could be enforced.

What would happen if it proved impossible for the members of the NCRD to get the necessary 95 per cent majority vote in favour of a recommendation to Parliament? It would be essential that the Act setting up the NCRD contained clauses that:

(a) Stated the sanctions the Government would use against those on strike for wage claims. For example, withdrawal of supplementary benefit or unemployment pay to those on strike.

(b) Made it clear that failure of the NCRD to agree on a recommendation to Parliament about wage differentials would result in the *status quo* on wages continuing until the NCRD could agree changes.

I have much experience of unanimous voting councils. Their

success depends on every member having to face the fact that no change can take place until all are agreed on some change. *This is the psychological factor that enables them to operate.* It forces protagonists in an argument to go on modifying their different attitudes until agreement is reached. I doubt if anybody who has not had experience of unanimous voting can have a realistic appreciation of the pressures that are set up towards agreement. The constitution of the NCRD would have to be such that there was no way out of disagreement except by somehow obtaining the necessary 95 per cent majority vote.

The unanimous voting procedure adopted by the members of the European Common Market and the events that have taken place as a result are illuminating. Many changes have been retarded, some changes have so far not proved possible, but many changes have been agreed that could not have been brought about by any other procedure. Many of these changes have been of immense economic and political importance and will affect the lives of tens of millions of people. It would seem very doubtful indeed if it would have been possible to form the Common Market at all without unanimous voting on all major changes. Would Germany or France have agreed to a majority voting procedure, which might have resulted in, say, Luxembourg's vote producing a majority that bound them to some important change? I think not. The power of veto that each possesses is the factor that makes association together and the introduction of common conditions and common change possible.

Committees, such as Parliament itself, whose decisions are reached by majority vote, have a culture of their own and rules of procedure to support it. A motion is put, after a debate, often of pre-determined duration, and is voted upon. The matter is decided. It cannot be re-opened next week.

A unanimous voting council works quite differently. Formal and informal votes have to be taken frequently to discover the state of opinion. If there is not unanimity the debate proceeds. It has to continue until such modifications are conceded by protagonists as will result in a unanimous vote.

To operate in this way the council has to have long sessions, with breaks. During the breaks compromises can be worked out between those who are not in agreement. The task imposed on the members of the NCRD looks immense; but theirs would be a paid and nearly full-time occupation. They would have time not only to know each other extremely well but also to keep in contact with their constituent trade unions.

If, for example, the NCRD differential-wage plan established an increase of £x per week on the basic rate of engineering operatives, then through what mechanisms would this national policy be translated into a wage adjustment for individual employees? This is a very difficult question. If the same question were asked today about how the results of a national bargain between employer and trade union were translated, then it would not be possible to give a general answer. The mechanisms and the results would vary greatly from company to company.

The question posed takes us into the area of intra-company differentials. One answer, therefore, is: Set up within each company an institution based on the same principles as the NCRD itself or based on the principles that operate in the Glacier arrangement already described.

A second answer is: Allow the same varied mechanisms that currently translate an employer-association–trade-union bargain into individual pay to continue.

Further research and consideration is needed. But confusion of thinking is likely unless it is clearly recognized that the entire psychological frame of reference within which discussions in individual companies (and other types of employment hierarchies) takes place would be different from the current frame of reference. For example, company strikes to enforce company wage-increases that did not accord with national differentials would be illegal. The existence of a court that could hear appeals about disputes on the manner of implementing NCRD plans would also produce some change of atmosphere.

Thus whatever mechanisms were used to translate the national plan for wage differentials into adjustments to the pay of individuals would have to be thought out against the background, not of the current situation, but of the new situation brought about by the move away from wage-bargaining based on the market concept of labour.

Surely the employers ought to elect representatives to the NCRD?[1] My answer would be an emphatic no. If we were to continue to regard labour as a commodity and its price a matter of a bargain

---

[1] Professor Phelps Brown in a *Times* article of 19 November 1970 proposed a National Council for Pay, 'which would bring together representatives of management, employees and the public. . . .' I agree with much of the thinking in this article but I part company with Professor Brown on the composition and the functions of the council that he proposes.

between 'supplier' and 'seller' then we do not need an NCRD. We would continue as now. But if labour ceases to be regarded as a commodity then the bargain between 'seller' and 'buyer' also ceases and the presence of 'buyers' on the NCRD is unnecessary.

The work of the NCRD would be to arrive at 95 per cent agreement about 'felt-fair' differential pay as between one occupation and another. Employers have no contribution to make in such a debate. Once a pattern of differential pay has been established by law then any employers would have to pay employees in accordance with that pattern. I believe that this would relieve employers and managers from many problems and would release great energies for the performance of managerial tasks in a manner that would promote more efficiency and more contentment of employees. I think it would be appropriate for the secretariat of the council to be in constant communication with employers so that their reactions to draft proposals could be obtained. But that is quite different from having employer representatives on the NCRD.

As soon as the focus of both employers and trade unions was taken off the battle over wages by the operation of the NCRD then other matters of great importance would take their place in negotiation: for example, appeals systems, real joint participation in the agreement of operating policies, and individual promotion mechanisms. The latter would become much more important then they are today. With national law in existence governing the differential pay of occupations the means by which individuals would improve their personal pay would be by promotion to a higher level of work. I believe that these matters would receive much more attention from employers once the daily wage-battle had receded.

Would employers be able to make voluntary wage awards in excess of the results of the NCRD procedure? I see no cogent reason why employers should not have this degree of freedom. I say this on the assumption that company strikes to enforce company wage increases would be regarded as illegal. If they were not illegal and if employers were permitted by law to grant increases in excess of NCRD recommendations to Parliament then while *national* wage bargaining would have been displaced by NCRD operations, bargaining at company level would be intensified.

Given however that wages strikes were illegal then I can see no reason why an employer, who would be under limited pressure only, should not agree with representatives to pay wages above national norms.

Are our current problems of an order that warrants consideration of such far-reaching change? The economic problems deriving from potential and actual wage inflation have probably lowered our standard of living in this country below its maximum potential by a very substantial amount since 1946. The precise figure is almost anybody's guess. But most economists would agree, I think, that had we been able to run the economy considerably nearer to its maximum potential for the last twenty years without wage inflation (and therefore without balance of payments difficulties) then our material wealth would have been very substantially greater than it is today. And yet I doubt if the implied potential material benefit will prove sufficient incentive to get acceptance of the changes I suggest. If, however, fears of still greater deprivation based on still higher rates of inflation grow in the next year or so then economic factors alone might drive us to great changes.

But my case for an NCRD does not rest solely on the economic effects of avoiding inflation. I think that failure to solve this problem is making us into an increasingly unhappy society. Most people recognize that unresolved wage problems breed greed and hostility in employment. But few believe as I do that these employment attitudes are bleeding over into society at large.

I see a direct connection between unresolved employment problems and racial intolerance, increasing crime, majority support of policies against the taxation necessary to succour the old, and the danger of a general regression in the behaviour of citizens such as is already observable in the USA.

I do not think this is fanciful. Over 90 per cent of our working citizens are employees. Many of them have no sense of participation in the organization that employs them, no sense of a just environment, many are employed on occupations that do not fully utilize their creative capacity, and most are anxious about their earnings as compared to others.

Organizations have grown so rapidly under the pressure of technological advance that they have failed so far to provide an environment at work that prevents acute feelings of frustration and hostility. If millions of people continue to spend much of their time in these situations is it reasonable to expect society in general to be insulated from the results?

Many changes in employment conditions are required, but the major change would be to deal effectively with wage differentials. The solution of that problem would reduce tension and enable full-employment policies to be pursued. Fuller employment without wage inflation would put pressure on managements to create the organizational and sociological changes in conditions of employment that would begin to change the attitude of people to their daily work. My reasons for wanting an NCRD are therefore much broader than those that may perhaps appeal to most people.

I do not think society will vote for the changes I want until we are in very serious trouble. I hope this turns out to be a pessimistic view. The prizes of reform are so rich. It would be such a pity if we allowed ourselves to sink too deeply into the pit of trouble before we belatedly decided to act.

Part Three

Operational Work and Techniques

CHAPTER TWENTY-THREE

Product Design

In PART THREE of this book I intend to discuss, firstly, industrial operational work under its three sub-divisions of Product Design, Manufacturing and Marketing. I shall then discuss personnel specialist work. I begin with a discussion of the *organization* of Product Design in industry.

I have already made the point in chapter seven that the economic conception of industrial activity (and, indeed, of all employment-hierarchy activity) always comprises the development, manufacture and marketing of goods. In many companies the idea that product development is a specialist type of work dies hard. It may appear pedantic to emphasize this false perception. Some might suggest, for example, that the only matters of real importance to an organization are the quality, ingenuity and quantity of product development, and not its relationship to other functions. It is my belief, however, that putting product development on to a wobbly pedestal exercises a profound effect on the people engaged in it, and that this is likely to lead to counter-productive consequences like this:

(*a*) If product design is seen as a non-operational or 'non-line' function then it is likely to be regarded as concerned only to advise the company on product design instead of being accountable for providing for the market those designs that the market requires and which can be manufactured and sold at a profit.

(*b*) Product design is likely to lack the authority to insist that product specifications, once accepted by the chief executive, are adhered to by those who manufacture the product, and that those who sell it do so with full understanding of its nature, and the functions it is designed to perform.

(*c*) It is likely that if the accountability for product design is not clearly seen by the whole company to be an operational function equal in importance to manufacturing and marketing, then both manufacturing and marketing personnel will begin dabbling in this area and trying to introduce modifications by stealth instead of facing those engaged in product design with their views on the importance of such modifications.

(*d*) The product design function is likely to be confused or inter-mingled with that specialist function that is concerned (within the company's manufacturing organization) with the Development of Manufacturing Techniques (T).

(I shall refer from here onwards to Product Design and Development as D and Manufacturing Technology as T.)

I am concerned with the particular form of confusion that is most likely to arise when the profession to which those responsible for D and for specialist support for a Manufacturing Manager (T)[1] belong is the same.

In many companies D and T functions are both manned by engineers. Both teams know a great deal about each other's work. There are strong collateral relationships between them in that new product design usually demands changes in manufacturing tech-nique, and the reverse is sometimes also the case. If, however, the teams and the functions are not kept separate then they must jointly come under the command either of the chief executive, or of the D manager, or of the manufacturing manager. None of these arrange-ments meets the case. Each will result in either D or T being put at a discount.

In the past many industrial companies had a role in their hierarchy entitled 'Chief Engineer', which very often was accountable for both D and T. If the role was accountable to the chief executive, as was the case in some shipbuilding and heavy engineering companies, then D received most of the chief executive's attention and the develop-ment of improved manufacturing techniques often languished. Where the role was accountable to the manufacturing manager, then D languished. There appear to have been (and maybe still are) many cases of this, which resulted in a lack of success causing the company finally to 'sub-contract' D by manufacturing under licence goods designed by another company. Role clarification of D accountability is not, therefore, unimportant.

---

[1] In chapter twelve I described the three dimensions of all operational work as personnel work (P), programming work (Pr) and the tech-niques of doing work (T). Managers in charge of manufacturing work are almost always assisted by specialists in manufacturing techniques (T staff officers) who advise the manager on new and better methods of *manufacturing* products. This is *not* product-development work—though it has a strong interaction with product design.

In major areas of industry the phrase 'Research and Development' is used to describe D. Again, it may be felt that this is a purely semantic issue, but words alone sometimes start a pattern of thought and behaviour that can be unfortunate. I am critical of the use of 'Research and Development' for the following reasons.

(1) It suggests that research is a technique to be used, at least primarily, in the D part of the organization, whereas research is a technique that should be used in all phases of work—research into the market, into maintenance, into manufacturing technology, etc.

(2) The term 'research' carries the very important connotation that the research-worker must be free to follow his intuition and pursue that type of work which seems most likely to yield the most knowledge. For many people research is linked with academic freedom to follow one's own line of thinking. The word stands, in some minds, for an untrammelled search for greater knowledge. In this latter sense industrial firms do not carry out research, because their efforts are necessarily bent towards profitably, satisfying the needs of a market. D departments use research techniques in the course of doing their work, but D is not a department set up to do research any more than a factory that uses electro-deposition as *one* of its manufacturing techniques is an electro-deposition factory.

(3) Because the most dramatic outcome of pure research in universities and scientific institutions is the discovery of something new, the use of the term 'research' to label a D department tends to make others believe that the department's essential work is to discover new things, to produce 'break-throughs', and to be 'creative' in a special sense. This leads to the idea that the ordinary disciplines of conserving resources and focusing them on the priority needs of the company are not altogether appropriate in a research and development department. Some of the incoming new staff of such departments join the company with the notion that they will be free to follow the lines of research that fit their personal skills, knowledge and aspirations. Such ideas orientate the department away from its real operational function of keeping the company in the forefront of the competitive battle (by product development) and result in a waste of resources, because the department follows up ideas which, from the point of view of the company and its market, are off-centre.

All this may look like mere semantics and, indeed, in many companies who use the term 'research and development' the actual operations are beyond criticism. But for others the change of the term would signal a re-orientation of attitude towards product development. It would mean ceasing to regard 'R&D' as:

(a) an expensive investment made necessary to maintain the image of the company;

(b) useful for impressing customers;

(c) hopefully brought into existence because it might in the future produce some real winners;

(d) of current value because it can help to solve many problems of function and testing of the product;

(e) responsible for the laboratory (which, in fact, is often a manufacturing inspection function);

(f) giving service to customers in helping them to understand how to use the product, and

(g) analysing failure to perform to specification.

These are important but, nevertheless, peripheral functions of a D department, whose essential task is to improve existing products and to design new products in accordance with the total future plans of the company as a whole and the needs of its market.

The Organization of the Product-Design Function

The term 'Product Design' covers a vast range of work, involving people of many divergent disciplines, using widely varying techniques.

The continuum of work stretches from consumer goods, fashions, foods, books, random luxuries, furniture, dishwashers, motor cars, housing, industrial consumer goods, chemicals, tools, to scientific and capital goods at the other end of the continuum. To generalize about the organizational structure that embraces the work of designing such a range of products, it is necessary to keep comment at a high level of abstraction.

D usually requires the pulling together of ideas arising from many different experiences and types of knowledge. This experience and knowledge, assembled in the mind of one person and successfully projected on to paper or into models, is rightly regarded as creative genius. As products grow in complexity the possibility of one person being able to model the whole product in his own mind becomes increasingly remote. Such products require technical knowledge beyond the compass of one mind, and their complexity makes the total imaginative concept too broad for one man to conceptualize at that level of detail that is the stepping stone from an idea to a product design.

The range of product complexity explains the very different types of product-design organization found in different companies. We find the individual shoe, fabric, furniture or fashion designer, working in one company perhaps alone or possibly supported by assistants who make up the models, research the available materials, or work out detail, but whose work does not affect the general design concept very much. At the other end of the scale we have the product composed of an assembly of perhaps electrical hydraulic and mechanical sub-assemblies, each using intricate components and all integrated together by an all-over design. Such products require a knowledge of mechanical engineering, metallurgy, electrical engineering, ergonomics, cybernetics, production technology, and many other applied sciences.

It is a short step to think of mixed 'teams' of people engaged on product design. The increasingly emphasized cliché about invention or innovation today is that instead of being the product of one brain it is the result of team-work by groups of scientists. But team-work can mean two different things. Firstly it can mean the delegation of one responsibility to be shared by a number of people occupying different roles; this group of roles then shares a corporate responsibility for producing results. The second meaning can be that clear-cut individual responsibility for separate tasks is allotted to each role, but that those occupying roles responsible to the same manager are expected to keep each other fully informed of what they are doing, and of the results obtained, and generally to meet and discuss the total task of their manager so that by interaction, ideas can emerge that will widen horizons, throw up fresh leads to problems, and so on.

I will discuss team-work first in its connotation of 'corporate responsibility'. I do not believe that product design (or for that matter any other type of employment work) can best be carried out by team-work in this corporate sense. There is often a high level of collateral relationships between those who are not working as a team but who carry quite explicit personal responsibility, and the result is often described as team-work. I have defined collateral relationships in chapter eleven as 'the relationship between people of the same rank when exercise of the authority delegated to them can impinge on the effectiveness of each other's activity'.

Work in employment systems is invariably carried out by individuals in distinct roles; but much interaction usually takes place between these individual roles (because of the increasing extent to which the work decisions of one role impact upon those of the work being done by colleagues in other roles).

I believe these observations may have an important bearing on the structure of product-design organizations. The manager B may have been given the task of designing an improved type of product, which itself is composed of a number of components. It may be necessary to experiment with new materials for some of the parts. It will be necessary to test the manufacturability of some of the parts, and research into the finer points of their function may be required. These are tasks that can be separated and delegated to subordinates. But each separate task is intimately related to the total task at a series of interfaces. Each part of the total task can and certainly will be delegated to an individual (who may himself have subordinates). He will be working on his own task, but his decisions are also circumscribed to some extent by the work decisions of his colleagues, each of whom is engaged on his own and separate task. Much interaction, discussion and, at times, reference to manager B, who carries the responsibility for the total design, will be necessary, *but this is not corporate responsibility.*

Corporate responsibility carries the connotation of a group compromising with each other or even voting when they disagree. (Or it may imply that the member of the group with the highest status makes the decisions—a sort of *primus inter pares* conception, which is itself inconsistent with joint or corporate responsibility.) This way of organizing work shields the individual and allows him to evade personal accountability by taking shelter within the group. Thus the ablest members of this sort of 'team' will be frustrated because they feel that their own contribution does not stand to their own credit. They feel pulled down to the level of the group. The less able tend to welcome the situation because it can cover up their own inadequacies.

An unfortunate characteristic of a great deal of product design and development work is that the original budget usually turns out to have been an under-estimate. It seems probable that in many cases this is due to lack of individual responsibility and too much reliance on 'team-work'.

Another field of endeavour provides another example that helps to demonstrate the dangers of group responsibility for resources. If a number of separate companies bring a loosely knit consortium into being to quote for what is nowadays referred to as 'a package deal' (that is, the supply of a total process involving different items of equipment separately supplied by each member of the consortium), then the final price is likely (initially at any rate) to be surprisingly high. The reasons for this are known. If each company were to quote separately for its separate items to a main contractor or directly to the potential buyer the company would know that the sub-contract will be won or lost basically on price. The individual company will sharpen the price sufficiently, in the light of market knowledge, to give its bid a good chance of success. If, however, the price is simply going to be one to be added into the total price for the package deal, then the company is in a difficult situation. If the company keeps its price low other members of the consortium may use this highly competitive offer to allow them to gain higher than normal margins of profit for themselves. In other words, the individual company responsibility is at a discount and the total price rises. I believe that 'group' responsibility in product design has the same sort of effect.

In some product-design organizations the lack of clear-cut roles and of defined individual responsibility breeds irresponsibility about the spending of resources. If three individuals within a group each suggest different approaches to a problem the tendency will be to keep the peace by following up all three. If the decision rested with one individual he would choose the approach that seemed best to him, and only attempt a second or third approach if the first failed. If three people in individual roles responsible to the same manager produce different ideas for solving problems and each persists in his choice, then they will have to take their disagreement to their manager, who will have to decide which to back. Thus the blurred responsibility induced by trying to set up teams with some sort of corporate responsibility can be highly wasteful of resources. It can result in an inability on the part of the manager in charge of product design to pinpoint weaknesses in his organization. This leads to bad design, failure to keep to time targets, and the wasteful expenditure of resources on non-priority projects. The 'team spirit' will cover up the failures of its individual 'team' members.

Team-work in the second sense of the word—that is, constant interaction between people who are working on individual tasks—is, on the other hand, a way of working that is necessary to many types of product development. But it operates best where colleagues have mutual respect, where there is a feeling of security, where each feels that his manager is capable of recognizing his own unique contri- bution, and where jealousy is absent. Clear-cut role definition, allocation of tasks to individuals, individual responsibility and, in fact, explicit organization are the necessary conditions if confidence between persons is to grow. This confidence allows free and creative discussion—which is what is sometimes referred to as good team-work.

Growing percentages of those employed in companies' 'Research and Development' organizations come from universities. This may be one reason for the absence of clear manager–subordinate relationships, individual responsibility, and the tendency towards group responsibility. The idea of 'academic freedom' can hardly be regarded as a boundary-defined conception, and its full meaning in practice is variable. Nevertheless, it is regarded as a principle of university life and is inconsistent with the sort of managerial–subordinate relationships that exist in industry. In a university the amount of research and the resources spent on it may be under the control of the head of a university department; but the nature of the research and the approach to the problems involved seem to be entirely at the discretion of the research-worker. This freedom to choose one's own research targets and the methods of carrying them out, if carried into industry, can be very wasteful. The university does not go bankrupt if its research fails to help to earn income. Its income is independent of the success of these efforts. But if the members of the organization of an industrial company carry over into their work the behaviour-patterns arising from university research, then there is no guarantee that the kind of product development that matches the manufacturing and marketing plans of the company will be achieved.

If I may risk a rash generalization I would suggest that one of the characteristics of industrial organization is too *little delegation* of the use of judgement to *manufacturing* managers and too *few bounds* to the use of discretion by managers in control of *product development*. Many companies seem to assume that manufacturing processes can be specified, timed, mechanized, and implemented, on the basis of a plan. But often in practice the use of discretion by craftsmen, supervisors and foremen is essential to overcome uncatered-for variables, which would bring the process to a standstill if a sort of technical 'working to rule' attitude were adopted.

But in product development the opposite attitude often prevails. The assumption there is that the setting of specific tasks to be attempted according to a timed programme within specified budgets of cost would interfere with creative effort and could not, therefore, be imposed.

I am sure that if chief executives were to work out with their operational subordinates broad specifications of the future new products (or the developments of existing products) which they thought would be required (in the light of their markets and manufacturing capacity) and set these as tasks to be attempted at a given cost on a timed programme, then they would get more benefit from the resources they spend on product development.

D departments of industrial companies often come under great pressure from M and Mk to provide a wide range of services. They are asked to do chemical analysis, physical testing, to educate customers in the use of the product, or to help in trouble-shooting, repair and maintenance of the product in the field. These services are necessary; sometimes the provision of them is welcomed by D personnel because it means travel and contact with the market. Performing these services generates a feeling that they are making an immediate contribution to the work of the company, as compared to the longer-term contribution involved in the design and development of future products.

I found, as a chief executive, that as soon as manufacturing or marketing managers gained confidence in the ability of this or that 'boffin' from the product-development organization they tended to lure them away from urgent work on new products on to a wide range of peripheral problems. There is need for D personnel to visit markets under the control of marketing personnel and to get involved in the problems of manufacturing processes. They must do this in order to gain the experience that will help them with their own tasks. But it seems to me that a strong tendency exists to overdo it.

Central Product-Design Organization

Chief executives of parts of large companies or of subsidiary companies sometimes have special problems because of the organizational placing of the D function inside the total structure of an industrial group.

Groups of companies with many subsidiaries have an important choice to make about the product-design function. The choices are shown in the figures that follow:

If the D organization is centralized and responsible to the chief executive as in Fig. 26, then the managers in charge of the subsidiary companies have been relieved of the responsibilities for their own product design. They are not, therefore, in terms of my definition, chief executives. They cannot be held accountable for the

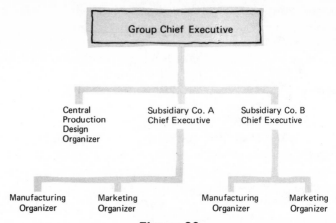

Figure 26

success of the subsidiary companies they command, because their results will be materially affected by product-design decisions that lie outside their field of responsibility. I am not implying that this situation is either good or bad. The decision to adopt this organization might, for example, be forced on the company by circumstances. For example, the subsidiary companies A and B may be making such closely related products in terms of end-function (though with differing designs of product for different markets) that product design aimed at the needs of A will overlap the design effort for the products of B to an extent that makes it uneconomic to operate a separate product-design organization for each of them.

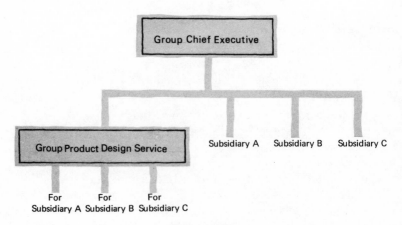

Figure 27

The organization shown in Fig. 27 also centralizes D. But the manager in charge of D is accountable for providing a product design *service* to the managers of the subsidiary companies A, B, and C. This service is provided on demand from the subsidiary companies up to limits of product design expenditure set by the group chief executive.

The rationale of such an arrangement will normally lie in the fact that the type of products made by the subsidiaries are related to each other, and involve in their design and development similar knowledge, skills, equipment, test rigs, or materials. Where this is the case the grouping together of the design effort on the products of all three subsidiaries will lead to more economic use of resources.

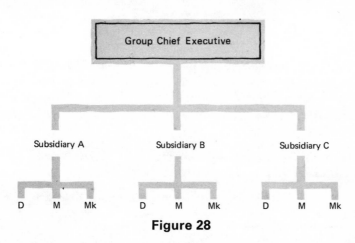

Figure 28

The organization in Fig. 28 places the managers of the subsidiary companies quite clearly in the position of being chief executives of their respective companies. It is in my view the best form of organization when the products of the subsidiary companies are highly differentiated. To group product design when this is so, is simply to centralize the function for the sake of centralizing it.

CHAPTER TWENTY-FOUR

Manufacturing Work

NEARLY EVERYTHING I have written so far applies as much to manufacturing organization as to any other part of the employment hierarchy, but there are some particular problems that arise either uniquely or more often in manufacture than in other areas, and this chapter is devoted to them.

Product or Process Organization

In discussing the issue of collateral relations in chapter eleven I described the manner in which some tool-manufacturing departments were at one time organized. A tool-maker was given a drawing, and he proceeded personally to subject a piece of steel to all the processes such as milling, turning, grinding, drilling and fitting, that were necessary to complete it. In doing so he used various types of machines in the department. This is the ultimate form of *Product Organization*. The accountability for production of the complete product in this case was delegated down to the last level in the hierarchy. I do not know a factory that organizes its operational work in this way today. One can imagine a factory engaged on unique pieces of furniture employing highly skilled craftsmen, each of whom works exclusively on the completion of a single piece of furniture, but even when I visited a small factory making exquisite reproduction furniture of very high quality, each piece was worked upon by several craftsmen, each of whom specialized in some part of the manufacturing process.

An extreme form of *process organization* would be exemplified where four or five factories, each under the command of, say, a

Rank-4 manager,[1] each separately specialized in a process necessary to the manufacture of the finished product. For example, the first would produce castings, the second would carry out preliminary machining operations, the third finish machining, and the fourth would chromium-plate the product and deliver it to the customer. This would be an extreme form of process organization. Figures 29 and 30 depict the two forms of organization.

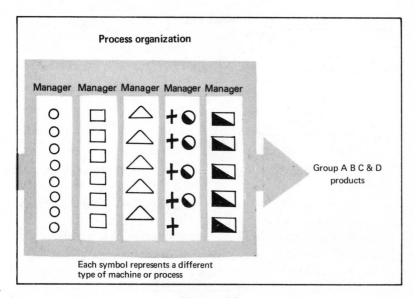

Figure 29

Product organization enables accountability for finished goods to be held at a lower rank in the employment hierarchy than process organization. At some rank in the structure someone has complete accountability for the product. Beneath that level organization breaks down tasks into process organization or into manufacture of component parts of the product.

---

[1] I discuss 'ranking' in Chapter thirty-one. Briefly, if we consider a machine operator as Rank 1; his foreman manager as Rank 2; the foreman's manager as Rank 3, then a Rank-4 manager would be at the third level of management. In manufacturing, I would expect the *average* Rank-4 manager to have an extended command ranging from 500 to 1000 employees.

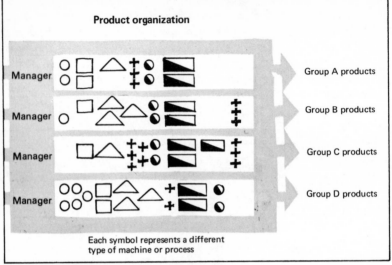

Figure 30

Two major influences are at work that push towards process
organization:[1]

(a) The economic gains from the specialization of managers and
operators on a narrow range of skills and tasks.

(b) The economic gains from higher utilization of expensive equipment and machines.

If all the machines of one type are assembled together in one department, perhaps three of them may be adequate to perform a given
quantity of work. But if there are five product departments, each
may need one such machine, and machines will necessarily lie idle
for some part of their life.

Three major influences are at work that push towards product
organization:

(a) The economic gains through very large reductions in the total
production time-cycle, because of the ability to move *single units*

---

[1] Exact definition is difficult. Every factory uses both process and product organization. The issue is how far down the employment hierarchy
it is possible to establish managerial roles that are accountable for a
finished product. Establishing them at relatively low level is a move
towards product organization. When product accountability remains
at a relatively high level in the hierarchy then that is what I mean by
using process organization, because in that latter situation few managers
will hold product accountability.

of the product from one machine to another as each process upon each unit is completed. In process organization each process is under the command of a different manager, perhaps in a different department. This means that the work has to move from one process to another in batches, so that the first unit of the batch to have a process completed upon it has to wait to move on to the next process (in a different department) until the whole batch has been completed. The difference in the total time taken to produce a given quantity can be hours as against weeks.

(b) The sociological and psychological gains (which in turn give rise to economic gains) arising from the association of employees at low levels in the hierarchy with the finished product, and the opportunities which arise in a finished-product department of moving, promoting and educating personnel over a wider range of skills and tasks.

(c) The economic gains that arise from the degree of mechanization that product organization makes possible when the length of 'run' of a particular product is sufficiently large to warrant the linking together of machines. This enables conveyors and transfer mechanisms to be used, which eliminates much manual labour or even all of it.

Product organization is increasingly adopted for goods that are produced in large volume. Process organization tends to continue as the basis for the production of industrial and capital goods.

These matters are very familiar to production managers and production engineers, but I have set them out (in somewhat over-simplified form) because the organizational effects of the economic decisions that bring about greater or lesser degrees of the two modes of organization are not always, in my view, sufficiently considered.

Before proceeding further there is a need to establish some clear language. We have, in industrial hierarchies, a conglomeration of terms used to describe various managerial and quasi-managerial roles, such as charge-hand, supervisor, assistant foreman, foreman, superintendent, production manager, factory manager. Such terms would convey different meanings to those who read them according to their own past experience. I propose, therefore, to discuss production organization in terms of Rank 1 (operators), Rank-2 managers (equivalent to foremen or supervisors who hold managerial authority), Rank-3 managers (equivalent possibly to superintendents in large companies or production managers in smaller companies).

The steadily growing tendency towards product organization

places on the shoulders of managers in charge of manufacturing departments increased accountability and requires a wider range of knowledge and experience. They have under their command more types of machinery and processes of which they must have knowledge, and they are accountable for co-ordinating these processes and the people deployed upon them. This is work that would be done at a higher level of the hierarchy if they were in command of processes instead of complete products.

I will now risk a generalization. Nevertheless, I believe it to be true in a large percentage of situations. Product responsibility is tending to move from Rank-4 down to Rank-3 managers. Where Rank-4 managers are accountable for co-ordinating the production of complete products they are often assisted by specialists in staff roles. For example, a Rank-4 factory manager might have the assistance of a personnel officer, a production engineer in charge of a work-study department and perhaps a jig-and-tool drawing office, and a production scheduling specialist. Or at least he may have some of these specialists. When, however, responsibility for the finished product moves down to Rank 3 such specialists usually remain responsible to Rank-4 managers.

I am not suggesting removal of all specialists from Rank 4, nor am I necessarily suggesting an increase in the number of specialists. Figures 31 and 32 depict what I am suggesting. I have, for simplicity, confined the diagrams to one type of specialist only.

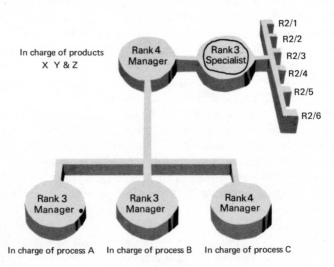

Figure 31

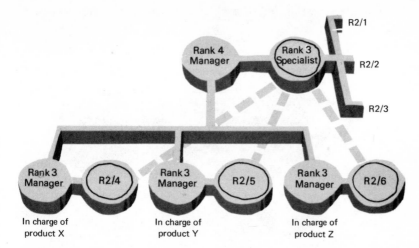

Figure 32 Illustrating delegation of product accountability to Rank-3 managers, with attachment of specialists by specialist R3 to R3 operational managers.

I have already described in chapter twelve, in general terms, the function of the R2 attached specialists and their relations to both R3 operational managers and to R3 specialists.

I think that many companies are paying a high price for failing to support some operational managers with specialist staff officers. The increasing complexity of both products and manufacturing processes demands ever more attention from operational managers. As a result administrative, personnel and programming problems sometimes receive too little attention. When, as a result, there is trouble, specialists from higher up in the organization move in to 'sort things out'. This is not always very helpful. The manager of a department then finds 'his boss's specialists monkeying about with the work of his own foremen'! Had this irate manager been given one or two specialists of his own, he could have mastered the problems that are bothering the factory manager. Fig. 33 illustrates what happens.

I have examined situations where all specialist staff are attached at R4 level. One finds, however, that though the manifest situation is that these specialists are accountable to a Rank-3 specialist, as in Fig. 31, in fact some of them are actually working most of their time to the instructions of operational managers at R3 in charge of departments of the factory as in Fig. 32. The pressure of the work situation has provided them 'informally' with staff officers as in Fig. 33. But of course the situation is not a clear one and it does not work very well.

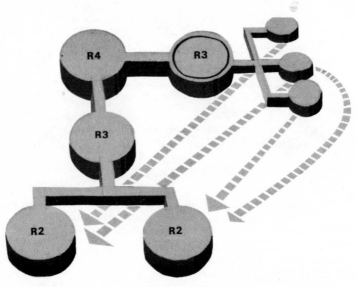

Figure 33

Much has been said about the better state of relations in the small company, and it is probably true that the average factory of up to 400 people is better off in this respect than larger units. Instead of leaving it at that (and accepting the prospect of increasingly unsatisfactory relations as companies grow larger), we ought to examine those aspects of smaller companies that help to bring about sound relations at work, and consider ways of creating those conditions in larger companies. While much of this book is an attempt to do just that, this is the first chapter in which I have discussed sheer size (in terms of number of employees) as one of the criteria.

A battalion in the army comprises up to about 700 men, and because they not only work together but also live together, each man tends to know who does or does not belong to the battalion. But others from higher commands do not know, and this leads to the practice of wearing on uniforms some type of insignia, which identifies soldiers as members of their battalion. It is the property of recognizability that makes this unnecessary below battalion strength.

This phenomenon is familiar in industry. If you are chief executive of a company employing a few hundred people you know a large number by name, you know still more by sight, and you ask about the newcomers whom you do not recognize. I speak from personal experience. When you can do this you are probably in a Rank-3 managerial position. The company grows; your role becomes Rank 4 or 5 and (if you have the capacity) you move up to work at a new level; you begin losing touch with the majority of people. You are accused of having become distant and your extended command has ceased to have the property of 'recognizability' for you.

Now consider, say, the Rank-3 managers who are subordinate to you, some of whom are responsible for finished products. They will be the managers with the largest extended commands at that level. If these do not exceed about 350 employees then they probably have the property of 'recognizability'. But the Rank-3 manager's task is harder than yours used to be. You had, as chief executive, no manager above you. Your 350-employee command embraced the whole company.

Your Rank-3 subordinate has colleague managers who also have large commands. His is one unit in the conglomeration of units that forms the company. You, as chief executive, had command of all the specialists and the services in the company. His unit is constantly invaded by specialists and others 'from the main office' or 'from upstairs' or from 'headquarters'.

It is possible, however, by adjustment of organization, to go some way, in a Rank-3 product unit within a larger company, towards creating within it some of the 'feel' of a separate small company. This can be achieved by providing the manager of the unit, by attachment, with those specialists who would otherwise be constantly invading the department from a higher level, by placing the unit manager's office as near as possible to the production area, and by accommodating the attached specialists around the unit manager so that all of them are physically a part of the unit. This sort of arrangement enables specialists—designers, draughtsmen, production engineers, rate-fixers, progress-chasers, personnel officers, inspectors and others—to be known personally and to be felt, as in the smaller company, to be part of the team who are sharing in the job. In addition, if such a product unit can have immediate contact with customers over issues of quantity, delivery, and quality, then the feelings of wholeness and departmental cohesion will be further strengthened.

I have observed the effects of moving towards this form of organization in several companies. They are impressive not only in their impact on managers and specialists but on the rank and file as well.

Foremen
There are probably more foremen in industry than the total of all other persons in command positions. The number of employees accountable to foremen is certainly larger than the total of all others because foremen's commands are usually large. Foremen are the link between millions of craftsmen and other employees of many types and the rest of management. I have already pointed out that if a hierarchy employs 1000 people it includes 999 manager–employee relationships. If foremen are managers then they are parties to most of these relationships. The question is, however, are they managers?

Some years ago I addressed a large gathering of senior industrial people and I defined the term 'manager' as I have done in chapter three (i.e. a manager minimally has the authority to veto appointments, to make assessments of and to de-select people in immediately subordinate roles).

One man said he would have liked to accept my definition because it was logical but he had difficulty in doing so. He was the senior man in one of the largest banks in that area. He had always assumed that he was a manager but he said that if he accepted my definition, he was not. The reason was that he had no authority to de-select immediate subordinates. All he could do was to report his dissatisfaction to the central establishment branch of the bank and they—not he—decided what was to happen to the individual. I asked him if he had recently wished to de-select any subordinate and he informed me that over the last three years he could think of four. 'What happened to them?' I asked, and he replied: 'They were transferred elsewhere.' 'And supposing', I asked, 'the establishment branch had said—"No you must keep them in their present positions"?' He replied: 'That would have created an impossible position for me and I should have resigned.'

This story highlights the danger of confusing the assumed situation with the extant position. The bank manager in my story *was* a manager. The need to report his wish to de-select a subordinate to the establishment department of the bank was because they were going to have to handle the problem. This had given rise to an untenable regulation that the decision lay with them. Clearly the decision to de-select lay with the manager, but he had to report his decision in advance to the establishment branch of the bank so that they could arrange a transfer.

Few senior civil servants would classify themselves as managers within the terms of the definition, but if one questions them closely they will agree that 'if they feel sufficiently strongly' they can veto appointments, they can influence promotion and they can have people removed from subordinate roles—'but it takes time'. There is vagueness about the authority of their roles in this respect (and it would do a great deal of good to remove it) but they are, in my opinion, not nearly so far-removed from the possession of managerial authority as most of them assume.

The situation is the same for some foremen, but I believe that the majority are not granted full managerial status. This situation is so familiar in many companies that its validity is not even questioned. But it is not valid. For though they are often not managers, most of those foremen will be held fully accountable for the activities of their 'subordinates'. There are many reasons for this failure to make the role of foreman a full managerial role, and I will list some of them.

(1) The absence of formalized appeals systems would make it dangerous. Without them foremen granted managerial authority could make unjust decisions, which could lead to strikes and distress.

(2) Failure of companies to commit to paper much of their policy concerning conditions of work means that decisions by foremen about such matters would probably be inconsistent one with another. This would lead to labour problems.

(3) In many cases foremen would not be able to exercise managerial authority unless it had been sanctioned by representatives. The idea of representatives being invited to debate and agree what are, in many companies, regarded as 'managerial prerogatives' is regarded by many senior managers as repugnant.

(4) Many foremen today are not capable of, or ready to use, managerial authority. The importance of the role has been and continues to be seriously under-rated, with the result that many such roles are manned by people who lack the capacity to hold them.

(5) Lack of clear policy, of training in the meaning of policy, and of managerial authority itself, has led many foremen to act in a cautious and indeterminate way. This is frequently accepted as a reason for not giving foremen managerial authority—though the argument is of course circular.

My personal experience in getting a range of policies written and sanctioned, getting an appeals system operating, and *then* setting up foremen as managers, was that many rose to the job, but around

30 per cent did not. They lacked the psychological capacity that enables one man to take command of others.

Other situations render the use of managerial authority by foremen difficult. Two examples are payment-by-results systems and 'clocking in'. It is unfortunate that while it is difficult to get rid of direct-incentive methods of payment without sound managerial control on the shop-floor, it is equally difficult to establish such managerial control in the presence of such payment methods.

Piecework is, in one sense, an attempt to turn employees into quasi-entrepreneurs. It engenders the attitude, when a foreman gives directions about work, of 'mind your own business, the task I am engaged on is my business, not yours. If I do not carry it out properly I lose, not you: what are you worrying about?' I am not suggesting that operators give expression to that attitude, but it exists and influences their relationship to authority in the presence of direct-incentive payment methods.

Much the same attitude arises over 'clocking-in' procedures. The practice is that if employees are more than five minutes late then *the wages office* (not the foreman) deducts a quarter of an hour's pay as a penalty. Thus a foreman who criticizes a subordinate for being late is likely to encounter the unexpressed attitude: 'What has it got to do with you? I'm late, but I've paid for it; the company hasn't lost, they've deducted a quarter of an hour's pay.'

These are two examples of de-personalized authority reaching down on to the shop-floor and endeavouring to exercise control otherwise than through the authority of those who should be exercising that control. I certainly found that the abolition of both of these things improved the situation. But the abolition of these remote controls was not possible without, at the same time, giving foremen full managerial authority and laying the burden of control on their shoulders. They had to assess and criticize both the time-keeping and the work activity of their subordinates. It took much training and general upgrading of the role to achieve this situation. I know of some other companies who have had similar experience.

In many manufacturing companies brackets of hourly pay are attached to different types of hourly paid occupations. Decisions have to be made about the individual employees' level of pay within the bracket. The foreman should be responsible for making these decisions. But although apparently this is often the situation, in fact the foreman will need to obtain sanction from his manager (the superintendent) to award increases within the bracket of pay.

This situation can arouse the most bitter feelings in the foreman's subordinates. An operator asks for an increase of rate of pay and argues his case with the foreman. The foreman says that he will consider the matter. He sees the superintendent, who decides on quite general grounds (perhaps that total expense in the department is already at too high a level) that the increase sought should not be granted. Perhaps the foreman feels that the operator's case is a just one, and he argues the case but the answer is still negative.

If the foreman were now to see the operator and state precisely what had led to the refusal then the operator would probably wish to argue his case to the superintendent. This would have to be refused, because if the superintendent once got himself into the position of being openly acknowledged as the arbiter on individual issues of this kind he would be inundated with similar problems. In any case, he does not know enough about the work-performance of individuals to be able to decide such issues intelligently. So the foreman is not permitted to tell the operator that the operator's arguments and his own, in support of a wage increase, have been overridden by the superintendent. The foreman, therefore, refuses the operator's claim on some insincere basis. Experience in the department has probably led to a situation where the actual process whereby these matters is decided is known. So cynicism and frustration are born.

The solution is to give foremen discretion to make decisions about individual claims within a bracket of pay. It is not difficult for the personnel office to watch the distribution of individual pay-levels within the bracket that arise from the decisions of each foreman, and to inform the superintendent which foremen tend to pay all their operators at the top of the bracket.

I have set out in detail this case of an individual pay-rate claim as an example of many other types of decision which should lie within the discretion of foremen, but which often in fact lie at higher levels in the hierarchy. Other examples are concerned with holidays, absence from work, promotion, change of job, over-time, and night-shift work. Decisions about all of these matters can cause great ill-feeling if an employee is unable to discuss them directly with his own 'manager'. As long as the lowest level of supervision is denied managerial authority (and trained in how to use it) then we shall have trouble over such matters on the shop floor.

Supervisors
The term is used by some companies as an alternative to foreman or manager. But in other companies 'supervisor' is a position junior to foreman, half-way between him and his subordinates.

The term 'charge-hand' is used in a similar way. Some companies appoint assistant foremen. In short, in many companies there is a woolly stratum of semi-managerial roles at the base of the hierachy. It certainly ought to be cleared up. I am going to use the term 'supervisor' to refer to all these in-between roles. Foreman-managers frequently have very large commands ranging up to fifty people. They need help in the management of these commands, and supervisory roles have come into existence to fill this need. But the authority of these supervisory roles must be explicitly described and defined if the authority of foreman-managers is not to be confused and diluted. Employees need to know who is their real boss. Undefined supervisory roles interfere with this.

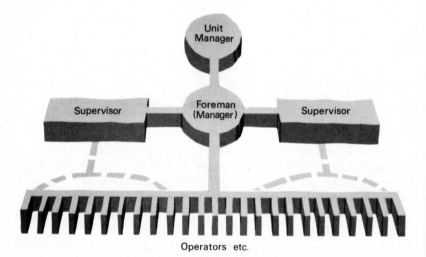

Operators etc.

Figure 34

In Fig. 34 the foreman is shown as the manager of twenty-five subordinates. The supervisors are shown as assistants to the manager, exercising the following accountability and authority.

(1) They are accountable to their manager for the quality and quantity of work done by operators while they are supervising them.
(2) They are assigned tasks by the manager and decide how these shall be apportioned between the operators.
(3) Subject to general work-methods decided upon by the manager, they decide detailed methods to be used, how to overcome problems, when to seek help from others.

(4) They are accountable for ensuring that operators adhere to these methods and for such discipline on the job as will ensure the required standards of quantity, quality and safety.

(5) They are accountable to their manager for assessing the work done by operators, for reporting to their manager if they feel that his managerial authority is necessary to solve problems, and for providing an assessment of each operator allotted to them when required to do so by their manager.

Thus, in more general terms, supervisors exercise on-the-job discipline, but they do not have the authority to veto appointments, to make overall assessments of operators, or to de-select. They are not managers.

Having often discussed such a definition of supervisory authority, I know well that many managers will regard such detail as fussy and unnecessary. But many managers would admit to a very strong dislike of being placed in a situation where they are uncertain whether someone senior to them in the hierarchy is or is not their own manager. Placed in such a situation they say: 'He gives you an instruction. You aren't certain whether he has the authority to do so; you aren't sure whether you can challenge his authority; if you carry it out you may be in trouble with the man you regard as your manager; if you don't carry it out you may equally be in trouble.' This is precisely the situation in which many operators and office-workers find themselves *vis-à-vis* supervisors, charge-hands, leading hands, assistant foremen, etc. This is a problem that needs attention in many sections of industry and commerce.

More generally, it may be stated that it is a problem of half-ranks. By that I mean that for a true managerial–subordinate relationship to exist there must be a specific degree of difference of psychological capacity between the manager and the subordinate. Wherever this does not exist we get a situation of half-ranks. I shall discuss this in a later chapter.

Few would deny that the lower strata of managers, and particularly the lowest stratum, are of the greatest possible importance to efficiency and satisfaction for all at work. But it is among these ranks that the greatest confusion and uncertainty often exists. Time and again one hears managers claim variously that six, seven or eight immediate subordinates constitute the maximum viable size of an immediate command. Yet, in the hierarchies of those same managers there are foremen in charge of thirty, forty or even fifty operators. The managers will also argue against the idea of giving those foremen managerial authority. The situation that they unwittingly disclose is that some higher-level manager who has responsible to him, say, four foremen each with, say, thirty operators is in managerial command of over 120 immediate subordinates! Thus decisions about individual employees at Rank 1 are made by managers who are far removed from them, have little personal experience of their work and who, to them, are often simply names. If you are a clerical worker in an office, or a machine operator in a factory, and you know that the decisions about your pay, your change of job, your promotion or your de-selection are being made by a man to whom you seldom speak and to whom you have no access, then you begin to feel that you are dealing with an authoritarian system from which you need protection.

Leadership, if it means anything, is a combination of the wise use of authority and a humanitarian interest in the individual person. A combination of good selection and training of managers can begin to achieve this at the lower strata of the hierarchy, but continued organizational ambiguity will inhibit it. It seems to me that organization is not sound unless a situation has been created where:

(*a*) The men in charge are managers, in the fully defined sense of the term.

(*b*) These managers are well-chosen, highly trained, *and paid a salary appropriately above that of all their subordinates.*

(*c*) Every Rank-1 employee has a manager whom he knows personally and to whom he has easy access.

(*d*) Every Rank-1 employee has the assurance that the assessment of his work, behaviour and progress is decided by his known manager, and not by others.

CHAPTER TWENTY FIVE

Measuring a Mixed Output of Products

In *Product Analysis Pricing*[1] the writer and Elliot Jaques have described an objective method for the calculation of standard selling prices. The method is based on measurement of the properties of the article. The technique was developed to assist pricing decisions in a company making products to the designs of its customers. Many new prices for different designs had to be established every day, and the previous practice of estimating prices and adding percentages was seen to be unworkable and unrealistic.

Towards the end of *Product Analysis Pricing* we discussed the use of the method as a means of measuring output, but did not explore this use deeply. I now believe that the use of the technique as a means of measuring a mixed output is more important than its use as a means of controlling selling prices.

It surprises me that so many senior people in industry seem to be unaware that they have no objective means of measuring their output and no means, therefore, of comparing their efficiency from one period to another. Because misconception seems to be so widespread I shall run briefly through the methods that are sometimes assumed to be appropriate for making such measurements.

Total sales value as a measure of output

Sales turnover is not an index of the total output of the manufacturing activity of a company, for the following reasons:

(1) Sale values contain the value of materials, components and sub-contracted work not produced by the manufacturing

---

[1] Wilfred Brown and Elliott Jaques, *Product Analysis Pricing*, Heinemann Educational Books, 1964.

activity of the company. I shall refer to these as 'bought-out' values.

(2) Sale prices vary as a result of competition, negotiation, shortage or surplus of goods in the market.

(3) Sale prices vary in many industries according to the quantity ordered.

(4) Sale prices vary according to factors such as the changing image of the company, advertising, promotion, etc.

(5) Sale prices vary according to the country, type of market, or customer to whom they are sold and in accordance with different pricing policies for different products.

These factors causing variation in sale prices also apply where sale prices are netted by deduction of bought-out values (except of course for (1) above).

I have tried to dispose briefly, and perhaps too didactically, of the idea that sale values are an index of output. I know that what I have stated has long been accepted by most industrial executives. I would refer those who continue to doubt to documents such as: *Pricing: Policies and Practices* by Jules Backman.[1]

Added value as a means of measuring output?

Added value is usually defined as:

$$\left(\begin{array}{c} \text{Total Sales} \\ \text{Value} \end{array} \right) \text{minus} \left(\begin{array}{c} \text{Value of bought-out materials, com-} \\ \text{ponents and sub-contracted work.} \end{array} \right)$$

Added value is the price recovered from the market for all the work done by the manaufacturer in turning bought-out items into the products that he sells. It is one means of stating the total of a mixed output of different products, but it has a grave defect.

Assume the example of a manufacturer who produces *each* year 1000 items of a single uniform product. Assume that the added value of each item is £100. Then in year one his total added value will be £100 000. But in year two the market price drops for each item by £10. Assuming that other factors remain unchanged, then the added value in year two will be £90 000.

---

[1] Professor of Economics, New York University. Published as 'Studies in Business Economics' Number Seventy-one, by the USA National Industrial Conference Board, 1961. Obtainable from the British Institute of Management.

I know of no company that produces only one uniform product, and my example is therefore unrealistic. But it discloses the fact that the total added value can vary while the total physical output remains constant. This fact is disguised in real situations where many products are being produced and where the mix of products varies from year to year. It is impossible in these circumstances to state what the physical total output is because it is not possible to add different products together.

A manufacturer who assumes that his physical output has risen when the total of his added value has risen (or vice versa) may be deceiving himself. Added value is no indication of physical volume of output, because it is not directly related to the number or to the physical nature of what is produced.[1] I shall describe, in this chapter, a method of measuring output that has these characteristics.

Standard hours as a measurement of output?

Most manufacturing companies set work-targets for machine-operators in terms of the hours of work required to perform specific processes. Thus, the total target to complete all manufacturing processes on a specific product may be stated as ten standard hours per unit of finished product. But standard hours are a target of *input*, not of *output*.

The use of standard hours as an index of output is very common, and it produces some extraordinary results. For example, assume that a company is producing each week 1000 units of Product A, each of which is targeted to take ten standard hours to complete, and 1000 units of Product B, each of which is targeted at twenty standard hours. If an attempt is made to obtain an index of total output by the use of standard hours, we get the following:

1000 Product A at 10 hours each	=	10 000 Std Hours
1000 Product B at 20 hours each	=	20 000 Std Hours
Total index of output	=	30 000 Std Hours

Now assume that as a result of a change of manufacturing method involving new machines and new tools, the target number of standard

---

[1] It is also worth noting, in passing, that our method of valuing Gross National Product (GNP) is not related directly to the number or physical nature of what is produced. I often wonder when I see figures of British percentage increases of output compared to the increases of other countries whether the figures rest on a secure basis.

hours for Product B is reduced to ten hours each from twenty hours each. We then get:

1000 Product A at 10 hours each = 10 000 Std Hours
1000 Product B at 10 hours each = 10 000 Std Hours

Total index of output = 20 000 Std Hours

Apparently output has fallen by one-third as a result of an improvement of method, although the number of units produced has remained constant. Or we get:

1000 Product A at 10 hours each = 10 000 Std Hours
2000 Product B at 10 hours each = 20 000 Std Hours

Total index of output = 30 000 Std Hours

In this case though the number of units of product B has doubled, standard-hour index of output remains constant.

I apologize for the elementary nature of the example I have given to demonstrate what happens when an attempt is made to state output in terms of input. The fact is, however, that this practice is very widespread, particularly in the engineering industry.

I think people often fail to see the errors of this approach because even in a relatively small factory producing a limited range of products there may, nevertheless, be many thousands of different operations, each of which carries a target, set in standard hours. With so many separate targets, the elegant simplicity of the conceptual error is overlooked.

Use of the total of unit costs as a measurement of output?

This method suffers from the same defects as those that arise in the case of standard hours. A unit cost is a statement of the *input* of the resources used up in producing an output, and I hope I have successfully demonstrated that inputs cannot be used to measure outputs.[1]

---

[1] In a company producing a stable range of proprietary products, where only small changes occur from year to year, unit-costing systems can be useful. If the same basis of overhead-expense distribution is maintained, then the comparison of unit costs from one year to another can yield useful data. But I think there are easier ways of obtaining data, which serve the same purpose.

In any case, unit costs are not objective; they are arbitrary because they arise from *arbitary* loading of parts of the overhead expense of the company on to specific products.[1]

Use of single properties of products as a means of measuring output?

We frequently talk of *tons* of coals; *gallons* of oil; *yards* of cloth, etc. What we are doing is taking a single property of a product and stating the total quantity of output in terms of that single property. We realize that the product has other properties by referring to cloth, for example, as being thick or thin, wide or narrow, fine or coarse weave, cotton or wool, black or red, etc. But we have selected a dominating property to give a rough approximation of quantity.

Such rather crude statements of quantity serve social purposes and are useful in industry for general statements, not intended to be highly accurate, but they are seldom useful for measuring a mixed output of different products.

One can state the volume of a mixed output of various types of textiles in yards, but such a means of measurement is insufficiently accurate for economic purposes because the other properties such as width, thickness and weave are so important.

Product analysis as a means of measuring output

I now want to describe a somewhat sophisticated method by which it is possible to measure a mixed output of different products. I will base it on a simplified example, but the technique can be used on almost any range of products.

I choose mild steel in flat lengths. There is an almost infinite variety of these. This variety can be regarded as different combinations of properties that are of significance to the market. These properties are taken as width, length and thickness. Those familiar with the art will be able to state other significant properties, such as composition, hardness, accuracy of width, and so on, but as I shall show, the technique can handle any number of such properties, and the explanation will be simpler if I assume a rather more limited range of significant properties than those that actually exist.

I propose to express these properties in terms of the single

---

[1] See, for example, Jules Backman, *Pricing: Policies and Practices*, op. cit., p. 36.

parameter of apparent market value at a given point of time, so that they can be added together.

(1) The first step is to select at random a number of sample sizes and to obtain for each the current average market price at which the company is actually selling them.[1] I shall refer to these as standard values.

(2) If any particular size is regarded as a special case in terms of its sale price, I exclude it from the sample.

(3) I shall now give the properties the following symbols:

$$\text{Length} = L \qquad \text{Width} = W \qquad \text{Thickness} = T$$

(4) I state the *value of each unit of length* as Vl, of each unit of width as Vw, of thickness as Vt.

(5) I can now write a general formula for each sample:

$$(L \times Vl) + (W \times Vw) + (T \times Vt) = \text{Standard Value}$$

This formula simply states that the number of units of a particular property multiplied by the value per unit of the property gives the value of the amount of the property in that specific sample; the total of these property values equals the standard of that particular value size.

(6) I must now deal with a complication. If one takes a number of examples of flat mild steel all with common length and width, but each sample varying in thickness, and plots on graph paper the sales price against the varying thickness, then the answer would probably not be a straight line but more like that illustrated in Fig. 35.

This quadratic relationship between some properties of products and sales price is typical, but the equation

$$(L \times Vl) + (W \times Vw) + (T \times Vt) = \text{Standard Value}$$

would allow only of a linear relationship. We must therefore allow of a quadratic relationship by amending the equation. This is done by subjecting each property to the power of a different constant $(k_1, k_2 \text{ and } k_3)$, to provide the formula

$$(L \times Vl^{k1}) + (W \times Vw^{k2}) + (T \times Vt^{k3}) = \text{Standard Value}$$

---

[1] I must approach description of the technique in stages, and the first step is, for the present, to ignore change in price, which often arises from the placing of contracts for different quantities. I shall deal with this point later.

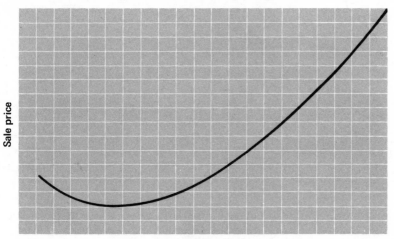

Thickness (T) (with L and W constant)

Figure 35

(7) The next step is to take each sample in turn. Measure the amount of the properties L, W and T in each; fill these values in the general formula; fill in the standard value (i.e. the current sale price) and thus produce an equation for each of the samples.

For example, if in one sample L $=$ 72 cm, W $=$ 3 cm and T $=$ 0.5 cm and the current selling price of that sample of flat steel is £1 then the equation would be as follows:

$$(72 \times Vl^{k1}) + (3 \times Vw^{k2}) + (0.5 \times Vt^{k3}) = £1$$

(8) If originally we selected, say, twenty samples then we will have twenty simultaneous equations. Computer programmes are available that will solve these equations to give values for Vl, Vw and Vt and for k_1, k_2 and k_3. Suppose that the values that fitted these simultaneous equations were as follows: Vl $=$ 14, Vw $=$ 1.6, Vt $=$ 9; $k_1 =$ 1.2, $k_2 =$ 1 and $k_3 =$ 2, then the general formula for flat steel lengths would read

$$(L \times 14^{1.2}) + (W \times 1.6^1) + (T \times 9^2) = \text{Standard Value}$$

(9) When it is necessary to obtain a standard value for *any* size[1] of flat mild steel in the future, all that is necessary is to fill in the

---

[1] Within the range of the original samples on which the formula was based.

values of length, weight and thickness and perform a simple calculation.

This technique is based upon the recognition that the production of a range of products involves the generation in each of a varying quantity of different properties—a product is a combination of quantities of different properties.

The quantity of each property present in a product will bear a direct relationship to the input required to generate it if the efficiency in the use of the input remains constant.[1]

(The relationship may be a linear one or subject to some power but it will be a direct relationship.) Thus variation in the resources used to produce a product of a given design is a function of variation in the efficiency of the use of the input.

The values per unit of the various properties are derived from market values of that class of product at one given point in time. These values are therefore independent of the resources used to produce the products (input). They are also independent of subsequent changes in market value. The only variables in the formula affecting the standard values that they calculate are the quantities of the various properties present in the specific product being studied. These standard values are therefore a direct function of the physical nature of the product valued at market prices at a given moment in time.

It will be noted that having derived the value per unit of property from current sales values I have referred to them as standard values. This sleight of hand merely signifies that the starting point to obtain values per unit of property is originally based on current selling price. As time moves on, however, standard values can become a constant basis against which selling prices can be varied in a known ratio according to varying market conditions, varying total expense arising in manufacture, and so on. Thus, as the years go by, selling price may progressively change from the original standard value to

---

[1] It is difficult in a brief account of this technique to answer all the questions that may arise. Some might contend that though the *amount* of resources devoted to the production of a product might remain constant, the *cost* of those resources would rise, and that this would constitute a drop in efficiency. I am using the term efficiency to refer not to the cost of the resources used but to their quantity. In my terms, therefore, efficiency remains constant if, for example, the number of standard hours used to produce a given product remains constant, even though the wages paid to those who work those hours rises.

standard value plus or minus a percentage, which varies through time. Despite the fact that many new products, which were not being produced at the time when the formulae were devised, have come into manufacture, *they can all have standard values calculated on precisely the same basis as for products made in the past*. We have thus established a constant datum line in relation to which variations in selling price, stock values and quantity of output, valued at standard value, can be stated.

(10) My simple example excluded a circumstance that arises with most products. Most products include bought-in materials and/or components, which are assembled into the product without work being done upon them. This circumstance can be catered for by deducting from the selling price of the samples used for deriving the formula, the cost to the company of buying the material *actually included* in the product (not the amount used up during its manufacture),[1] or the cost of the *finished* components added to it that have been bought from an outside source. These deductions give what I call the *net* standard value. The addition of these bought-out items to net standard value to produce standard values makes it possible for the effect of changes in the price of bought-out components and materials to immediately affect the standard values directly.

(11) There is yet another circumstance I have not dealt with, that is, variation of selling price arising from variation in the quantity ordered. This can be treated separately by setting up a curve plotting percentage additions to standard value against quantity, as in Fig. 36. The values of the percentage additions can be derived from the past commercial practice of the company.

Up to this point the technique may well appear to be concerned with setting sales prices rather than with the measurement of output, but this is simply because in order to obtain values per unit of property it is necessary to go to market figures.

---

[1] The material 'used up' in producing a product includes the amount of material in the finished product plus any turnings, trimmings, melting loss, etc. arising during the process of production. These marginal 'losses' of material vary according to the techniques used in production. If the gross amount of material 'used' by the production process were valued and deducted from the selling price to give net selling price the latter would vary according to changes in production techniques. In other words gross material value is an input. The output is the actual amount in the product.

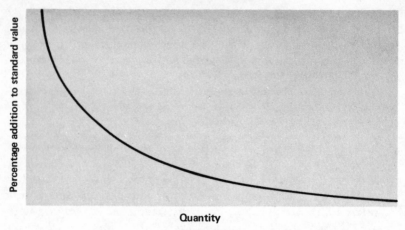

Figure 36

There is no other set of values that are relevant to the valuation of output. Production is designed to satisfy the consumer. Value, in its absolute meaning, is the differential value placed on it by the consumer.

The factory manager needs to be able to measure the variations in his total output over different periods of time. Without an objective technique of stating this he does not know whether his efficiency in the use of resources is rising or falling. The current methods in use are not objective, for the reasons stated earlier. What the manager needs is a series of yardsticks that measure the quantities of properties that his resources generate, stated in a form that enables them to be added together to give him a measured figure of total output.

The technique I have described provides this measure of output by:

(a) Taking market prices at a given point in time to establish the differential value of a range of products of the same class.

(b) Deriving from these market prices (after deducting from them the cost of those materials and components bought from external sources by the producer), the value per unit of each of the properties that have been generated to form the product.[1]

---

[1] It is possible for the differential value placed upon each property (as deduced by the solution of the simultaneous equations) by the values given to V_1, V_2, etc. to change. The evidence that may indicate that this is happening arises when the price quoted for designs of products

(c) Establishing formulae that enable future products, as yet un-designed, to be valued on the same basis as current products.

(d) Enabling any mix of products to be measured, valued and added together to give a total of output over a given period.

Measuring output by product analysis avoids the fundamental fault of other techniques used with the same objective. The fault is to include in the calculation of output some elements of input. It is easy to agree that such a practice is fallacious. But I found in practice that it was difficult to make certain that those who assembled the data on which the formulae were to be based did in fact exclude these elements of input. The minds of all kinds of staff, particularly accountants, are so orientated towards considering how to recover resources expended by including them in market prices, that they become conceptually confused. There is, for instance, a constant bias, from previous thinking, to include in the standard value the bought cost of the actual material *consumed in the production* of the product instead of the *amount present in the final product*. If the amount of material used up in the production of the product is included, then each time that a change of production method takes place the amount of material included in the calculation of standard value may change. If this conceptual deviation is not spotted, then we have drifted back into including input into the valuation of output. Any method of output valuation that results in measurement varying with changes of production method introduces elements of input into the valuation of output. To the extent to which this happens the 'measurement' is distorted.

This technique, by providing a basis upon which sales prices can be built, eliminates the necessity both for price estimates and for the calculation of unit costs of production. It can increase effectiveness not only by the elimination of the work involved but also by creating a situation where:

(a) Price quotations can be given very rapidly, simply by the use of drawings of the product, market prices of materials and bought-out components, and the formulae.

---

that include specially large amounts of one property consistently prove to be uncompetitive. If this happens it is necessary to re-constitute the formula for that class of product. Changes of this sort are not likely to happen. If they do, the change in differential value of properties will take place over a long period of time.

(*b*) It can very rapidly provide accounting departments with stock values, and ensure their consistency.

(*c*) It can give insight into trends of productivity and efficiency.

Many managers initially criticize the technique on the grounds that if unit costs cease to be reflected in sales prices, then the possibility of unit losses arises. My answer to such misgivings is as follows:

(*a*) Prices, if based on estimates, will vary very widely from one estimator to another. Production target times upon which estimates are built are usually no more consistent from one estimator to another than is rate-fixing.[1]

(*b*) Unit costs can be based on *actual* operator time or process time, but the allocation of overhead charges, which nowadays largely exceed the cost of direct labour, is arbitrary.

No objective basis for allocating overhead expense to the cost of specific products exists. Thus, the manager who feels confident that a specific sale price on a product will yield a profit because it exceeds unit cost by some given percentage, is comforting himself with an illusion. The fact is that profit or loss is the result of deducting total expense from total revenue. A breakdown of expenses as between specific products is not possible on an objective basis.

Product-analysis techniques can be used in a manner that will produce additional data, which is much more helpful than the false reassurance of comparison between price and unit cost.

The Return Index

If actual average-operator, or machine, or process time is established for each unique product from time to time and divided into the net sales price received (actual sale price less bought-out items) then we get an index figure of x new pence per direct hour recovered from the market for each product. I call this the 'return index'. It will vary through time. An average 'return index' for groups of similar products can be established. This also will change over time. If the return index on a specific product deviates largely from the average current return index of the group of products then it must be caused by one or other of the two reasons given below, or by a combination of both:

(*a*) The production methods employed on the product are less or more efficient than the norm for that group of products.

---

[1] I have already commented on the degree of inconsistency in the setting of target times upon which payment-by-result schemes are based.

(b) The sale price is less or more than the norm for that group of products.

Investigation into these two possible factors will disclose the reason for the departure of a specific return index from the average return index. Rigorous use of the return-index notion will exercise more control over loose prices or loose use of resources to produce particular products than conventional unit-cost techniques, and should prove, with experience, much more reassuring to managers.

This is a brief account of a complex technique, which is rooted in the idea that social utility, market price and the relation of output to input must all be based not on cost but on the intrinsic nature of the article produced. Confused semantics have, in the past, led us into the error of thinking that cost is a property of an article; it is not. If it were, it would be possible to derive the cost from an examination of the article. Some people think that they can, in fact, derive 'cost' from the article, but what they do is to derive an estimate of input from a knowledge of the manufacturing method they assume will be used to produce it.

The only properties of articles are their physical characteristics, and these are measurable. That is where we must start if we are to achieve more objectivity in thinking about situations that involve production of articles, measurement of output, market prices, and the like.

CHAPTER TWENTY-SIX

Aspects of Organization Unique to Marketing

THIS CHAPTER IS about the marketing of capital and industrial goods (non-consumer goods). I confine my comments to that area because I have insufficient knowledge of consumer goods marketing.

Most companies have come to realize over the last thirty years that the primary aim of their existence is to provide goods or services *for a market*. Despite this there remains, however, some confusion about the manner in which the accountability and authority for attracting customers and for meeting their demands is structured into the organization. A wide range of sophisticated marketing techniques, and a conviction that the organization must be market-oriented in all that it does, are not enough. I have seen countless companies engaged in export marketing that have lost important contracts, not on the grounds of price, design, delivery or enthusiasm, but simply because it was not possible to marshal the necessary company resources at the right moment to bring to bear on a customer that array of information, persuasion and decision that could have won the order. The resources I refer to are such things as demonstration of the article, availability of technologists to put the technical arguments, quick decisions about finance, credit, modification of design and delivery dates, and authority to negotiate about price, terms of contract, and so on.

Working at the Board of Trade on exports I had exceptional access to the opinion of overseas purchasers about British suppliers from a wide spectrum of markets. I was able to sift these opinions in discussion in order to try and separate out sincere opinion from the conventional critical comments that most buyers will make of all suppliers as a sort of opening gambit.

It was always a source of deep frustration to me that the United Kingdom mass media consistently failed to appreciate that the task of professional buyers is to obtain goods of maximum quality at minimum price in minimum time. By definition, therefore, they can almost never express satisfaction. Any questions addressed to them about performance of suppliers will always draw criticism. The mass media often accepted such conventional criticism without investigation and published the results as a condemnation of United Kingdom suppliers' performance. This had the result of convincing many members of our public that *comparatively*, British suppliers were deficient on practically all counts, in spite of the fact that from 1965 to 1971 they had increased the value of goods shipped from £4600m to nearly £8000m per annum. This could not have happened unless their performance had been above average.

Such mass-media coverage, reflected back into the foreign press via foreign trade correspondents in London, in fact did great damage to the image of the British exporter. Many British mass-media reporters lack sophistication in commercial matters and fail to realize that some buyers' criticism is simply a technique for blaming suppliers for faults that originate in their own organizations. On countless occasions, when I personally followed up serious complaints, I discovered that failure to deliver on time often arose from long delays in placing contracts by the buyer; failure on quality was sometimes due to interference with the supplier's design by the buyer; failure to offer a bid was due to the design required having been orientated to a competitor's designs; and failure to win contracts too often due to plain corruption overseas.

All this is not to whitewash British suppliers' faults, but I have to state the facts as I saw them in order that when I do criticize marketing organization I can avoid being seen as just another naïve person who has joined the band of ignorant critics.

The reiterated criticism was (a) apparent lack of a sufficient number of personnel to take part in sales negotiation, and insufficient availability of technical personnel to back up their efforts and (b) lack of 'flexibility' in negotiation. Exploration of what was meant by flexibility left me with the strong impression that it was lack of ability by negotiators to vary the terms offered, even over small issues, without reference back to headquarters, and slowness by H.Q. in giving decisive answers. The dangers of generalizing over such issues are obvious, but I have to record that while many other initial comparative and general criticisms melted in the light of discussion and questioning, these two issues did not.

Both of them, to me, seemed to stem from organization of the marketing effort rather than from the personality of the suppliers' marketing personnel. Indeed, I have heard high tribute paid in many informal conversations to British personnel, in terms of their frankness, integrity and ability. One commentator from an Eastern European government buying department summed up a considerable general impression by stating that some countries seemed to believe in frequent visits of quite large groups of salesmen endlessly extolling the virtues of their products and denigrating their competitors. British personnel generally seemed to know their products, talked of them objectively, argued logically and could, even if apparently fairly junior in rank, discuss technical issues of design and performance with great knowledge and assurance.

The feeling, and it is no more, generated in me by that experience is the background to this chapter. It causes me to believe that in spite of the marketing function of business having come right into the centre of the stage of management thinking in recent years, it has been denied resources and has received insufficient study in terms of role-structure and allocation of decision-making accountability between roles. Time and again reports were received in the Board of Trade from our Foreign Office Commercial Officers overseas that negotiations were coming to a head, and that there was urgent need for a visit by negotiators of the British supplier, or that questions about delivery, credit, price or design awaited urgent decision by the British supplier if success was to be achieved. I have contacted firms personally by telephone and on thousands of occasions contact was made by Board of Trade officials over similar issues. But often it was very difficult indeed to discover the individual in a supplier company who could decide such issues, or who had the authority to send people overseas. There was frequent reference to being short-handed, and evidence of internal argument in the company, which was the cause of prolonged delay about surprisingly trivial issues.

Finally, when large contracts had been lost, the buyer would make the statement that the British bid was not competitive on price, or on credit terms, or on design. But I would be left with the impression that often such comment was a superficial statement, and that if there had been greater availability of personnel to make more frequent visits, and capable of taking decisions on the spot, then the contract might have been won without alteration to the factors stated as reasons for failure.

I have defined the role of chief executive as one accountable for the development, production and marketing of specific goods or services. As all employment hierarchies are brought into being to supply a body of consumers,[1] then the whole organization must be orientated towards their market. This implies that one of the primary responsibilities of a chief executive is to bring market considerations appropriately into play in every decision he makes, and to insist that his operational subordinates, whether concerned with D or M or Mk, do likewise.

In chapter sixteen I pointed out that executive hierarchies exist in the presence of three power-groups—the shareholding system, the employee–representative system and the customer system, and that the chief executive cannot introduce change without the tolerance of all of these power-groups. Thus, market orientation is simply an acknowledgement of the existence of the customer power-group.

It is fashionable today for chief executives to say that their organizations exist to make profits, and for nothing else. But if a company is to be relatively successful, it must make profits to maintain the support of shareholders, it must create satisfactory working conditions to retain the support of employees, and it must be market-orientated to maintain the support of customers.

The chief executive's task is, therefore, concerned with the maintenance of the primary balance between the rights and entitlements of these three power-groups. This requires threefold orientation in order to make profits.

When, however, we come to consider the issue of market orientation in its own right, semantics tend to prejudice thinking towards acceptance of the idea that this is solely the task of the marketing manager. It is not; it is the task of the chief executive and all of his operational subordinates. The danger is that while all managers work in the daily presence of employee pressures (and are indeed employees themselves) and all managers are under constant economic pressures from higher authority to work towards profits, some of them can become shielded from market pressures, through the semantic escape of accepting the fallacy that satisfying markets is the task of their marketing colleagues. But, unless all managers are orientated

---

[1] This may seem to be a very wide generalization, and yet I can think of no employment hierarchy that escapes it. Even the armed forces are there to supply protection to the citizens of a country. I have explored the idea at somewhat greater length in chapter seven.

towards all three power-groups, then optimum decisions will not be made.

If all managers are to be required to consider market needs, what, then, is the special function of a marketing department? Let me put my reply to this question in context by pointing out (*a*) that accountability for the orientation of the organization towards the shareholder power-group is borne by the chief executive with special assistance from the company secretary and his accounting hierarchy; (*b*) that the chief executive's accountability for orientating the organization towards the employee–representative power-group is specially assisted by his personnel officers. Seen in this perspective the task of the marketing organization falls into two parts. The first is the recognized one of finding the facts through market research, planning the company's strategy towards the market, and the use of a wide range of attraction, persuasion and negotiating techniques. The second part of the task is less explicitly recognized. It is to assist the chief executive to take appropriate account of the importance of market considerations in the policies he sets, and *to influence every other manager in the organization to do likewise.*

If under the stimulus of the marketing manager the other operational managers become as responsive to market pressures as they are to profit pressures and employee-satisfaction pressures, then the marketing manager will have achieved one of his primary objectives. Marketing departments do not design goods, they do not manufacture them. It is not the decisions of marketing personnel that decide whether the price, quality, design, delivery and performance of goods are satisfactory: those decisions are made elsewhere. If other considerations in the minds of managers in charge of design and production outweigh market considerations, then marketing men have failed in a vital area. They can only get for their customers in the market what they feel is needed by stimulating the chief executive to set appropriate policies, and by continuously influencing their colleague managers.

Customers are never fully satisfied. When one standard of stated requirements is achieved the standards are immediately raised, particularly by professional buyers. In a rather bizarre sense, therefore, marketing men obtain contracts and orders in spite of the 'failure' of the rest of the organization to match the ever-rising demands of the market, and they do so by persuasion in all its various forms.

Where the marketing department succeeds then those considerations that affect design, quality, reliability, credit, delivery, and after-service, take their rightful place in the decisions of all operational

managers. Calls on the services of design and manufacturing personnel to visit the market are met with due priority. Authority is allocated in such a manner as to allow rapid decisions to be communicated to customers, and an image of a flexible fast-moving
supplier is created in the minds of customers. Market orientation is
not simply a state of mind, or a resolve to spend enough on persuasion
of the customer, but the availability throughout the organization
of sufficient resources to be able to respond rapidly to demand in a
wide variety of ways. But where the internal impact on a company
of the demands of the market are weak because the marketing department lacks status or resources, then the shortcomings about which
I generalized at the beginning of this chapter will exist.

Evidence of this lack of impact of the marketing department arises
when suppliers inform complaining customers of the *reasons* of their
failure to achieve what they have contracted to do. The statement
that one of the supplier company's sub-contractors has failed to
deliver a vital component on time, and that therefore delivery will
be delayed, is analogous to a manager saying to the chief executive:
'I have not completed your job on time because one of my
subordinates let me down.' This would properly evoke the response
from the chief executive: 'Why tell me that? You have failed. You
have control over your subordinate and you have permitted him to
fail. If that is all you have to say then I must take over that
subordinate from you and get a better performance out of him.'

The transmission of 'reasons' to a customer is, in effect, simply an
acknowledgement that 'my organization has been unable to solve the
following problems and to that extent it has failed.' The customer
has his own problems to solve and is quite uninterested in those of
his supplier and, in any case, probably does not believe what he is
told. He is interested solely in remedial measures to put matters
right. Quoting reasons for failure to customers always, to me,
indicates a failure on the part of the marketing function to make the
reality of the company's relationship to its customers clear to the
rest of the organization.

Basis of delegating Marketing Accountability

I wish to elaborate the general statement made in chapter seven on
operational work in order to comment on the organizational positioning of the marketing function.

There are, in principle, three ways in which operational work can
be split up and delegated. It can be split up by process, by product

or by market. D tasks are almost invariably split up by product or sub-product, and delegated in that form. M tasks can be split by product or by process, though with modern production methods, product delegation is the more usual method. Mk tasks are best split by Market. A process split is only possible if the company is engaged not only in selling products but also in marketing its manufacturing processes, and that is a separate issue. The delegation of marketing by products is viable only when the different products each sell to quite different groups of customers. Where this is so then the possibility arises of delegating D, M and Mk work on each separate product to subsidiary chief executives, as in Fig. 37 below.

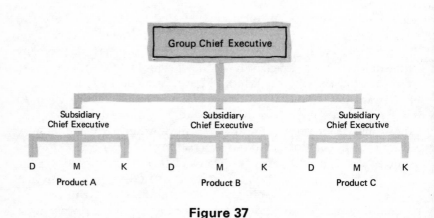

Figure 37

But if nearly all the company's customers are potential consumers of most of the company's products, then Fig. 37 is not viable, because none of the three subsidiary chief executives can be held personally accountable for the company's relations with its customers. Any one of them can, by his decisions, interfere with the goodwill built up with the common customers by his colleague subsidiary company chief executives.

A second alternative is set out in Fig. 38.

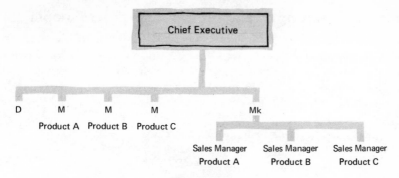

Figure 38

But Fig. 38 again creates a situation where three sales managers are each sharing accountability for all the company's customers. The organization pattern that usually emerges is therefore to subdivide marketing work by market, as in Fig. 39.

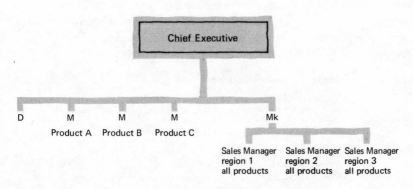

Figure 39

Model 1 will result in a higher degree of awareness of market needs on the part of all operational managers than Fig. 39. But it is frequently not possible to organize in this way, because particular products are seldom consumed only by particular groups of a company's customers.

Varying meaning of the term 'Marketing Manager'

The term 'Marketing Manager' is currently being used, particularly in the industries producing consumer goods, in three additional ways. This is apt to cause confusion. I therefore describe these three additional uses of the term in the diagrams below.

Figure 40

Fig. 40 shows the use of the term 'Marketing Manager' to describe a role that I think would be more accurately referred to as 'Company Planning Staff Officer to the Chief Executive'. This is a very important post, from which the occupant can give decisive assistance to the chief executive in effectively orientating all of his operational subordinates towards the market and assisting the chief executive to co-ordinate their efforts.

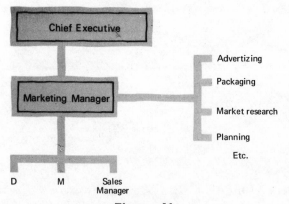

Figure 41

Fig. 41 uses the term 'Marketing Manager' to describe a role that is, in fact, that of a chief executive. It will often be found where the 'marketing manager's' own manager is in fact also responsible for other subsidiary companies. Unfortunately Fig. 41 organization is sometimes depicted in a misleading fashion as in Fig. 42. Such a presentation manifestly shows the marketing manager as a colleague of those in charge of Product Development, Manufacture and Sales when in fact he often has authority over them, as in Fig. 41.

But Fig. 42 may in other cases show the actual position. In such a case the marketing manager is genuinely a colleague of those in charge of D, M and Sales. But in this case the selling aspect of marketing has been hived off under a separate manager. Such an

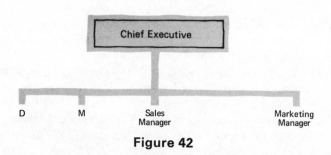

Figure 42

organization pattern would give rise to very high collateral relations between the 'marketing' manager and the sales manager. The task of co-ordinating these two roles now falls on the shoulders of the chief executive. In addition the latter cannot hold one subordinate accountable for the company's relations with its customers.

Thus, the first additional use of the term really refers to a very high level planning staff officer, and this use should be dropped in favour of a more accurate term. The second use of the term is inaccurately used to describe a role which, in effect, is that of a chief executive, and should be dropped. The third use of the term refers to a 'part-marketing' role, which creates organizational difficulty.

Some readers may have in mind still further variations on the way in which the term 'marketing manager' is used. But I have commented on these three uses because, in the course of meeting several hundred 'marketing managers' I have become aware that they are in common use. In many cases it has been difficult to discover from the 'marketing manager' precisely what his duties are. This confusion I believe to be particularly harmful to the export activities of companies, where the need for speed in the making of decisions is greater than in home markets.

The Status of Salesmen

It is significant that product-producing organizations, as opposed to service-producing organizations, continue to be referred to as 'Manufacturing Industry'.[1]

Manufacturing is one aspect only of the operational work involved in supplying goods, the other two aspects being product-design and marketing. For many years in the past, books on management consistently treated manufacturing as 'being the central task of management'. Manufacturing involved 'line' managers, and other activities were regarded as being performed by 'functional' or 'specialist' managers. Various meanings can be attributed to the terms used, but the central feature of such comment was the relegation of product-design and marketing or selling to a less important place in the scheme of things than manufacturing.

Product design, or 'Research and Development' as it continues to be referred to, maintained its psychological status, I think, because it often employed highly trained people, often university graduates, and these were sometimes referred to as scientists. 'Selling', the term that was always used before 'marketing' became the accepted word, lacked and continues to lack status in many areas of industry.

Values are changing, but I believe it still remains true that in a British social group the pecking order allotted would place the salesman very low compared with lawyers, doctors, teachers, production managers, designers, civil servants, etc., without reference to the level of work that each might be carrying out. But I doubt if this is true of the USA, Germany or Japan.

In the company that I managed, the salesmen insisted on being referred to as Technical Representatives. I was constantly distressed

---

[1] There was an interesting governmental confusion when Selective Employment Tax was first introduced. The intention was to tax service industries, but not to tax product-producing industries. But when the Government wishes to refer to product-producing industries it invariably uses the term 'manufacturing industry'. So the product-design and marketing departments of companies that had established these functions in premises separate from their manufacturing activities were not exempt from Selective Employment Tax. This naturally produced intense resistance, and the Government finally conceded the point. I doubt if the misuse of a single adjective in an Act of Parliament has ever caused quite so much concern. I relate these events, however, to draw attention to the fact that the manufacturing function of industry has long been regarded as the major function. I think this is one of the reasons why the other two functions have for so long been neglected.

to hear officials in the Board of Trade refer somewhat disparagingly to 'salesmen'. I heard the comment: 'He is only a salesman' too often. The public image of marketing and salesmen is distorted, and the tendency is to regard them as being people who are ebullient, extrovert and insincere, as though these are the prime qualities required for the activity of selling. These are socially unacceptable attributes.

I have heard repeated comment on the fact that the Institute of Marketing is a much more important body than it used to be 'when its membership chiefly consisted of sales managers'! Whereas in fact I suspect that the change of title from 'The Institute of Sales Managers' to the present 'Institute of Marketing' was not so much a change of function or membership, but simply a move away from a title that produced an unflattering image in the public mind.

It would be very interesting to see research on the career-choice preferences of parents for their children, in order to discover the percentage who had aspirations to see their children become salesmen. I would prophesy that selling would come low in the order of choice. The low status still accorded to the term 'salesman' has counter-productive effects:.it tends to limit the number of able and intelligent persons who take up selling as a career. This is, I think, a special problem of our country, and is damaging to our national prosperity.

Organization for the Marketing of Technology

Many companies, both large and small, market not only their products but—as the situation demands—the technology and machinery by which that product is made. The process is variously referred to as licensing, sale of know-how, etc. This can be called the marketing by a company of its technology as opposed to the products of that technology.

Many companies fail to appreciate that, in addition to their normal products, they possess in their own technological knowledge an important asset, which is highly saleable and can produce a great deal of revenue. This saleable technology can take many forms— patents and trade-marks, unpatented product designs, manufacturing techniques, machinery and process plant developed for their own use, and so on.

Some companies refuse to sell their own technology on the grounds that this will create overseas competitors and diminish the sale of their products. There are, however, strong counter-arguments. Many companies who have established licensees for the manufacture of their products have actually increased the sale of their products even in the countries where their own licensees operate. If a company refuses a licence then some other competitor company may grant one, and they will have lost not only the market for their products but also the compensating alternative of selling technology in its place.

This is only a very brief synopsis of some of the factors that have to be taken into consideration when a company is deciding whether it should embark on technology marketing or not. Much more could be written. Here I will confine my comments to the organizational aspects of the matter.

When a company enters into its first licensing negotiation this is often conducted by its product-marketing organization. I risk the anger of product-marketing men by saying that I believe that a product-marketing organization is often ill-fitted to conduct such a negotiation. My reasons are:

(a) Product-marketing men are steeped (rightly so) in the business of maximizing the volume of products sold at remunerative prices. When an overseas manufacturer, or perhaps one of their own distributors or customers in an overseas market who wishes to manufacture the product approaches them, their first reaction is often great anxiety about loss of product sales. Their initial response is often to try to turn down the approach and to rebuff it. They have visions of the licensee invading other markets, and they become anxious.

(b) Product-marketing managers are seldom knowledgeable in the field of their own company's manufacturing technology, patent procedure, or the negotiation of the complex legal agreements upon which sound licensing agreements are built.

(c) It is difficult for product-marketing personnel to shift their thinking to the new frame of reference into which a company must move if it is to give proper consideration to its own future as an exporter of technology.

(d) The sale of technology, and the long-term operation of a series of licensing agreements, involves the employment of people with skills and experience that are different from those normally possessed by product-marketing managers.

Thus, delegating the task of selling technology involves grafting on to the product-marketing department what is really a new type of marketing department, which requires to be led by a person of similar capability to the chief product-marketing manager himself—but a man with different skills and experience.

I am an active advocate of every company giving serious consideration to the marketability of its technology. Theirs may well be in advance of the standard available to prospective licensees from other sources, and capable of earning, by its sale, large revenue which can be used still further to advance product design and manufacturing methods. If they are in this position a failure to embark on the marketing of their technology will simply result in other companies doing so instead. If their competitors at home and overseas do, in fact, become licensors then the effect on those competitors will be to stimulate greatly their product and process development. Thus, in due course, the company which, for insufficient reason, turns its back on technology marketing, will find that it has been outstripped by its competitors, has lost the opportunity to establish overseas licensees, and is also beginning to experience a fall in the volume of sales of its own products because of the increased manufacturing activity of licensees appointed by other companies.

I would suggest that any company which, after due consideration, decides that it will attempt to market its own technology should, before it enters into licensing activities or negotiations, set up at least the skeleton of a new technology-marketing department, whose manager should be immediately responsible to the chief executive. I now set out my reasons for holding such a view.

(1) If a company had designed a new range of products, which were functionally entirely different from anything it had sold before, and whose potential customers were entirely different from the customers with which it had dealt previously, it would not necessarily delegate accountability for sales to its existing marketing department. By the same token it is unlikely that a product-marketing organization will be successful in handling the marketing of technology.

(2) A technology-marketing department will be negotiating not single contracts or annual contracts, but contracts that will be binding for up to ten years and more. The original terms of licence will have decisive effects on continuing licensing contracts stretching far out into the years ahead. The manager who leads it should have a legal turn of mind, and experience in manufacturing methods, as well as negotiating ability.

(3) The original negotiation and subsequent operation of manufacturing licences will certainly involve much discussion and decisions about product design and/or manufacturing method. A technology-marketing manager must have available to him

either subordinates with knowledge of these matters or *formal access* to the services of people who have such knowledge in the commands of colleague managers in the company.

I have emphasized the term 'formal access' above because informal arrangements by the chief executive that 'Mr X the chief production engineer' or 'Mr Y the head of product design will be available to assist you' are, in my experience, not good enough. If a technology-licensing department is to be an active operational department, vigorously pursuing a policy established by the company, then it requires to have its own resources, or to have access to resources under the command of others when it requires them and not at someone else's convenience.

Eventually, if it is successful, a technology-licensing department will have to include engineers, chemists, etc. (as appropriate) who can speak foreign languages, and mechanics able to travel abroad and provide installation, maintenance and fault-finding skills.

A company should not drift into granting a licence here or there with its product-marketing department playing the major role. Instead I would envisage a company reviewing its situation, deciding that it will market its technology, establishing a role immediately subordinate to the chief executive to head an embryonic new department, filling the role with a person with the necessary basic knowledge and training and letting the new department grow as it gains experience and begins to bring returns. It would also have to bear in mind that this is a long-term operation and that it will take some years for it to become an important earner of revenue.

I write with enthusiasm about this not only because of my experience as chief executive of a company which, after initial mistakes, became a successful exporter of technology, but also because of the insight I later gained in the Board of Trade. The marketing of technology by sophisticated, dynamic companies is a future growth export of our country. But companies that fail to assess its importance and try to invade this important field by delegating the job to managers whose training and skills are fitted to quite different functions, are putting this important activity at risk.

This chapter may seem scant treatment of a very important subject, but this book as a whole is concerned with organization, and almost everything in it is of equal importance to marketing, as it is to the organization of any other type of work carried out by employment hierarchies. In this chapter I have simply tried to set down some aspects of organization that are unique to marketing activities.

CHAPTER TWENTY-SEVEN

Product Analysis, a Technique for Setting Prices

IN CONJUNCTION WITH Elliott Jaques, I have described else-where[1] the technique of arriving at market prices by product analysis, and I have described in chapter twenty-five the method of creating formulae that will enable a mixed group of products to be valued for the purpose of measuring output.

This chapter is about the relevance of this technique to market operations, for which it was originally developed. *What I have to say will not be relevant, as far as pricing is concerned, to those companies who have a finite number of products that they are marketing.* If a company is marketing, say, a hundred products, then the chief executive and his subordinates can decide the range of prices at which these will be sold to various types of customers in different markets. The basis upon which these decisions are taken will involve knowledge of the total input of resources required to produce the products, the current profit-trend of the company, the cost of advertising, packaging and servicing, knowledge of prices of competitive goods, and so on. With this information available the price-levels set are based on intuition. The main point I wish to emphasize, however, is that the chief executive is able to take the pricing decisions and is thus in control of his revenue. *Though product analysis is not useful to such a company in this position as an aid to price-setting, it is useful nevertheless for measuring output.*

Many companies, however, manufacture products that are

---

[1] Wilfred Brown and Elliott Jaques, *Product Analysis Pricing*, Heinemann Educational Books, 1964.

designed differently for each of their customers. Most of these companies are producers of components and assemblies to be included in finished products marketed by their customers (who are themselves manufacturers). Terms such as 'bespoke', 'tailor-made', 'specially designed', are variously used to refer to such companies' products. These companies cannot predict at the commencement of a year how many different products they will make before the year is over. Their current output may contain tens of thousands of different products. These will probably be variations on a much more limited series of basic designs. But, because each is different from the others and liable to be ordered in different quantities, each will have to be the subject of different pricing decisions.

A company like this, depending on its size, may be faced with a large number of pricing decisions *each day*. Each decision will require serious study, and it becomes impossible for the chief executive to take part in those decisions, despite their importance to company revenue. The chief executive has thus lost personal control over company revenue. This is the situation that has forced a large number of companies to adopt routines concerned with unit costing, marginal costing, standard costing, and estimating. The task of setting prices is delegated by the chief executive to others, who are usually free to act within policies that confine prices within some bracket of percentage additions to the estimated or 'calculated' unit cost of production.

In my experience this method of delegating the setting of prices is unsatisfactory, for the following reason:

(a) Though direct labour input can be ascertained with reasonable accuracy from past data, estimates of direct labour input on new designs are likely to vary widely as between one estimator and another. Notwithstanding the use of sophisticated techniques (involving the use of what are known as 'synthetics' and other methods) the estimates are likely to be no more accurate than the target-hour figures produced by rate-fixers for direct monetary incentive schemes.[1]

(b) Even if direct labour cost is accurate, the allocation of overhead charges is arbitrary, and thus historical costs, standard costs, or marginal costs, are not objective but are based on decisions made largely by accountants. I shall not argue the validity of the

---

[1] I have already referred in chapter twenty-one to the fact that several researches undertaken indicate variations between individual skilled rate-fixers of the order of plus or minus 40 per cent.

foregoing statement, but refer readers to many writings on the subject.[1]

(c) Thus a chief executive who sets for his subordinates a policy such as 'Sell at prices of estimate plus 10 per cent up to plus 20 per cent according to your judgement' is, in fact, adding a fixed percentage bracket on to a highly variable base.

(d) The task of sales negotiators is to gain as much insight as possible into the market prices obtainable. They may find on a large and important contract that estimated cost plus 10 per cent will lose the contract. This can happen very frequently, particularly when the market is passing through a period of weakness. But chief executives cannot spare time for these decisions nor, if they did have time, would they have any better basis for deciding than their subordinates. Those responsible for setting prices and negotiating contracts find themselves in a very difficult position. The estimate of cost is £1. If the minimum margin of profit of 5 per cent is added, the sale price ought to £1.05. But perhaps the negotiator knows that the contract cannot be gained at any price above 95p. The negotiator knows that loss of the contract will result in serious under-use of the company's production capacity and consequent loss of profits. If he is sophisticated, he will also know that there is a strong probability that his company will be better off if it accepts the contract at a sales price of 95p than if it loses it by quoting a higher price. In order to get round the dilemma he puts pressure on the estimator to 'think again'. Under pressure, the estimator bases his estimate on cheaper but more speculative methods of production, though there is no certainty that they will, in the event, reduce expense.

This is an area of conflict between entrepreneurial business decisions and the advice given by accountants. The accountants say: 'Don't accept the order, because it will cost more to make than you will get for it.' But the accountants do not know (though they think they do) what it will cost. The chief executive says: 'I must accept the order for despite the "costs" being apparently more than the sales price, I know that the company will make less profit without the order than it will if the order is accepted; without it my volume of production will drop, the percentage of overheads will rise, all my

---

[1] See, for example, *Product Analysis Pricing*, op. cit., p. 29, or *A Report on Marginal Costing*, Institute of Cost and Works Accountants, Gee & Co (Publishers) Ltd, London, or *Pricing: Policies and Practices*, op. cit., p. 36.

prices will go up and we will have entered a vicious circle of declining business. My task is to recover in total from the market enough money to make a total profit—not a unit 'profit' on every contract or on each individual product. If I add a pre-determined percentage margin to 'unit costs' as a means of establishing sales prices I will not only lose contracts that help to keep the show going, but I will fail to obtain, on some products, the full margins that the market is prepared to pay.'

Cost accounting is essential to efficient management. But its real value is not to produce 'unit-cost' data but to provide managers with an analysis of how much they have spent over given periods, how they have spent and, importantly, the trend of these various types of expense. These analyses lead to changes of strategy, changes of production methods, reduction of variety, the use of different materials, changes of design, changes of organization and changes of market policy. But the attempt to divide up all overhead expense into neat parcels and charge one of them to each product achieves nothing except a dangerous basis for setting prices. The custom of trying to divide overhead expense into neat parcels continues, in my view, simply because chief executives have not been offered an alternative basis for pricing. Businessmen face a real dilemma here. Experience tells them that cost-plus pricing is not a sound practice. Yet they dare not give it up.

Two incidents stand out in my mind. The first was when my chief cost-accountant presented me with the 'expense budget' for the coming year. In one of our factories there were two departments, each making a different range of products. Department A had been overloaded with work for two years. The prices of its products were apparently very competitive, but I knew that future demand was likely to decline. Department B had been short of work, though future long-term demand looked promising.

The 'budget' showed a rise in the total hourly operating rate of Department B and a fall in the rate of Department A. Clearly, on this basis the 'estimates' (on which we based our sales prices at that time) of Department A products would fall and those of Department B would rise. Our efforts of the previous year to improve the efficiency of Department B did not seem to have achieved what was required.

I thought about it and did the obvious thing. I instructed the accountants to reduce the overhead burden allocated to Department B by £X thousand pounds and to increase the allocation to Department A by a similar amount. The protests from the accountants were vociferous. But at the end of the year the overload in Department A and the shortage of load in Department B had gone. A quite arbitrary decision (which I was informed at the time 'ignored the facts and undermined cost-accounting principles') had proved of substantial benefit to the company.

The second incident made me make a stern personal resolution to find some way out of the pricing dilemma which at that time dogged our business activity.

I left my office rather late one evening and noticed lights burning in the production engineering office. I decided to pay it a visit. I asked why it was working overtime and was shown product A, which was being urgently re-tooled. I asked what the cost of the re-tooling was likely to be and was told about £1000. I asked why we were re-tooling product A and was told that it was *because it was being sold at a loss*. I picked up another product, B, which happened to be lying on the desk of the chief production engineer and asked which would save the most—spending £1000 on re-tooling A or £1000 re-tooling B. He said he needed time to study this question. Two days later he informed me that the alternative proposal I had suggested would save twice the resources. I asked how he had calculated that, and he replied that A and B were very similar but we were producing twice as many of B as of A. I asked: 'Why then are we not re-tooling B instead of A?' and was told that it was because *we were making a profit on B*! The chief production engineer said to me: 'It is completely stupid. I admit we are following the least economic course, but we are producing A in substantial volume and the cost office were very concerned about the *losses* arising on it.'

As we were clearly working on the basis of two sets of contradictory notions I decided that the time had come to tackle the whole issue frontally. Some years of thought led to the methods of deriving standard values from the product itself (already described in chapter twenty-five). Their introduction as a basis of pricing led to the abandonment of *unit-costing* altogether (but not to the sacrifice of the analysis of expense, which is a different matter altogether) and to the closing of the estimating department (but not to a cessation of the planning of the manufacturing methods for each unique product).

It became possible to calculate a standard value very rapidly for each new product from its drawing. I was able to set a policy for my subordinates of quoting prices on the basis of standard value plus x to y per cent, and to say that any important contracts that could not be gained by using the lowest percentage addition were to be referred to me. The number so referred was small because all the standard values were consistent with the nature of the individual product.

The use of formulae had cut out the arbitrary variations introduced by estimating and unit-costing. Instead of adding a percentage 'profit' to a variable figure (which had been based on judgement or on the choice of a particular production technique) we were adding a percentage to a constant level of value derived from the product itself.

Our entire price-structure gradually became consistent with the nature of the individual products to which it applied. That is what a market wants. The market does not welcome surprise variations in price that are inconsistent with the nature of the product, and which arise from changes in the supplier's annual revision of the expense budget or from the application of different methods of production on similar products. The market wants prices that are consistent with the nature of the product, and product analysis pricing provides this.

A company has a product which is selling in a growth market whose design is acknowledged to be competitive but whose price is not. If its cost-accounting and pricing mechanisms are conventional it will assume that its competitors have found a means of producing at lower cost than it has. It may, however, be quite wrong, because each competitor may be making the same assumptions about his competitors.

If a company is using product analysis pricing methods it is able to compare the prices in the market of all of its products with a value for each of those products derived from their intrinsic nature. These variations between market prices and standard value provide objective data, which indicate those products that are currently underpriced by the market in relation to their intrinsic content.

Many companies who manufacture 'bespoke' products for other companies use a range of plant and processes, which produce at different levels of efficiency. The most efficient machinery is heavily loaded with work and the less efficient takes the rest. The decisions as to which products are made by the most efficient methods generally stem from the timing of the placing of orders, the size of the initial orders placed, and problems of delivering the goods according to programme. These decisions, based on factors other than the cost of production, have a decisive effect on unit costs. Most of those products made on the slower processes or on the older machinery will 'cost' more. To reflect such variations in price quotations is absurd, but it happens. If prices are consistently related to standard value this absurdity will be avoided.

I have seen instances when companies have decided, on a basis of comparison of unit cost with sales price, to cease accepting orders from particular customers or for specific products because 'losses' are being made. The fact was, however, that the unit costs arose from the initial arbitrary decision to use low-efficiency plant on those contracts. Had it been possible to find production time for those same contracts on their high-efficiency plant, then they would have become 'profitable'.

A company that markets the same finite range of products to all of its customers knows which customer is paying the highest or lowest price. On the other hand, a company that supplies each customer with different unique designs does not know this with any certainty. I have had the experience of believing, on the basis of cost-plus pricing, that we were obtaining better prices from customer A than from customer B, only to find that on the basis of comparison of margins obtained over standard value the position was reversed. Product analysis pricing makes it possible to state that products 1, 2 and 3 sold to customer B are at higher prices, relative to the nature of these products, than products 4, 5 and 6 sold to customer A.

Equally it is possible to compare the margin obtained over standard value by different negotiators, or in different territories, or for different groups of product. What is perhaps even more important is that it is possible to compare the success of market effort in selling in terms of margins obtained over standard value between different time-periods that contain quite different mixtures of product sales.

The third important result of using this technique is to make presentation of the accounts of different departments of a company more meaningful. It is not unusual for companies to treat the expense incurred in their marketing division as an overhead. The marketing manager will no doubt receive a full analysis of his expenses, but this cannot be related in a meaningful way to any other sets of figures to provide an index of marketing proficiency. The manufacturing department accounts will show allocated overheads and direct expenses in analysed detail, and will compare these perhaps with the total of the targeted unit costs of all products produced. But, owing to the variability of targeted costs or estimates, this is not an objective comparison. In addition, the factory manager is frequently in a situation where the 'value' of his output is being compared to the expense that he controls, inflated by allocated overhead charges over which he has no control.

Product analysis pricing enables factory expense to be compared with total standard values, and enables marketing expense to be compared with the difference between total standard values and total income. This difference is, in fact, the margin of income 'created' by the marketing department for the company. It is one vital indicator of the proficiency of the marketing department in its role as negotiator.

Finally, standard values can be used in connection with the values placed on products when they are interchanged between departments of a company or between subsidiary companies in the same group. The difficulty of establishing these interchange values is a widely recognized problem.

Subsidiary companies A and B supply sub-assemblies and components to subsidiary company C, which assembles and markets the completed product. Subsidiary C wants to keep the price low and competitive. It will bring pressure to bear on A and B to transfer their sub-assemblies or components to C at as low a price as possible. A and B want as high a price as possible so that their accounts will show up favourably. To say that tension can arise is an under-statement.

If A and B succeed in obtaining high interchange prices then these, increased still further by margins added by C, may render the resulting market prices uncompetitive. The volume of business will then fall and the product will begin to look 'unprofitable'. It may even be discarded.

If C succeeds in extracting low interchange prices from A and B this will affect the 'profits' of A and B, which may attract criticism from the group chief executive.

Product analysis pricing provides a means of dealing with this problem if the following policies are followed by the group chief executive.

(1) The 'accounts' of manufacturing activities should be based on a comparison of that total of manufacturing expense that is under the control of the factory manager with the total standard value (or some constant derivative of standard value).

(2) All interchange of products, components and sub-assemblies between divisions and subsidiary companies should be at the same derivative of standard value as in (1) above.

(3) Marketing activity 'accounts' should be based on a comparison of marketing expense with the difference between the actual sales value and the derivative of standard value used for the manufacturing activity 'accounts'.

When the internal accounts of subsidiary companies are drawn up in this way then standard values (or some derivative that has a consistent relationship to standard values) can be used as a base for all interchange prices between subsidiary companies. Because it is an objectively fair basis the group chief executive will be able to instruct that these values are to be used without the danger of starting up a host of arguments among his subordinates. (I must add however that semi-processed products or components cannot be valued by the technique I have described; except by taking intuitive decisions to the effect that they are finished to the extent of x per cent and taking that percentage of their standard value as the interchange price.)

I have described a range of uses to which product analysis can be put to provide objective information. My account has been curtailed and I have not explored some quite intricate problems to which the technique gives rise. For example, the treatment of bought-out components and materials, the fact that standard values cannot be calculated for unfinished products, and so on. But these are subsidiary problems, which can be catered for and are discussed in greater detail elsewhere.[1]

My purpose in writing this chapter will have been served if I have stimulated interest in a technique which can bring a degree of objectivity to the pricing problems of unlimited product companies that is at present missing.

[1] Brown and Jaques, *Product Analysis Pricing*, op. cit.

Part Four

Personnel Work and Techniques

CHAPTER TWENTY-EIGHT

Personnel Work (P)

IN ONE SENSE the whole of this book is concerned with personnel work. A more objective phrase would be 'organization and manning'. It has often occurred to me to label it in this way, but it would quickly become O & M work and would then be confused with Civil Service O & M work, which is something else again. Civil Service O & M is concerned with organization and *Methods*, which is not the same area of activity.

The subject of Organization and *Manning* does, however, touch upon nearly all that I have written, and is relevant to the work of all operational managers. I must therefore justify a special section entitled 'Personnel Work' by including in it a number of special techniques concerned with selection, appraisal, progression, ranking, and grading, and these will form the subject of separate chapters of part four. This chapter is more a general comment on the work of personnel departments of employment hierarchies.

As various branches of knowledge have advanced it has become necessary to employ specialists to be accountable for keeping abreast of current knowledge and its further advances, and for using the authority of the chief executive to try to get the results of this knowledge applied. Personnel specialists have been gaining in knowledge and status rapidly since the last war. But organization and management have not, in many instances, been treated as the areas of knowledge in which personnel specialists are the special guardians. For example, it is often assumed that there are no technical criteria that can be brought to bear on decisions about the structure of roles required to do given work and the relation of one role to another. For lack of expert guidance, decisions about such matters often offend against the realities of a situation. If the resulting decision is ineffective the shortcomings of the people involved are blamed. (This is one of the main themes of this book.)

If this sort of mistake is to be avoided then the accountability for advising chief executives and for helping them to ensure that their subordinates take into account all available knowledge should lie, in my opinion, with personnel specialists.

Employment hierarchies face the fact that the reaction of people to their work and to their work environment dominates the hierarchy itself. But the study of the institutional environment in which people work continues to be neglected.

In the past personnel work often got off to a bad start because its first specialist manifestation was the 'Welfare Officer'. The work of those who held such roles was often extremely valuable. The nature of the work attracted many sensitive people of humanitarian outlook whose chief aim was to alleviate what they regarded as the necessary evils of employment, rather than to study the conditions of employment objectively. The work had fewer attractions for those whose capacity tended to run rather more to analytical thinking.

I know that many personnel specialists may dislike what I have written, but I have no intention of denigrating the profession. Instead I want to persuade others that the potentiality of their expertise has been seriously undervalued, and that a disciplined study by personnel officers of the matters discussed in this book has been rendered difficult because they have not been required to advise on such matters. Had personnel specialists been recognized by operational managers as the people who ought to be generating a whole series of concepts and ideas about organization, then I think the profession would have attracted more people who were prepared to do the analytical research that is necessary if we are to solve the relationships and earnings problems of employment hierarchies.[1]

In addition to what is today regarded as their proper work (selection, training, progression, negotiation, work conditions, payment policies) personnel specialists must become the 'structural

---

[1] Even today establishment branches of the various government departments are manned not by specialists but by 'generalists'. Officials are drafted into the establishment branches not because they are believed to have personal qualities or knowledge suited to personnel work but because it is held that it is good experience for any official to spend two or three years in such a branch. In other words, it is used as a training ground. The result is that the establishment branches of the Civil Service are the subject of more open criticism by senior officials than any other branch, and many officials posted to such branches for a term of experience regard it as an unpleasant interregnum in their career.

engineers' of the employment hierarchy. They must possess the expertise that allows them to advise managers on the institutions they should or should not use, on how to structure roles in relation to each other (in order to get work done most effectively), on how many levels of management are required, on the arrangements required if managers are to obtain effective sanction for the changes they seek to introduce, on the need for and the effective working of appeals systems. Personnel specialists must, in short, give their managers an objective description of the real nature of the sociological environment in which they and their subordinates work.

Other important aspects of the operation of employment hierarchies receive too little attention because the accountability of personnel departments is not made explicitly clear. These are concerned with the representative system and the institutions through which negotiation is carried out, and the writing up and agreeing of the operating policies of the company *vis-à-vis* its employees.

Most personnel departments meet representatives, carry on negotiations with them, are concerned with policies affecting employees, and hear appeals. But what is not always clearly expected of personnel specialists is that they should analyse, codify, describe and propose changes in the structures of the institutions through which these activities take place. For example, I know of literally hundreds of companies who have no written and agreed policies on overtime, redundancy, holidays, night-shifts, appeals, representative activities, appointments, etc. Policies do exist in these companies but they are often vague and inconsistently administered. Managers would be hard put to it to describe how they had come into being and whether they were sanctioned by those whom they affect. The rectification of these vague arrangements is, in my view, a pre-condition for the relaxation of tension and hostility in any employment hierarchy. Making a personnel department explicitly accountable for such matters would give it the opportunity of getting to work on them. Great benefits would flow from this if the work were intelligently done.

One might almost say that personnel work, which has been concerned with the psychological reaction of people to work, must now add a dimension to its activities and become the repository of knowledge about organization, and advise on the *sociological* as well as the psychological impact of the environment on work activity.

In chapter twelve I set out a general specification of the work of the head of a personnel division. I think it is appropriate to close this chapter by repeating the first part of that long specification.

Responsibilities of the Personnel Divisional Manager

In general terms, he is responsible for advising the managing director on those policies for the structuring, manning and operation of the organization of the Company that (in the light of its product development, manufacturing and marketing activities) will make an optimum contribution to the managing director's total plan of operations. To discharge this general responsibility he will need to advise the managing director continuously on the following matters:

(a) Whether the current organization and its manning are actually helping to achieve the current planned programme of activity.

(b) Changes which ought to be made to ensure that the structure of the employment hierarchy stays matched to the requirements of a changing company work-load and of its forward planning.

(c) Policies for the manning of roles in the hierarchy that take account not only of current, but also of future requirements.

CHAPTER TWENTY-NINE

The Progression-Curve Technique

WE HAVE NO means of measuring the capacity of individual people for carrying out employment work,[1] but we make too little use of the data that is available to us about the changing rate of earnings of people during their employment career, where it is based on managerial assessment of the level of their work. (Where pay is dominated by power bargaining, as is so frequently the case with hourly rated occupations, the data of changing pay through time is often so divorced from consideration of work capacity as not to be susceptible to the treatment by the technique I shall describe. In view of the increasing extent to which 'hourly rated' wages are dominated by power bargaining, my comments apply mainly to 'staff jobs', where regular managerial assessments of work done takes place.)

Suppose we take the case of an employee who has worked in one employment hierarchy for a number of years, and during that time has taken up roles in the immediate commands of a number of different managers; each of those managers has had to assess the work of that employee frequently. The results of these different managerial assessments of the rising work-capacity of that person have been expressed in a series of changes to his wage or salary, which have taken place at different ages of the individual. That is raw data which, if appropriately processed, can yield substantial insight into human capacity.

---

[1] Though, as I have described in chapter twenty-one, the correlation discovered by Jaques between felt-fair pay and the maximum time-span of decisions gives us indirect insight into human capacity; if a person not only feels that the pay he is receiving for the work he is doing is fair *but also feels that the same work reasonably employs his full capacity* then the measured time-span of that work is an indication of his capacity.

Wherever there is reasonably full employment those who are dissatisfied with their current employment roles have an opportunity to seek new positions, either within the hierarchy that employs them or in others. The choice of role and occupation lies open within the constraints of personal skills, experience, and acceptability to prospective employers. Given a sufficient degree of dissatisfaction with their current work or current earnings, people will be stimulated to seek change of role. Is there, therefore, a case for saying that people remain in roles so long as the levels of work and pay seem satisfactory to them? And can one turn this statement upside down and say if people stay in a role this must mean that the level of work and pay does satisfy them?

When talking to their friends, many people will claim that they are underpaid. Asked why they do not seek another post they will, however, give a variety of answers: 'I find the work very interesting although I am underpaid' or 'I have been so long with the company that I cannot take the risk of moving out of a job that is secure into one that contains risk of loss of employment' or 'I can't find alternative positions that suit me, which are paid at a higher level'. I believe that such statements are often a rationalization of an unwillingness to change, the reasons for the unwillingness being that the degree of 'felt underpayment' is insufficient to produce the necessary motivation.

Another common reason for statements of felt underpayment by people who, nevertheless, do not seek to change jobs, is envy of people in other occupations who are intuitively thought to be overpaid. What the complainants seem to be saying is: 'I am not prepared to seek another job, but the fact that excessive wages are being earned by people in some other occupations around here for work that looks less responsible than my own, is making me feel discontented with my own earnings.'

I think there is enough evidence to suggest that in the presence of reasonably full employment people who remain in specific roles can be said to find their earnings tolerably consistent with what they think their own personal ability should enable them to earn. But if their earnings are out of balance with their felt capacity, they will usually pursue and achieve a change of role. This leads to the general proposition that the majority of people in 'staff jobs', barring the presence of unemployment, and excluding those whose earnings are dominated by power bargaining, tend to get paid in accordance with their innate ability to do work.

There are two major arguments against this proposition:

(a) The current differential pattern of average earnings (as between different types of occupations) is not equitable. The immediate examples of differential inequity that spring to the mind are some public performers employed on employment contracts by films, television, etc.,[1] car-assembly workers, dockers, and some employees of the printing industry on the one hand, and nurses, young doctors, teachers and social workers, on the other hand. This means that those in the lower-paid occupations do not have the opportunity for employment at a level of equitable differential earnings implied by the term 'full employment' unless they take the drastic step of changing their profession.

(b) The term 'unemployment', crudely used, means fewer vacancies than there are people to fill them. Clearly, however, it is possible to have a shortage of employment opportunities for particular groups within a total situation of full employment. For example (and ignoring geographical unemployment) people in the 55–65 age-groups often lack the opportunity to work at their full capacities. Such lack of opportunity likewise, from time to time, affects those in some types of specialized occupation.

Thus I agree that there are many exceptions to my general proposition, but let me test my proposition further by considering what would happen if it were generally *untrue*. The proposition that would then have to be supported might be stated as follows: 'Most people's pay is not related to their innate capacity and where a correlation does exist it is fortuitous.' This statement can be attacked on the following grounds:

(a) If large samples of individuals are asked what they expect to be earning within a given number of years, they usually give quite positive replies. These replies fit into a pretty consistent pattern, which indicates that the higher the existing pay, the higher the percentage addition expected in the future, and vice versa.[2]

It is difficult to avoid the conclusion that people base these consistent predictions on self-assessment of their own capacity. If there were no relationship between self-assessed capacity and pay

---

[1] This is not a reference to self-employed performers, who are not employees and whose high earnings are the result of variation in public taste and are always at risk.

[2] This is a crude statement of findings described by Jaques in *Equitable Payment*, based on 650 discussions with individuals about their future earnings.

their future expectation would be tied to circumstances over which the individual would exercise no control. One would not expect people to be able to answer this sort of question except in terms of wild guesses, which could not be expected to show any consistent relationship to current earnings.

(*b*) Employment hierarchies are based on the general principle that the nearer a role is to the chief executive the higher the capacity of its incumbent. (We are all aware of deviations, but they do not invalidate the general principle.) If pay were not related to capacity then one could not expect to find the existing pattern, i.e. the nearer the role is to the chief executive the higher the earnings of the incumbent. In fact, of course, this pattern does exist.

(*c*) If there were no correlation between individual capacity and earnings what would be the criteria that would influence future pay? I can only think of chance, personal magnetism, patronage, or power. I know of no evidence to support the idea that individual pay is decisively influenced in a generality of cases by these criteria, except to the extent that it is influenced by the use of power by highly organized groups.

(*d*) Thousands of highly paid roles are advertised every week in the press. If pay were unrelated to capacity then the current pay of applicants would bear no consistent relationship to the pay offered for the vacant role. But, as every personnel officer knows, the advertisement of a vacant role at, say, £5000 per annum, may produce an occasional application from a person with current earnings as low as £2500 but virtually no applications from those earning, say, £1000 per annum. The reason is that those on the lower earning levels know, intuitively, that a £5000 role calls for a level of capacity higher than their own and that they have no chance of being selected. (I must add however that in a developing country where gross under-employment of capacity exists, such an application might well succeed.)

If these arguments are accepted then the record over the years of the changing salary of an individual has a relationship to his changing capacity for work. But these data on earnings contain random variables arising from the effects of inflation on the one hand, and generalized increases of earnings on the other. If the effect of these variables is not corrected then the data are not useful. For example, a manager looking at the salary progression of a subordinate over a ten-year period may note increases each year of £50 and feel that increased level of work taken on during that period has been suitably recognized. In fact, the apparent progression may be a regression in terms of buying power, or in terms of comparison with rising general wage-levels.

I shall now describe a technique developed by Jaques in collaboration with personnel specialists of Glacier for presenting salary data in a form that makes them useful.[1] The Department of Employment publishes each month a wages index derived from the current average of negotiated and standard minimum wage rates for manual work. It is an index of the average national minimum wage for a normal working week. The crude salary data of individuals are first corrected by the use of this wage index. If, for example, the index has risen by 5 per cent over a year and the individual's money salary has risen by 10 per cent, this indicates a corrected real increase of 5 per cent. Corrected in this way, the salary increments awarded to a person are an important indication of the changing level of payment that the employee finds tolerable. The fact that he has stayed in the company indicates that (in normal circumstances) the level of work he has been given to do is a reasonable match with his level of capacity. Such broad assumptions will not be valid in all individual cases, but they are, in my experience, of sufficient general validity to support the use of a technique that can be of great value to personnel officers. The technique is particularly useful because it is capable of showing up cases where there has in the past been a continuous over- or under-assessment of the capacity of individuals.

Fig. 43 shows two plots. The dotted line is the money wages of a single employee plotted against his age. The other plot is his money wage corrected by the varying wage-index percentage rise since June 1955. At the point where a wage increase is made the pre-existing money wage is corrected and plotted and, at the same time, the increased wage arising from the wage increase is also corrected and plotted. These corrections by the ever-changing wage index cause the fall in the corrected salary levels that takes place between the increases of money wage plotted in Fig. 43.[2]

---

[1] See also *Equitable Payment* and *Progression Handbook*, both published by Heinemann Educational Books Ltd.

[2] Thus a person may be earning a money wage of, say, £30 per week from 1 January 1970. Since June 1955 the wage index has increased by $x\%$, which produces a corrected salary of £30—$x\%$. By January 1971, when his next wage increase takes place, the wage-index increase is $(x + 3)\%$ and his original corrected salary at January 1971 is £30—$(x + 3)\%$. He is given a money increase of £4 per week, making his

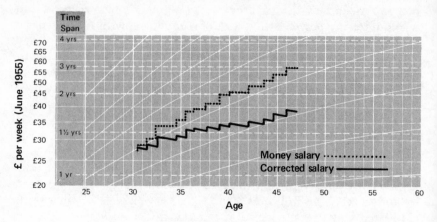

Figure 43

The plots are made on logarithmic graph paper, which has the result of showing a rise from, say, £20 to £25 per week (25% increase) as the same vertical distance on the scale as a rise from £40–£50 (25% increase).

Fig. 44 shows a more dramatic result, where money wages (dotted line) have risen but corrected wages have fallen over the period. It

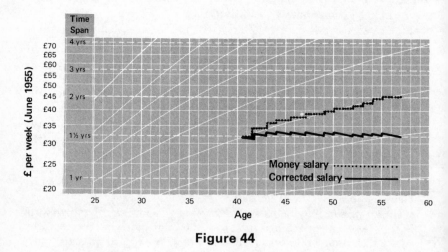

Figure 44

money wage £34 per week, which is corrected to £34—$(x + 3)$%, giving the new corrected salary.

graphically demonstrates the misleading result of simply consulting a record of money earnings over a period of time.

Note that the vertical rises are salary increases corrected on the dotted plot but not on the other plot. The horizontal lines on the uncorrected plot are the stable *money* wages that the individual receives in between money-wage increases.

Jaques originally plotted the corrected salary against age of 250 people from five different companies. These plots are shown in Fig. 45.[1]

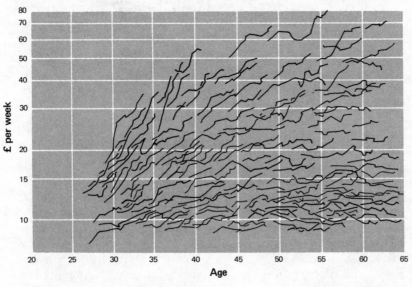

Figure 45

Jaques then drew through the plots on Fig. 45 a series of smooth curves, as in Fig. 46.

Readers would be entitled to doubt whether this rather arbitrary

---

[1] The method of plotting differs from that described because the existing corrected salary before each increase is not plotted, only the corrected salary resulting from the salary increase. Women were excluded from these plots. If people were in receipt of emoluments other than salary, such as private use of car, etc., these were valued and added to the salary.

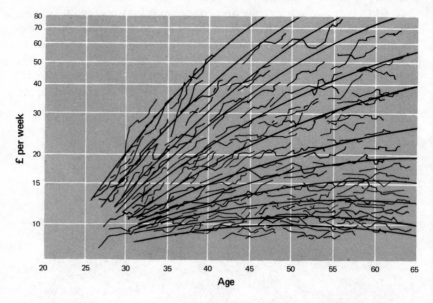

Figure 46

method of arriving at a field of curves had any validity. The fact is, however, that the 'corrected salary against age' plots from a large number of companies in nineteen other countries all showed conformity with this field of curves.[1]

These smooth curves were given the label 'Capacity Growth Curves', and data sheets containing the curves, and a conversion rule to aid plotting, were put on sale. Since then a large number of employment hierarchies have made use of them.

I am not trying here to validate the accuracy of these capacity growth curves. Those who wish to delve more deeply into the degree of rationale that can be attached to them must turn to Jaques's writings. I simply want to indicate the existence of a technique which, in my own experience, is exceedingly valuable and which has proved valuable to other companies both in the United Kingdom and overseas. For even if managers reject the claim that these individual plots and their coincidence with 'capacity growth curves' indicate growth

---

[1] Considerable research was done in order to obtain for other countries their equivalent of the British National Wage Index.

in the capacity of individuals they may, nonetheless, find that this method of displaying salary data of individuals is highly illuminating and useful.

There were several different ways in which I found this technique useful. All the examples are based on the supposition that if an individual's corrected salary progression has followed roughly one of the capacity growth curves for a few years, then that curve is an indication of the past and future capacity for work of the individual. I am convinced that this supposition is correct in *general*, but I think that it may not be correct for a minority of cases. If it is not correct it means that most of the many different managers who have made assessments of that individual in the past have been wrong. That can happen. But it is unlikely to happen. If a process of *under-assessment* continues too long the individual is likely to leave the hierarchy and seek employment elsewhere. If, on the other hand, the assessment of a series of managers have been too high there is no automatic corrective process (except scrutiny of the comparison of the work of that individual with the pay and work of others). Thus it is necessary, each time a curve is examined, to consider whether the ability shown by the individual is consistent with the salary pattern as shown by his individual curve in his previous career. Having said that it must now be made clear that what follows in the examples is based on the assumption that the career progression of each individual discussed is roughly correct. I do not wish to have to pepper each example discussed with cautionary notes about the possibility that he is on the wrong curve; this must be a general consideration in the minds of all who use this technique for examining the progress of individual careers.

Looking at those who have left the company

It is instructive to take a sample of men or women who have left an employment hierarchy in the past, whose exit was regretted by management, and to plot their salary progression up to the point at which they left. I show in Fig. 47 the possible results of doing so with two cases.

It will be noted that in the case of A the corrected salary towards the end of his career with the company has levelled out, and in the case of B it has actually fallen. I have also shown the result of plotting these individual progressions with uncorrected salaries, and it will be noted that the uncorrected plots each show a consistent upward rise in salary. Thus, a manager can be deceived into believing that the

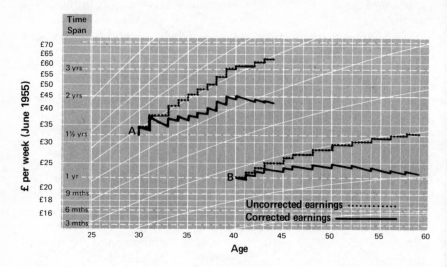

Figure 47

salary of one of his subordinates is steadily advancing when, in terms of corrected salary, it may be flattening out or falling. In many cases where valuable people leave the company the reason is a failure to perceive what lies behind the monetary figures of the salary progression.

Basis of over-promotion

Fig. 48 shows cases of over-promotion in terms of salary.

In the case of A, he was promoted at point Y and given a substantial rise in salary. Subsequently, over a period, although his monetary salary continued to rise at a slow rate, his corrected salary did not progress, and later it fell slightly until, at point Z, it was back on the basic curve that appeared to have been indicated by his earlier salary progression. He then proceeded along this curve.

In the case of B, he proceeded up a curve until at point W he received promotion and a steep rise in salary. Subsequently he received very small further monetary increases and his corrected salary actually fell until at point X, feeling distressed about the receipt of no increments of pay, he left the company. This was the case of an individual who could have progressed usefully up the curve indicated by his earlier career and stayed with the company to

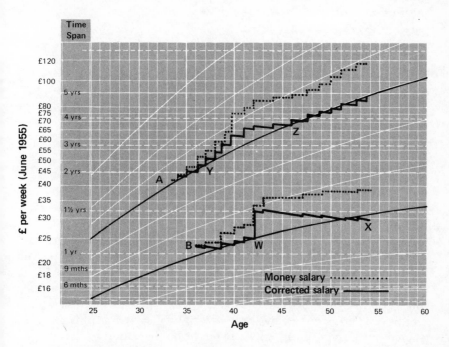

Figure 48

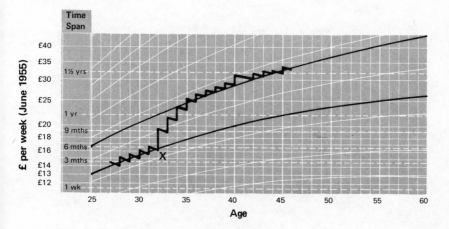

Figure 49

do useful work but who was, in fact, caused to leave by over-promotion, over-payment for a period, leading to subsequent disillusionment.

Early under-payment

This is the case of a young man who, in the early part of his career, appears to have been underpaid; but promotion took place at point X and subsequently he established a satisfactory career on the new part of the field of curves. (Fig. 49)

The use of fixed salary scales during a learning period and their effects

Fig. 50 depicts a curve stretching from X to Y, which is the age–wage progression chosen by a company. Such uniform progressions are customarily used during the initiation period for young entrants in a company. Subsequently, individuals A, B and C progress at quite different rates in terms of salary, according to their individual innate ability. Clearly, A might well have become dissatisfied during the period X to Y because it would appear that his innate earning ability was not satisfied by the wage–age scale, but, in this case, he stayed on through that period. It might be that another individual, with a still higher capacity than A, might have left during the period

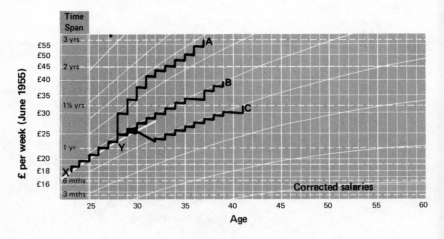

Figure 50

because of felt underpayment. The importance of plotting these uniform progressions in corrected form will be understood.

Caution in use of salary progression curves in the initial part of employees' careers

The capacity for work of young men and women who enter employment is often an unknown quantity. There is no back history of previous managers' decisions to guide their existing manager. They are very often learning and are not making a major contribution to the employment hierarchy, but are using a certain amount of the employer's time preparing themselves for their own future. This can, therefore, be a period when some people are underpaid in comparison with their innate ability, and this need do no harm. On the other hand, many younger people today are much more mature and capable of carrying responsibility than is generally assumed, and this undervaluation particularly applies to the more intelligent. For these reasons the assumption that young people, whatever their apparent qualities, should be paid on a wage-for-age scale until they reach a given age, may result in some young people becoming very frustrated because the discrepancy between this wage-for-age scale and their innate abilities may be too great. People in this situation will seek employment elsewhere, and some of the best may be lost to the company.

It is clear, on examining the early progression curves of young people in many hierarchies, that tendencies both to underpayment and overpayment exist frequently. In some hierarchies, for example, training salary-scales for graduates are too low for the more able and more mature. Before such graduates emerge from the training period and can be paid a level of salary commensurate with their ability, they have left the hierarchy. Guide-lines are difficult to draw. But I emphasize the need to keep an extremely watchful eye on young men and women in an endeavour to spot high potential at an early stage and not to lose it.

Use of single-point plots to consider the availability of possible talent

It is a useful and very informative exercise for a personnel specialist to take a group of staff in a particular command, or belonging to a particular discipline, or in a certain age-bracket, or in a specific salary bracket, and to correct their current salaries, plotting them against their current age.

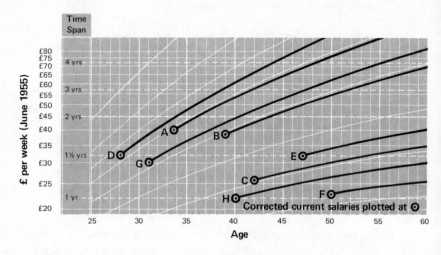

Figure 51

Fig. 51 depicts the possible result of doing this. On the assumption that these individuals are roughly on their correct curves, the differentially higher levels of work that they may be able to do in the future become apparent. A manager, in the knowledge of the indicated potential abilities of all those plotted, can begin making comparisons between what these plots indicate and his intuitive expectations about those individuals. For example, he might look at C and F on Fig. 51, which indicated that C has got considerably more potential than F, and he might come to the conclusion that, in his experience, this is not so. He then might begin wondering about the individual salaries paid to C and F, and begin looking at their career curves and consider whether in the past he had been doing the right thing with the salaries and responsibilities of these two individuals. He might similarly look at D and G; the potential progressions of these two might be consistent with his own judgement but, on the other hand, they might not be. Where what is displayed does not coincide with his intuitive assessment he may wish to reconsider the situation.

Use of curves at salary-review time

There is a strong tendency among managers responsible for review-ing the salaries of their immediate subordinates to give the same increment of salary to each of them, with the exception of any who are clearly unsatisfactory or those who are very clearly showing pronouncedly greater ability than the others. The effects of this tendency towards equality of annual or bi-annual salary increments can be disastrous.

Fig. 52 shows the corrected salary plots of A, B, C and D, who constitute the immediate command of one manager, Mr X. I have squared off the graph paper and inserted a percentage figure. This

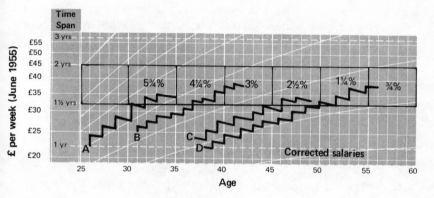

Figure 52

is the average percentage increase of corrected salary required to maintain any corrected salary within that box on its current progression curve. Thus, for example, if A is given a percentage increase on his current corrected salary of $5\frac{3}{4}$ per cent his salary will rise, approximately, along the progression curve on which it is currently situated. The equivalent percentage for B is 3 per cent.

Assume that Mr X, their manager, gives a real increase to A, B, C and D of $2\frac{1}{2}$ per cent.[1] The effect will be to over-increase the salary of D grossly. B and C will remain approximately on their current progression curves. The effect on A is likely to be highly discouraging. If his previous salary record is a fair reflection of his rising capacity then, as a man of 35, he shows considerable promise for the future. A $2\frac{1}{2}$ per cent increase of salary will fail to keep him on the progression

---

[1] That is, an increase of such a percentage that, after taking into account the movement of the wage index since the last salary review, the corrected salaries increase by $2\frac{1}{2}$ per cent.

curve along which his corrected salary has been rising. My experience is that without any knowledge whatever of the technique I am describing, he will intuitively feel that his progress is 'losing way'. He may start thinking about looking for a role outside the company.

If this policy of equal percentage increases of pay at salary reviews is continued by Mr X, then A will leave the company and D will become progressively over paid. The company will then have lost a person with high potential for the future and over-rewarded others.

Before using this technique I had found it very difficult to influence the managers in the company towards realistic policies at salary-review times. I had issued guidance notes saying that I wanted employees who were considered to be of future high potential capacity to be the recipient of generous salary increases, and those for others to be more moderate. But such guidance did not produce the results I sought. It makes a manager feel much more comfortable in his relations with his subordinates if he feels he has been 'fair' to all. Too many managers satisfy this feeling of 'fairness' by the policy of equal increments of salary increase to all their immediate subordinates at salary-review time.

This 'fairness' policy can have a crippling effect on the future of the company. One of its effects is to give the impression to many members of the staff that the company's policies suffer from 'lack of opportunity' for younger men and women.

This progression-curve technique suggests a viable and clear-cut salary policy, by means of which managers can consider the performance, the potential ability and the salaries of their immediate subordinates. I would sum it up as follows:

(*a*) A manager should have before him, when he reviews the salary of his immediate subordinates, the career-progression curves of each of those subordinates.

(*b*) The earning progression data sheets now in general use have printed on them dotted lines connecting all capacity curves at the point at which they have the same degree of slope.[1] The manager can, at a glance, see what percentage increase is required to maintain each subordinate on his existing curve (to which I refer as the 'indicated percentage salary increase').

(*c*) The manager is now required to consider whether the basic curve

---

[1] My diagrams do not show these (and indeed omit other detail also) because they are on a much smaller scale than the earning progression data sheets. (These are available in pads from Heinemann Educational Books.)

of progression indicated by the individual's past salary progression is correct. If it is not correct (in the manager's view) then the indicated percentage salary increase will not be the amount by which the salary ought to be adjusted at this review. The manager will have to state why he thinks the individual has been progressing in the past along the wrong curve, suggest what his correct curve should be, and indicate a recommended salary increase consistent with that judgement.

(d) If the manager comes to the conclusion that individual subordinates are roughly on the correct curve, then he must consider the performance of each during the period under review. If he finds that the performance has been up to expectation, then he will recommend an increase of salary in accordance with the indicated percentage salary increase. If he considers that the performance has fallen off from what could reasonably be expected, then he may perhaps indicate a lower percentage increase, and undertake to discuss the situation and the individual's performance with him. If the performance has been exceptionally good during the period under review but he still thinks the individual's curve is correct, he may recommend an *ad hoc* bonus for this special effort during the period.

In short, what managers are required to do is either to award indicated percentage salary increases or to say why they should not be awarded. Such a policy will obviate the tendency to give equal percentage increments to the immediate subordinates of a manager and the counter-productive consequences that can flow from such a policy.

Budgeting the cost of salary reviews

If one of the earning progression data sheets is divided into squares, then it is possible to put a percentage figure in each square that approximately indicates the gradient of the curves passing through that square. Fig. 53 depicts a progression-curve sheet so divided up, with percentages inserted.

Each square also represents an average corrected salary at a bracket of age. If all members of the staff who are subject to the salary review are then placed in the appropriate square (according to age and corrected salary) it is possible, (a) by counting the number of staff in each square, (b) by multiplying this by the average salary per square, (c) by taking the appropriate percentage of the result, to

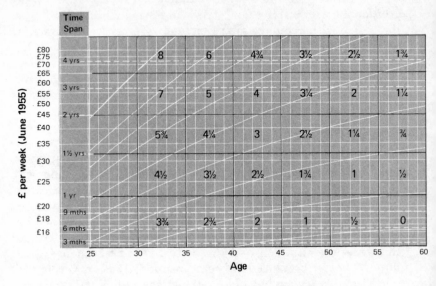

Figure 53

deduce for each square the amount of the increased salaries arising from the review; subject to the assumption that every member of staff has his salary increased by the indicated percentage salary increase. By the addition of the calculations in each square it is possible to arrive at the indicated percentage addition to the wage-bill that will come about if every member of the staff is paid in accordance with the indicated percentage salary increase. This is an extremely useful figure to compare with the actual results of the salary review in terms of addition to the total salary bill.

The comparison of the two resultant totals will indicate the extent to which the proposed policy outlined above has been adhered to on average.

People in the 45–60 age-range who are on the lower curves of work capacity

The fact that the plotting of corrected earnings against age shows that at the lower ranges of capacity individuals' corrected salaries begin to drop over the age of around 50, will strike many people as being extraordinary or even immoral. But the data show this to be so. What is surprising is that the phenomenom has been hidden from view in the past because the technique of plotting corrected earnings against age has not been used. Inflationary effects and money rises in earnings have produced a situation where most men whose corrected salaries drop are not explicitly aware of the fact.

The interesting question is why (if the general field of progression curves is looked at) men with high ability experience an increase of that ability up to late ages, whereas men of low working-capacity experience a decline in their capacity from an earlier age. These indications of the data can only be compared with the intuitive experience of managers and personnel specialists. But is it not the experience of industrial managers that some operatives and craftsmen seem to decline in ability as age advances through the fifties, whereas managers and others occupying positions of greater responsibility do not suffer this decline? When we look at the Churchills, the de Gaulles, the Adenauers, we see that the ability of such men was probably curtailed, not by a decline in intellectual growth, but by sheer physical deterioration. These curves take no account of physical effects, and physical factors can clearly take effect at any period in a man's life. Some of the deviations on the plots in Fig. 46 may well be explained by this. A manager who looks at a large number of career curves in his extended command will spot somewhere that an early downward trend (away from the expected trend indicated by the progression curve) has taken place and he may, knowing the individuals, be able to correlate this with a deterioration in that individual's physical health.

The newcomer effect

There is a shortage of able and experienced persons in many areas of industry and commerce. If a firm is expanding and engaging such people to fill gaps, then many individuals will not leave a previous post without a fairly large increment of salary. They want this to compensate them for the upset to their domestic life and the expense incurred of moving from one area to another, plus the emotional problems of taking on entirely new responsibilities in a new company. Thus one gets a situation where the starting salary that proves acceptable to a newcomer often shows a substantial increase on his previous corrected earnings curve. Has he then achieved an appropriate place on a new curve in the field of curves? The answer is that often this initial jump to a new progression curve tails off to the original curve along which his previous salary was progressing. This will come about if his new employer is, for a year or two, cautious about giving large annual salary increases to a man who has not yet proved himself. If his salary curve is looked at four or five years later it will be found that he has resumed the original curve on which his previous record placed him.

This also explains the phenomenon of people leaving a company and beginning a post elsewhere at a much higher salary than was thought justified by his previous employers. The salary increase may be justified because his previous employers had, in fact, been under-paying him. This may have been the reason for his search for another post. On the other hand, his employer may have been unable to offer him future prospects of rising accountability and, although the individual was reasonably well-paid and satisfied, he found the forward prospects discouraging. So he sought a change of occupation.

Used with due caution, this technique of plotting corrected salaries will be found to increase insight into the interaction of the three variables affecting people at work—the capacity of the person, the level of work in the role, and the wage paid.

The many combinations of these variables have been depicted by Jaques in the rather novel way shown in Fig. 54.

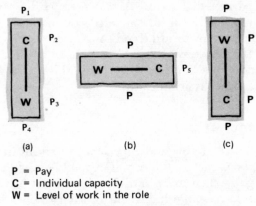

P = Pay
C = Individual capacity
W = Level of work in the role

Figure 54

Fig. 54 (*a*) shows the capacity of the individual as being in excess of the level of work he is given to perform, and the different levels of pay that can exist in this situation, i.e. he can be paid above his level of capacity (P_1) or consistent with his capacity (P_2), or consistently with the level of work (P_3) or below the level of the work (P_4). Fig. 54 (*b*) at the (W–C–P_5) position represents the ideal. Fig. 54 (*c*) shows the situation where the capacity of the individual is below the level of work in his role.

Finally, this technique can help subordinates. I cannot give first-hand examples, but I know that thousands of career discussions between employees and their managers, or with personnel officers, have been helped by a discussion based on salary-progression curves. Data presented in this way encourage much franker and more realistic discussion than would otherwise be possible.

I can quote one general example. Some years ago in one company a number of young chemists claimed, as a group, that they were underpaid and that their salary progression was lower than others doing the same level of work. A discussion took place based on their progression curves. What emerged was as follows. The maximum level of work available for chemists was relatively low. The company did not produce chemical products and the function of chemists was largely centred round various forms of chemical analysis. The capacity growth curves that some of these young chemists' salary progressions were following would rise well above the level of work available in the near future. But for other younger members of this group there was still ample opportunity for growth in their level of work for some years to come.

The upshot was that it became clear that unless some of the senior members of the group were prepared to change their profession as chemists, then their capacity would very soon grow beyond the work available and they ought, therefore, to seek employment elsewhere. It was possible to reassure the more junior members of the group. The discussion was calm and objective, and the company helped some members of the group to seek other employment. They left the company with goodwill.

I have referred constantly in this chapter to managers and very little to personnel specialists, but it must be clear that the progression-curve technique, which covers the career of an employee during his passage from one immediate command to another, can only be introduced, maintained and interpreted by personnel specialists. It must be centralized to some extent in their hands because of its nature. Furthermore, it is not feasible to load every manager with the need to understand the principles lying behind the technique. What managers need is the advice and the data that arise from its use, and this is best conveyed to them by personnel specialists.

CHAPTER THIRTY

Selection of Personnel

'. . . There is a story attributed to King Henry II of England (1154–89) and a certain clerk who had long besieged him for a bishopric. A see fell vacant; the chapter met, and elected another. The clerk in some fury taxed Henry with perfidy, in that he had not lifted a finger to secure his election, to which the King replied that it was so: he had not judged it necessary, having observed that a chapter, left to itself, invariably chose the worst. But lo! they have found a worse than thee. Have courage brother, it cannot always be thus.'—HELEN WADDEL, The Wandering Scholars

SELECTION OF PEOPLE for appointment to important positions remains, unfortunately, one of the great gambles. Unsound decisions leading to the appointment of people who later prove incapable of carrying the accountability of the role lead to great inefficiency and to unhappiness on the part of subordinates. At worst, bad decisions can threaten the continued life of the organization. They inevitably lead to all the problems associated with de-selection.

Much diligent research into selection methods has been carried out in the armed forces, in the Civil Service, and in industry, by a formidable array of social scientists, psychologists, and others. These have led to beneficial changes in tests, interview techniques and the general criteria used in selection. What I have to say is not in contradiction of the work done, but by way of supplement to it.

Despite all the efforts deployed on selection, human judgement in choosing the right person continues to play a central part in the appointment. That judgement is concerned basically with a comparison of the characteristics and experience of applicants with the nature of the work of the role. In chapter twenty-one I briefly described Jaques's time-span method of measuring the level of work in a role. In chapter five I discussed the nature of work in terms of its prescribed and discretionary content and, in the last chapter, I described an indirect way of obtaining insight into the capacity of people for work. In this chapter I want to bring these things together and show how they may be able to aid the process of selection.

Role specifications

Most advertised specifications name and describe the type of work in terms, for example, of 'Marketing', 'Production Engineering', 'Product Designing', 'Workshop Management', and so on, or call for specific qualifications such as, 'chartered accountant', 'mathematician', 'chemist', 'civil engineer', etc. They provide only an initial basis on which people can decide whether or not they are potential appointees.

Some advertisements specify the range of salary or wage offered, but this is usually the only objective guide to the level of the work involved. Where salary is not stated then the only indication of level of work may be the size of the employment hierarchy that seeks applicants, and this is likely to give rise to very inaccurate predictions by potential applicants.

One way of overcoming this difficulty about providing better indications of the level of work for which applicants are required is to draw up a more detailed role-specification, and to describe the work in terms of its prescribed and its discretionary content. Having already discussed work in these terms in chapter five I shall move straight away to the description of a general matrix upon which such a specification can be built.

(1) *Organizational setting of vacant role*

(a) Main operational activity of the employment hierarchy. Total number of employees. Whether private or public. Financial results (if public) in recent years. Export results (if relevant).
(b) The area of the organization in which the vacant role exists, e.g. whether in Product Design, Production or Marketing or in Service Provision, or in a specialist branch, or in accounting.

(2) *Specification of the vacant role*

(a) Whether managerial or not.
(b) If managerial, size of immediate and extended command.
(c) Brief details of function of members of immediate command.
(d) Manager to whom appointee will be accountable.

(e) *Prescribed elements:* brief reference to the main types of policies limiting decision-making by the appointee.

(f) *Discretionary elements:* examples of the more important decisions that will have to be taken by the appointee.

(g) *General responsibilities* for which appointee will be held accountable.

(h) *Conditions of employment:* salary, other emoluments, pensions, holidays, use of car, place of work, any special working conditions.

(i) *Qualifications sought in candidates:* experience, training, certificates, degrees, age-range, any special physical characteristics.

I suggest that the production of a role-specification based on the foregoing matrix would be justified to help potential candidates for all vacant roles of Rank 2 and above.

I am sure that many managers, and perhaps some personnel officers, will feel that this goes into too much detail, but the fact is that a wise candidate for a role (and nobody wants unwise people) would do well to elicit all the foregoing information during his interview. But even sophisticated candidates will probably not do so because the stresses of being interviewed make this difficult. If the candidate is appointed he will discover the answers later, and these may cause grave disappointment, with unfortunate results.

The work involved in preparing a specification like this is heavy at first, but it is possible to produce such specifications with greater ease as experience grows. The act of preparing them can, in many instances, have a most salutary general effect; it may be discovered, for example, that lack of clarity in the organization has made it difficult to fill many of the sections of the matrix. For example, is it a managerial post or is it not? What are the policies to which the appointee must conform? What are the main types of decisions for which he will be accountable? Personnel officers who insist on answers to such questions will be forcing on managers a degree of objective thinking that could be good for them and good for the company. Clearly, it is not possible to provide all the details of such a specification in the advertisement for the vacancy. Instead, a much briefer description can be given, and those interested can be invited to write and ask for a job-specification and an application form to be sent to them.

My experience of the use of this procedure is as follows:

(a) If the procedure is followed when important vacancies arise it persuades management of the need to be much clearer about organization.

(*b*) Press advertising can be concise and money can thus be saved.

(*c*) The volume of replies to an advertisement that specifically makes the offer to send a job-specification to candidates is, in my experience, higher than the response to advertisements that do not include such an offer.

(*d*) A high percentage of those requesting the specification do not complete the application form. This implies that having viewed the role in detail they decide either that they are not suitable or that the role is unattractive. It seems likely that the opportunity of reading the job-description prior to making application saves expense and time by obviating the interview of candidates who would turn the job down after hearing its details verbally. Some might want to argue that candidates who did not apply after reading the specification might, if interviewed, have proved acceptable. This I doubt.

(*e*) I have interviewed many candidates who have applied after asking for a role-specification, and frequently the interview has commenced by the candidate congratulating the company on its procedure and stating that he feels that he already has quite a clear grasp of what the job is all about. I have often asked candidates what particular feature of the specification seemed most helpful in this respect. The answers usually referred to the details given of the immediate and extended command and the data on the prescribed and discretionary elements of the role.

(*f*) If one compares the calibre of the candidates responding in the first case to a conventional advertisement, and in the second case to a role-specification, one finds in the second case fewer applications that can be dismissed without interview and more candidates who are, on the face of it, suitable for consideration as potential appointees.

Advertising vacant roles within the employment hierarchy

When I started to work in the Board of Trade it was interesting to come face to face with an organization that regarded advertising of roles to candidates outside the hierarchy as exceptional, and where nearly all vacant roles were filled by promotion from within. Such promotion to vacant roles is not reserved to members of the particular government department within which they arise. This means of filling vacancies by promotion is, of course, a function of the very large numbers employed in the Civil Service, where the likelihood of there being nobody suitable for transfer or promotion to a vacant role is remote.

Contrast this, however, with a company employing a few hundred people or less. In such a case a search for *external* candidates will be necessary more frequently if roles are to be adequately filled, because smaller numbers reduce the chances of finding suitable candidates among existing employees. Thus, the relevance of internal advertising of vacancies depends partly on the numbers employed in the hierarchy. In the small company with, say, three ranks only, managers ought to have a fairly realistic idea of the potential capacity of every employee. Appointments from within can be based on this knowledge.

Advertising within is thus a search for *unknown* talent. This is unlikely to exist in the small firm, and the act of internal advertisement (because it will seldom produce a successful applicant) may come to be looked upon as a farce by employees. In larger concerns this is certainly not so, and the felt injustice of appointing an outsider without first providing opportunity to employees to apply can be most damaging to morale.

In the absence of such fair opportunity, representative power has already intervened in some companies and has forced a situation where supervisors' or even foremen's roles are allocated on the basis of seniority. I would regard this means of filling such roles as potentially damaging to the future of the organization, for mere seniority, in terms of length of employment or age, is an inadequate criterion for such choices.

I would strongly advocate the commitment to paper of realistic policies providing first opportunity for internal applications in large concerns. The detailed procedure should be agreed by representatives and thereafter carried through with integrity. I have experience over many years of such procedures. They are quite onerous and often involve providing interview time for candidates whose abilities are already known, by long experience, not to measure up to the vacant role. Nevertheless, discoveries are made that would not otherwise be made, and this is a safeguard against losing able people from the organization.

The other, possibly more important, result is the effect on total morale, and the creation of an atmosphere that discourages representative pressures towards damaging procedures founded on seniority or other superficial criteria.

In the absence of agreed and understood procedures, and in the absence of any real contact with the criteria, the methods and operation of appointment procedures, employees generate fantasy notions about such matters. It only requires a few cases of real internal talent to be overlooked for the belief to spread that most appointments are made on the basis of patronage, or because 'your face fits', or because promotion goes only to those who 'play up' to management, and so on. These ideas are usually ill-founded but, very damaging nevertheless, to relationships in general.

Using capacity growth curves to aid selection

The previous employment career of external applicants for vacant roles is one of the main criteria for selection, but it is very difficult to discover, from the descriptions given by applicants, what *level* of work they have done in previous posts. I have described in the previous chapter Elliott Jaques's technique of plotting the corrected salaries of people throughout their careers against their age. This technique can help selection.

It is necessary for the applicant to supply data of his actual salary at the commencement and termination of each different role he has held in the past, the relevant dates of entering and leaving those posts and his age at those times. The salary data are then corrected and plotted. Such salary plots are not as detailed as the plots that can be kept for employees of a hierarchy, because the data on every separate adjustment of salary are missing. Nevertheless, they do yield a picture of comparative progression from one level of work to another, which is helpful.

I set out in Fig. 55 below the type of result that emerges. This is not based on actual data, but gives an impressionistic idea of what emerges.

The following tentative conclusions could be drawn from these plots.

A is already working at a level above that of the work in the vacant role. He will probably want a higher salary than that proposed, and even if he obtained it he would not stay long in the role, unless its work level rises in the near future or he is promoted.

B and C look like possible candidates for further consideration.

D is unlikely to be able to perform at the required level.

E This is an unusual plot. His earlier career was at a lower level, which suggests that he has been underpaid or given too low a level of work in the past. Cautious examination is indicated.

These plots represent a first approximation of the level of capacity.

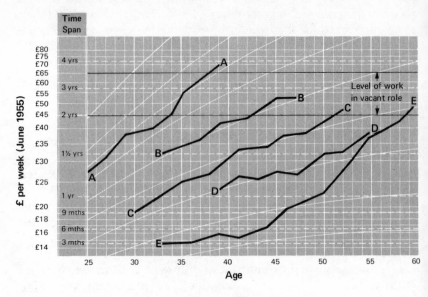

Figure 55

They do not represent more than that, because it is difficult to obtain all the data about other emoluments from candidates on their initial application, and these can change the picture. Furthermore, some candidates may have remained in posts below their real level of capacity because of lack of opportunity in their area, domestic ties to a particular town, or a desire to remain in a profession where the general level of salaries is depressed. These factors can give false readings. On the other hand some people may have worked for companies whose salary levels are in excess of the general norm, and their plots will also give false readings. Nevertheless, where large numbers of applications are involved it is a useful initial means of classification provided it is used with caution.

In a large employment-hierarchy where even internal candidates (who come from some other part of, say, a group of companies) are not well known, then such progression curves may form a useful guide.

Measuring the level of work as an aid to selection

If a large employment-hierarchy adopts the practice of taking maximum time-span measurements of the level of work being done by salaried employees, then this can yield very useful data to aid selection. I have advocated giving the first opportunity to internal candidates to apply for vacant roles that constitute promotion for them. But in large hierarchies such as the Civil Service, or in the case of a group company with many subsidiaries, the issue of comparability of work in different divisions can make selection difficult. There are currently no criteria in general use to help selectors to compare the degree of accountability previously carried by applicants from different parts of a large group. Nor is there in general use any method of objectively stating the level of work that will arise in the vacant role.

If, however, the measuring of the time-spans of roles becomes a consistent practice, then both of these needs can be met. The level of work in the role can be stated in terms of time. In addition, if many companies adopted this practice then meaningful objective data about the level of work in the advertised vacant role would become available to candidates. The other result arising from time-span measurements would be to enable the salary-progression plots of internal candidates to be used with more assurance, because time-span constitutes objective comment on the validity or otherwise of salary-progression plots.

I do not know of any research done to discover the cost of making bad selections, enduring them for perhaps a year or so, de-selecting and starting the process of selecting again. But the cost must be immense if one takes into consideration such matters as loss of morale in the command of a badly selected manager, the reduction of efficiency, and so on. I have always felt that selection decisions are crucial. The techniques I have described—which bring into use role-specifications, salary-progression plots and time-span measurement—though time-consuming, could save hierarchies from many problems, save money and increase human satisfaction at work.

CHAPTER THIRTY-ONE

Ranking and Grading

I HAVE DEFINED the term 'manager' as one who has the minimal authority (*vis-à-vis* his immediate subordinates) to veto appointments, to make differential assessments and to de-select (chapter three). I have discussed the different strata of roles that occur in employment hierarchies in terms of the different levels of abstraction at which people in different strata are able to think and do work (chapter six). I have described a method of measuring the level of work in terms of the maximum time-span of discretion of that work (chapter twenty-one). I have discussed the basis upon which managers assess their subordinates (chapter nine).

Using all these ideas, I now want to discuss grading and ranking of roles in employment hierarchies. The subject is important because the 'distance' set between ranks in building a hierarchy will not only determine the number of levels of management between the chief executive and roles at the base of the hierarchy, but will also decide whether or not managers really manage their immediate subordinates, and thus affect the morale of those subordinates. If we were to take two men, B and C, of equal capacity for work, and make B the manager of C, we know in advance that it will be, at best, a very uncomfortable arrangement and, at worst, a disaster. It would represent a waste of the capacity of C, because he is capable of working at the same level as his manager B and yet is called upon to do work at a lower level of abstraction. If B, the manager in this situation, is being trusted by *his* manager, A, to work on an array of tasks in a manner that entails his carrying on using resources and making decisions for maximum periods of, say, six months without the results being reviewed, then the time-spans of the sub-tasks that B gives to his subordinate C will be shorter than six months. If B were to allot C six-month tasks then the effect would be that A (B's manager) would be reviewing the subordinate's work, not B.

If a manager feels that one of his subordinates is equal in work-capacity to himself then the manager will be reluctant to assess the work of that subordinate. People do not accept criticism or praise or evaluation of their work even in the most neutral terms from 'managers' to whom they consider they are equal in capacity.

If, on the other hand, we have a manager with a group of immediate subordinates, one of whom (X) is clearly of considerably lower capacity than the others, then the manager again will be in difficulty.

The manager meets his subordinates to discuss a plan of work, but X has difficulty in understanding. The manager gives general instructions to his subordinates, but he has to have a special session with X in which he goes into much more detail. He has to keep a very special eye on the work of X, and review what he is doing at much shorter intervals.

I have postulated two situations, which imply in each case the appointment of unsuitable immediate subordinates, and such cases would in reality arise, I hope, infrequently. What can happen much more frequently is the case of the bright young subordinate whose rapidly increasing capacity catches up and becomes equal to that of his manager. In other cases the capacity of the manager increases markedly and some of his subordinates cannot, so to speak, keep up with him. One can see this happening in small companies where the chief executive is very able and his rising capacity is making the company grow at a rapid rate. Some of his brighter subordinates can keep up and are able to take on more important tasks as the company grows. But we also see the rather sad situation where one member of the original team of subordinates who helped the chief executive to build up a company, is falling behind his colleagues' rate of advance in capacity and producing the situation of X described above.

Somewhere between having subordinates too close to their 'manager' in terms of their capacity and too far away, there is an optimum distance. This statement is no doubt a platitude but it is, nevertheless, exceedingly important.

Millions of people are employed in hierarchies. A vital aspect of the structure of those hierarchies is the number of levels of 'management' that exist within each. Usually there are too many such levels. I have already referred to the charge-hand—supervisor—foreman—'managerial' structure on the shop floor. But over-proliferation of 'management' levels does not stop there. It is rife in the executive grades of the Civil Service. It frequently exists at the higher levels in industry and commerce. It separates managers from their real subordinates by interposing 'half-managers' between them. It is extremely expensive. It is commonly referred to, where it is recognized, as 'over-management', but it actually produces 'under-management' because it creates situations where 'subordinates' are too close, in terms of personal capacity, to their 'managers', and those 'managers' do not manage. It has the result of denying subordinates close personal contact with the real managers who actually decide their tasks, assess their progress and decide their promotion.

The company that I managed apparently had nine managerial levels at one time. As a result of thinking about the idea of managers and subordinates being separated by 'one-rank distance' it was later being more effectively managed by six levels of management and, by that time, it was employing a considerably larger number of people.

Those who create employment hierarchies must have the idea of required distances in capacity between subordinates and managers in mind. There are no other criteria on which to base decisions about the number of levels of management. But these ideas have not been worked out explicitly.

I shall refer to this optimum difference between a manager and his subordinates as 'one-rank distance'. But to give precise meaning to the phrase I must first establish what I mean by 'rank'. Jaques has put forward an elegant but still tentative set of proposals. These are based on the taking of measurements of the level of work being done by real managers and their real immediate subordinates in terms of time-span. I require Fig. 56 below to assist my further explanation.

The empirical data showed that large numbers of persons holding full managerial roles at the first level of management (Rank 2) were doing work that varied between a three-month maximum time-span and a one-year maximum time-span.

Similarly, the second level of full managers who had managers as their immediate subordinates were doing work between the one-year and the two-year level, and so on up to Rank 6, where managers were found to be doing work in excess of the seven-and-a-half-year time-span level.[1]

The data showed that in many companies the time-span differentials between 'managers' and 'subordinates' was much smaller. But in such companies there was more confusion about 'who

---

[1] My terminology can be confusing, because I designate non-managerial people working at the base of the hierarchy as Rank 1 personnel. Thus the first level of *managers* becomes Rank 2, the second level of manager is at Rank 3, and so on.

managed whom' and the number of levels of 'management' was greater (sometimes much greater) than appeared to be effective in other companies where the level of work of the chief executives was similar.

In short, these data point to the following ideas: that there is an optimum number of levels of management, which can be defined in

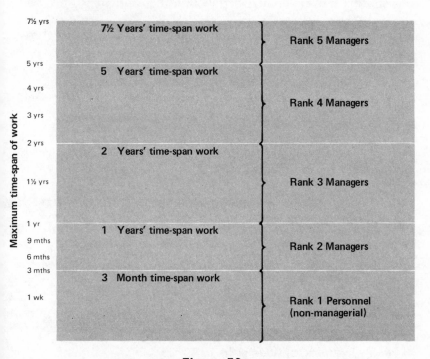

Figure 56

terms of time-span brackets of work level; that if the number of management levels exceeds this number then managerial–subordinate relationships are weakened; that once the level of work required to be done by the chief executive is established in terms of time-span measurement, then it is possible to derive the number of managerial levels required to operate the employment hierarchy effectively from that single fact.

It might have been assumed from what I have written that 'one-rank distance' means a relationship where manager and subordinate were at the same relative positions in their respective time-span rank-brackets (i.e. that a rank-3 manager whose most important area of work was near the two-year time-span level would be at a one-rank distance from a rank-2 subordinate working near to the one-year level). In fact, Jaques defines one-rank distance as the relationship between a manager working anywhere within his rank-bracket with a subordinate working anywhere within the contiguous rank below that manager.

In chapter six I discussed the different levels of abstraction of work that seem to characterize different levels of management. These have a bearing on the use of the idea of one-rank distance as a parameter for the building of organization. I repeat a short description of these levels of abstraction, to save the reader from having to refer back.

Rank 1. 'Perceptual-concrete thinking.' The mind is dealing with work in the restricted sense of what the eye can see.

Rank 2. 'Imaginal-concrete thinking.' The mind is dealing not only with what the eye can see but also at the image-making level.

Rank 3. 'Conceptual-concrete thinking.' The mind, being unable to cope with a rapidly expanding array of data at the concrete or image levels, moves into thinking about classes of things and concepts.

Rank 4. 'Abstract-model thinking.' The mind casts off its attachment to the concrete and is able to build complete mental models of current and future situations.

Rank 5 and above. 'Theory and strategy construction.' The mind is able to deal with the interaction of models and systems of thought as a means of constructing theories and of planning future strategies.

Using these descriptions of levels of work it is possible to define one-rank distance alternatively as the relationship between a manager working at one level of abstraction with a subordinate working at the next level below.

As I have indicated, the data to support these notions are sparse and the ideas are put forward tentatively. But in spite of their tentative nature I found them to be useful. The fact is that some hunch or theory is used by everybody who takes decisions about structuring employment hierarchies. People who take these decisions think of themselves as using experience or intuition, but each has a hunch theory operating at some level in his mind. The ideas about ranking that I have described are really an attempt to make explicit notions that exist already, but at a sub-conscious level.

I turn now to a short discussion of some practical examples of the use of these ideas. My first concerns the Civil Service. The first impact on me when I entered Government was the proliferation of grades and ranks. The theoretical potential maximum number in any one hierarchy of the Civil Service is twenty, because there are twenty grades of employees. But grades are not at one-rank distance. The 'executive grades' in particular are much nearer to each other than that. These grades are required as designations of different salary brackets and other entitlements. But in the absence of explicit ideas about ranks and differences in personal capacity between superiors and subordinates, they have been used as ranks.

The Fulton report says in Paragraph 221, referring to this grading system: 'This is essentially a pay structure; it is not designed to determine the actual organisation of work'—and yet there is no reference to ranking in the report.

The primary *administrative* grades of the Civil Service are as follows:

Permanent Secretary
Deputy Secretary
Under-Secretary
Assistant Secretary
Principal
Assistant Principal

The principal *executive* grades are as follows:

PEO   (Principal Executive Officer)
SCEO (Senior Chief Executive Officer)
CEO   (Chief Executive Officer)
SEO   (Senior Executive Officer)
HEO   (Higher Executive Officer)
EO   (Executive Officer)
CO   (Clerical Officer)
CA   (Clerical Assistant)

These fourteen grades are generally treated as ranks—though this is no longer a consistent practice. The situation is at its worst when PEO, SCEO, CEO, HEO, EO, CO and CA are set up, one on top of the other, in a series of 'superior–subordinate' relationships. These relationships are at half-rank distance or less.

A tentative assessment of the real position suggests that Permanent Secretary, Deputy Secretary, Under-Secretary, Assistant Secretary, and Principal, refer to five *ranks* of management, whereas the

Administrative grades		Executive grades	Rank	Time-span
Permanent Secretary	A		} 6	↑
Permanent Secretary	B			10 Years
Permanent Secretary	C			
Deputy Secretary	A		} 5	↑
Deputy Secretary	B			5 Years
Deputy Secretary	C			
Under-Secretary	A		} 4	↑
Under-Secretary	B			2 Years
Under-Secretary	C			
Assistant Secretary	A	Principal E.O.	} 3	↑
Assistant Secretary	B	Senior Chief E.O.		1 Year
Principal	A	Chief E.O. Senior E.O.	} 2	↑
Assistant Principal	B	Higher E.O.		3 Months
		Executive Officer	} 1	1 Month
		Clerical Officer		1 Week
		Clerical Assistant		Days

Figure 57

executive titles refer to *grades*, and that the underlying structure is more like that illustrated in Fig. 57.[1]

I have shown sixteen grades organized into six ranks. I do not know whether time-span measurement of a random sample of these ranks would coincide with Jaques's findings, but I would expect this

---

[1] Since writing the above I have read a press release from the Civil Service department (30/12/70) detailing the abolition of the old divisions of the Civil Service into Administrative, Executive and Clerical groups. This is certainly a step forward. It states equivalents as between existing Administrative and Executive grades. The statement is complex (no doubt as a result of bargaining with representatives) but the equivalents stated seem to coincide with my own instructions as set out above. For example 'PEO' will be re-titled 'Assistant Secretary' and the distinction between CEO and Principal will cease.

to be the case on the basis of intuitive judgement after working within Government for a considerable period.

Though there is widespread proliferation of superior–subordinate relations separated by less than one-rank distance in the executive part of the Civil Service the situation appears to be more realistic in the administrative part. Between Permanent Secretary and Deputy Secretary, between Deputy and Under-Secretary, between Under-Secretary and Assistant Secretary there often, but not always seemed to be something like a managerial–subordinate relationship. But the relations between PEO and SCEO, or lower down the scale between, say, SEO and HEO, gave me the same feeling of close non-managerial relationships that I have noticed in industry between foreman, assistant foreman, supervisor, charge-hand, and leading hand (not in terms of level of work but in terms of psychological feel). There seemed to be a decided lack of readiness for a superior to take personal responsibility when things went wrong at levels lower than his own. There was ambiguity, and whereas when things went wrong at the senior administrative levels remedial action was pretty prompt, at the lower levels it was not.

I have already commented on the extent to which younger people at the lower levels of the service sometimes seem to be seriously under-employed in terms of the quantity or level of work they are asked to do and become bored. This, I believe, is nearly always one of the results of under-management of people, arising from unclarity about managerial authority or lack of psychological distance between superior and subordinate. I certainly formed the opinion that this was not due to the calibre of those employed in the executive grades (many EOs have passed A level examinations) but to the many overlapping superior–subordinate relationships.

I have seen the effects of cleaning up a similar situation in industry, particularly the proliferation of half-rank managers in the superintendent, foreman, assistant foreman, supervisor, and charge-hand area. Such an operation produces better relationships between manager and subordinates, better assessment of subordinates, crisper work, speedier attention to problems, less neglect or overlooking of young people with talent, and more effective utilization of the time and the work capacity of subordinates.

I choose the example of the Civil Service to delineate these problems, not because its situation is worse than that of industry, but because consistent titling of roles makes it easy to describe the problem. It is much more difficult to use industrial examples, because although fairly commonly used terminology exists, such as chairman, managing director, general manager, production manager, works manager, superintendent, foreman, supervisor, etc., each of these titles is liable to mean something quite different according to the notions of different companies.

If the ideas about establishing ranking (in terms of time-span brackets) could be validated, then employment hierarchies could begin discussing the structure of organization in terms of Rank 1A, 1B, 1C, Rank 2A, 2B, 2C, etc., using the numbers to indicate managerial rankings and the letters to designate grades within each rank.

The grade sub-division of each rank sets brackets of salaries. The various entitlements of a non-salary nature concerned with such matters as holidays, pensions, sick pay, allowances, etc. can also be attached to grades. The function of such a payment structure is simply to have a sufficient number of internally published brackets to allow employees to compare their position with others in terms of categories—instead of allowing inaccurate rumours of what people are paid to develop. Clearly established grades enable people see the ladder of promotion that is open to them. Grades help managers to think of individual salaries in terms of whether or not a subordinate is in the correct salary position compared to others in different parts of the hierarchy.

Fig. 58 shows the organization of a group of companies containing three subsidiaries. No. 1 is working at the highest level, contains employees organized in five ranks, and may, if it grows, have to become a six-rank company in the near future. No. 2 has recently grown rapidly from a four-rank to a five-rank company. No. 3 is still a four-rank company.

All ranks in these companies would be at one-rank distance from each other. I am discussing perfect models, and I know that perfection is unattainable, because the changing level of work, changing capacity of people and the need for different grades of people in different parts of the same company, make constant adjustment inevitable. It is useful, nevertheless, to have a model at which to aim.

If companies had clear ideas about grading and ranking they could probably make reductions in the numbers of 'levels of management' and in the number of people involved in administering the work of others. This would not only save personnel but would, in my experience, lead to more efficient work and more satisfaction on the part of all employees.

If managers are regarded by their subordinates as having wider vision or greater maturity or more experience than subordinates

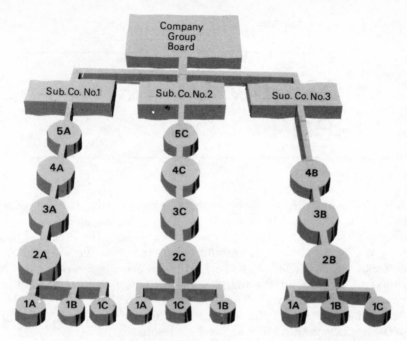

Figure 58

possess themselves then those subordinates will accept instructions, praise, criticism, assessment or training from those managers. But where this situation does not hold there is cynicism on the part of the subordinates. The concept of 'one-rank distance', even if it is not at present objectively definable except in these very tentative terms is, nevertheless, an important one for those who design the structure of organization to have in mind.

CHAPTER THIRTY-TWO

Glossary of Terms Used

ACCOUNTABILITY : *the quality of a role (or group of roles) that determines that the incumbent shall be answerable for the consequences, directly or otherwise, of his use of authority.* Accountability varies with the nature of the role, with the policy of the organization, and with the instructions given by the manager of the role. He who accepts the role can be called to account for the manner in which he has carried out the policies of the hierarchy and the instructions of his manager. Accountability implies the use of the authority of the role to make decisions, act upon them and produce results.

ACCOUNTING SYSTEM : *a role-system attached to an employment hierarchy, which is accountable to representatives of the association that set up the employment hierarchy. The function of the accounting system is:*

(a) *To provide economic and financial reports on the results of the operation of the employment hierarchy.*
(b) *To report on any deviations by the chief executive and his managers from association policy or from the law.*
(c) *To provide a range of services to representatives of the association.*
(d) *To provide a range of services to the chief executive and his managers.*

This definition is stated in general terms to include accounting systems that serve boards of directors and shareholders, and also other types of associations. For example, 'association policy' covers not only shareholder policies and board of directors' policy in the case of a company, but Government policy in the case of the Civil Service, and the policy of members and their management committee in the case of a club.

APPEALS PROCEDURE : *the process whereby an employee can cause a decision of a manager to be reviewed by a higher manager.* This definition implies that an employee who is dissatisfied with the decision of his manager may cause it to be successively reviewed by ever higher managers until it reaches the chief executive.

ASSUMED ORGANIZATION: see ORGANIZATION.

ATTACHMENT: *the organizational mechanism by means of which an operational manager is provided with assistance in the co-ordination of his operational subordinates in a specific dimension of his work by attaching to him a specialist staff officer from a specialist command.*

AUTHORITY: *that quality of a role (or group of roles) that sanctions the incumbent to make decisions and act within defined limits.* Authority in a chief-executive role is derived from those power-groups, mainly the owners, customers and employees, who possess the power to prevent the incumbent from acting without their sanction.

CAPACITY-GROWTH CURVES: see POTENTIAL PROGRESS ASSESSMENT.

CENTRALIZATION OF ORGANIZATION: *refers to a process whereby a manager restricts the degree of discretion of his subordinates or gives contraction instructions (which see) that apply to more than one level of his extended command.*

DE-CENTRALIZATION: *the reverse process to centralization, and particularly applies when a manager withdraws contraction instructions and relies instead on instructions to his immediate subordinates only, leaving them to use discretion with their commands in carrying out the tasks and policies that he specifies.*

COLLATERAL RELATIONSHIP: *that relationship obtaining between employees of the same rank who work within the same immediate or extended command when their work is interdependent.* Collateral relationships arise between members of a manager's command when decisions they are authorized to make can affect the performance of each other.

COLLATERAL MEETING: *a meeting of persons between which collateral relationships exist.* Collateral meetings are very frequently referred to as committees under the mistaken assumption that they carry corporate accountability and can come to decisions by majority vote (see COMMITTEE).

COMMITTEE: *a body of people who are collectively accountable and are authorized to come to decisions by majority vote.* Members of committees can be appointed by those with authority or elected to represent others.

CO-MANAGER : see SPECIALIST CO-MANAGER and OPERATIONAL CO-MANAGER.

CONCEPTS : *generalized ideas based on relationships that are deducible from a specific range of perceptions, data, observations or assumptions, stateable in terms that make it possible to know what lies within or without their ambit.* In this book I have also used the phrase 'Boundary-Defined Concepts'. Concepts must always be stated in boundary-defined form. Unfortunately the word 'concept' is frequently used simply to refer to ill-defined ideas. If the real meaning of the word 'concept' were more widely understood it would not be necessary to add 'boundary-defined' to the noun 'concept', because real concepts are only stateable in terms of their boundaries. To be useful for the purpose of communication or of building mental models the perceptions from which the concepts are deduced must be first agreed by those who wish to share the use of the concepts in a meaningful way. (See *The Grammar of Science* by Karl Pearson, pp. 49–51 of Everyman's Library Edition, J. M. Dent & Sons Ltd., London.)

CONTRACTION : *occurs when a manager makes any communication, verbal or written, to any levels lower in the employment hierarchy than his immediate command.* If a Rank-4 manager gives an instruction to a Rank-2 member of his extended command he has issued a contraction instruction. (In such a case he should immediately inform his Rank-3 managerial subordinate in charge of that Rank-2 subordinate of what he has done.) If a plant manager has a discussion with the whole of his extended command in order to clarify his plans to them, then he is making a contraction communication.

COUNCIL : *as used in this book is a body composed of elected representatives of the whole of a manager's extended command plus that manager, which arrives at decisions (apart from those concerning procedure) by unanimous vote of its members.* It has been established by experience that such councils can work effectively if comprised of representatives of an entire company, or of an entire part of a company established in a specific geographical area. If two councils attempt to operate within the same geographical area then differences in the decisions arrived at will cause dissension.

CROSS-OVER POINT MANAGER : *in relation to any two or more roles the cross-over point is the lowest rank of manager whose extended command embraces those roles.* Stated in another way, a cross-over point manager is the lowest-level manager whose extended command embraces all the employee roles involved. This is a concept which has not been the subject of explicit recognition. But the idea is used with great frequency and the absence of a term for it hinders communication.

D: a symbol used to denote Product Design and Development.

DIFFERENTIAL ENTITLEMENTS: *a statement of the full range of the economic benefits to which different groups of employees are entitled by agreement or contract.* The term 'differential wages' (or 'salaries') is widely used, but there is no term in general use to refer to the other benefits, such as pensions, holidays, sick leave, expenses, use of cars, share options, etc. The term refers to a statement of all benefits including the wage or salary.

DISCRETIONARY CONTENT OF WORK: *those aspects of a task or a policy about which a subordinate must exercise discretion in order to fulfil his manager's instructions to him.* It is the discretionary content of work that carries the feeling of weight of responsibility. The person doing the work is on his own, choosing a course of action, within limits set or implied by the organization or his manager (prescribed limits of discretion), with no certainty that his choices will be satisfactory until the results have been reviewed by inspection, or by the use of what he has done, or by his manager. In any kind of work requiring manual manipulation (for example, machine-operation, typing, etc.) discretion manifests itself in the form of judgements about pace, quality and means of application of physical skill.

EARNINGS PROGRESSION CURVE: *the line resulting from plotting on a logarithmic vertical scale the total money earnings of an individual, corrected by use of the wage index, against the person's age at the time of the plot on the horizontal scale.*

EARNING PROGRESSION DATA SHEET: *sheet on which earnings progression curves may be plotted.* The vertical scale is a financial scale of earnings and is logarithmic. The figures refer to equitable payment scales in June 1955 and all plots are corrected by use of the Wages Index (which see in this Glossary) on a basis of the percentage increase of national earnings since that date. The horizontal scale refers to the age of the employee. Also on these data sheets appears a series of capacity growth curves (see Potential Progress Assessment in this Glossary of terms).

EARNINGS INDEX: see WAGES INDEX.

EMPLOYMENT HIERARCHY: *that structure of work-roles (set up by an association to give effect to the latter's aims) within which people take roles up by entering into employment contracts.* The term 'employment hierarchy' embraces all the employment roles in a hierarchy responsible to its chief executive. I have drawn attention in my chapter on Accounting Work to the fact that accountants and their subordinates are, *de facto*, responsible to some authority higher than the chief executive because they carry accountability for reporting on his activities. In fact, therefore, an association often sets up two employment hierarchies, one to carry out work to achieve their objectives, and another to audit the results of that activity and provide financial reports upon it.

EMPLOYMENT WORK: *the application of knowledge and the exercise of discretion within limits prescribed by the immediate manager and by higher policies, towards an objective set by the immediate manager, the whole being carried out within an employment contract.*

EQUITABLE PAYMENT: *the common norms of payment that have been discovered to be held by individuals in roles of the same maximum time-span, when asked under confidential conditions to state what they would consider to be fair pay.* Contrary to what might generally be supposed, individuals possess common standards as to what constitutes fair pay for given levels of work measured in time-span, regardless of their occupation, actual current earnings, previous earnings or income-tax levels. These norms of fair pay are relative, i.e. they indicate what differentials in payment are felt to be fair in relation to differentials in level of work. (See Elliott Jaques, *Equitable Payment*, Heinemann Educational Books, London.)

EXTANT ORGANIZATION: see *Organization.*

EXTENDED COMMAND *of a manager comprises all those employees for whose work activities he is accountable.*

FELT-FAIR PAY: a more colloquial term for Equitable payment, which see.

IMMEDIATE COMMAND *(of a manager): comprises all those employees whose, manager he is.*

INDEX OF AVERAGE EARNINGS: see WAGES INDEX.

INSTRUCTION: *any communication from a manager to one or more of his immediate subordinates when they are in their employee roles.* This definition includes not only orders but also requests for information, advice or assistance, the passing of information, etc., which always contain an instruction, either explicitly or implicitly.

POLICY INSTRUCTION: *a communication from a manager to any or all of his subordinates, or to those in his extended command, stating the actions that they must or must not take under given circumstances in the future.* Policy statements that set out standing orders, procedures, physical controls, signals, routines, are the rules that circumscribe the area over which an employee is expected to use his own discretion. Failure to conform to policy statements thus defined constitutes negligence or insubordination. Failure to use discretion, take decisions and act within the boundaries set by policy instructions, constitutes abdication from accountability.

STAFF INSTRUCTION: *one given by a staff officer (within his own manager's policy) to any other of that manager's immediate subordinates.*

TASK INSTRUCTION: *a task is a specific item of work and a task instruction is a communication from a manager to a subordinate instructing him to carry out that specific item of work.*

TECHNICAL INSTRUCTION: *an instruction given by a staff officer to a lower-rank staff officer who has been attached by him to a manager.*

'LEGISLATIVE' SYSTEM: *the interaction between the shareholder's system, the customer system, the representative system and the chief executive.* The 'legislative' system is an interaction of role-systems rather than of individual roles. The formal institution within which this interaction can take place is a council. It is to be noted, however, that whether or not a formally constituted council exists, the interaction of role-systems takes place and that, in this sense, every employment hierarchy works within an environment of rules, policies, etc., created by this interaction of role-systems.

M: a symbol used to denote Manufacturing Work.

MANAGER: *an employee whose role requires subordinate roles, over which he wields the minimal authority to veto appointments to those roles; to assign work; to assess the relative performance of subordinates; and to de-select subordinates from those roles if their work performance is, in his judgement, not up to the required standard.* This definition is not a description of a manager's work but simply states those facets of the authority of a manager that distinguish his role from other types of role. By asking three questions relating to appointment, assessment and removal of subordinates, it is possible to determine whether or not a specific role does or does not fall within the ambit of the definition.

CO-MANAGER: see Specialist Co-manager and Operational Co-manager.

Mk: a symbol used to denote Marketing Work.

MANIFEST ORGANIZATION: see ORGANIZATION.

NET STANDARD VALUE: see STANDARD VALUE.

NET TARGET PRICE: see STANDARD VALUE.

OPERATIONAL CO-MANAGER: *that part of a managerial role which an operational manager takes up in relation to a specialist attached to his command from a specialist division.*

OPERATIONAL WORK *is the design, production and supply or marketing of goods or services.* Employment hierarchies are always set up with the specific objective of designing, producing and supplying goods or services, and these are referred to as its operational work. An employee carrying out some aspect of any of those types of work is in an operational role, in contrast to others who are concerned with the supply of some service to operational roles or whose work is concerned with the Personnel, Programming or Technical dimension of operational work. I have used the symbols D, M and Mk to refer to Design, Production, and Supply or Marketing of goods or services.

ORGANIZATION

MANIFEST ORGANIZATION: *the situation as formally described and displayed.*

ASSUMED ORGANIZATION: *the situation as it is assumed to be by the individuals concerned.*

EXTANT ORGANIZATION: *the situation as revealed by systematic exploration and analysis (it can never be completely known).*

REQUISITE ORGANIZATION: *the situation as it would have to be to accord with the real properties of the field in which it exists.*

If Manifest, Assumed and Extant organization coincide, then it can be said that an exceedingly high state of practical awareness of organization exists. Requisite organization is unlikely ever to be achieved because all the real properties of the situation will not be known. It is useful interpreted as the organization required in the light of a knowledge of the extant situation.

P: a symbol to denote the specialist work concerned with organization, manning and personnel phases of operational work.

POLICY INSTRUCTION: see *Instruction.*

POTENTIAL PROGRESS ASSESSMENT (PPA): *the assessment of employed persons' rate of growth in capacity and future capacity to do employment work.*

CAPACITY GROWTH CURVES: I have referred in the text to the technique of plotting the corrected earnings of employees against their age on the earnings progression data sheets devised by Jaques. On these data sheets there appears a series of curves derived from empirical data, which indicate the probable growth (and decline) in the capacity of individuals as their age changes. These are referred to as capacity growth curves.

POWER: *those qualities of a person or associated persons that enable him or them to cause other persons to act.*
  SOURCES OF POWER: *lie in the capabilities of individuals (knowledge, charisma, ideology, etc.) and in the capabilities and degree of cohesion of associated persons.*
  MODES OF EXERCISING POWER: *persuasion—the exercise of power by impact on the minds of others; coercion—the exercise of power by threat of control or deprivation.*

PROGRAMMING WORK (PR) (I am using this term in a rather wider sense than is usual): *that phase of all operational work concerned with the timing, progression, quantification, assembly of supplies and balancing of the work-pattern required to get work done.*

PROGRESSION CURVES: see EARNINGS PROGRESSION CURVE.

PROPERTY VALUE: seè STANDARD VALUE.

RETURN INDEX: *a term used in the description of the technique of Product Analysis Pricing, defined as follows—the resultant of dividing the net sales price (sales price less the value of bought material and bought components included in it) of a product by the target input of direct labour hours to be used in its manufacture.*

RESPONSIBILITY: *that quality of a person or persons that determines how he or they will exercise their authority or their power.* The words 'responsibility' and 'accountability' are often used interchangeably. I have reserved the use of the word 'accountability', together with 'authority', as referring to properties of a role. I use the word 'responsibility', together with 'power', as qualities of a person or a group. The terms are linked as follows: persons, power, responsibility; roles, authority, accountability. The sanction of a power-group endows a role with authority. It is to be noted, however, that persons in roles use not only the authority of the role but also the personal power deriving from their acknowledged experience, skill, reputation, etc.

ROLE: *a position in a system, filled by election or appointment, which carries accountability and authority, to be assumed by the person taking up the role.*

SALARY PROGRESSION CURVE: see EARNINGS PROGRESSION CURVE.

SERVICE ORGANIZATION: *a role or structure of roles set up by an organization to provide specific assistance of a non-operational kind to other specified members of that organization.* The provision of services to customers is today widely recognized as an essential part of good marketing, but there is a lack of clarity in thinking about the internal services that exist within hierarchies to assist operational work, in spite of the fact that they are sometimes responsible for substantial expense. I refer to such services as building and machine maintenance, canteen facilities, tool design and manufacture, office cleaning, telephone and postal services, transport, etc.

SPECIALIST CO-MANAGER: *the part-managerial role that a specialist manager takes up in relation to another specialist whom he has attached to an operational manager.*

SPECIALIST ROLE: *A role from which the occupant is accountable for giving advice to his manager within a specific field of expertise.*

STAFF INSTRUCTIONS: see INSTRUCTION.

STAFF OFFICER: *a specialist who is also accountable for assisting a manager in the co-ordination of that manager's immediate subordinates in a specific dimension of his work by exercising authority and issuing instructions on his behalf.*

STANDARD VALUE: *the total of the values of the material content, the bought components, and the properties of a finished product.*
   NET STANDARD VALUE: *the standard value minus the sum of the material value and the bought value of a finished product.*
   NET SALES PRICE: *the actual price realized less the value of the bought material and bought finished components included within it.* (Note that the material referred to is the amount actually present in the product, not the amount used up in its manufacture.)
   TARGET PRICE: *the sales price to be quoted, which results from the addition of a specific percentage decided by the chief executive to the standard value.*

SUPERVISOR: *an employee who assists his manager by assigning work to those members of his manager's immediate command allocated to him and seeing that this work gets done.*

T: *a symbol used to denote the specialist work concerned with the techniques used in carrying out work.*

TARGET PRICE: see STANDARD VALUE.

TASK INSTRUCTION: see INSTRUCTION.

TECHNICAL SPECIALIST WORK (T): *that phase of operational work concerned with the development, modification and exploitation of methods of carrying out the work.* Technical specialists seem to be consistently necessary in product manufacture, but are seldom found assisting managers in charge of product development or marketing. This is probably because managers in these two types of operational work are almost invariably expert in the technique of product development or of marketing, whereas in manufacturing work the variety of techniques required is so great that specialists are required.

TECHNICAL INSTRUCTION: see INSTRUCTION.

TIME-SPAN OF DISCRETION: *the longest period that can elapse in a role before the manager can be sure that his subordinate has not been continuously exercising marginally sub-standard discretion in balancing the pace and quality of his work.*

UNANIMOUS VOTING COUNCIL: see COUNCIL.

WAGES INDEX: a reference to the Index of Average Earnings of all employees published monthly by the Department of Employment and quarterly in *Statistics on Incomes, Prices Employment and Production.*

WAGE PROGRESSION CURVE: see EARNINGS PROGRESSION CURVE.

WORKS COUNCIL: see COUNCIL.

WORK: see EMPLOYMENT WORK.

Bibliography of the Glacier Project

BROWN, WILFRED

'Principles of Organisation', *Monographs on Higher Management No. 5*, Manchester Municipal College of Technology, December 1946.

'Some Problems of a Factory', *Occasional Paper No. 2*, Institute of Personnel Management, London, 1952.

Exploration in Management, Heinemann Educational Books Limited, London; Southern Illinois University, Carbondale, Illinois, 1960; Penguin Books, Harmondsworth, Middlesex, England, 1965.

In Swedish translation—*Forskning l Företagsledning*, Strömberg, Stockholm.

In French translation—*Gestion Prospective de L'Entreprise*, Les Editions de la Baconnière, Neuchatel, Switzerland, 1964.

In German translation—*Unternehmensfuhring Als Forschungsobjekt*; Verlag W. Girardet, Essen, 1964.

In Dutch translation—*Nieuwe Wegen in Het Bedrijfsbeleid*, Spectrum.

In Spanish translation—*Dirreccion Empresarial*, U.T.E.H.A., Mexico.

'Selection and Appraisal of Management Personnel', *The Manager*, Vol. XXVIII, No. 6, 1960.

Piecework Abandoned, Heinemann Educational Books Limited, London, 1962.

'What is Work?', *Harvard Business Review*, September 1962; *Scientific Business* August 1963.

'A Critique of some Current Ideas about Organisation', *California Management Review*, Fall (September) 1963.

'Judging the Performance of Subordinates', *Management International*, 1964, Vol. 4, No. 2.

Organisation—Heinemann Educational Books Ltd, London, 1971.

BROWN, WILFRED AND JAQUES, ELLIOTT

Product Analysis Pricing, Heinemann Educational Books Limited, London, 1964.

'The Business School Syllabus—A Systematic Approach', *The Manager*, April 1964.

Glacier Project Papers, Heinemann Educational Books Limited, London, 1965; Basic Books, New York, 1965.
'Consent or Command in Committee', *The Manager*, January 1965.

BROWN, WILFRED AND RAPHAEL, WINIFRED

Managers, Men and Morale, MacDonald and Evans, London, 1943.

HILL, J. M. M.

'A Consideration of Labour Turnover as the Resultant of a Quasi-Stationary Process', *Human Relations*, Vol. IV, No. 3, 1951.
'The Time-Span of Discretion in Job Analysis', *Tavistock Pamphlets No. 1*, Tavistock Publications, London, 1957.
'A Note on Time-Span and Economic Theory', *Human Relations*, Vol. XI, No. 4, 1958.

JAQUES, ELLIOTT

'Studies in the Social Development of an Industrial Community', *Human Relations*, Vol. III, No. 3, 1950.
The Changing Culture of a Factory, Tavistock Publications, London; Dryden Press, New York, 1951.
'On the Dynamics of Social Structure', *Human Relations*, Vol. VI, No. 1, 1953.
Measurement of Responsibility, Tavistock Publications, London; Harvard University Press, Cambridge, Mass., 1956.
'Fatigue and Lowered Morale Caused by Inadequate Executive Planning', *Royal Society of Health Journal*, Vol. 78, No. 5, 1958.
'An Objective Approach to Pay Differentials', *The New Scientist*, Vol. 4, No. 85, 1958.
'Standard Earning Progression Curves: A Technique for Examining Individual Progress in Work', *Human Relations*, Vol. XI, No. 2, 1958.
'Disturbances in the Capacity to Work', *International Journal of Psycho-Analysis*, Vol. XLI, 1960.
Equitable Payment, Heinemann Educational Books Limited, London; and Southern Illinois University Press, Carbondale, Illinois, 1961.
And in French translation—*Rémunération Objective*, Editions Hommes et Techniques, Neuilly-sur-Seine, 1963.
'Objective Measures for Pay Differentials', *Harvard Business Review*, Jan.-Feb. 1962.
'A System for Income Equity', *New Society*, 12th December 1963.
'Economic Justice—by Law?', *The Twentieth Century*, Spring 1964.
'National Incomes Policy: A Democratic Plan', *Pamphlet Published by K.-H. Services Ltd.*, May 1964.
Time-Span Handbook, Heinemann Educational Books Limited, London, 1964.

And in French translation—*Manuel d'Evaluation des Fonctions*, Editions Hommes et Techniques, Paris, 1965.

'Level-of-Work Measurement and Fair Payment: A Reply to Professor Beal's Comparison of Time-Span of Discretion and Job Evaluation', *California Management Review*, Summer 1964.

'Two Contributions to a General Theory of Organisation and Management', *Scientific Business*, August 1964.

'Social-Analysis and the Glacier Project': *Human Relations*, Vol. XVII, No. 4, November 1964.

'Too Many Management Levels', *California Management Review*, 1965.

In Preparation

BROWN, WILFRED

Exploration in Management, in Japanese and Italian translations.

JAQUES, ELLIOTT

Equitable Payment, in German, Italian and Spanish translations.

Index